THE CHANGING RACIAL REGIME

National Political Science Review

Volume 5

NATIONAL POLITICAL SCIENCE REVIEW

EDITOR
Matthew Holden, Jr.
University of Virginia

EDITOR-DESIGNATE
Georgia Persons
Georgia Institute of Technology

ASSOCIATE EDITOR
Robert C. Smith
San Francisco State University

ASSISTANT EDITOR
Cheryl M. Miller
University of Maryland-Baltimore County

BOOK REVIEW EDITOR
Paula D. McClain
University of Virginia

EDITORIAL BOARD

Julian Bond
University of Virginia

William V. Crotty
Northwestern University

Steven E. Finkel
University of Virginia

Dennis Judd
University of Missouri
St. Louis

Lois Moreland
Spelman College

Ronald E. Brown
Wayne State University

William Daniels
Rochester Institute of Technology

Charles Hamilton
Columbia University

Edmund Keller
University of California
Santa Barbara

Kathie Stromile Golden
Morgan State University

Michael Combs
University of Nebraska

Richard Fenno
University of Rochester

Mack Jones
Prairie View A&M University

Mamie E. Locke
Hampton University

Katherine Tate
Harvard University

THE CHANGING RACIAL REGIME

National Political Science Review

Volume 5

Matthew Holden, Jr., Editor

Transaction Publishers
New Brunswick (U.S.A.) and London (U.K.)

Copyright © 1995 by Transaction Publishers.
New Brunswick, New Jersey 08903.

All rights reserved under International and Pan-American Copyright Conventions. No part of this book may be reproduced or transmitted in any form or by any means, electronic or mechanical, including photocopy, recording, or any information storage and retrieval system, without prior permission in writing from the publisher. All inquiries should be addressed to Transaction Publishers, Rutgers—The State University, New Brunswick, New Jersey 08903.

This book is printed on acid-free paper that meets the American National Standard for Permanence of Paper for Printed Library Materials.

ISSN: 0896-629-X
ISBN: 1-56000-814-8
Printed in the United States of America

Contents

Acknowledgments	ix
Editor's Introduction *Matthew Holden, Jr.*	1
Slavery and the Platonic Origins of Anti-Democracy *Cedric Robinson*	18
Abram Harris, E. Franklin Frazier, and Ralph Bunche: The Howard School of Thought on the Problem of Race *Charles P. Henry*	36
Organizational Character and Interest Group Strategies *Katherine A. Hinckley and Bette S. Hill*	57
Regimes, Party, and Federal Budgeting: Presidential Estimates, Appropriations, and Expenditures *Edward James Mullen*	75
Ethics and Budgeting: Comment on an Integrity Model *Marjorie Lewis*	90
The Rehnquist Court's 1990 and 1991 Terms: The Constitutional Politics of Federalism and its Consequences for Black Americans *Barbara L. Graham and Abraham L. Davis*	93
Agenda and Roll-Call Responsiveness to Black Interests: A Longitudinal Analysis of the Alabama Senate *Mary Herring*	117
Race, Abortion, and Judicial Retention: The Case of Florida Supreme Court Justice Leander Shaw *Susan A. MacManus and Lawrence Morehouse*	133

Mayoral Politics Chicago Style: The Rise and Fall of
a Multiethnic Coalition, 1983–1989   152
Paul Kleppner

Party Sorting at the Local Level in South Carolina   181
Robert P. Steed, Laurence W. Moreland, and Tod A. Baker

Boston's *Mandela* Referendum: Urban Nationalism and
Economic Dependence   197
Nancy Haggard-Gilson

Minority Business Enterprise Set-Aside Programs, Disparity
Fact-Finding Studies, and Racial Discrimination in State
and Local Public Contracting in the Post-*Croson* Era   215
Mitchell F. Rice

Racial Formation in Zimbabwe   241
Vernon D. Johnson

BOOK FORUM

Review Essays

Affirmative Action: The Quality of the Debate   263
Sue Davis

Mozambique's Descent into Hell   270
Robert Fatton, Jr.

Democracy in America and the Representation of
African Americans   276
Robert C. Smith

Book Reviews

Decision and Structure: U.S. Refugee Policy in the
Mariel Crisis *and* The Paper Curtain: Employer
Sanctions' Implementation, Impact, and Reform   283
reviewed by James A. Regalado

Political Liberalism   287
reviewed by George Klosko

Monitoring Government: Inspectors General
and the Search for Accountability   289
reviewed by Dennis J. Palumbo

Researching the Presidency: Vital Questions, New Approaches   291
   reviewed by Ryan J. Barilleaux

The Promise and Paradox of Civil Service Reform   293
   reviewed by N. Joseph Cayer

Black Families: Interdisciplinary Perspectives   296
   reviewed by Howard A. Palley

Parties and Leaders in the Postreform House   299
   reviewed by Bruce Oppenheimer

The Poverty of American Politics:
A Theoretical Interpretation   301
   reviewed by William W. Ellis

The Fragmental Metropolis: Political
Fragmentation and Metropolitan Segregation   303
   reviewed by Floyd W. Hayes, III

America's Strategy in a Changing World   306
   reviewed by Walton L. Brown

Issues in Democratic Consolidation:
The New South American Democracies in
Comparative Perspective   310
   reviewed by Michael Mitchell

Editor's Postscript: Regime Issues and a Study Agenda   313

Invitation to the Scholarly Community   321

NATIONAL CONFERENCE OF BLACK POLITICAL SCIENTISTS OFFICERS

President
William H. Boone
Clark-Atlanta University

President-Elect
Lenneal J. Henderson
University of Baltimore

Immediate Past President
Mamie Locke
Hampton University

Executive Director
Lois Hollis
Albany State College

Secretary
Cheryl M. Miller
University of Maryland-Baltimore

Treasurer
Sheila D. Ards
University of Minnesota

Membership Secretary
Robert C. Smith
San Francisco State University

Parliamentarian
Nolan Jones
National Governor's Association

Historians
Jewel Prestage
Prairie View A & M

Alex Willingham
Williams College

Executive Council
Maurice Woodard
Howard University

Sheila Harmon-Martin
University of District of Columbia

Mary Nell Morgan
Skidmore College

Earl Picard
Clark-Atlanta University

Rudy Wilson
Norfolk State University

Zaphon Wilson
Appalachian State University

Zelma Mosley
University of Delaware

---

*Contributions for future volumes of the *NPSR* should be sent to the new editor, Georgia A. Persons. (See the invitation to the scholarly community.)

Acknowledgments

The Editor would like to offer a special thanks to the editorial assistant, Vivian M. Brailey, for her contributions to the completion of this volume.

Special thanks to Steven C. Tauber, the assistant to the Book Review Editor.

The Editor also thanks the following reviewers, without whose advice and counsel the volume could not have been produced: Nola Allen, Gabriel Almond, Elsie Barnes, Pamela Carlin, William J. Daniels, David Dickson, Lawrence Hands, Ricky Hill, Oliver Jones, Willard Johnson, George Klosko, Burdett Loomis, Paula D. McClain, Cheryl Miller, K.C. Morrison, David O'Brien, Lawrence O'Toole, Roger Oden, Jim Savage, Robert C. Smith, Pauline Stone, Cedric Robinson, Pearl T. Robinson, Mylon Winn, Louis Wright.

Editor's Introduction
"Regime" and "Race" in Political Science

The Purpose of the *National Political Science Review*

The following papers can be read each one standing alone, as they initially were written. Each serves its own intellectual purpose, according to the method and theory of the author in question. As presented here, however, they also lend themselves to a broader treatment of race and the political order. This form of presentation should be understood against the purpose of the *National Political Science Review (NPSR)*. The *NPSR* is sponsored by an organization—the National Conference of Black Political Scientists (NCOPBS)—most of whose members share the social experience of being African American. It is almost inevitable that a scholarly publication so sponsored would be particularly oriented to "information, insights, findings" that deal with "the ongoing problem" of race and the political order. There is, of course, no intellectual uniformity among those political scientists who share the social history of being African American. Not all are committed to research on subjects related to race. Some find such a concentration on issues of race to be itself a form of intellectual and professional imprisonment that they would seek to escape or refuse in any way to countenance. But if African American political scientists, taken as a group, had no interest in such matters, they would deem themselves, and others would deem them, lacking in self-respect.

Suffice it to say, a social science interest arising from some experience or thought about moral problems is by no means unusual. While social science can arise from pure curiosity, and may often be generated by some existing theory, that is not the only way. Social science is often—though, one emphasizes, not always—a moral perception, a purpose, or a strategic objective armored with a methodology. The powerful influence of the cold war and the nuclear threat upon international relations is one example. The fear of chronic unemployment that dominated England from the 1920s onward, and that dominated the United States from the 1929 depression through World War II, is another. When the *NPSR* was initiated, Lucius Barker wrote of the ultimate hope that "this venture will lead to new information, insights, and findings that add both to our basic knowledge as well as prove helpful in understanding and dealing with important ongoing problems in our politics and society" (Barker, 1989: 3). The subordinate position of African Americans—and, in varying degrees, of other ethnic groups—is what is here seen through moral perception. The trouble with moral perception is that one can become so committed to the problem, or to the answer, that one deceives oneself about data and consequences. Thus, writing can become little more than the grinding of self-confirming propaganda. If methodology is good enough, one will not deceive oneself. If intellectual integrity is present, one will deceive no one else.

Albert O. Hirschman once introduced a volume on Latin America by attempting "to review the principal ideas on the character of Latin America's development problems which have been put forward by Latin American writers and social scientists." The reason he thought it worthwhile was that

> when we are called upon to advise a Latin American country on economic policy it is only natural that, hard pressed, we should first of all attempt to get the "facts," a difficult enough undertaking. But frequently our advice will be futile unless we have gained an *understanding of the understanding* Latin Americans have of their own reality. (Hirschman, 1961: 3–4; emphasis mine)

The Editor is convinced the Hirschman dictum (this volume) is particularly relevant. It is likely that many, perhaps most, white scholars do not comprehend, or actively disagree with, what African American scholars intend to say on the subject of race. The converse may also be true. There is an intellectual central tendency among African American political scientists that is different from the intellectual central tendency of other political scientists when the subject matter is the ill-defined phenomenon called "race."

Different Central Tendencies

The difference in central tendencies is reflected, first, in the claim that the discipline is inhospitable to themselves, and the belief still more that it is inhospitable to matters that they really wish to examine. The evidence most often cited is the claim that the journals were not open to them because the journals were not interested in the things about which they wished to write.

Ralph Bunche was, so far as one has ascertained, the first scholar to articulate this difficulty in a form that is still available for us to read. In 1941, he commented that "there isn't a very cordial reception for papers dealing with the Negro" (Herskovits, 1941). To be fair, this criticism is not properly limited to political science. Abram Lincoln Harris said, "One of my friends? an editor? told me when I published *The Negro as a Capitalist*, the technique is all right, but all this stuff about Negroes is outside my interest'" (Herskovits, 1941).

Jewel L. Prestage spoke precisely in the Bunche vein. In her 1979 Presidential address to the Southern Political Science Association, Dean Prestage said: "[O]ne might wonder aloud if the profession at large does not have some responsibility for creating an atmosphere in which there is *confidence on the part of scholars, in the willingness of those who control the media of dissemination to examine seriously, for purposes of publication, works focusing on the types of concerns which are central to Black political scientists,* women political scientists, and other 'out groups'" (Prestage, 1979: 769; emphasis mine.) Prestage continued to say, "To what extent must the profession bear a responsibility for the feeling of Black political scientists that their legitimate concerns are not considered 'becoming' by the profession at large?"

Walton, McLemore, and Gray went beyond the Bunche-Prestage criticism just four years ago. They make the dual case that the discipline is ill-grounded in the relevant intellectual and political history, and that it sustains work that they deem grossly inadequate. In volume 2 of the *NPSR*, these three authors review some ninety-two books. They show rather decisively that literature on the politics of African Americans, however defined, did not pass through the professional screens of the discipline, in that it did not even make it to the book reviews. There were but ten books reviewed on the subject of African American politics in a period of sixty-two years.

> Needless to say, not much on black politics, or Negro politics as was called, reached the academic community via its major journals. What did reach the academic community were monographs, and these were regional and spotty, if not scattered. At best these books represented a factional, if not highly limited, picture of this area, with several books promoting a distinct racial ideology that gave a negative portrayal of black politics. (Walton, McLemore, & Gray, 1990: 210)

The cited paragraph has one further sentence that represents a point of view very similar to that in Dean Prestage's address: *"There is, then, little wonder that black politics was imbued with such a stigma, and almost no commitment and/ or support from the general academic community"* (emphasis mine).

Walton, McLemore, and Gray return to the topic in volume 3 of the *NPSR* with their claim that the discipline gives sanction support to the wrong kind of work. To make this case, they focused attention upon the Chicago-based books of Harold F. Gosnell and of James Q. Wilson. While Gosnell receives, on the whole, favorable evaluation, both as to methodology and end result, Wilson is subject to severe critique as to methodology ("essayistic," based too much on interviews, saturated with preconceived perceptions that are inaccurate) and affiliated to his "neoconservative" politics (Walton, McLemore, & Gray, 1992: 217–29). Rickey Hill appears to be in the same general mode as Walton, McLemore, and Gray. In a review of *Slavery and Its Consequences* (Goldwin, ed.), Hill writes that it "suffer(s) from the failure to lay bare the truth about the continuing consequences of slavery—the domination of African Americans under explicit racial and class domination" (Hill, 1990: 267).

If Bunche and Prestage criticize the apparent difficulty in securing publication outlets, and Walton, McLemore, & Gray criticize what is published, Mack H. Jones (1992: 3–12) engages in the most far-reaching criticism, which may contain the virtual denial of the possibility of relevance in conventional political science.

> The move toward a political science with descriptive relevance and prescriptive utility for black Americans can only be undertaken by those who see the full liberation of black Americans as the ultimate objective to be served by their work. Scholars so committed would not begin their critique of mainstream political science simply by looking for procedural errors, biases, misplaced emphases, ulterior motives, or similar academic transgressions. Instead they would begin by challenging the existing corpus of political science literature in its entirety. The quest for relevance would begin with a systematic examination of the con-

sciously normative assumptions upon which American political science rests. (Jones, 1992: 36)

If that were done, Jones argues, it would be possible to construct a new paradigm, based upon the worldview of black Americans, and lead to different analyses ending in "empirically useful descriptions" and "more promising prescriptions for action" (Jones, 1992: 38).

It would be impossible to assent to all such criticisms. The criticisms referred to cannot systematically be discussed here. Perhaps the Bunche-Prestage criticism is no longer so valid as it used to be. Technique, it is true, is more important to political scientists than it ever has been, but the scope of American political science surely includes a great deal more material than it did even five years ago (Abramowitz, 1994; Barker, 1994; Beck, Allen, & Rainey, 1993; Glaser, 1994; Harris, Frederic C., 1994; Merelman, 1994; and, Terkildsen, 1993.) This apparent increase in publication, however, may not meet the criticisms being put forth by Hanes Walton and others. It cannot, in and of itself, meet the Jones criticism. If one accepts Jones's premises, then one has to imagine an entirely different intellectual realm. (One may, indeed argue that Jones is in error. Much of what he argues may be far less radical than he would agree, unless one makes "nationalist" or socialist assumptions. In fact, one could argue that the logic of the conventional political science he attacks can be utilized without those assumptions, but that is another matter for separate discussion—although this is part of a critical debate between friends that the Editor and Jones have had informally over some years.)

Whether one agrees or disagrees with any of the particular criticisms—Bunche-Prestage, Walton-McLemore-Gray, or Jones—all converge on one point. Most political scientists do show by example that African American subject matter ("all this stuff about Negroes") has little or nothing to do with their ideas of their own normal work. If this is a correct statement of what political scientists do—and it is empirically testable by content analysis—then it is legitimate to say that political science, as a discipline, appears not to agree with the claim that race has been (Robinson, 1971), and remains, something without which the American polity cannot be explained. Absorbed in their own social worlds, their own work, and themselves, as most of us are, most political scientists leave this to someone else. The same self-absorption characterizes a significant proportion of the African American political scientists. There is a strong tendency to display little interest in other aspects of the discipline, unless and until the connection to the status of African Americans is explicitly made. The structuring of this volume represents an effort to get the phenomenon more overtly before the discipline and, thus, to seek an overlapping of the central tendencies.

This influences the purpose of the *NPSR*. The task of the *NPSR* is, if one may so summarize, partly to enhance the general professional understanding of the understanding that African Americans have of their own reality. But it does not turn it into an organ of propaganda. Authors, however, are not necessarily connected to the NCOBPS. Nor are they necessarily African American in social identity ("race"). Nor are they committed to a predetermined methodology or doctrine. The present volume is specifically designed, choosing from the papers received, in accord with the interest in African Americans,

Africa, and what some colleagues (Hamilton, 1994; Harris, Joseph E., 1994) call the *African diaspora*. At the same time it contains papers about broad generic subjects such as budgeting and interest groups. We thus use "racial regime" as a linking term to engage both types of papers. The authors wrote their papers individually and independently, to fit their several intellectual and professional agendas. Some authors (e.g., Hinckley & Hill; Steed, Moreland, & Baker; and Mullen) wrote with no explicit racial relevance. They did not set out to discuss the theme that has been chosen here. Indeed, for all the Editor knows, some might well dispute it, as is their right.

The Use of the Term *Regime*

There can be occasions when group X and group Y tend to always be in the same relative position. In the extreme case, Y is a permanent *political* minority unable to have its material values—wealth, income, physical security, or of deference values and social respect (Lasswell & Kaplan, 1950)—values defined as prime values that will be safeguarded and not sacrificed in the polity. This signifies an extreme tendency toward stability in the coalitions of winners and the coalitions of losers. There have been circumstances where the active leaders of one political party knew that they could not defeat the leaders of the other party in any significant election. They worked in "modified one party systems" (Ranney & Kendall, 1956) and had to make such benefit-sharing deals as the majority party was willing, for its own convenience, to concede. There have been situations in management-labor relations where union leaders have had, however unwillingly, to stand as dependent allies of management.

No existing usage in political science is conventionally accepted to describe this situation. Therefore, we adapt an old word, *regime*, which political scientists have used in many situations before (Greenstein & Polsby, 1975). To define such more or less persistent—though not necessarily permanent—orders of precedence. While we here speak of regime, the term is not a substitute for protest literature. Nor is it a disguised restatement of the populistic model of "the power structure" (Hunter, 1957). Nor is it any more a term of opprobrium than a term such as *elite*. It is an indication of a more or less definitive political type, and has little or nothing to do with whether a given regime is approved or disapproved. We draw on T. J. Pempel, who himself draws on Easton: "[R]egimes represent a particular social order with what Schattschneider has called a prevailing 'mobilization of bias'" (Pempel, 1992: 120; Easton, 1965: 116–17).

The regime has predicates, or doctrines, that are more or less taken for granted, processes for decision making, institutions through which people act, and policies. It is very unlikely that the results they yield will render *notable* change in the distribution of benefits and burdens except in the very long run.

Extreme rigidities can exist in the middle of competitive fluidity. [This *may* be what is implied in William Ellis's review (see this volume) of a recent work by Mark Roelofs.] This is one of those important problems, implicit in Barker's comment. There are, in some respects, remarkable degrees of fluidity in the American political process. But there are also remarkable rigidities.

In order to illustrate the term, let us think of the economy and the economic regime. The economic regime of the United States is centered upon private ownership of property. The economy is also not some free-standing entity, but a set of transactions bounded by the exercise of power. Property is chiefly organized through the large-scale corporation, capital-aggregated remote trading systems represented by stock markets and other methods. The courts and arbitration methods are the chief means of resolving the number of disputes, which is so large that it is virtually impossible to calculate accurately. In 1963, Berle represented it as having "integrated the democratic process by which we operate our politics with visible or indirect controls of the private decisions by which we work our economics" (Berle, 1963: vii). Berle thus continues to describe the private decisions:

> These [private decisions] run all the way from decisions made by a woman buying groceries at a supermarket to those governing great plants like General Motors in manufacturing and selling automobiles. They include policies adopted by United States Steel as it produces iron and steel and decisions by the Department of Agriculture affecting the western plains in raising wheat and food. The decision-making includes department-store policies in granting credit to consumers, as well as policies of great banks in taking deposits and making loans. The sum total of all economic operations creates and distributes wealth and income, and feeds, clothes, and supplies the United States. (Berle, 1963: vii)

Berle's characterization would be modified in the present because the international facet is so much more emphasized now, since the role of government in some respects is so much more limited as to the regulation of business entries and pricing. The role of government is so much greater now as to regulation of production processes and waste disposal; it is also bigger as to the regulation of hiring, promotion, and discharge practices. But the essentials are that the economic regime is as strong as a private property regime, that any idea of converting it into, say, a socialist system is, and has always been, sheer fantasy.

We could also say that there are cultural regimes. To be more exact, the hypothesis would be that the United States is in its third linguistic-cultural regime. The English-speaking Protestants dominated the regime at the foundation of the republic (Jay: 9), the German and Irish Catholics being incorporated by the Civil War so that Christian was a more adequate definition; Jews and the Southern and East Europeans being incorporated essentially since the election of Franklin Delano Roosevelt, in a regime of Ellis Island cultural pluralism. In other words, the populations so described are no longer within a *political* minority, the prime interests or prime values of which will be sacrificed.

By the same token, we can inquire into the modalities of a "racial regime." If significant benefits and burdens are allocated in accord with some racial hierarchy then—however harsh it may seem—we may characterize the regime as racial. If no significant benefits and no significant burdens could be forecast by knowledge of the social identity called race, then the regime could be seen as nonracial. In American experience the regime was, at one time, purposeful and sustained white advantage. The "white race" (and its preferential standing) was central to virtually all institutional practice, both public and private. [Moreover, the idea of the natural and legitimate primacy of "the white race" has been notably important in the United States, but has not been limited to the question of white over black. Evidences are strong in the history of domestic politics as to the controversy about Chinese (Swisher, 1969; Ringer, 1983: 564–680), Japanese (Daniels, 1968; Grodzins, 1974; Ringer, 1983: 681–943); as recently noted in the *NPSR*, Native Americans (Chaudhuri, 1989: 190–200; McCool, 1992: 249); and Latinos (de la Garza, 1992; Fraga, 1992; Garcia, 1992; Hero, 1992; Jennings, 1993; Schmidt, 1992; Sierra and Sosa-Riddell, 1994: 297–317; Torres, 1992.)]

White advantage in 1994–1995 is not some inexplicable result, but the continuing consequence and explicit *realpolitik*. There was without question Pempel's "sustained fusion between the institutions of the state and particular segments of the socio-economic order" committed to white priority. When scholars at the University of Virginia said, in the early 1900s, that it was foolish to educate the blacks who were then being disfranchised, or that it made no sense to remove the blacks as a current political menace and educate others to be a future economic menace, (Henry, 1994), there can be no doubt that the intention was to argue for a policy of educational disadvantage for African Americans. The policy of many states, not merely Virginia, was over many years purposely to provide a poorer education for African Americans. The consequence was to ensure that, for a number of years after any given decision date, there would be an undereducated population.

The civil rights controversy of the 1960s, as it emerged, was a controversy not only about altering public practice, such as the admission of African Americans to the franchise, but about employing public authority to alter private institutional practice. The advantage is similar to the advantage of inherited financial capital. If an ancestor three generations back acquired the capital, and one has the capital and interest so far accrued, the advantage that one has today exists no matter how the ancestor first acquired the capital. The system of unofficial apartheid that existed at the time of Gunnar Myrdal's project, at of the decision in *Brown v. Board of Education*, of the civil rights movement, or of the adoption of the Civil Rights Act of 1964 and the Voting Rights Act of 1965 is no longer to be seen.

The complete disappearance of the racial regime obviously has not occurred. It has demonstrably been reduced. Except by unusual definitional exercises, as to what is "important," no one can validly claim that the racial regime has not changed in the past century, and in the past twenty-five years. The argument can even be made that it has changed within the past decade. White advantage remains to some substantial degree. It may result from some current purpose, the inheritance of prior privilege, or from belief in principles that stand in the way of alteration (Sniderman & Piazza, 1993). The challenge to racial stratification could not, in the short period and under the circumstances, have overcome all stratification. Nor, in the dynamics of group conflict, could it have entirely prevented some new forms of racial stratification.

Predicates of the American Racial Regime

Contemporary students of American political thought might place more attention upon the intellectual foundations of the American racial regime. It is hardly possible to discuss that regime without discussing slavery. Yet, students of American politics have proceeded as if slavery were a minor matter to which early thinkers had devoted no time. Cedric Robinson's article is necessarily controversial. Robinson proposes a connection between the concept of slavery in Greek political theory and in American politics. Robinson argues that in classical Athens, the upper classes, "the political interests most dependent on slavery," perceived intuitively that democratic values would inevitably mature in antislavery, while democrats saw that slavery would subvert their freedom. Robinson theorizes that an analogy occurred in the American framing. The product, Robinson claims, was a "counterfeit democratic discourse masking republicanism," often articulated by reliance upon Plato's ideas. The *Republic,* "a conflicted text...provided a rhetorical cornice for later disputants."

Robinson asserts a view that is consciously the opposite of the view most commonly held in contemporary American political science. (A quite different view of Greek political thought is represented in Klosko, 1991). Robinson deals not merely with racism, but goes further to criticize "a fabulist academic literature [that] has enveloped the 'Founding Fathers,' nurturing a science of pseudo-democracy whose *metier* is the electoral phenomena associated with "representative democracy." Thus, there is, he sees, a "counterfeit democratic tradition . . . openly hostile to the periodic outbreaks of what it redundantly terms 'participatory' or 'direct' democracy."

Robinson's treatment of Greek political thought deals with what he perceives as the racist implications of a concept of a people being slaves by nature. Whatever is to be said of Greek political thought, that idea reappears in the United States, especially in the nineteenth century, in the claim that Africans were inherently inferior human beings. Biology became a presumptive means of defending slavery. Black scholars, even before the Civil War, had to contend with the means by which they were characterized, and this need continued afterward. The black intellectuals, like their white counterparts, tended to accept the idea of inherent racial differences. What they rejected was that the differences defined superior and inferior or provided a basis for allocating rights and exercising power.

There was an important turn when African American scholars came to the new social science that grounded human action in something other than biology. Charles P. Henry offers a treatment of "the Howard school of thought," which broke with the biologistic interpretation. Henry thus examines the intersecting work of the sociologist E. Franklin Frazier, the economist Abram Lincoln Harris, and the political scientist—better known as world statesman—Ralph Bunche. These young scholars attempted to demonstrate that it was the socioeconomic factors of black urban existence that explained differences between the races. As is often to be expected of scholars from groups under pressure, their work was seldom "pure," but reflective of their own moral engagement. They mounted an attack, in the early 1930s, on longtime race leaders, such as W. E. B. DuBois and James Weldon Johnson, whom they thought afflicted with racial provincialism. Bunche, Frazier, and Harris said the existing leaders were caught up in the needs of the black business elite, ignored the economic needs of the black masses, and were lacking the perception, ability, and understanding to form black-white labor solidarity to force through the necessary reform legislation.

Henry's interpretation is that "the Howard school" promoted a class analysis of race relations, favored the unity of black and white workers in opposition to capitalism, and saw black culture as dysfunctional. They contributed to a paradigm that remained dominant until the 1960s. These views, as interpreted by Henry, constitute only a transitional paradigm. Henry deems their racial paradigm—the only one that black scholars would participate in developing—a theory of assimilation that would call for their disappearance as a racial group. Yet, in Henry's view, these scholars were undoubtedly reflecting the views of a significant segment of the black community in the 1930s.

These differences convince one that there is, indeed, a good deal to study both in knowing what are the predicates of the American racial regime, and in knowing what sustains or alters them.

Processes and Institutions

The regime issue can be examined by generic questions that need not be put in race-specific or race-conscious terms. The mixture of generic and race-conscious questions about processes and institutions is presented in the next section with articles by Hinkley and Hill; Graham and Davis; Herring; Steed, Moreland, and Baker; Kleppner; and McManus and Morehouse. The interest group is a critical institution in the American polity, and need not be approached in race-specific terms. This is part of the appeal in Hinckley and Hill's piece on organizational and interest group strategies where they develop a conception of the role that nonresource organizational characteristics play in the determination of central strategic choices, a role they distinguish from that of resources in the political world. Their argument is that "most central strategic decisions of a group are embedded in that group's character as an organization than in the extent of its resources." The hypothesis bears close scrutiny within the interest-group politics of the African American population. Nothing is more apparent than the extreme discomfort and dissatisfaction likely to be found within such interest groups as the National Association for the Advancement of Colored People (NAACP), the National Urban League, and others that lay claim to African American leadership functions. Political scientists, African American no less than others, have largely left aside the theoretical and practical examination of this issue, and the question of whether Hinckley and Hill are correct and applicable is of major importance.

One indicator of the character of the regime is what happens as issues are presented and processed in the official decision-making entities. Barbara Luck Graham and Abraham Davis examine the 1990 and 1991 terms of the Supreme Court and its decisions affecting racial and ethnic minorities. The specific subjects they examine are voting rights, the discriminatory use of peremptory challenges, secondary and higher education desegregation cases, and *habeas corpus* law.

The decisional propensities of the Rehnquist Court are examined against a federalism framework where a solid majority on the Court gives considerable weight to state sovereignty at the expense of limiting federal powers in the area of civil rights. Graham and Davis argue that the Supreme Court can no longer be viewed as the institution that will be consistently sensitive to the rights of victimized minorities. Only major shifts in the current composition of the Court are likely to reverse this trend. Graham and Davis say their "analysis does reveal a centrally important theme present in many Rehnquist Court decisions which have profound consequences for racial and ethnic minorities' quest to obtain equality before the Court—the Court's adherence to federalism as a mechanism for limiting the role of the federal government in safeguarding minority rights." There is some need for closer attention to federalism and its consequences (Zimmerman, as cited in Harris, Charles W., 1994: 331–33). The Editor would remind political scientists of the analysis of federalism by the late William H. Riker, who wrote, "the main beneficiary throughout American history has been the Southern whites, who have been given the freedom to oppress Negroes, first as slaves and later as a depressed caste" (Riker, 152).

Mary Herring, in a quantitative analysis of the Alabama state senate, provides another way of thinking about the racial regime and its persistence or alteration. She quite expressly posits "that elites may act to prevent serious discussion of some issues is acknowledged as a problematical part of the democratic process." At the same time, she notes that what is kept off an agenda is not there to study. In this paper, she seeks to discern what might have been kept off legislative agendas, comparing agendas before and after implementation of the Voting Rights Act. Herring applies a variant of the issue-domain typology developed by Aage Clausen, in order to define agenda content. She applies this to the Alabama senate sessions of 1961, 1971, 1981, and 1991. On the issue dimensions of civil rights, government intervention in the economy, and social welfare, the content changed in a direction that can be interpreted as more favorable to black constituents. Her roll-call voting scores show a change in the effect of the racial composition of the constituency: in 1961 the percentage of blacks is strongly and negatively associated with anti-black voting, but by 1991 the effect is positive. The race of the legislator has an impact on responsiveness when an issue dimension is dominated by bills with a highly salient racial component.

The potentiality for diminishing the racial quality of the regime is called into question by the implications of Steed, Moreland, and Baker in an examination of party sorting at the local level. What the authors discuss overtly is the withdrawal of local-level party activists from one party and their migration, so to speak, to the opposite party. If this makes parties potentially more coherent in local politics, it also makes them potentially more policy oriented. If the local political constituency, however, is divided on racial grounds, it follows that the party receiving younger white members will, over the next two decades or so, become more resistant to what African Americans would think are their legitimate aspirations. One might expect that this would be especially important in the "hundreds of smaller towns" in the South where the strongest effects of the Voting Rights Act have yet to be felt, "the areas of the South least affected by the civil rights revolution of the 1960s and most in need of minority officeholders to protect the interests of black citizens" (Davidson & Grofman, 1994: 386).

Regimes are sustained, in large measure, by public opinion, and the reshaping of the racial regime in the second half of this century can be conceived as a reshaping of public opinion, both white and black. Two papers here deal with public opinion, in very different ways. Paul Kleppner deals with the regime problem (though nowhere does he adopt the language) by an analysis of the coalition process that resulted in two elections of Harold Washington as Mayor of Chicago. Washington's multiethnic coalition is reported to originate in actions by a previous mayor, Jane Byrne, who was elected with African-American votes, but whose policies there embroiled her administration in virtually continuous battle with the African-American community. That coalition collapsed and was displaced by another in 1989, with the election of Richard M. Daley six years after Harold Washington. Implicit in this analysis has to be the assumption that the subordination of black to white is not a more-or-less inevitable result, but that victory or defeat depends on strength or weakness of strategies. The Chicago experience between 1983 and 1989 is taken to illustrate the possibilities and problems involved in constructing and maintaining multiethnic coalitions. Such coalitions and are said to require cohesiveness within the African-American community and links to potential allies. They do not maintain themselves automatically.

Struggles around seemingly isolated and discrete issues provided African-American leaders with opportunities to develop cohesiveness within their own community, to building links between themselves and both white and Latino activist communities, to define the problem as Byrne and the Democratic machine, and the solution as a reform candidate. The collapse of the Washington coalition, after his death, provided the basis for a return to office of a mayoralty based upon a highly cohesive white electorate.

Susan MacManus and Lawrence Morehouse provide material for further examination of the public opinion structure by examining a judicial retention election in Florida. They set a context by saying that, in any event, "judicial retention elections are becoming more controversial," that they are increasingly subject to "negative advertising." The judge in question was the chief justice of the Florida Supreme Court and was both African American and the author of "a controversial liberal abortion ruling." He was the subject of the closest retention vote in Florida history. A seven-variable, multivariate model explains 65 percent of the variance in the vote for Shaw's retention. Shaw's support was strongest in large, heterogeneous counties where electronic and print media advertising *for* him was heaviest. Opposition was strongest in smaller counties with larger proportions of conservative white voters—those for whom Shaw's abortion ruling and race may have been viewed with the most contempt. The study also examines the correlates of rolloff. An eight-variable, multivariate model explains only 10 percent of the variance in rolloff. The strongest predictor is the "Yes" vote for Shaw's retention.

Policy and Regime

Budgeting could as well be studied as "process" or "institution." But the definition of "regime" takes for granted that policy (the *product* of politics) is vital, and the budget can be seen as the most specific and regular authoritative allocation of policy values. We can ask, then, To what degree are the interests and values specific to African Americans protected by being securely incorporated in budget decisions? Edward Mullen's article (written as a generic inquiry) on federal budgetary decision making, provides one point of departure. Mullen examines the effect of regime composition—using the term *regime* more narrowly than the Editor uses it—and the effect of the electoral cycle on budget decisions. If these electoral events affect budget decisions, they will create temporal patterns in outcomes. Regime composition is divided or unified, depending on whether the same party controls of the Congress and the presidency. In unified regimes, when one party controls both branches, spending is hypothesized to be greater than in divided regimes. The second independent variable is the electoral cycle. Spending patterns should follow the relative importance of electoral years defined by Tufte.

The unit of analysis is the rate of change of individual budget functions. This avoids the effect of monotonic patterns caused by annual spending increases and allows comparisons of the relative strength of different forces on policymaking. Mullen reminds us of researchers who argue that budget analysis presents unique problems because of small samples, non-normal distribution, and wide variability. He thus uses more than one technique to describe the data. This paper uses a variety of tests designed to compensate for limitations in the data caused by distribution, size, and composition.

The analysis indicated that both regime composition and electoral cycle significantly affect spending decisions. Temporal patterns are evident in 40 percent of the functions examined, some affected by regime composition, some by the electoral cycles, some interrelated. If one takes the analysis that Mullen develops, one can begin to think about the consequences for African Americans. In the particular case, the appropriation items studied do not include items that yield a sustained discussion of the implications for African Americans as a somewhat subordinated part of the population. Even education has limited value in this regard, and the data in Mullen's article do not reveal what happens in the social programs at the detailed level, so that one could identify African American-specific relationships. In this regard, Mullen is in the normal pattern of budgetary analysis.[1]

Marjorie Lewis, on invitation of the Editor, sets forth an "integrity model" of the budgetary process. *Integrity*, as she uses the term, does not refer to "good," instead of "bad," as in common speech. Rather, it has to do with optimality and consistency. The budgetary practices of an entity represent its level of integrity. If the budget does not follow the mission, then the integrity is questionable. Integrity may be defined as an instance where the mission is optimal. Integrity is a function an entity's correlation between its mission, goals, and objectives and its budgetary decisions. The question that the note raises, and by implication refers back to Mullen, is what the "mission statement" is for the government as a whole. Moreover, if the racial regime is one of white preference, how does the budget reflect that mission? If, on the other hand, as some critics assert, national policy now incorporates "reverse discrimination," how would that be shown in the budgetary process?

Formal subordination in law no longer exists. Actual subordination, under a pretense of formal equality, no longer receives constitutional sanction, though it would be rash to say that the fabric of segregation is entirely rent. There is a high degree of black entry into governmental competition, when compared to the situation in 1965 or thereabouts. The stress of the African American middle class (Cose, 1993) arises precisely from the fact that it is present in the economy in a manner that seems extraordinary, compared to the same baseline of the 1960s.

Hardly anywhere do African Americans agree that racial stratification is so far removed as to be a minor irritant and nothing more. Whether they are susceptible to a "politics of resentment"—the term used by one critic of this Introduction—might be examined. But African American scholars, who share some of the same perceptions, are open to a variety of approaches to achieve material and deference values they deem essential. Two papers here provide some analysis of different policy approaches.

Nancy Haggard-Gilson examines an attempt to emphasize claims of uniquely black interests by a referendum to detach a poor and black portion of the city of Boston and create a new municipality. This is the "Mandela" referendum, on which Haggard-Gilson offers a substantive analysis of the circumstances leading to the referendum and culminating in its rejection. The original conception was to create a predominantly black city in which black empowerment and autonomy could be achieved. Haggard-Gilson's analysis concludes that the referendum campaign exposed the difficulties of racial or ethnic nationalist politics, showing the complexity of the current political environment of American cities and the rise of the economic and political strength of the suburban areas and private businesses in urban policymaking. The "Mandela" referendum leads, among other things, to opportunities to think about achieving policy by modifying institutions. (One of the most successful such ventures was the creation of the United States, substituting for the institution of the Confederation, in order to achieve a policy of coordinated military defense and to facilitate commercial growth. Urban government reflects institutional modification, including the creation of multiple governmental units, which leads to the situation reviewed by Floyd W. Hayes, III (this volume).

"Affirmative action" is a policy—in national government and in many states and localities (Davis, 194)—that tests the degree of partial change in the whiteness of the regime. The test is severe, and is further analyzed in the article by Mitchell Rice. Rice examines procurement policy designed to aid African American beneficiaries. This is the policy of setting aside (reserving) for African American competitors a designated portion of public contracts. In 1989, the United States Supreme Court pronounced a very restrictive interpretation of the constitutionality of such policies by requiring very strict showing of disparities between white and black claimants. Mitchell Rice examines the consequences of the procedural change, namely "disparity fact-finding studies," as a basis for state and local government set-aside policies. Disparity fact-finding studies have been conducted or are underway in some sixty jurisdictions around the United States. This article discusses set-aside programs after *Croson*, disparity fact-finding studies as mechanism for justifying the adoption or continuation of such programs, and the specific analyses that have been major components of disparity fact-finding studies. It particularly emphasizes disparity fact-finding studies conducted in five jurisdictions.

Change in the "Racial Regime": Zimbabwe

The idea of the racial regime sets up the question of the degree of white dominance over nonwhite groups. But that idea occurs to us only because of the experience of the United States and other white majority countries, especially of Anglo-centric past. However, the problem can be turned upside down. The whole world is still influenced by the consequences of European imperialism in Africa, and in the travails of independence. (Fatton, book review, this volume). But there are the special cases in which the issue is how a white minority will function in a regime dominated by nonwhites. Vernon D. Johnson brings some perspective to this problem in the case of Zimbabwe, formerly known as Southern Rhodesia. (Johnson, "Racial Formation in Zimbabwe.") Johnson, taking his conceptual departure from Omi and Winant (1986) defines "racial formation" as "the process by which social, economic and political forces determine the content and importance of racial categories, and by which they are in turn shaped by racial meanings"(61).

The two peoples who lived in the area, the Ndebele and the Shona, did not then think and act in "racial" terms, but for the most part, cultural and ethnic terms. The growth of colony-wide racial consciousness among Africans was accelerated by the establishment of a responsible settler government that consolidated racial, political, and economic institutions. Modern interest groups expressed an inchoate black nationalism, social welfare association overlapping the Shona and the Ndebele, and early trade union activity.

Some Africans began to think racially, but had yet to mobilize the peasant masses. The Second World War involved Africans in a way that was empowering, and the idea of a white-controlled federation of Northern Rhodesia (Zambia), Southern Rhodesia (Zimbabwe), and Nyasaland (Malawi) became the issue that allowed African nationalism to mature. The Central African Federation, which it is not Johnson's purpose to analyze, did not work and the three units went their separate ways. In Southern Rhodesia, Europeans and Africans coalesced around mutually antagonistic, racially based programs, at least by 1962. The Unilateral Declaration of Independence by the whites led to an independence struggle by the Africans. The emerging nationalist movement was divided, in part by Ndebele and Shona ties, but chiefly between those who sought international support for majority rule, and a government in exile (Nkomo), in contrast to those who emphasized building a stronger base inside the country. In the end, the latter prevailed when the supporters of Robert Mugabe won a clear majority in the first independence election.

The Mugabe government embarked upon a policy of "national reconciliation" in order "to try and unite Zimbabweans in spirit, one might say, and make them accept one another" (Mugabe, in Novicki, 1982: 5). Within this overall framework of national reconciliation there has been political contestation, and some of it has been over matters of race: the raising of minimum wages for farm, domestic, and industrial workers and an increase in the percentage of Africans in the civil service went from 40 percent in 1980 to 60 percent in 1982, with Africans holding roughly half of the senior positions (Curtin, 1987: 107; *Africa News*, 1982: 4–5).

Land reform is, for many Africans, the test of the degree of whiteness or blackness in the regime. At the same time, sweeping land reform was precluded until 1990 by the constitution. The existence of a great deal of unused and underused land in commercial farming areas left the government some room for maneuver. It would acquire this underused and unused land, while leaving white farmers who have continuously occupied and worked their land alone. Johnson also refers to another implicit compromise. He quotes the idea that there is an agreement "which is never discussed but is generally understood," that the present generation of white industrial and agrarian entrepreneurs and managers can stay, but their children should be encouraged to make their lives outside of Zimbabwe. This can be called delayed displacement of the white population. If this were to prove to be the effective policy, in another generation or so race would cease to be an issue in Zimbabwean politics. Johnson concludes that as long as whites retain the socioeconomic advantages created by settler colonialism, racial political contestation will continue to haunt the country. In other words, though Johnson does not say so, the logic of his analysis is that a biracial country must have biracial politics.

Notes

1. In this respect, the Editor is very much indebted for comments of an anonymous reviewer, from which he has abstracted, and which he has incorporated.

References

Abramowitz, I. 1994. "Issue Evolution Reconsidered: Racial Attitudes and Partisanship in the U. S. Electorate." *American Journal of Political Science 38*, 1 (February): 1–24.
Barker, Lucius J. 1994. "Limits of Political Strategy: A Systemic View of the African American Experiences." *American Political Science Review 88* 1 (March).
1989. "New Perspectives in American Politics." *National Political Science Review*.
Beck, Paul Allen, Hal G. Rainey, and Carol Traut. 1990. "Disadvantage, Disaffection, and Race as Divergent Bases for Citizen Fiscal Policy Preferences." *Journal of Politics 52*, 1 (February): 71–93.
Berle, Adolf A. 1963. *The American Economic Republic*. New York: Harcourt, Brace & World, Inc.
Chaudhuri, Joyotpaul. 1989. "Indians and the Social Contract." In *New Perspectives in American Politics*, Lucius Barker, ed. New Brunswick, N.J.: Transaction Publishers.
Cose, Ellis. 1993. *The Rage of a Privileged Class*. New York: Harper Collins.
Daniels, Roger. 1968. *The Politics of Prejudice: The Anti-Japanese Movement in California and the Struggle for Japanese Exclusion*, chap. 1. New York: Atheneum.
Davidson, Chandler, and Bernard Grofman. 1994. "The Voting Rights Act and the Second Reconstruction." In Davidson, Chandler, and Bernard Grofman, eds. *The Quiet Revolution in the South: The Impact of the Voting Rights Act, 1965–1990*. Princeton, N.J.: Princeton University Press.
Davis, Sue. 1994. "Affirmative Action: The Quality of the Debate." In *The Racial Regime: Rigidity within Fluidity*, ed. Matthew Holden, Jr. New Brunswick, N.J.: Transaction Publishers.
Easton, David. 1965. *A Framework for Political Analysis*. Englewood Cliffs, N.J.: Prentice-Hall, Inc.
Ellis, William. Review of Mark Roelofs, *The Poverty of American Politics: A Theoretical Interpretation*. In Matthew Holden, Jr., ed., *The Racial Regime*. New Brunswick, N.J.: Transaction Publishers.
Fatton, Robert, Jr. 1994. Review of William Finnegan, *Mozambique's Descent into Hell*, this volume.

Fraga, Luis. 1992. "Self-Determination, Cultural Pluralism, and Politics." In *Ethnic Politics and Civil Liberties (National Political Science Review 3)*. Lucius J. Barker, ed. New Brunswick, N.J.: Transaction Publishers.

Garcia, F. Chris. 1992. "Introduction." In *Ethnic Politics and Civil Liberties, (National Political Science Review 3)*. Lucius J. Barker, ed. New Brunswick, N.J.: Transaction Publishers.

de la Garza, Rodolpho O. 1992. "Latino Politics: A Futuristic View." In *Ethnic Politics and Civil Liberties*, Lucius Barker, ed. New Brunswick, N.J.: Transaction Publishers.

Glaser, James M. 1994. "Back to the Black Belt: Racial Environment and White Racial Attitudes in the South." *Journal of Politics 56*, 1 (February).

Greenstein, Fred I., and Nelson W. Polsby, eds. *Handbook of Political Science*. Reading, Mass.: Addison-Wesley.

Grodzins, Morton. 1974. *Americans Betrayed: Politics and the Japanese Evacuation*. Chicago: University of Chicago Press.

Hamilton, Ruth Simms. 1994. *Creating A Paradigm and Research Agenda for Comparative Studies of the Worldwide Dispersion of African Peoples*. East Lansing: Michigan State University, African Diaspora Research Project.

Harris, Charles W. 1994. Review of Joseph F. Zimmerman, *Federal Preemption: The Silent Revolution*. In *The Challenge to Racial Stratification (National Political Science Review 4)*, Matthew Holden, Jr., ed. New Brunswick, N.J.: Transaction Publishers.

Harris, Frederic C. 1994. "Something Within: Religion as a Mobilizer of African-American Political Activism." *Journal of Politics 56*, 1 (February).

Harris, Joseph E. 1994. "Ruminations on the African Diaspora in World Politics." *CONEXOES 6*, 1 (April): 2.

Hayes, Floyd W., III. 1994. Review of George R. Weiher, *The Fragmented Metropolis: Political Fragmentation and Metropolitan Segregation*, this volume.

Henry, A'Lelia R. "Virginia's Higher Education Policy Toward Blacks: A Pluralist Critique." Ph. D. dissertation, Government and Foreign Affairs, University of Virginia, 1994.

Hero, Rodney. 1994. "Questions and Approaches in Understanding Latino Politics: The Need for Clarification and Bridging." In *The Challenge to Racial Stratification (National Political Science Review) 4*. Matthew Holden Jr., ed. New Brunswick, N.J.: Transaction Publishers.

Herskovits, Melville J., ed. 1941. *Interdisciplinary Aspects of Negro Studies*. Washington, D.C.: American Council of Learned Societies.

Hill, Rickey. 1990. Review of Robert A. Goldwin, et. al., *Slavery and Its Consequences*. In *National Political Science Review*.

Hinckley, Katherine A., and Bette S. Hill, "Organizational Character and Interest Group Strategies," this volume.

Hirschman, Albert O. 1961. "Ideologies of Development in Latin America." In Hirschman, Albert O., ed. *Latin American Issues: Essays and Comments*. New York: Twentieth Century Fund.

Hunter, Floyd. 1957. *Community Power Structure*.

Jay, John. *The Federalist* (with an introduction by Edward Mead Earle) 2. New York: Modern Library: 9.

Jennings, James, ed. 1993. "A Special Issue on the Political and Social Relations Between Communities of Color." *Trotter Review 7*, 2 (Fall).

Jones, Mack H. 1992. "Political Science and the Black Experience: Issues in Epistemology and Relevance," In *National Political Science Review 3*. New Brunswick, N.J.: Transaction Publishers.

Klosko, George. 1991. "'Racism' in Plato's Republic." *History of Political Thought XII*, 1 (Spring): 1–13.

Lasswell, Harold D., and Abraham Kaplan. 1950. *Power and Society: A Framework for Political Inquiry*. New Haven, Conn.: Yale University Press.

McCool, Daniel. 1992. Review of Linda S. Parker, *Native American Estate: The Struggle Over Indian and Hawaiian Lands*. In *National Political Science Review 3*. New Brunswick, N.J.: Transaction Publishers.

Merelman, Richard M. 1994. "Racial Conflict and Cultural Politics in the United States." *Journal of Politics 56*, 1 (February).

Morris, Richard B. 1969. "Introduction." In Matthew Mellon, *Early American Views on Slavery: From the Letters and Papers of the Founding Fathers*. New York: Bergman Publishers.

Mullen, Edward. "Regimes, Party and Federal Budgeting: Presidential Estimates, Appropriations, and Expenditures," this volume.

Pempel, T. J. 1992. "Restructuring Social Coalitions: State, Society, and Regime." In Rolf Torstendahl, ed. *State Theory and State History*. Newbury Park: SAGE Publications.

Prestage, Jewel L. 1979. "Quelling the Mythical Revolution in Higher Education: Retreat from the Affirmative Action Concept." In *The Journal of Politics 41*.

Ranney, Austin, and Willmoore Kendall. 1956. *The American Party System*. New York: Harcourt Brace.

Riker, William H. 1964. *Federalism: Origin, Operation, Significance*. Boston: Little, Brown and Company.

Ringer, Benjamin. 1983. *"We The People" and Others: America's Treatment of Its Racial Minorities*. New York: Tavistock Publications.

Robinson, Donald L. 1971. *Slavery in the Structure of American Politics 1765–1820*. New York: Harcourt, Brace, and Jovanovich.

Schmidt, Ronald J. 1992. "Latino Politics in the 1990s: A View from California." In *National Political Science Review 3*.

Sierra, Christine M., and Adaljiza Sosa-Riddell. 1992. "Chicanas as Political Actors: Rare Literature, Complex Practice." In *National Political Science Review 3*. New Brunswick, N.J.: Transaction Publishers.

Sniderman, Paul M., and Thomas Piazza. 1993. *The Scar of Race*. Cambridge, Mass.: Belknap Press of Harvard University Press.

Steed, Robert P., Laurence W. Moreland, and Tod A. Baker. "Party Sorting at the Local Level in South Carolina," this volume.

Swisher, Carl Brent. 1969. *Motivation and Political Technique in the California Constitutional Convention, 1878–79*. New York: DaCapo Press.

Terkildsen, N. 1993. "When White Voters Evaluate Black Candidates: The Processing Implications of Candidate Skin Color, Prejudice, and Self-Monitoring." In *American Journal of Political Science 34*, 4 (November): 1032–53.

Torres, Maria. 1992. "Will Cuba Be Next? What About Miami?" In *National Political Science Review 3*. New Brunswick, N.J.: Transaction Publishers.

Walton, Hanes, Leslie L. McLemore, and C. Vernon Gray. 1990. "The Pioneering Books on Black Politics and the Political Science Community, 1903–1965." In *National Political Science Review 2*. New Brunswick, N.J.: Transaction Publishers.

———. 1992. "The Problem of Preconceived Perceptions in Black Urban Politics: The Harold F. Gosnell, James Q. Wilson Legacy." In *National Political Science Review 3*. New Brunswick, N.J.: Transaction Publishers.

Slavery and the Platonic Origins of Anti-Democracy

Cedric Robinson

University of California, Santa Barbara

> ...there was no action or belief or institution in Graeco-Roman antiquity that was not one way or other affected by the possibility that someone involved might be a slave.
> —M. I. Finley[1]

The Twinned Discourse of Slavery and Democracy

The present essay elaborates on ancient Greek thought, and especially upon Plato's *Republic*—a conflicted text, a work that not only surreptitiously recomposed the oppositions of freedom and slavery faced by Plato and his contemporaries, but also provided a rhetorical cornice for later disputants about democracy. For the Greek philosophers of the fifth and fourth centuries, a political theory of democracy was unimaginable. T. H. Irwin tells us that "the best of them failed even to take up the task, since they thought that the Athenian democracy was theoretically indefensible." Instead, the gravity of philosophy was employed to absolve the failure. Two thousands years later, "the loss to political theory" was still being assessed, "for the assumptions of Greek democracy are in some ways similar to, but in many important ways different from, those of what might loosely be called the modern liberal tradition."[2] M. I. Finley also argues that no democratic theory survives from fifth-century Athens,[3] a view rejected by Cynthia Farrar, who maintains that a "version of democratic theory is to be found in the ideas espoused by Protagoras, Thucydides, and Democritus."[4] In classical Athens, slavery and the discourse of democracy were twinned. As historical forces, however, they were opposed. The Athenian upper classes—the political interests most dependent on slavery—intuited that democratic values would inevitably mature in antislavery; the democrats were just as certain that sooner or later slavery would subvert their status as free citizens. More than two thousand years later, again under the pall of a slave economy, an accommodation between slavery and liberty was attempted by the framers of the American Constitution. A counterfeit democratic discourse masking republicanism was substituted in order to reconcile the competing economic and moral claims of liberalism.

The monumental intelligence of Plato, the fourth-century Athenian philosopher, proved to be significant in both instances. Plato's articulation of a racial social order convalesced the proximity of slavery and liberty. No longer, perhaps, the "divine Plato" celebrated during the Italian Renaissance, his *episteme* survived to fertilize and dominate the conceits masqueraded as American democracy. Of his numerous works opposing democracy, none is more central than the *Republic,* his ingenious architecture of a Just Order. In looking at this work, I agree with Irwin and Fisher. Irwin's lament assumes a particularly greater poignancy when we resituate the Hellenic failure as a portent of the moral catastrophes that attended the antinomies of American liberty and slavery.

Ideology and Textual Interpretation

The interpretation of historical and literary texts is a daunting exercise. Evidently, the more disciplined the intelligence behind a work and urgent the anxiety surrounding its subject, the more fugitive its meaning may be. We require a method of excavation that neutralizes the encoded snares, narrative seductions, and elegant blandishments with which the text is salted. If we approach the *Republic* as the work of a political as well as philosophic imagination, Fredric Jameson might urge that we attempt to reveal the terms of Plato's ideological system, which the text represses. We should expect that these "nodal points" will be "unrealized in the surface of the text [and] the logic of the narrative."[5] Typically, the closed text obscures its ideological purpose and represses opposing discourses. But like the compulsive analysis of psychoanalytic literature, the text scatters clues about. In its repetitiveness, its silences, and its corrupted, disjunctive "speech," the text reveals what it was intended to conceal.

Jameson refers to an "ideological system," and the clearest presentation of the notion of ideology he employs is provided by James Kavanagh:

> *Ideology*...does not primarily signify a consciously articulated set of ideas that form the explicit basis of a political "world view," but a system of unconscious or preconscious image-concepts that form the implicit basis for a "lived" relation to the real. Ideology identifies a system of representations through which men and women *imagine* and *experience* as well as *think about* their relation to, and their place within, a given socioeconomic mode of production and its class structure. Indeed, strictly speaking, *ideology* signifies no "thing" at all, but a *type of relation,* "indispensable in any social formation," an "imaginary" relation of individuals to their real conditions of existence.[6]

Ideology provides the inventory of the imagination, the symbolic itinerary of thought, the sensed representations of the real. These elements will constitute our interpretive "system." With it we may determine whether the rudimentary evidence of the *Republic's* partisan character is substantiated by deeper interrogation, and what germ accounts for Western civilization's recurring susceptibility to the work.

After several centuries, the interpretation of Plato has amounted to an industry. This is not quite as forbidding as it might first appear since at least one extensive division of the industry is derisive, having been devoted to preserving particular traditions in the misinterpretation of Plato.[7] Nevertheless, the boundaries are broad and, as E. N. Tigerstedt concludes, "To decide in each controversial case how Plato should be interpreted, is a matter of personal judgement and responsibility.

We are in duty bound to do our best to ascertain, in accordance with the rules of historical and philological criticism, what Plato's words mean, but we have to make sure that we have exhausted the possibilities of objective interpretation before abandoning ourselves to the lures of subjectivism."[8] So let us proceed, as Socrates might have said.

Situating Plato

The first step is to situate Plato. For that we will need instrumentation. Antonio Gramsci's reconstruction of Italian history provides us with the notion of "organic intellectuals," individuals generated from particular activities of their social class whose ideas provided for their class "homogeneity and consciousness of its function...in the economic...social and political field."[9] Pythagoras, Plato, and Aristotle might be usefully thought of as such organic intellectuals, produced in the praxis of training the young and advising the powerful. Their class was characterized by Thomas Africa as "a leisure class [which] reflected the views of a defunct aristocracy [disdainful of] labor and commerce."[10]

On that assumption, Plato's *Republic* might simply be read as a manifesto of this "defunct aristocracy" following upon its defeats at the end of the fifth century (the oligarchic revolutions of 411 B.C. and 404 B.C.), the vanquishing and subsequent disintegration of the Athenian Empire, and the further commercialization and democratization of Athens in the first decades of the fourth century. Starting in 380 B.C. and for the next fifty years, the writings of Socrates catalogue the stasis of fourth-century Greece: "The enumeration of the evils from which Sparta was exempt is, and is meant to be, a roll of the major evils besetting the other states of the Hellenic World. These are: internal strife...slaughter and unlawful exile of citizens...seizure of property...revolutionary changes of constitution...abolition of debts...and redistribution of land."[11]

However, as John Bremer has demonstrated, the *Republic* is no simple political tract.[12] Greek literature (and later Roman literature) was meant to be read aloud, recited in the company of friends, at public occasions (trials, legislative debates, festivals, etc.) or within the academies of Plato, Socrates, or Aristotle. In the oral culture of the Greek *poleis*, oration, recitation, and rhetoric were the commanding forms of thought and expression. The *Republic* is a masterpiece of the form. As Africa implies, such a deliberate style required the existence of leisure (which Greeks referred to as *schole*)—freedom from the preoccupations of labor, commerce, or the management of property and household affairs. In short, literature like the *Republic* or Aristotle's *Politics* emanated from an intellectual strata supported by "unfree" labor: "[T]he propertied classes in the Greek and Roman world derived their surplus, which freed them from the necessity of taking part in the process of production, not from wage labour, as in capitalist society, but mainly from unfree labour of various kinds [i.e. slavery, debt bondage and serfdom]."[13]

The *Republic* is one of the thirty-odd survivals of Plato's didactical lectures on conduct, effective thought, and the state of Athenian (or Greek) affairs. As a cultural, historical, and literary text, its interpretation requires an interpretive system conscious of the work's hegemonic authority (the *Republic* assumes a commanding position in our own civilization). That system must also reveal the minimal "units" or *ideologemes* of its discursive structures, what Jameson terms its *pseudo-idea* systems (conceptual and belief systems, abstract value, opinion, and prejudice) and its *protonarrative* systems (social fantasy).[14]

As a dialogue, the work resonates with a particular stratagem of argumentation and demonstration. *A propos* of the employment of the binary opposition, perhaps the "signatory" logical form found in the *Republic* and Plato's truer dialogues. Only Book I of the *Republic* corresponds to the dialogic form familiar to readers of Plato. For that and other reasons, some scholars have argued that Book I was written much earlier than the rest of the work and existed for some time as "thrasymachus," an independent dialogue.[15] We must be wary of the boundaries imposed by the social and political oppositions which hover beneath the work's surface. As we shall see, Greece was racked by the opposition between poverty and riches (*penia kai ploutos*). Plato transcribed this social opposition between the few and the many into a philosophic contradiction between a chaotic injustice and moral perfection, and a political contradiction between democracy and rule by philosopher kings. He proposed an opposition between the divine orderliness that an imagined hierarchy might achieve and the messiness of actual democracy. Addressing the construction of dualities, Fredric Jameson warns that "the political imagination seeks desperately to transcend, generating the contradictories of each of these terms, mechanically generating all the syntheses logically available to it, while remaining locked into the terms of the original double bind."[16]

Plato's *Republic* as a Guide to Political Discipline

Keeping Jameson's remarks in mind, it is more than possible that the *Republic* is less about philosophic discovery than political discipline. Plato's choice of disputants in the first book of the *Republic* provides the initial hint of the political purpose of the work. Though largely lost on his later audiences and modern commentaries, the small group gathered at the home of Polemarchus was an unlikely social aggregate. Plato's select audience in the Academy understood this. But even for his original, intended audience Plato was satisfied to use "cultural persuasion," signification drawn upon overdetermined or prepacked symbolic materials, rather than resort to overt exposition. He counted on his audience's shared class prejudices, its shared political experiences, and its inventory of cultural-political narratives.

The aged Cephalus and his sons, Polemarchus, Lysias, and Euthydemus were *metic* manufacturers and merchants. As resident aliens in Athens they were denied the political rights and protection afforded to citizens.[17] This would have fateful consequences. They were also a family long associated with Athenian democracy. Cephalus had emigrated to Athens from Syracuse at the behest and sponsorship of his friend Pericles, the prominent Athenian democratic leader in the middle third of the fifth century. Already affluent, Cephalus indicates he had accumulated even greater wealth as an arms manufacturer (presumably with profits from the campaigns of the Peloponnesian War). However, during the oligarchic rule of the Thirty Tyrants (404 B.C.) in Athens, Polemarchus and Lysias were among the wealthy metics arrested by the extremist junta. "Lysias and his brother Polemarchus may have been among the richest men in late-fifth-century Athens, and in 404 B.C. they are certainly said to have owned the largest number of slaves which can be reliably credited to any Greek of the Classical period, but in Athens they were metics (resident foreigners) and enjoyed no political rights."[18] Polemarchus was executed by the Board of Eleven and his property (the largest Athenian manufacturing establishment mentioned in the literature) confiscated. After his own arrest, Lysias barely escaped with his life. But with the democracy restored, and upon his return from exile with the victorious *demos*, Lysias had prosecuted Eratosthenes at the court of accounting in 403 B.C. for his role in Polemarchus's execution.[19] Another (but silent) witness to the *Republic's* dialogue, Niceratus, was the son of the rather wealthy Athenian leader Nicias and had met the same fate (through association?) as Polemarchus.[20]

Among the remaining prominent participants in the dialogue were Plato's brothers, Glaucon and Adeimantus (Athenians) and the foreigner, Thrasymachus, the Chalcedonian teacher of rhetoric. Plato's family was aristocratic. His uncle Charmides and great-uncle Critias had been prominent in the extreme oligarchic rule of the Thirty Tyrants. As the discussion in the *Republic* runs its course, it becomes clear that Socrates's attention is largely directed to the instruction of Glaucon and Adeimantus since the resident aliens and committed democrats alike are irrelevant to the future ideal polis.

In view of these familial identities and political persuasions, it is possible to understand how Plato's aristocratic audience accepted Socrates's obviously facile refutations of the conjectures of Cephalus, Polemarchus, and Thrasymachus. Annas concludes: "Socrates may be right, but his method of discussion and argument are not adequate to deal with someone who disagrees with him in a basic and systematic way. In Book I of the *Republic* we see the ineffectiveness of Socratic methods in dealing with the powerful claim of the moral skeptic, that there is really no reason to be just, and that one should, if one is rational and intelligent, look after one's own interest."[21] The first two were (1) supporters of the democracy; (2) metics; and (3) manufacturers whose interference in Athenian politics had been at the cost of Polemarchus's life and the loss of much of the wealth Cephalus so valued. Finally, Lysias had publicly prosecuted a representative of Athens's aristocracy. Plato's original audience would have debased Cephalus and his sons on all four accounts.[22] Finally, Thrasymachus, Socrates's most persistent and rude interrogator in the dialogues, was both foreign and so arrogant as to demand payment for his thoughts. The Academy knew on both scores that Thrasymachus the sophist was unworthy to challenge Plato's master.

The physical and temporal locations of the dialogue were also significant. Athenian law forbade metic merchants to reside in Athens. Polemarchus resided with his fellow tradesmen and manufacturers in Peiraeus, the "licentious" and prostitute-ridden seaport five miles southwest of Athens.[23] The port was thus associated with just the sort of self-indulgence and moral pollution which Socrates and Plato so frequently lamented. More importantly, in 403 B.C., it was from Peiraeus that the democratic resistance supported by metics and slaves successfully besieged Athens and fought off the army of the Thirty Tyrants and their Spartan allies.[24] The dialogue itself, Plato hinted, had taken place in the late 420s.[25] Situating the Republic at Peiraeus in the period preceding the oligarchic revolutions of 411 B.C. and 404 B.C. thus added a certain foreboding to the dialogue.

In light of this indirect evidence, one might suspect the author of the *Republic* of special pleading. Our interpretive instrument, fortunately, generates a much more profound and substantial penetration of the text. This is particularly important if we pursue the *Republic* less for its peculiar notion of a Just Order or its Pythagorean metaphysics of Absolutes than for its justification of the stratification of domination.

One rather glaring instance of an "unconscious or preconscious image-concept" in the *Republic* is Plato's evocation of Hesiod's myth of the origins of human development. Plato first advocates it as a "noble lie" ("noble falsehood" or "magnificent myth") with which to fashion the civic identity of his "republic":

> "We shall," I said, "tell our citizens the following tale: 'You are, all of you in this community, brothers. But when god fashioned you, he added gold in the composition of those of you who are qualified to be Rulers (which is why their prestige is greatest); he put silver in the Auxiliaries, and iron and bronze in the farmers and other workers.'" (415a)

"In the interests of unity," Julia Annas remarks, "the citizens are to be brought to accept a story which is avowedly not true."[26] Plato's unity, his Just Order, acquires its legitimation in part through the introduction of a racial protonarrative.

The "Racial" Character of Plato's Myth

Scholars disagree strongly as to whether the ruse, the noble myth, reveals a sinister intent on Plato's part. The racial character and social imaginary of the myth itself are troubling.

The social imaginary of Plato's racial myth is a slave society, the social order long familiar to Greeks of the Classical Age and before. Classical Athens, like the other leading Greek city-states, was a slave society. Slave labor was exploited in agriculture, industry, commerce, domestic service, private and public management, entertainment, state service, and war by the *rentier* and hoplite classes, by small farmers and artisans, *metic* merchants and manufacturers, as well as by the State.[27]

The documents from the period indicate a general acceptance of slavery. "Even when crisis turned into civil war and revolution, slavery remained unchallenged."[28] For Attica, two *fourth*-century sources—the census of Demetrius of Pharlerum and Hypereides—put the number of slaves at 400,000 and 150,000, respectively.[29] Finley accepts a total between 60,000 to 80,000 for the period, while the most conservative surmises are as low as 20,000.[30] Desmond Lee estimates that the total population of Plato's Athens was between 200,000 to 300,000; 60,000 to 80,000 slaves, 35,000 to 40,000 metics, and 35,000 to 45,000 male citizens.[31] Though it is not certain, the majority of slaves were apparently non-Greeks, a good proportion of those Thracians.[32]

Gregory Vlastos has persuasively demonstrated, taking to task John Wild, that the presumption of slavery in the Just Order of the *Republic* is so unremarkable for Plato that his few references to that aspect of the economy are casual.[33] More significant, however, are Plato's justifications for slavery found scattered in his other works, particularly the *Laws* and *Timaeus*. In the *Republic*, the gold which racially distinguishes those "qualified to be Rulers" from the bronze of laborers, elsewhere in Plato are signified by *logos* (reason) and *doxa* (belief). Vlastos drew attention to the importance of the "slave metaphor" in Plato's work by asserting: "Plato uses one and the same principle to interpret (and justify) political authority and the master's right to govern the slave, political obligation and the slave's duty to obey his master." For Plato, Vlastos understood, slavery was a key to the necessary *(ananke)* order of the world:

> [H]is views about slavery, state, man, and the world, all illustrate a single hierarchic pattern; and that the key to the pattern is in his idea of *logos* with all the implications of a dualist epistemology. The slave lacks *logos*; so does the multitude in the state, the body in man, and material necessity in the universe. Left to itself each of these would be disorderly and vicious in the sense of that untranslatably Greek word, *hybris*. Order is imposed upon them by a benevolent superior: master, guardian, mind, demiurge. ...In such an intellectual scheme slavery is "natural"; in perfect harmony with one's notions about the nature of the world and of man.[34]

Vlastos argued that the transference of the slave metaphor between Plato's anthropology, political theory, and ethics—*logos*—and his metaphysics (the Forms) and cosmology (the soul) was the elementary premise of Plato's refutation of the "contract theorists" and their "subversive view that slavery was unnatural." His attack extended to Ionian physics (with its imposition of an autonomous nature and denial of superior agency) as a consort to democratic theorists. The debate between Plato and those intent upon trivializing slavery as a mere convention concerned the economic basis of Athenian (and Greek) society. "Their conflicting idealism," Vlastos insisted, "mirrored the real contradiction in Athenian society: a free political community that rested on a slave economy."[35] No wonder, then, despite his objections to Plato's Just Order, Aristotle felt compelled to reaffirm Plato's argument, instituting natural law to justify slavery: "Therefore whenever there is the same wide discrepancy between human beings as there is between soul and body or between man and beast, then those whose condition is such that their function is the use of their bodies and nothing better can be expected of them, those, I say, are slaves by nature" (*Politics*, 1254b16).

So "normal" was the inferiorization and omnipresence of slaves to Plato and his contemporaries that "but for a few scattered texts in the Athenian orators and a handful of inscriptions we should have hardly any specific evidence of the central role played by slaves in production even in Attica itself."[36] S. Douglas Olson informs us that the protocols of power relations and social discourse between Athenian citizens and slaves are preserved in Aristophanes's comedies:

> The fact that mute slaves often have names while slaves with speaking parts do not...suggests that something important is at stake here.... Silent slaves can accordingly be allowed [a name], not only for the sake of social verisimilitude but also in order that vocatives can be used against them to determine their behaviour. Servile characters who can speak (and thus potentially speak back) to their masters, on the other hand, are apparently best kept anonymous and thus prevented from wielding their names in potentially subversive ways.[37]

In the *Republic*, the determinant place of this racial fiction as a conceit in Plato's own ideology is revealed later when it rather surprisingly resurfaces as a part of Plato's *political theory!* In Book Eight of the *Republic*, we discover Plato resorting to the same mythic material as a means of explaining the beginnings of "imperfect societies" or "imperfect constitutions." Plato asserts that "change in any society starts with civil strife among the ruling class" (545d). Confronted by the self-invented paradox[38] that his perfect State has changed (a contradiction), Plato sought to escape responsibility by momentarily surrendering instruction to the Muses: "Shall we invoke the Muses, like Homer, and ask them to tell us 'how the quarrel first began'?" (545e). According to the Muses, the first instance (timarchy) of such division within the ruling class results from the trespass against the myth:

> This whole geometrical number, controlling the process, determines the quality of births, and when the Guardians ignore this and mate brides and bridegrooms inopportunely, the resulting children will be neither gifted nor lucky.... In the next generation Rulers will be appointed who have lost the true Guardian's capacity to distinguish the metals from which the different classes of your citizens, like Hesiod's, are made—gold, silver, bronze and iron; and when iron and silver or bronze and gold are mixed, an inconsistent and uneven material is produced, whose irregularities, wherever they occur, must engender war and hatred. That, then is the pedigree of strife, wherever it happens. (546c–547a)

In similar fashion, Plato (reassuming authority for his opinions) then determines that the next degradation of society—from timarchy to oligarchy—is again a responsibility of the ruling class. Timarchy degenerates into the further concentration of wealth and the eventual disfranchisement of the poor through oligarchic legislation, armed violence, and terrorism. In time, oligarchic society, split into two factions, inevitably nurtures the seeds of its own destruction—a class of renegade, impoverished oligarches: "This neglect [of self-discipline] and the encouragement of extravagance in an oligarchy often reduces to poverty men born for better things.... Some of them are in debt, some disfranchised, some both, and they settle down, armed with their stings, and with hatred in their hearts, to plot against those who have deprived them of their property and against the rest of society, and to long for revolution" (555de). From these embittered elites emerge the leaders of the democratic revolution (564b).

Finally, unavoidably (even for Plato), it is only in the ultimate degeneracy (from democracy to tyranny) that the demos becomes the culpable class. The *demos,* reacting to the counterrevolution of the wealthy, "put forward a single popular leader, whom they nurse to greatness...this leadership is the root from which tyranny invariably springs" (565c–d). Democracy and its issue, tyranny, spring from miscegenation and fractures of the ruling class.

Of course, Plato's political theory is a total fiction. It corresponds to neither the surviving testimony of revolutionary change in Greek societies nor to the documented reconstructions of later ancient Roman historians and modern classicists. For one instance, Solon, an oligarch credited with laying down the founding codes of Athenian democracy, indicates that it was a popular rebellion rather than factionalism in the ruling class that compelled radical changes in the Athenian *polis* at the beginning of the sixth century. In the midst of Solon's boasts, we find a rebellion: "[H]ad another than I taken the goad in hand, a wicked and avid man, he would not have been able to keep the people in check. For if I had wanted what those who were in revolt were wanting then, or again what their opponents would have wished for them, the city would have been bereft of many men."[39]

Plato's historical environment was full of counterinstances to his political theory: the oligarchies' massacre of 700 *demos* at Aegina in the early fifth century; the oligarchic destruction of the democracies in Samos (404 B.C.) and Rhodes (391 B.C.); the aristocratic defense of Phlius (the site for Plato's *Phaedo*) in 369 B.C.; the democratic example of Plato's aristocratic contemporary Empedocles at Acragas; the *skytalismos* democratic revolt in Argos (370 B.C.); and earlier the tyrannies of the sixth century, which were "quisling" regimes for their Persian masters.[40] Modern historians like A. Fuks,[41] Finley,[42] Sealey,[43] and St. Croix confirm similar problematics in the fifth and fourth centuries for Plato's political theory. According to Paul Cartledge, the "Age of Revolution" preceding the appearances of democracy in the fifth century was conditioned by "relative overpopulation leading to settlement abroad and stimulating a decisive switch from pasturage to arable farming at home; growth of overseas trade, especially in metals and luxury goods and raw materials; decline of monarchy; full development of the *polis;* questioning of social and political values; and contrivance of new political expedients."[44]

Almost exclusively, Plato draws attention to the ruling classes in both his political theory and philosophy. It is as if the rest of Greek humanity was not real to him. For Plato, the lack of discipline within the ruling classes was a sufficient explanation for the successive appearances of imperfect constitutions—each more degraded than its predecessor. Plato's political theory thus repressed the history of popular rebellion and with it the recognition that social agency might have its genesis from the general populace. Even in his "treatment" of the degeneracy of democracy to tyranny, the *demos* is denied true agency through the selection of a demagogue. In his philosophy, "justice" (permanent order) is opposed to liberty and equality. Logically, then, he is compelled to substitute theory for the literary and cultural record that revealed the long history of popular rebellion in the Greek experience. This repression was one aspect of his political *imagination,* his *experience* of the real, his *ideology.*

One other aspect of his political theory was its manufacture of the historical origins of power. For Plato, power (rule) was identical to nobility (gold). In his presentation, the concentrations of power in Greece were totally divorced from an association with the ill-remembered centuries of tribal warfare, organized violence, pillage, exploitation of agrarian cultivators, colonization, piracy, and migration—in short, all we know of Greek dynastic history from the Dorian invasions (sometime before 1200 B.C.) to the fourth century. On the issue of these events as sources of timarchic, oligarchic, and tyrannical societies, Plato is silent. He suffocates a Thucydidean history by substituting a fabulous and theoretic construction of antecedent events. The mythical terms through which he relates to the real are ideological. Plato's contemporary, Isocrates, embellished a similar fabulous history.[45] The *Republic* is a *protonarrative* system: a "social fantasy" proceeding from the "preconstructed reality" that the aristocratic classes are the descendants of the gods.

Why Plato's Influence Persists

Plato's fascinating deceits in the *Republic* were inspired by the supersession of a narrow class partisanship. The deficiencies which have so frequently subverted modern Western commentaries on Plato are of a different order. Yet the two are related. If we are to understand a fundamental reason for the appreciation of Plato's work after the passage of more than two millennia, it becomes necessary to assemble Plato's moral and social philosophical thought with the historical provenance of modern Western civilization.

From the time of Aristotle to the present, the presence of slave systems, slave trades, and slave economies was nearly a constant in the historical record of the West. In Europe itself, in the eastern, Mediterranean, and western regions, large- or small-scale slave systems occur from the Roman Imperial era down to modern times.[46] During this 2000-year period, and beyond the European peninsula itself, Western economies have either cohered to, appropriated, or invented slave systems in Asia, Africa, or the Americas. Though, obviously, slavery was not a uniquely Western institution, the "problem" of slavery in Western culture (as David Brion Davis has supposed) manifested itself in particular forms. It concerned the contradictions between slavery and the ethical, philosophical, and social impulses coalescing into "Western humanism." The presence of slavery in Western civilization has, as Finley persuasively shows, played havoc with modern Western historiography. Assessing the most important studies of slavery in the past three hundred years, Finley remarks, "men of firm belief were compelled to find some sort of explanation of the long survival of slavery after the triumph of Christianity."[47] For example, that discursive practice which Hayden White maintains is "inextricably bound up with modern Western culture's notions about its own identity, its status as a (or rather *the*) civilization."[48] Similarly, in the most eminently authoritative moral, theological, political, and juridical discourses spawned in the West, the rationalizations of slavery were legion. The scholastic defenders of slavery could be found in every epoch: pagan or Christian, ancient and medieval, feudal and bourgeois, the Enlightenment and its successors. In sheer number and resourcefulness, if not in conceptual consistency, the apologists—among them Plato, Aristotle, Cicero, Augustine, Aquinas, Thomas More, Las Casas, Grotius, Hobbes, and Locke—easily overwhelmed their formal opposition, just as earlier Plato had vanquished the antislavery Sophists.[49]

After the fourteenth century, as the more powerful European states became implicated in world-systemic slave systems, the utility of Platonic and Aristotelian thought became greater. "The *Philosophy* of Aristotle had such an authority in sixteenth and seventeenth century Spain, that any attack on him 'was regarded as a dangerous heresy,' and the *Politics* enjoyed a *respecto casi supersticioso*."[50] David Brion Davis acknowledges that the "frigid sympathy" for the slave, which W. L. Westermann had ascribed to the Roman world, seemed all but extinguished. "Throughout Europe scholars debated the relation of slavery to divine and natural law as an exercise in dialectic; it was as if the learned volumes on law and statecraft had been produced in a different world from that which contained the Negro captives awaiting shipment at Elmina Castle, the disease and sickening stench of the slave ships, and the regimented labor of colonial plantations."[51] Davis continues that "the inherent contradiction of human slavery had always generated dualisms in thought, but by the sixteenth and seventeenth centuries Europeans had arrived at the greatest dualism of all—the momentous division between an increasing devotion to liberty in Europe and an expanding mercantile system based on Negro labor in America." Paradoxically, the unprecedented breadth of the debates around African slavery which raged in Europe and the New World in the eighteenth and nineteenth centuries concealed a deeper cultural consensus: the recession to a racialized discourse.

Vlastos concluded from his critique of Plato "that a consistent democratic philosophy would repudiate slavery altogether."[52] The abolition of slavery proclaimed in 1794 by the National Convention during the French Revolution can be read as a confirmation of that view.[53] That this was not the case with the founding of the American republic, a decade earlier, suggests (if Vlastos is correct) that something other than "a consistent democratic philosophy" informed North American republicanism. Democratic philosophy was subverted by plutocracy: the construction of a politicoeconomic order whose rulers depended on the preservation of a slave economy, the exploitation of "white" laborers (male and female), the severe restriction of women's political rights, and the expropriation of native Americans.

During the eighteenth and nineteenth centuries, the Hellenism of the Anglo-Saxon world—as articulated in its moral and aesthetic literature and its social thought—centered on Plato, Aristotle, and Homer. Coleridge narrowed that list even further when he declared, "Every man is born an Aristotelian, or a Platonist.... They are the two classes of men, beside which it is next to impossible to conceive a third."[54] Aristotle, in particular, fell on fertile soil in the racialisms of Anglo-Saxonism in Victorian England and plantocracy in America and the British West Indies.[55] Mavis Campbell[56] discusses in detail the Aristotelian influence on George Fitzhugh,[57] George Frederick Holmes (professor of history at the University of Virginia),[58] John Calhoun,[59] and Arthur Lee.[60] The presence of Aristotle's *Politics* was so ubiquitous among the numerous defenses of slavery that Campbell suggests, "It would be too extensive a list to name all the nineteenth-century Southerners who were influenced by Aristotle."[61] Others argue along the same line. W. S. Jenkins says that "the Aristotelian influence upon Southern thought was strong and may be traced through much of the pro-slavery literature.[62] James Oakes similarly says: "Alfred Taylor Bledsoe, Thomas R. R. Cobb, and other pro-slavery writers...gave prominent display to quotations from Aristotle's *Politics*.... Antebellum Southerners were apparently more receptive to Aristotle's extreme pronouncements than were the philosopher's fellow Athenians."[63]

In late-eighteenth-century America, democracy was abhorrent to the most prominent and influential revolutionists.[64] As Edmund Morgan observed: "The key to the puzzle, historically, [was] Virginia. Virginia was the largest of the new United States, in territory, in population, in influence—and in slaveholding."[65] Thomas Jefferson and James Madison acquired slaves while opposing slavery, and like most in their fraternity, they fought and spoke for liberty while opposing democracy. Jefferson, intimately familiar with the "antients," was very critical of Plato. In his private correspondence, Jefferson frequently referred to Plato's "foggy brain" and his abuse of Socrates.[66] In a letter to John Adams in 1814, Jefferson commented on the *Republic*: "While wading through the whimsies, the puerilities and unintelligible jargon of this work, I laid it down often to ask myself how it could have been, that the world should have so long consented to given reputation to such nonsense as this?.... And particularly, how could Cicero [Jefferson's favorite 'antient'] bestow such eulogies on Plato?"[67] Fitzhugh, who edited this correspondence, himself enthuses over "our Indoeuropean stock, that masterful race of tall, blue-eyed, blond-haired Northmen, whose European beginnings we have now learned to identify with the Greeks and Romans of antiquity themselves, but whose spiritual and racial unity had scarcely been established in the science of Jefferson's day."[68] Yet he, one of the most precocious intellects of his generation (he began his study of Greek, Latin, and French at age nine), reconciled these contradictions through race. However critical he was on other matters, on slavery and racial superiority Jefferson never issues a challenge to Plato. Instead, Jefferson wholly mimicked the "antient's" construction of doctrines supportive of a racial order:

> Comparing [blacks] by their faculties of memory, reason, and imagination, it appears to me, that in memory they are equal to the whites; in reason much inferior.... Many millions of them have been brought to, and born in America.... Some have been liberally educated, and all have lived in countries where the arts and sciences are cultivated to a considerable degree, and have had before their eyes samples of the best works from abroad.... But never yet could I find that a black had uttered a thought above the level of plain narration; never see even an elementary trait of painting or sculpture.[69]

Jefferson thus complemented the race discourse fertilizing in race science[70] and popular culture (minstrelsy)[71] in eighteenth and nineteenth centuries Europe and America. Among the ruling classes as well as the laboring classes, the inventions of the white and black races rationalized the suturing of liberty, freedom, domination, and oppression.[72] Winthrop Jordan provides an artifact of the moral and political system being displaced by race discourse in the eighteenth century. In the Virginia code of 1705 "negroes, mulattos, or Indians, although christians, or Jews, Moors, Mahometans, or other infidels" were barred from purchasing "christian servants." The "invention" of the idea of a race, along with the idea of ineradicable differences between races, made it possible for people who believed in "liberty" and in "freedom" to also believe simultaneously in "liberty" and "freedom" for themselves and in their right to "dominate" and to "oppress" others. The social imaginary of a slave order enveloped morality and consigned the reciprocal principles of community to a select few. Many scholars concerned with the anomaly between the American Revolution and slavery still insist the problem was reconciling natural rights philosophy and slavery: "Eighteenth-century science had concluded that Negroes were, like the whites, homo sapiens; but this conclusion did not conflict with the reality that Negroes were men, 'persons,' who were legally property.... In the colonial ideology the right of property was central."[73] Juxtaposed to the older and more local signs of difference—the racial codes assigned to previously enslaved peoples in Europe—the invented races brought to the "white" imagination a sociology of desire perhaps more accessible than Christian community. The new difference permitted suspension of the reach of the moral, gentle protocols lurking within Christianity. But simultaneously, within the embrace of the White Race, the new difference affirmed and conditioned the fraternal kinship between the superior and less-privileged strata.[74]

The constitutional debates read as if they were drawn directly from the *Republic*. This is not surprising since much of what passed for learning in the period (some of the conveners had attended British universities, others American colleges, and quite a few were autodidacts) stressed the classics.[75] As Pierce Butler (South Carolina), one of the framers, assured a friend in October, 1787, "We tried to avoid what appeared to us the weak parts of Antient as well as Modern Republics."[76] Apparently, they believed they had discovered what Fustel de Coulanges later drew from the Greek experience, "The ruling class would perhaps have avoided the advent of democracy if they had been able to found what Thucydides calls [oligarchia isonomos],—that is to say, the government for a few, and liberty for all."[77]

Most certainly, a strong antidemocratic spirit enveloped the proceedings at Philadelphia in 1787.[78] Sherman of Connecticut abhorred direct elections: "The people" he said, "[immediately] should have as little to do as may be about the Government. They want information and are constantly liable to be misled." Elbridge Gerry (Massachusetts), who refused to endorse the Convention's agreement, suggested, "The evils we experience flow from the excess of democracy." Madison (Virginia) warned, "Democratic communities may be unsteady, and be led to action by the impulse of the moment."

At the close of the convention, George Mason, the wealthy Virginian who also opposed the final constitutional draft, reported on its handiwork: "This government will set out a moderate aristocracy: it is at present impossible to foresee whether it will, in its operation, produce a monarchy, or a corrupt, tyrannical aristocracy; it will most probably vibrate some years between the two, and then terminate in the one or the other."[79] Madison, his social and political junior, agreed: the new state was an "oligarchy" (*Federalist Paper*, No. 59). In the discussion regarding Senate terms of office, Madison suggested that long terms provided necessary "permanency": "Landholders ought to have a share in the government, to support these valuable [landed] interests.... They ought to be so constituted as to protect the minority of the opulent against the majority."[80]

Many constitutional scholars for whom Madison's words are normally authoritative routinely ignore such sentiments. They prefer the interpretation of the Constitution which ennobles its architects: "[T]here is one fundamental truth about the Founding Fathers...they were first and foremost superb democratic politicians."[81] Over the years, then, the ignominy of the oligarchies and their governing machinery has been concealed. Indeed, a fabulist academic literature has enveloped the "Founding Fathers," nurturing a science of pseudodemocracy whose *metier* is the electoral phenomena associated with "representative democracy."[82] This counterfeit democratic tradition is openly hostile to the periodic outbreaks of what it redundantly terms "participatory" or "direct" democracy.[83] Ironically, the tradition and its techniques often parrot the corruption of philosophic instruction which Plato criticized in the *Republic:*

> Suppose a man was in charge of a large and powerful animal, and made a study of its moods and wants; he would learn when to approach and handle it, when and why it was especially savage or gentle, what the different noises it made meant, and what tone of voice to use to soothe or annoy it. All this he might learn...and then call it a science, and reduce it to a system and set up to teach it. But he would not really know which of the creature's tastes and desires was admirable or shameful, good or bad, right or wrong...remaining quite blind to the real nature of and difference between inevitability and goodness. (493b-c)

It was to this "queer" (Plato's term) procedure that Finley addressed himself in a severe critique of the pseudodemocratic subterrain he uncovered in Seymour Martin Lipset's *Political Man* (1960). Finley suggested:

> Both Plato and Lipset would leave politics to experts, the former to rigorously trained philosophers who, having apprehended the Truth, will thereafter be guided by the Truth absolutely; the latter to professional politicians (or to politicians in consort with the bureaucracy), who will be guided by their expertise in the art of the possible and be periodically checked by an election, the democratic device that gives the people a choice between competing groups of experts, and, to that extent, a measure of control...both agree that popular *initiative* in political decisions is disastrous...naive ideology."[84]

(Referring to Lipset's contemporaries, Quentin Skinner remarked: "[T]he operational definition of democracy supplied by Dahl and the other empirical theorists is in fact perfectly adapted to performing precisely [its] ideological task.... For its application suggests that the existence of a ruling elite may be compatible with the maintenance of a genuinely democratic political system.")[85] The elitist theory of democracy which Lipset championed did not so much appropriate Plato but rather mirrored its Platonic genealogy.

It has long been evident that the *Republic's* purpose was to mount a sustained attack on democracy. But its durability as an eminent work in modern liberal democratic society has been taken as a testament to the recognition of its literary, philosophical, ethical, and historical merits rather than its ideological prosecution. Such is not the whole explanation. In its antidemocratic plutocratic prejudice, the *Republic* provides an authority rich in intellectual stratagems a propos to the political discourse embedded in the American political order. Plato survives because if he had not existed, he would have had to be invented.

Notes

1. M. I. Finley, *Ancient Slavery and Modern Ideology* (New York: Viking Press, 1980), 65.
2. T. H. Irwin, "Socrates and Athenian Democracy," *Philosophy & Public Affairs* 18, 2 (Spring, 1989): 205.
3. M. I. Finley, *Democracy, Ancient and Modern* (New Brunswick, N.J.: Rutgers University Press, 1985), 28.
4. Cynthia Farrar, *The Origins of Democratic Thinking* (Cambridge: Cambridge University Press, 1988), 1.
5. Fredric Jameson, *The Political Unconscious* (Ithaca, N.Y.: Cornell University Press, 1967), 48.
6. James Kavanagh, "'To the Same Defect': Toward a Critique of the Ideology of the Aesthetic," *Bucknell Review* 27, 1 (1982): 103.
7. E. N. Tigerstedt, *Interpreting Plato* (Stockholm: Almquist & Wiksell International, 1976), chaps. II and III; the examples of Ronald Levinson, *In Defense of Plato* (Cambridge: Harvard University Press, 1953); Irwin, "Socrates and Athenian Democracy," page no. passim.
8. E. N. Tigerstedt, *Interpreting Plato*, 107.
9. Antonio Gramsci, *The Modern Prince and Other Writings* (New York: International Publishers, 1967), 118.
10. Thomas Africa, *Science and the State in Greece and Rome* (New York: John Wiley & Sons, 1967), 35–36. See also F. L. Vatai, *Intellectuals in Politics in the Greek World* (London: Croom Helm, 1984).
11. Alexander Fuks, "Isokrates and the Social-Economic Situation in Greece," *Ancient Society*, 3 (1972): 19.
12. John Bremer, *On Plato's Polity* (Houston, Tex.: Institute of Philosophy, 1984).
13. G. E. M. de Ste. Croix, *The Class Struggle in the Ancient Greek World* (Ithaca, N.Y.: Cornell University Press, 1981), 39.
14. Jameson, *The Political Unconscious*, 87.
15. "Thrasymachus". Cf. Julia Annas, *An Introduction to Plato's Republic* (Oxford: Clarendon Press, 1981), 17; George Klosko, *The Development of Plato's Political Theory* (New York: Methuen, 1986), 16.
16. Jameson, *The Political Unconscious*, 48.
17. For the relationship between citizenship and land in classical Greece, see T. E. Rihill, "EKTHMOPOI: Partners in Crime," *Journal of Hellenic Studies* CXI (1991): 104–5.
18. Ste. Croix, *The Class Struggle*, 92.
19. David Whitehead, "Sparta and the Thirty Tyrants," *Ancient Society* 13/14 (1982/83): 127ff; A. R. Burn, *The Pelican History of Greece* (Harmondsworth: Penguin, 1982), 301–2; Charles Darwin Adams, ed., *Lysias* (Norman: University of Oklahoma Press, 1970), 38ff.
20. Bremer, *On Plato's Polity*, 5–6.
21. Annas, *An Introduction*, 56–7.
22. "Aristotle's argument, which leads to the condemnation of all forms of manual labor as banausic, harmful to body and soul, is the clearest and most logical statement of a view which seems to have been commonly held by the intelligentsia of the late fifth- and fourth-century Athens." Maurice Balm, "Attitudes to Work and Leisure in Ancient Greece," *Greece & Rome* XXXI, 2 (October, 1984): 140–1.
23. The description of Peiraeus is Thomas Pangle's, cf. *The Laws of Plato* (New York: Basic Books, 1980), 381; see also, Eva Keuls, *The Reign of the Phallus* (New York: Harper & Row, 1985), 153ff.

24. For the defeat of the Thirty Tyrants, see Raphael Sealey, *A History of the Greek City States* (Berkeley: University of California Press, 1976), 379ff.
25. A. E. Taylor, *Plato: the Man and His Work* (Cleveland and New York: the World Publishing Company, 1966), 263–4.
26. Annas, *An Introduction*, 107.
27. Ste. Croix, *The Class Struggle*, 138ff; M. I. Finley, *Economy and Society in Ancient Greece* (Harmondsworth: Penguin, 1983), Part Two; Michael H. Jameson, "Agriculture and Slavery in Classical Athens," *Classical Journal* 73 (1977–78): 122–45.
28. Finley, *Economy and Society*, 106.
29. A. H. M. Jones, *Athenian Democracy* (Oxford: B. Blackwell, 1957), 77.
30. Finley, *Economy and Society*, 102; Jones, *Athenian Democracy*, 79; Desmond Lee, "Translator's Introduction," in *Plato: The Republic* (Harmondsworth: Penguin, 1986), 26.
31. Lee, "Translator's Introduction," 26.
32. Finley, *Economy and Society*, 104; Ste. Croix, *The Class Struggle*, 227.
33. Gregory Vlastos, "Does Slavery Exist in Plato's Republic?," in Gregory Vlastos, ed., *Platonic Studies* (Princeton, N.J.: Princeton University Press, 1973), 140–46. Cf. John Wild, *Plato's Enemies and the Theory of Natural Law* (Chicago, Ill.: University of Chicago, 1953), 50–1.
34. Gregory Vlastos, "Slavery in Plato's Thought," (orig. 1939) in M. I. Finley, ed., *Slavery in Classical Antiquity* (New York: Barnes & Noble, 1960), 137 and 147.
35. Ibid., 138.
36. Ste. Croix, *The Class Struggle*, 171.
37. S. Douglas Olson, "Names and Naming in Aristophanic Comedy," *Classical Quarterly* 42, ii (1992): 311.
38. Plato's philosophy of knowledge founded on his theory of the Forms provided him no alternative but to presume the "imperfect societies" of his age were *derived* from an earlier, *perfect* society.
39. M. M. Austin and P. Vidal-Naquet, *Economic and Social History of Ancient Greece* (Berkeley: University of California Press, 1977), 211; Rihill, "EKTHMOPOI," 120–21.
40. Ste. Croix, *The Class Struggle*, chap. V.
41. Alexander Fuks, "Plato and the Social Question: the Problem of Poverty and Riches in the Laws," *Ancient Society* 10 (1979): 39.
42. Finley, *Democracy Ancient and Modern*, 28.
43. Sealey, *A History*, chap. V.
44. Paul Cartledge, "Hoplites and Heroes: Sparta's Contribution to the Technique of Ancient Warfare," *Journal of Hellenic Studies* 97 (1977): 21; Alexander Fuks makes similar observations in "Patterns and Types of Social-Economic Revolutions in Greece from the Fourth to the Second Century," *Ancient Society* 5 (1974): 54ff.
45. Fuks, "Isokrates and the Social-Economic Situation in Greece," *Ancient Society* 5 (1974): 21.
46. Orlando Patterson, *Slavery and Social Death* (Cambridge, Mass.: Harvard University Press, 1966); David Brion Davis, *The Problem of Slavery in Western Culture* (Ithaca, N.Y.: Cornell University Press); J. Thorstein Sellin, *Slavery and the Penal System* (New York: Elsevier, 1976).
47. Finley, *Ancient Slavery*, 16.
48. Hayden White, "Between Science and Symbol," *Times Literary Supplement* 31 (January 1986): 109.
49. Cf. Davis, *The Problem of Slavery*, chaps. 3 and 4.
50. Mavis Campbell, "Aristotle and Black Slavery," *Race* XV, 3 (1974): 285–86.
51. Davis, *The Problem of Slavery*, 108.

52. Vlastos, "Slavery in Plato's Thought," 148.
53. C. L. R James, *The Black Jacobins* (New York: Vintage Books, 1963), 137ff.
54. Richard Jenkyns, *The Victorians and Ancient Greece* (Cambridge, Mass.: Harvard University Press, 1980), 227.
55. Jenkyns, *The Victorians*, 166–68; Campbell, "Aristotle and Black Slavery," 289ff; Eric Williams, *Capitalism and Slavery* (New York: Capricorn Books, 1966).
56. Campbell, "Aristotle and Black Slavery," 285–86.
57. George Fitzhugh, *Cannibals All! Or Slaves Without Masters*.
58. George Frederick Holmes, *Observations on the a Passage in the Politics of Aristotle Relative to Slavery*.
59. On Calhoun, cf. Clement Eaton, *The Freedom-of-Thought Struggle in the Old South* (New York: Harper Torchbooks, 1964), 144 and 349.
60. Ibid.; Davis, *The Problem of Slavery in Western Culture*, 440.
61. Campbell, "Aristotle and Black Slavery," 295.
62. W. S. Jenkins, *Pro-Slavery Thought in the Old South* (Chapel Hill: University of North Carolina Press, 1960), 137.
63. James Oakes, *Slavery and Freedom* (New York: Alfred A. Knopf, 1990), 30–31.
64. R. R. Palmer, "Notes on the Use of the Word 'Democracy,' 1789–1799," *Political Science Quarterly* LXVIII, 2 (June 1953): 203–26.
65. Edmund S. Morgan, *American Slavery, American Freedom* (New York: W.W. Norton & Company, 1975), 5; Linda Grant DePauw, "Land of the Unfree: Legal Limitations on Liberty in Pre-Revolutionary America," *Maryland Historical Magazine* 68, 4 (1973).
66. Madison was also skeptical of Plato; Morton White, *Philosophy, The Federalist, and the Constitution* (Oxford: Oxford University Press, 1987), 113.
67. Thomas Fitzhugh, ed., *Letters of Thomas Jefferson Concerning Philology and the Classics* (University of Virginia, 1919), 36–7.
68. Ibid., 72.
69. Thomas Jefferson, *Notes on Virginia* quoted by Winthrop Jordan, *White Over Black* (Baltimore, Md.: Pelican, 1968), 436–37.
70. The term "race science" is adapted from studies of Nazi science. Michael H. Kater, *Doctors Under Hitler* (Chapel Hill: University of North Carolina Press, 1989); George L. Mosse, *Toward The Final Solution* (London: J.M. Dent & Sons, 1978). For discussions of race science, see George Stocking, Jr., *Victorian Anthropology* (New York: Free Press, 1987) and John Trumpbour, "Blinding Them With Science: Scientific Ideologies in the Ruling of the Modern World," in Trumpbour, ed., *How Harvard Rules* (Boston: South End, 1989).
71. For working-class racism and black-faced minstrelsy, see David Roediger, *The Wages of Whiteness* (London: Verso, 1991); Michael Rogin, "Black Masks, White Skin," *Radical History* 54 (1992): 141–52.
72. Jordan, *White Over Black*, 94.
73. George Levesque and Nikola Baumgarten, "'A Monstrous Inconsistency': Slavery, Ideology and Politics in the Age of the American Revolution," *Contributions in Black Studies* 8 (1986–87): 28.
74. Race science excluded women from the white race. Cf. Nancy Leys Stepan, "Race and Gender: The Role of Analogy in Science," in David T. Goldberg, *Anatomy of Racism* (Minneapolis: University of Minnesota, 1990).
75. Ferdinand Lundberg, *Cracks in the Constitution* (Secaucas, N.J.: Lyle Stuart Inc., 1980), 114ff; Stephen G. Xydis, "Ancient Greece in Emergent America," *Greek Heritage* II, 5 (1965): 84–87.
76. Lundberg, *Cracks*, 76.
77. Numa Denis Fustel de Coulanges, *The Ancient City* (Baltimore, Md.: The Johns Hopkins University Press, 1980), 320.

78. William Riker, "The Heresthetics of Constitution-Making," *American Political Science Review* 78, 1 (March 1984): 6; Helen Meiksins Wood, "Oligarchic 'Democracy,'" *Monthly Review* 41, 3 (July 1989): 48.
79. All quotes are from Lundberg, *Cracks*, 157–71.
80. Ibid., 163.
81. John L. Roche, "The Convention as a Case Study in Democratic Politics," in Leonard W. Levy, ed., *Essays On the Making of the Constitution* (New York: Oxford University Press, 1978), 179; Lundberg, *Cracks*, chap. one.
82. Bernard Crick, *The American Science of Politics* (London: Routledge & Kegan Paul, 1959); Benjamin Ginsburg, *The Captive Public* (New York: Basic Books, 1986).
83. For a recent example, see Mostafa Rejai, *Comparative Political Ideologies* (New York: St. Martin's Press, 1984), 102.
84. Finley, *Democracy, Ancient and Modern*, 6–7.
85. Quentin Skinner, "The Empirical Theorists of Democracy and Their Critics," *Political Theory* 1, 1 (February 1983): 303.

Abram Harris, E. Franklin Frazier, and Ralph Bunche: The Howard School of Thought on the Problem of Race

Charles P. Henry

University of California, Berkeley

In late August of 1933, thirty-three young black intellectuals gathered at the Hudson River estate of NAACP president Joel Spingarn to discuss the problems of race in the midst of a depression. The meeting was planned by W. E. B. DuBois who, like other officers of the NAACP, was feeling increased pressure to adjust the organization's traditional legal and political approach to the economic reality of the thirties. In fact, longtime race leaders like DuBois and James Weldon Johnson would receive the brunt of the criticism coming from the young intellectuals.

Leading the attack were Abram Harris, E. Franklin Frazier, and Ralph Bunche. Charging the older men with racial provincialism, the young radicals advocated black and white labor solidarity to force through the necessary reform legislation. The older "race men" and the NAACP, they stated, were caught up in the middle-class needs of the black business elite, ignoring the economic needs of the black masses (Young, 1973: 3–5; Wolters, 1970: 219–23.)

Even though Harris, Bunche, and Frazier were appointed to a special investigative committee to follow up the Amenia Conference with specific recommendations for the NAACP, their report was debated but ultimately rejected. The young radicals went on to distinguished careers in academia and public service and their views began to diverge over the years. However, during the thirties they and other colleagues at Howard University produced a body of work that broke sharply with the preceding generation of black scholars and contributed to a paradigm that remained dominant until the sixties.

Race Relations Paradigms

There is a "mandatory requirement" that any discussion of paradigms begin with the work of Thomas Kuhn (Kuhn, 1970). This requirement is followed by social scientists even though Kuhn was writing about scientific revolutions. Perhaps this is because if Kuhn is right that normal science can only interpret a dominant paradigm, not correct it (ibid.: 122), how much more true is this of social science, dependent as it is on the dominant culture to give it legitimacy. In short, the social science community is less insulated from society than the scientific community and, therefore, its paradigms may be less likely to challenge mainstream social norms.

Of course, in the area of race relations, scientific, pseudoscientific, and social scientific theories have often merged to provide rationalizations for the racial status quo. According to Kuhn, any successful paradigm must attract an enduring group of adherents away from competing theories yet be sufficiently open ended to leave problems to be resolved by those adherents. The theory is learned through its application to problem solving even though practioneers may work on entirely different applications (ibid.: 10, 47). Social Darwinists, for example, accepted Darwin's paradigm but applied it to an entirely different set of problems.

Kuhn states that it is "particularly in periods of acknowledged crisis that scientists have turned to philosophical analysis as a device for unlocking the riddles of their field" (ibid.: 88). Almost all innovators, says Kuhn, are young with little commitment to prior tradition. In the social sciences, we might suspect that academics from marginalized groups would have less commitment to established views. However, the crucial question for both communities is, Who chooses the rules of debate when paradigms are in dispute or transition? As Kuhn states, more than logic and the impact of nature are at work in winning the paradigm wars (ibid.: 94).

Mack Jones has recently argued that the establishment of academic disciplines and the determination of their substantive content is a normative exercise that is necessarily parochial because a people's need to know is a function of their anticipation and control needs (Barker, 1992: 30). This means, says Jones, that a dominant paradigm "leads the practitioner to study the adversary community only to the extent that the adversary constitutes a problem" (ibid.: 32). For Jones, this explains why American social science generally sees blacks as a problem, but one which does not challenge the dominant paradigm of pluralist democracy. Such a paradigm conveys only a caricature of the oppressed or dominated people and hence has little prescriptive utility for their struggle to end their domination.

Jones's views help explain the paradox of the centrality of black politics yet its marginalization in the discipline of political science. Michael Dawson and Ernest Wilson III have documented this marginality as compared to the sister disciplines of history and sociology. Contending that the logical structure of a particular paradigm leads an analyst to structure the problem of racial or black politics in a particular way, they examine the dominant theoretical paradigm, pluralist theory, and its main challengers–social stratification (Weberian theory), Marxism, modernization theory, social choice theory, and black nationalist theory. Among scholars interested in black politics, they found that the most frequently used paradigms included pluralist, nationalist, and Weberian/modernization approaches. They also found that many of these scholars transcended paradigmatic differences and united their inquiries into black politics. Moreover, they found "that despite the paradigm or model in which black scholars worked, there were among many such scholars commonalties that transcended paradigmatic differences and united their inquiries into black politics" (Dawson & Wilson, 1990: 223). These commonalties include a concern with tactics or strategy, a concern with the internal dynamics of the black community, frequent reference to historical antecedents, a concern about the gap between the promise and the performance of the American political system, and a tendency to blame white racism for unequal societal outcomes (ibid.: 223-24).

Paradigms do indeed determine the approach we take toward defining and solving racial problems. Yet to fully understand contemporary paradigms we must examine their historical antecedents. None of the widely used modern paradigms on race relations in general or black politics in particular are new. Where they differ now and in the past is in the varying interpretations and applications given to them by black and white proponents.

The Religious Paradigm on Race 1619 to 1860

From the arrival of the first slaves at Jamestown, Virginia in 1619 until the Civil War, the dominant perspective on race was shaped by a religious worldview. The central text for this view was the Christian Bible. Both proslavery and antislavery advocates debated the issue within the parameters set by the Bible. A key event in the hegemony of this view occurred in Virginia during the mid-1600s when, after considerable debate, the colonial assembly decided that it was possible to convert Africans to Christianity and still keep them in bondage. This enabled white Christians to continue their conversion of blacks without opposition and indeed with some support from slaveowners. The opposite decision by the Lutheran Church in South Africa severely restricted the spread of Christianity among the African population (Raboteau, 1978; Levine, 1977; Fredrickson, 1981).

White proponents of slavery promoted a Christianity that rationalized the institution of black slavery. The most common justification for the subordinate status of blacks was the "curse on Ham." The favorite biblical texts for these proponents came from the New Testament, especially the letters of Paul calling on servants to obey their masters and give unto Caesar what is Caesar's. Biblical promises of rewards in heaven (one assumes a segregated heaven), were used to pacify slaves concerned about injustice in this life (ibid).

Developing simultaneously with "white Christianity" was a more radical "black Christianity." The slave's interpretation of the Bible often focused on Old Testament visions of "an eye for an eye and a tooth for a tooth." Heroes like Moses, Joshua, Daniel, Jonah, Gabriel, and David were preferred over Paul and the meek and mild Jesus. Obviously, the favorite book was Exodus and the spirituals were sometimes used to send secret messages. The best-known slave revolts of the nineteenth century were led by biblically inspired blacks—Denmark Vessey, Gabriel Prosser, and Nat Turner. Of course, "black Christianity" had to be practiced in secret and often co-existed with *vodun*. In fact, black Catholics in Louisiana integrated their Christianity with "voodoo" or "conjure" to produce a syncretic religion much like those found in Haiti and Cuba.

Almost all black political writings, from David Walker's *Appeal* through Reverend Henry Highland Garnet's call for slave resistance, use the Bible as the moral justification for action (Stuckey, 1972). From the earliest slave narratives through the most popular novel of the nineteenth century—*Uncle Tom's Cabin*—literature by and about blacks revolves around religious themes (Gates, 1988). Thus, while black and white applications of the Christian paradigm differ, the paradigm itself is not challenged.

"The Biological/Genetic Paradigm—1860 to 1930"

With the publication of Charles Darwin's *On the Origin of Species by Natural Selection* in 1859, a new paradigm rose to challenge and eventually replace the religious worldview on race. In the 1850s, Darwin's work had been preceded in Western Europe by a wave of racist literature claiming to be scientific. Thus, although Darwin's work was not specifically concerned with the origins of races, it was quickly applied to race.

Social Darwinists, led by Herbert Spencer and William Graham Sumner, soon equated the survival of the fittest with the right of superior races to rule. Social Darwinism and organicism also reinforced the economic liberalism of the day. Laissez-faire was reinterpreted as a mandate not to interfere with any form of human inequality and suffering. The poor were poor because they were biologically inferior and Negroes were slaves as a result of natural selection. Any attempt to interfere with "nature" through philanthropy or abolition would only hurt the superior race and lead to the multiplication of the inferior race (Van den Berghe, 1967: 17).

Natural scientists developed sophisticated craneological and phrenological tests to support sociologists and anthropologists in the establishment of a hierarchy of races and promotion of a eugenics movement. The black response was to deny the superiority or inferiority of any race but to acknowledge biological differences. Black leaders stressed the complementarity of the races. The warm, sensitive, emotional, artistic temperament of the Negro balanced the cold, scientific, industrious nature of Caucasians.

Perhaps the leading black intellectual of the nineteenth century, Edward W. Blyden, personified the black interpretation of the race paradigm. On the one hand, Blyden developed the concept of the "African personality." He stressed African religiosity, oneness with nature, and communalism as unique racial traits. On the other hand, he was a great admirer of European culture and supported colonization as a means for grafting "European progress wholesale on African conservation and stagnation." Blyden did not approve of racial mixing because it diluted racial traits (Mudime, 1988; Lynch, 1970).

In the United States, Alexander Crummell, a major early influence on W. E. B. DuBois, searched from the 1840s through the 1890s for the "innate" characteristics of races. Like his ideological opponent, Booker T. Washington, he tended to see blacks as an aesthetically gifted people, strongly enthusiastic, but lacking in discipline. Crummell acquired the reputation of championing blacks against mulattoes. His emphasis on race pride and race destiny led him to organize the black cultural and intellectual elite into the American Negro Academy in 1897 (Moses, 1978: 75).

It was at the first meeting of the Academy that its vice-president and social historian, DuBois, read his paper on "The Conservation of Races." In this paper DuBois sets forth a mystical notion of race, interchanging it with "nation." He believed that racially, growth was historically characterized by "the differentiation of spiritual and mental differences between great races of mankind and the integration of physical differences" (ibid.: 135). The German nation stood for science and philosophy; the English nation stood for "constitutional liberty and commercial freedom"; but the racial ideal of the Negro race had yet to be fulfilled (ibid.).

Only two years later in *The Philadelphia Negro*, DuBois introduces social science into his defense of the race. In a critical review of Frederick L. Hoffman's *Race Traits and Tendencies of the American Negro*, which asserts that Negroes were doomed to decline as a race because of weak genetic material, DuBois cites relevant comparative data from European cities with which blacks compared favorably in terms of health and crime statistics (Toll, 1979: 105). While his intellectual peers Kelly Miller and Carter Woodson continued to focus on the primacy of race (prior to World War I, only fourteen black Americans had Ph.D.s from recognized universities), DuBois began to give a class increasing consideration. Thus, while Miller and Woodson quarreled with the younger generation of black intellectuals, DuBois supported them and invited dialogue. As such, DuBois represents a transitional figure in the break from the biological paradigm (Young, 1973: 9–16).

The push of the Great Depression and the pull of new anthropological evidence mark the end of the dominance of the biological explanations for black subordination, though remnants of the biological/genetic paradigm remain today in the debate over IQ testing (Mensh, 1991). While DuBois now recognizes the importance of economics and encourages the NAACP to change its focus, he disappoints the "young radicals" by suggesting self-segregation in economic cooperatives as a viable economic strategy. Although DuBois is "convinced" of the essential truth of the Marxian philosophy, he asks, "Is there any automatic power in socialism to override and suppress race prejudice?"

There are those who insist that the American Negro must "stand or fall by his alliance with white Americans; that separation in any degree, physical or social, is impossible and that either, therefore, the Negro must take his stand with exploiting capitalists or with the craft unions or with the communists" (Aptheker, 1985: 144). DuBois says the question is already settled because Negroes form today a separate nation within a nation. What remains is to be organized along economic lines that benefit the great majority of blacks. At the same time, blacks would continue the fight for political and civil equality.

The overthrow of the biological paradigm removes the major obstacle to racial assimilation. Robert Park, a transitional figure who worked for Booker T. Washington early in his career and trained E. Franklin Frazier and Charles S. Johnson late in his career, provides a theory of assimilation based on urban racial contact. While the young black intellectuals who opposed DuBois assumed a Marxist posture throughout the thirties, by the early forties they had helped to shape a new dominant paradigm based on the social psychology of Gunnar Myrdal. This new paradigm was assimilationist at its core and therefore never acceptable to DuBois.

The Howard School

During the 1930s, Howard University was home for the most distinguished group of black scholars ever assembled on one campus. Of course, this concentration of intellectual talent was not coincidental. Segregation meant that the only positions available for black faculty, no matter how talented, were at black universities. In 1932, Bunche reported that of the 271 Howard faculty (including whites), 211 were Howard graduates (Bunche, 1932). As late as 1936, more than 80 percent of all black Ph.D.s were employed by Howard, Atlanta, and Fisk. By the 1940s, government service and elite white universities had lured away many of Howard's most noted faculty members.

Among the distinguished faculty at Howard in the 1930s were: Ernest Everett Just, an internationally known biologist; philosopher Alain L. Locke, the first African-American Rhodes Scholar and a leader of the Harlem Renaissance; Sterling A. Brown, English professor, author, poet, and critic; Law School Dean William H. Hastie, the first black governor of the Virgin Islands and the first black federal judge; Charles H. Houston, vice dean of the law school and architect of the NAACP legal strategy; surgeon Charles R. Drew, the pioneer developer of blood plasma; Merze Tate, historian and specialist on disarmament; historian Rayford Logan; Charles Thompson, founder of the *Journal of Negro Education*; theologian and president Mordecai Johnson; linguist and sociologist Lorenzo Turner; historian Charles Wesley; theologian Howard Thurman; chemist Percy Julian; William Leo Hansberry, a pioneer in African history; Kelly Miller, dean and professor of mathematics and sociology; W. Mercer Cook, professor of Romance Languages and later ambassador to Senegal and Gambia; economist Abram Harris; sociologist E. Franklin Frazier; and political scientist Ralph Bunche (Logan, 1968). These latter three—Harris, Frazier, and Bunche—were social scientists with advanced degrees from elite, white universities. They were active in campus politics and, as seen in the Amenia Conference, nationally known even though their careers were just developing.

Abram L. Harris

Harris was the first of the three to arrive at Howard in 1927. A native of Richmond, Virginia, Harris graduated from Virginia Union and then attended the New York City School of Social Work. While in New York, Harris worked as a research assistant for the National Urban League, came into contact with the city's left-wing intellectual community, and developed an interest in black workers in the labor movement. By 1924, he had completed an M.A. in economics from Pittsburgh with a thesis entitled, "The Negro Laborer in Pittsburgh." Around this time, Harris developed a warm friendship with DuBois that lasted until their separate splits with the NAACP in 1935. After teaching for a year at West Virginia Collegiate Institute (now West Virginia State) and a year as executive secretary of the Minneapolis Urban League, Harris began his doctoral studies in economics at Columbia. At the same time, he began teaching at Howard, commuting regularly between the District of Columbia and New York. Harris's best-known work, *The Black Worker* (1931), was written in collaboration with Sterling Spero and originally served as their joint doctoral dissertation.

DuBois had written an enthusiastic review of *The Black Worker* for *The Nation:* "One of the first attempts in the economic field to make a synthesis of the labor movement and the Negro problem so as to interpret each in the light of the other and show them to be one question of American economics" (Darity, 1989: 204). In his own journal, *The Crisis,* DuBois "strongly recommended this book for reading, particularly by those American Negroes who do not yet realize that the Negro problem is primarily the problem of the Negro working man" (ibid.).

In the chapters of *The Black Worker* written by Harris, he takes Booker T. Washington to task, emphasizing the old notion of the self-made man to the exclusion of the "problems peculiar to the wage earner in modern industry." Middle-class Negro leadership in general, Harris notes, always sided with capital and against organized labor. However, Harris urges blacks to try to avoid setting up separate unions, even if expedient, because it would hinder the development of class consciousness. Harris prefers the radical ideology of industrial unionism over more conservative trade unionism because the former must be more concerned about neglecting any large section of workers (ibid.: 41–42).

As early as 1927, Harris made it clear that class, not race, was the dominant force in black oppression. Writing in *Social Forces,* he states that "[s]lavery was an economic system which involved white freemen as masters and black men as slaves. The Negro was not enslaved because his complexion, and nose and lip formation differed from the white man's." He goes on to add that "both the lower white and black classes were weak…. For a short period white and black bondsmen were on the same indefinite legal footing." This brief equality in status among the poor changes because "Negro labor being cheaper (more plentiful) than cheap white labor was more desired" (ibid.: 169–70).

Harris's sharpest attacks on the racial paradigm come in response to DuBois. In 1935, DuBois published what some considered his finest scholarly work, *Black Reconstruction in America.* Despite DuBois's earlier praise of *The Black Worker* and Harris's stated admiration of DuBois as the Negro intellectual to whom his generation owes the most, he proceeds to launch a fierce attack on the work. DuBois, says Harris, is too bound by the racial paradigm of his generation to absorb Marxism:

> Dr. DuBois concedes the inevitability of socialism and even the desirability of it, but is at the same time distrustful of white workers. He cannot believe that a movement founded upon working-class solidarity and cutting across racial lines can afford any immediate relief to the Negro's economic plight or have any practical realization in the near future. By temperament and habituation to the Negro equal rights struggle he is wholly unfitted to join, to say nothing of initiating, such a movement. He is a racialist whose discovery of Marxism as a critical instrument has been too recent and sudden for it to discipline his mental process or basically to change his social philosophy. (ibid.: 209)

DuBois's ideological confusion, according to Harris, leads him to convert the wholesale flight of Negroes from the plantations into a general strike against the slave regime while in fact the slaves had no real class consciousness nor any idea of what impact their "escape to freedom" would have on the outcome of the war. Moreover, had they pursued a truly radical agenda during Reconstruction, says Harris, their plans would never have been supported by Stevens and Sumner, who were members of the capitalist class (ibid.: 211).

Harris would extend his criticism of DuBois's racial chauvinism in his other major economic study of the decade, *The Negro as Capitalist* (1936). This work came up just after DuBois had set his new program for a Negro economic nation within the nation. Harris argued that DuBois had not explained how a separate economy could function in the face of persistent industrial integration, business combinations, and the centralization of capital control. In fact, Harris links DuBois's proposal to those of the pre-Civil War proponent of a separate black economy, Martin Delany, whom he calls a "black Benjamin Franklin." The black businessman emerges as the villain who encourages black enterprise at the expense of white and black labor solidarity. Even groups like the New Negro Alliance who promote "Don't Buy Where You Can't Work" campaigns were categorized with DuBois as middle-class black chauvinists (Young: 43–44; Darity: 204). Throughout the thirties, then, Harris consistently rejects interracial conciliation as the strategy of Booker T. Washington and civil libertarianism and militant race consciousness as the program of middle-class blacks. The first actively supports capitalism while the latter left untouched the material basis for racial inequality. While maintaining that white trade unions must change their racial practices, he promotes class consciousness and class unity. In fact, blacks should pursue no actions that would inflame racial antagonism. Harris, unlike contemporary radical economists such as Michael Reich, argues that "if race prejudice is not accompanied with competitive activities or the subjugation of one group by the other it is soon removed through association" (Darity: 18). However, as blacks become more competitive with white workers, hostility between the races will increase. Harris never fully explains how this cycle of competition and hostility can be overcome, but perhaps we can gain insight into the process from Harris's colleague, E. Franklin Frazier.

E. Franklin Frazier

Frazier is more critical of the romanticism of race men like DuBois than Harris. In "The DuBois Program in the Present Crisis," Frazier not only joins Harris in attacking the legitimacy of DuBois's conversion to Marxism, but goes on to state that DuBois remained the "genteel" aristocrat who had no real conception or "sympathetic understanding" of the plight of the black proletariat. As for DuBois's ideal black society, Frazier gratuitously adds that "nothing would be more unendurable for him than to live within a Black Ghetto or within a black nation—unless perhaps he were king, and then he probably would attempt to unite the whites and blacks through marriage of royal families" (Young: 47). Like Harris, Frazier was concerned that DuBois's program would split black workers from white workers and create false hope among blacks for their survival in a capitalistic system. However, the bitterness of the attack is remarkable in that Frazier's early work on the family was much indebted to DuBois's 1908 report on the black family, and DuBois had hired Frazier in the early 1920s to do field work in the Deep South (Platt, 1991: 18, 133). (Frazier and DuBois established a better relationship in later years with Frazier chairing a controversial dinner honoring DuBois during the McCarthy era.)

Frazier was raised as one of five children in a stable and race-conscious family in Baltimore. Although his father was a bank messenger, three of the boys became professional men. Franklin won a scholarship that permitted him to enroll at Howard, from which he graduated cum laude in 1916. He did not take any formal courses in sociology even though Kelly Miller was offering them at Howard as early as 1903. He did read Gidding's *Principles of Sociology* at Howard and became a member of the Intercollegiate Socialist Society. He taught secondary school in Virginia and Baltimore during World War I and privately published a tract he wrote opposing the war entitled "God and War." In 1919, he won a scholarship for graduate study at Clark University in Worchester, Massachusetts, where he came under the influence of Professors Frank H. Hankins and G. Stanley Hall. He appreciated the objectivity of Hankin's statistical approach to sociology, but disagreed with his racism. Both Hankins and Hall were a part of the mainstream of scientific racists who supported benevolent social reforms (Blackwell & Janowitz, 1974: 89–90).

After receiving his M.A. from Clark, Frazier became a research fellow at the New York School of Social Work and was influenced by the psychological work of Bernard Glueck. Frazier's 1921 study of Negro longshoremen in New York City broke new ground in looking at the effects of migration at work and at home. These Southern migrants, Frazier reported, experienced problems in their families and failed to understand the nature of union organization in industry. Frazier was attracted by the socialists of *The Messenger*, supported the first Pan-African Congress, and attended the second Congress in 1921. The following year he spent in Denmark as a fellow of the American Scandinavian Foundation. Influenced by Booker T. Washington's praise of Danish Folk Schools he studied them and their role in the cooperative movement (by 1928 he had given up on co-ops). Returning to the United States, Frazier became professor of sociology at Morehouse College and later helped set up and then direct the Atlanta School of Social Work. It is during this Atlanta period that Frazier began writing on the disorganization of the Negro family and on the black middle class. In 1927 he wrote:

> The first fact that makes the Negro family the subject of special sociological study is the incomplete assimilation of western culture by the Negro masses. Generally when two different cultures come into contact, each modifies the other. But in the case of the Negro in America it meant the total destruction of the African social heritage. Therefore, in the case of the family group the Negro has not introduced new patterns of behavior, but has failed to conform to patterns about him. The degree of conformity is determined by educational and economic factors as well as by social isolation. (ibid.: 92)

Among the businessmen of Durham, North Carolina, Frazier found more stable family lives and disciplined individuals than among the poor of Atlanta.

Another work of Frazier's during the Atlanta years demonstrates the influence of psychology on his work. In "The Pathology of Race Prejudice" he compares the mechanisms that operate in prejudiced behavior with those that characterize mental illness. Frazier boldly refers to the operation of projective mechanisms in white women who accuse Negro males of attempted rape. The response to this 1927 article was so emotional (irrational?) among whites that Frazier's life was threatened and he was forced to leave Atlanta almost immediately after the article appeared (Edwards, 1968: xi).

By the time Frazier moved to the University of Chicago for two years of graduate study, his research focus was firmly fixed. Nonetheless, he came under the influence of distinguished teachers and fellow graduate students including Robert E. Park, Ellsworth Faris, Earnest W. Burgess, William F. Ogburn, George H. Mead, Louis Wirth, and Herbert Blumer. Frazier's dissertation, later published in 1932 as *The Negro Family in Chicago*, was clearly reflective of the Chicago tradition of empirical study of one aspect of community life to illuminate larger aspects of social reality (ibid).

Park, like DuBois, was a transitional figure who often intermixed biology and sociology. As late as 1931, Park was still attempting to provide a definitive statement on the issue of whether the superior achievement of mulattoes were due to their biological or to their cultural inheritance. Frazier disagrees with Park's contention that the two groups differed in temperament. In his writing on the black family, Frazier accounts for the deviation of the great majority of black families from the normative type of family behavior through environmental factors created by the experiences of slavery, emancipation, and urbanization. Older works on the black family insisted that racial or cultural differences in black families were African survivals. Using the recent anthropological work of Bronislaw Malinowski and Robert Briffault on the sexual behavior of primitive peoples, Frazier contends that there was no scientific basis for the belief that blacks and other primitive peoples had strong sexual impulses that could not be controlled by custom (Williams, 1989: 152). In short, Frazier denies the possibility of African survivals in order to refute the biological claims that black deviance from the middle-class family norm was due to the less-evolved status of the black race. By charging that slavery and urbanization had left the poor rural peasant with a folk culture unable to cope with city life, Frazier's view eventually won out over the biological determinists, but at the price of accepting conventional white standards of behavior.

For Frazier, Park's race-relations cycle of contact, conflict, and competition would more quickly lead to acculturation or even assimilation if the Negro became an industrial worker receiving an adequate wage that would enable the father to assume his position as chief breadwinner at the head of a stable, conventional family. At this stage, Frazier did not see any role for a unique black culture. In fact, his condemnation of the life-style behind the blues reveals more than a little of the capitalist ethos he condemned in others: "[T]he Negro has succeeded in adopting habits of living that have enabled him to survive in a civilization based upon laissez faire and competition, it bespeaks a degree of success on taking on the folkways and mores of the white race" (Young: 53). At least one writer states that "if Frazier wanted to see the end of the race in the future, Ralph Bunche often ignored its existence in the present" (ibid.).

Ralph J. Bunche

Bunche had gone to Howard from Harvard in 1928 where his in-campus home served as base for a small circle of progressive colleagues known as the "thinkers and drinkers." In fact, it was this group of scholar activists that helped attract Frazier to Howard in 1934. Yet, while all three of the core members of this circle had attended elite white graduate schools (Harris/Columbia, Frazier/Chicago, Bunche/Harvard), Bunche's background diverged sharply from theirs during his formative years. Ten years younger than Frazier and five years younger than Harris, Bunche was born in Detroit in 1904 rather than in the South of Harris and Frazier. Bunche's father Fred worked as a barber and the family lived in a mostly white neighborhood where Ralph's early friends were white. In 1914, after brief stays in Toledo, Ohio, and Knoxville, Tennessee, the family moved to Albuquerque, New Mexico, hoping the climate would help his mother's rheumatic fever. Unfortunately illness claimed both of Bunche's parents within two years leading his grandmother (the unquestioned head of the family) to move Ralph and his sister, Grace, to Los Angeles. In Los Angeles, the Bunche's were denied housing in a predominantly white neighborhood. However, Ralph did attend a predominantly white high school and won a scholarship to UCLA. He graduated magna cum laude and was valedictorian of his class. Bunche's academic success made him a local hero among Los Angeles blacks and won him a fellowship at Harvard (Haskins, 1992: 67–9; interview with Mrs. Ralph Bunche, 18 October 1985).

On the eve of his departure for the East Coast and his first contact with black leaders, Bunche outlined his goals in a letter to W. E. B. DuBois:

> But I have long felt the need of coming in closer contact with the leaders of our race, so that I may better learn their methods of approach, their psychology and benefit in my own development by their influence. That is why I am anxious to come east and anticipate enjoying the opportunity extremely. Now specifically, I would like to inquire if there is any way that I can be of service to my group this coming summer, either in the east or in the south? Admittedly my resources are limited, but I am willing to tackle any problems or proposition which will give sufficient return for bare living expenses. I feel that there must be some opportunity for me either connected with the NAACP or as a teacher. I have a liberal education, extensive experience in journalism, forensics and dramatics, as well as athletics, and am young and healthy. I can furnish the best of recommendations, both from the faculty of the University and from the Race leaders of the Pacific Coast. (Rivlin, 1990: 218)

Within a few years, Bunche would be a critic of DuBois and race leaders in general, although he was never as close to DuBois as Harris and Frazier. More perhaps than Harris and Frazier, Bunche was the logical successor to DuBois's intellectual legacy. Although separated by thirty years in their matriculation at Harvard, Bunche had completed the first doctorate by a black in political science at Harvard and the nation as a whole. (Aptheker reports that DuBois initially hoped to study political science at Harvard [private conversation, fall, 1988].) Bunche's scope of interests ranging from African-American politics to the politics of colonial African administration paralleled DuBois's expertise. Bunche cited philosophers at UCLA and Harvard as his most significant influences (Ralph Bunche Papers, "Letters to Dean Rieber", 10 June 1947, UCLA, Box 126). Remarkably his lecture notes from the early years at Howard reveal some of the racial sentimentality he so strongly attacks in DuBois:

> Fundamentally, the Negro is a being most sensitively sentimental; a being endowed with the most natural of artistic talents...(which historically leads to two very obvious truths)—one is that any distinction so far won by a member of our Race, here, has been in—variably in some one of the arts...the other is that any influence so far exerted by the American Negro upon American civilization has been primarily in the realm of art...the Negro Race of all races, whether it be generally known or not, is endowed with that greatest of racial blessings,—a *soul* (which might be poetically traced back to Africa)...—no race has ever,—nor race *shall* ever, rise to the heights of artistic achievement until it has suffered and mourned and received deliverance...(Given that every race has its outstanding trait of genius)—Then it appears from past indications that the American Negro is destined to attain his greatest heights of successful achievement in the realm of art—just as he has in the past—The final measure of the greatness of any people of whatever creed or race, religious or political affiliation, is the amount and standard of the artistic production of that people. (ibid., folder "Governments of Europe," lecture notes on "The American Negro and His Achievements")

It seems clear from these notes that Bunche did not fully reject DuBois's racial views until the onset of the Depression and under the influence of first Harris and then Frazier.

By 1936, Bunche has a decidedly different perspective on race as expressed in his only book-length publication, *A World View of Race*. Race, he says, first appears in the English language in the sixteenth century and has become an effective instrument of national politics. However, existing racial diversions are arbitrary, subjective, and devoid of scientific meaning. Thus, according to Bunche, all existing human groups are of definitely mixed origin (Bunche, 1936: 3–14).

Although much conflict is labeled as racial, its real causes are social, political, and economic. Racial attitudes are primarily social inheritances based on stereotypes. Like Frazier, Bunche sees racial prejudice and conflict existing as long as easily identified groups are forced into economic competition. Once society guarantees economic security to all peoples, the chief source of group conflict will be removed. Bunche implies that race war might be adverted by transforming it into class war:

> If the oppressed racial groups, as a result of desperation and increasing understanding, should be attracted by the principles of equality and humanitarianism advocated by the Soviet Union (and it is both logical and likely that they will) then racial conflict will become intensified. In such case, however, racial conflict will be more directly identified with class conflict, and the oppressed racial groups may win the support of oppressed, though previously prejudiced, working-class groups within the dominant population. (ibid.: 36)

Drawing on his dissertation Bunche cites Africa as imperialism's greatest and most characteristic expression. He condemns the "extreme egoism" of British and French culture as expressed in their colonial policies, yet he sees West Africans as culturally in a transition stage between primitivism and civilization (ibid.: 41–57). He ends the section on Africa by comparing Lord Lugard's views on "equality in things spiritual 'but' agreed divergence in the physical and material" to Booker T. Washington's famous "separate as the fingers of the hand" analogy and the familiar legal fiction of "separate but equal rights" (ibid.: 60). In the last chapter of his work, Bunche asks, "Is the plight of the Negro the plight of a 'race'?" He contends that the policies of Washington, Garvey, Kelly Miller, and others represent a plea for conciliation with the white moneyed class and at least a tacit acceptance of group segregation. "Dr. DuBois", says Bunche, "has differed from these gentlemen chiefly in the militancy of his tone in his insistent demand for fair and constitutional treatment of the Negro as a *race*." However, DuBois's attack was based on Washington's retreat from civil and political equality and not on Washington's economic philosophy or his misleading racialism. According to Bunche, such "racial" interpretations by Negro leaders and organizations "reveal a clear understanding of the true group and class status of the Negro in American society," leading him "up the dark, blind ally of black chauvinism" (ibid.: 83–84). On the positive side, "the depression, ably abetted by the policies of the New Deal, has made the American population white and black, increasingly class-conscious (ibid.: 90).

The same year that *A World View* appeared, Bunche published two articles sharply critical of the status quo. The first of these articles was perhaps the best critique of early New Deal social planning and its impact on blacks. In it Bunche contends that the New Deal represented "merely an effort to refurbish the old individualistic—capitalistic system and to entrust it again with the economic destinies and welfare of the American people" (Bunche, 1936a: 60). "Relatively few Negro workers were even theoretically affected by the labor provisions of Nation Recovery Administration," stated Bunche, and the Agricultural Adjustment Act deprived Negro tenants of his benefit from the crop reduction program (ibid.: 63–64). In short, the New Deal was a program to benefit the middle class, which barely existed in the black community.

The second article in this unusually productive year asks the question of whether separate schools for blacks raise any separate educational problem in terms of course content. In an article that reveals many of the issues that could arise after the *Brown* decision, Bunche writes:

> The fact is that under our present system it is impossible to achieve educational equality for all members of any group in the society. Public schools for example, are supported by taxation. The revenue derived from taxation will depend largely upon the relative prosperity of the propertied interests in the particular locality. Since wealth is unequally distributed in the country, the present glaring inequalities in the distribution of funds for the support of education will persist even for "White Education." The basic question for all schools is not one of copying the "white man's education," but one of developing a system of education which will afford both white and black students a sound basis for understanding the society in which they live and for attacking the problems confronting them. White as well as Negro schools are woefully deficient in this respect. (Bunche, 1936b: 355)

For Bunche, the culture of capitalism controlled Negro education as well as White education, and while Negro schools could be much more progressive than at present, they would never be permitted to remodel the position of the Negro in the social order (ibid.: 358).

By the mid-thirties, Bunche, Harris, and Frazier held identical views. While Bunche may have ranged across a wider scope of issues, they all gave primacy to class over race, thus breaking with the racial paradigm of the preceding generation of black intellectuals. The racial chauvinism and narrow legal and political orientation of the older race men was decidedly rejected. In its stead they offered not a program of minority advancement, but rather, a program of majority advancement through the vehicle of white and black labor solidarity.

Paradigms Lost

The Howard School of Thought represented one of several transitional theories that broke away from the dominant biological/genetic paradigm. New approaches to race problems included the Chicago School of Sociology, Donald Young's comparative analysis of minority groups, Howard Odum's regional sociology, Melville Herskovits's cultural anthropology, and John Dollard's "caste and class" approach. Perhaps the most challenging new approach from Bunche's perspective was the "immigrant analogue." The "immigrant analogue," which would gradually evolve into an ethnic analogy in politics, suggested that African Americans shared an experience and a destiny with recently arrived ethnic immigrants. In fact, during a period of immigration restrictions, blacks had moved in record numbers to the urban North occupying the cultural and social space that, twenty years earlier, had been claimed by the immigrant. According to Charles S. Johnson of Fisk University, who, like Frazier, had been a student of Robert Park, "both the theory and the machinery which has been developed for dealing with the immigrant are being transferred to the Negro" (Keppel, 1992: 94). For Johnson the "Harlem Renaissance" provided evidence of the new-found sense of "group respect" that Jews, Poles, and other oppressed groups had acquired.

A major intellectual leader of the "Harlem Renaissance" was Bunche's Howard colleague philosopher Alain Locke. Locke's *The New Negro* had defined the intellectual parameters of the era. Locke believed that African Americans, as the closest American equivalent to a peasant class, were the defining influence in the creation of a genuinely American culture. Moreover, as a student of William James and Josiah Royce at Harvard, Locke had developed a cultural pluralism that challenged the "melting pot" idea as another form of absolutism. For Locke, the solution to the problems of community life was not to change minorities from the top down through cultural domination, but rather to develop cultural tolerance and reciprocity from the bottom up (Washington, 1986: 45).

This early "multiculturalism" criticized the natural scientific and anthropological definitions of race as incomplete and overgeneralized. According to Locke, "the best consensus of opinion…seems to be that race is a fact in the social and ethnic sense [and not] in the physical sense." From his perspective culture sought to be inclusive while race operated to exclude. Thus, cultural assimilation and development, rather than a reinforcement of racial distinctiveness and separation, were the keys for ultimate aesthetic beauty and humanism (Linnemann, 1982: 69).

Locke insisted that the "New Negro Movement" of the 1920s had been much misunderstood as a racialist project. Instead, he preferred to compare it to the Irish Renaissance, which was a "revival of very admirable folk values" and "folk culture" (Keppel: 100). Locke constantly warned his students to avoid "racial isolationism" by continually moving beyond narrow racial boundaries toward cultural reciprocity and universality. In fact, he criticized his own teacher William James for not going far enough: "For the complete implementation of the pluralistic philosophy it is not sufficient merely to disestablish authoritarianism and its absolutes; a more positive and constructive development of pluralism can and should establish some effective mediating principles for situations of basic value divergence and conflict" (Washington: 41). In today's terminology, Locke sought to move from the negative of desegregation to a more positive integration, but not so far as assimilation. As such his views parallel those of DuBois in many ways. (According to Johnny Washington, DuBois and Locke differ in four ways. First, DuBois insisted that cultural values primarily pertained to the genteel tradition, and he encouraged the Elite to draw from that tradition rather than a Folk tradition. Second, DuBois insisted that black art should be conscious propaganda, while Locke promoted art for arts' sake. Third, DuBois tended to stress the role of political and civil equality in liberating blacks, but Locke believed cultural equality was equally important. Fourth, DuBois was more politically active than Locke who acted mainly through his scholarship [Washington: 15-16].)

The antiauthoritarian, pluralistic pragmatism of Locke would seem to have a lot to offer a young social scientist like Ralph Bunche. After all, Locke was a major figure on Howard's campus, influencing Bunche's close friends such as Sterling Brown and even Bunche himself. Moreover, Locke had praised works uncovering the economic components of the race question, while Bunche had been attracted to philosophy professors at UCLA and Harvard. (Bunche's favorite professors at UCLA and Harvard were both philosophers. See Bunche Papers, "Letter to Dean Rieber," 10 June 1947, Box 126; Linnemann: 60). Yet Bunche never adopted the immigrant analogue. (In *Beyond the Melting Pot*, Nathan Glazer and Daniel Moynihan try a 1960s synthesis of these political and cultural perspectives. They contend that the cultural pluralism of ethnic groups leads to political pluralism, which then transforms the ethnic group into a political interest group, losing its primordial base. [See Omi & Winant, 1986: 19].)

As the second generation of black scholars, the young men of the Howard School were anxious to break with the biological conceptions of race that so influenced their predecessors. They were also anxious to demonstrate that they were modern social scientists relying on empirical evidence, quantitative methods, and rational thought. However, Harris and Frazier had a distinct advantage over Bunche. Marxian theory had given Harris a radical alternative to mainstream economics and a "scientific" way to view the race problem. Frazier was also able to draw on the new thinking of the Chicago School of Sociology, which moved away from Social Darwinism and "custom" to view racial conflict as a product of urban contact and economic competition. Unfortunately for Bunche, political science as a discipline had little to say about race and had no radical alternatives.

Donald Matthews states that "[d]espite the fact that the Negro problem was the most important unresolved domestic problem confronting the nation, exactly six articles containing the word "Negro" in their titles were published in the *American Political Science Review* between 1906 and 1963" (Katz & Gurin, 1969: 113). Another four articles included the word "race," and three titles contained the phrase "civil rights," making a grand total of thirteen articles on this issue out of a total of 2,601 other articles in the profession's leading journal. (Matthews states that "the study of Negro politics is most likely to enter into the mainstream of American political science *if it can be shown that the subject can be analyzed in systems terms*" [emphasis mine].) and that problem does not itself challenge the pluralist (or systems) paradigm (Barker: 30–32). Michael Dawson and Ernest Wilson III have also documented the marginality of black politics compared to the sister disciplines of history and sociology. They also reveal significant differences in approaches to the subject between black and white political scientists (Dawson & Wilson: 223–24).

Seeking an approach to race from a broader perspective than the parochial views of his discipline, Bunche retrained himself in cultural anthropology over a period of two years, with the help of a grant from the Social Science Research Council (Edgar, 1992: "Introduction"). Studying with three leading anthropologists of the period—Melville Herskovits at Northwestern, Bronislaw Malinowski at the London School of Economics, and Isaac Shapera at the University of Cape Town—Bunche went on to do fieldwork in South Africa, East Africa, and Indonesia.

Despite his intensive training, Bunche rejected the "functionalism" of Malinowski, perhaps because its moral relativism conflicted with democratic theory as best for everyone. Like most American political scientists, he was committed to both the acceptance of scientific techniques and attachment to democratic ideals (Ricci, 1984: 24). The functionalist school would deny that democracy is necessarily the best form of government for all groups at all times.

As a rational social scientist, Bunche refuses to accept the irrationality of racial chauvinism. Even the inclusive cultural pluralism of Alain Locke is seen as a hindrance to the organization of groups around their "real" and "rational" class interests. Thus, Bunche is more likely to favor a Deweyian melting pot with science and technology fulfilling the community's aim. Locke saw himself as a cultural leader, but the younger Howard scholars (including Howard's famous law students and professors) viewed themselves as social engineers. Old primordial ties must give way to not the "New Negro," but to the new "rational man."

Still, what happens when scientific research continually denies central tenets of democratic ideology, such as the rationality of ordinary citizens? Bunche was no elitist as the Howard School had accused DuBois of being. How do we deal with the persistence of "irrational" behavior along race lines? For many, including Bunche, Gunnar Myrdal's social psychology provided an acceptable answer.

Howard and the Assimilationist Paradigm

When the Carnegie Corporation chose to fund a major study of American race relations in the late 1930s, it selected a Swedish economist with strong economic views to head the study, which also included Bunche as the principal black social scientist on the research team. Despite his socialist leanings, Myrdal focused the study on the alleged contradiction within American society between a strong commitment to democratic values on the one hand, and the presence of racial oppression on the other. The new paradigm had a number of important consequences. First, it moves the intellectual community away from biological and genetic explanation for racial difference. By posing a moral dilemma revolving around the gap between mainstream belief and practice, Myrdal shifts the debate to the area of social psychology. (Myrdal was influenced by John Dewey's *Freedom and Culture* (1939) [see Jackson, 1990: 105].) This moral emphasis could be used to combat any emergent Nazism, but it also moves away from social science neutrality. Myrdal believes that a social scientist should explicitly state his or her value premises. However, to be an effective social engineer, he argues, one must select as one's "instrumental norm" valuations held by a substantial proportion of the population (ibid.: 114).

Second, the shift to a focus on the social psychology of race relations submerges the emphasis on class put forward by the Howard school. While Bunche acknowledged the "American Creed," he found that most thinking is "largely reflex," and finds convenient streamlined expression through the "pat response" and "conventionalized stereotype." Myrdal had once held similar views, but his interviews with Americans convinced him that moral ideas were a real social force. The upper classes, in particular, were less racist because they were not in direct economic competition with blacks. According to Myrdal, the problem for the social engineer was "first to lift the masses to security and education and then to work to make them liberal" (ibid.: 129–30). In short, he agreed with DuBois that white and black unity under the banner of interracial unionism was premature.

Third, while DuBois agrees with Myrdal in the primacy of race over class, he fundamentally disagreed with the Swedish economist on the utility of black culture. Myrdal accepts the social pathology model of black culture suggested by Frazier. He saw black history as a "waste field," and, after witnessing the emotionalism of a black church service, suggested it be studied as abnormal psychology (ibid.: 107, 112). The emphasis of Herskovits, DuBois, and Woodson on the Africanness of American Negroes, Myrdal felt, was dangerous because it fed the tirades of extreme racists like Senator Bilbo (ibid.: 120). Thus, Myrdal and his Howard colleagues encourage blacks to adopt white middle-class behavior. Because they believe black status to be unique in that blacks accept mainstream values even though their environment sometimes effects their behavior, they do not develop a general theory of race or ethnicity. Instead, they promote what in essence is a theory of assimilation.

DuBois, on the other hand, disagrees with the cultural pathology model, although he chose not to publicly attack *An American Dilemma*. In his *Black Reconstruction*, DuBois enlisted the support of moral imperatives (over economic interests) as a prime motive behind the abolition movement. The class structure DuBois used was more complex than Marx or the Howard school was willing to admit. Although race was formed as a social category from economic conditions, it takes a central—partly subconscious—role due to the cultural milieu. (Antonio Gramsci's work accords culture a more central role in Marxism.) To counter the problem of discrimination in the ranks of organized labor, DuBois suggests support for a United Negro Trades modeled after the United Hebrew Trades, which would eventually allow blacks a chance to enter the labor movement with their own organizational power base. Moreover, DuBois believes his economic cooperatives could work because they were based on black culture, for example, the cooperative spirit of African tribes and Church groups (Demarco, 1983: 155). Thus, DuBois sought to use the given racial divisions to construct an economic alternative that might eventually serve a more general audience.

Fourth, by locating the fundamental problem in the attitudes of whites, the development by racial subordinates of power bases among themselves was obscured. This action serves to move political science to the margins in terms of analysis and replace it with social psychology. (Certainly the development of pluralist theory falls within the assimilationist framework that emerges during this period. See Robert Dahl's *Who Governs?* and Dianne Pinderhughes's *Race and Ethnicity in Chicago Politics*.) Modernization emerges as a model along with a theory of assimilation. Traditional values of social solidarity, ascriptive criteria, and religious orientations are to be replaced with secular, achievement-oriented, individualistic values of modern society. Of course, politics has a role in this process of transforming the rural peasants into urban workers. However, the emphasis is on leadership and political parties, not on values, culture, movements, or class. Thus, political science tends to focus on how well political elites and sub-elites function in guiding this transformation (assimilation) (Wilson, 1960; or Gosnell, 1967).

Conclusion

Why did the young Howard radicals moderate their views and accept Myrdal's analysis? The onset of World War II had a profound effect on Bunche and his colleagues. If fascism could rise up with such deadly consequences in Europe, could it not also engulf the United States? Bunche, Hastie, and a number of black scholars move to government service in defense of the "American Creed." Their work on the Myrdal study convinces Bunche and others that the New Deal had indeed brought a measure of progress to black America. Myrdal's influence as a social Democrat and social engineer led to a more evolutionary reform of American society. Finally, both Marx and Myrdal saw assimilation as the ultimate end. Neither Bunche, Frazier, or Harris saw in black culture a viable challenge to the status quo. Hence, it was DuBois and not the Howard radicals whom the scholars of the black power generation looked to for inspiration.

The social psychology approach or assimilationist paradigm remains dominant in the field of race relations until the mid-1960s. Bunche moves from Howard to the State Department to the United Nations where he won a Nobel Peace Prize for his mediation of the Palestinian conflict in 1950. Shortly after winning the Nobel Peace Prize, he is elected president of the American Political Science Association. Although he ceases to produce scholarly work after joining the U.N., his views remain closer to the assimilationist paradigm than Harris and Frazier. Indeed, in the eyes of many his fame became so great that he rose above race. Today, one might guess that the work of

William Wilson, a sociologist at the University of Chicago, would find favor with Bunche.

Abram Harris left Howard for the University of Chicago in 1945. He was the first black scholar to receive a teaching appointment at an elite white university. At Chicago his emphasis shifts almost entirely to the history of economic thought, specifically to the critical examination of proposals and schemes advanced by economic theorists for social reform. When he does write on racial matters he argues that the conferring of equal legal rights on blacks would be meaningless unless pre-existing racial differences originating in inadequate socialization of the young in black homes is addressed. Thus Harris's views bear a remarkable resemblance to these of another black economist trained at Chicago—Thomas Sowell (Darity and Ellison, 1990: 614–17). The market-oriented views of Sowell in economics have their counterpart in the individualism of rational or social choice theory in political science.

The only member of the Howard school to remain at Howard, with brief stints abroad, was E. Franklin Frazier. After his death in 1962, he was widely hailed by conservatives and praised by liberals for his social pathology model of the black family. This link to neoconservative thought is a misreading of Frazier, according to a recent biography. Frazier's goal in his work on the black family was to demonstrate that their problems were socially constructed rather than culturally inherited. In his latter years, he would move closer to DuBois's position and was attempting to formulate a set of values that would develop a notion of cultural self-determination in the context of American society.

The Howard School of Thought represents a clear break with the biological paradigm of the past. Bunche, Frazier, and Harris denied that there were any significant biological differences between the races. Using their training as social scientists, they attempted to demonstrate that it was the socio-economic factors of black urban existence that explained differences between the races. They promote a class analysis of race relations that favors the unity of black and white workers in opposition to capitalism and see black culture as dysfunctional. However, their views constitute only a transitional paradigm. They were rejected by mainstream black activists and later absorbed by the social psychological approach of Myrdal. World War II serves to further weaken their class approach and strengthen the importance attached to race. It is ironic that the only racial paradigm that black scholars would participate in developing, a theory of assimilation, would call for their disappearance as a racial group. Yet these scholars were undoubtedly reflecting the views of a significant segment of the black community in the thirties (Banks & Jewell, 1992).

References

Aptheker, Herbert, ed. 1985. *Against Racism*. Amherst: University of Massachusetts Press.

Banks, William M. and Joseph Jewell. "The Intellectual Society Revisited." Unpublished paper, Berkeley, 1992.

Barker, Lucius J., ed. 1992. "Ethnic Politics and Civil Liberties." *National Political Science Review*, vol. 3. New Brunswick: Transaction Publishers.

Blackwell, James E. and Morris Janowitz, eds. 1974. *Black Sociologists*. Chicago: University of Chicago Press.

Bunche, Ralph. 1939. "The Programs of Organizations Devoted to the Improvement of the Status of the American Negro." *Journal of Negro Education*, 8 (July): 3.

———. 1936a. "Education in Black and White." *Journal of Negro Education*, 5 (July): 3.

———. 1936b. "A Critique of New Deal Social Planning as It Affects Negroes." *Journal of Negro Education*, 5 (January): 1.

———. 1936c. *A World View of Race*. Washington: Lyon Press.

———. 1935. "A Critical Analysis of the Tactics and Programs of Minority Groups." *Journal of Negro Education*, 4 (July): 3.

———. "French Administration in Togoland and Dahomoy." Ph.D. dissertation, Harvard University, 1934.

———. Papers, UCLA, Collection #2051.

Dahl, Robert A. 1961. *Who Governs?* New Haven: Yale University Press.

Darity, William, Jr., ed. 1989. *Race, Radicalism, and Reform*. New Brunswick, NJ: Transaction Publishers.

Darity, William, Jr. and Julian Ellison. 1990. "Abram Harris, Jr.: The economics of Race and Social Reform." *History of Political Economy*, 22: 4.

Dawson, Michael C. and Ernest J. Wilson III. 1991. "Paradigms and Paradoxes: Political Science and African American Politics." In *Political Science*, ed., William Croty. Evanston: Northwestern University Press.

DeMarco, Joseph P. 1983. *The Social Thought of W. E. B. DuBois*. Lanham: University Press of America.

DuBois, W. E. B. 1968. *Dusk of Dawn*. New York: Schocken.

Edgar, Robert R., ed. 1992. *An African American in South Africa*. Athens, OH: Ohio University Press and Witwaterstrand University Press.

Edwards, G. Franklin, ed. 1968. *E. Franklin Frazier On Race Relations*. Chicago: University of Chicago Press.

Fredricksen, George M. 1981. *White Supremacy*. New York: Oxford University Press.

Gates, Henry Louis, Jr. 1988. *The Signifying Monkey*. New York: Oxford University Press.

Genovese, Eugene D. 1976. *Roll, Jordan, Roll*. New York: Vintage.

George, Hermon, Jr. 1984. *American Race Relations Theory*. Lanham: University Press of America.

Gosnell, Harold F. 1967. *Negro Politicians*. Chicago: University of Chicago Press.

Gramsci, Antonio. 1971. *Selections from the Prison Notebooks*. Edited and translated by Quentin Hoare and Geoffrey Nowell Smith. New York: International Publications.

Haskins, Jim. 1992. *One More River to Cross*. New York: Scholastic.

Jackson, Walter A. 1990. *Gunnar Myrdal and America's Conscience*. Chapel Hill: University of North Carolina Press.

Katz, Irwin and Patricia Gurin, eds. 1969. *Race and the Social Sciences*. New York: Basic Books.

Keppel, Ben Gareth. "The Work of Democracy." Ph.D. dissertation, Los Angeles: University of California at Los Angeles, 1992.

Kirby, John B. 1974. "Ralph J. Bunche and Black Radical Thought in the 1930's." *Phylon*, 25 (Summer): 2.

Kuhn, Thomas S. 1970. *The Structure of Scientific Revolutions*. Chicago: University of Chicago Press.

Linnemann, Russell J., ed. 1982. *Alain Locke*. Baton Rouge, LA: Louisiana State University Press.

Logan, Rayford, W. 1968. *Howard University*. New York: New York University Press.

Lynch, Hollis R. 1970. *Edward Wilmont Blyden*. London: Oxford University Press.

Martin, Robert E., ed. *E. Franklin Frazier, The Negro and Social Research*. Washington: Howard University Press.

Mensh, Elaine and Harry. 1991. *The IQ Mythology*. Carbondale: Southern Illinois University Press.
Morris, Milton D. 1975. *The Politics of Black America*. New York: Harper and Row.
Moses, Wilson Jeremiah. 1988. *The Golden Age of Black Nationalism*. Handen: Archer.
Mudimbe, V.Y. 1988. *The Invention of Africa*. Bloomington: Indiana University Press.
Myrdal, Gunnar. 1964. *An American Dilemma*. New York: McGraw-Hill.
Omi, Michael and Howard Winant. 1986. *Racial Formation in the United States*. New York: Routledge and Kegan Paul.
Pinderhughes, Dianne M. 1987. *Race and Ethnicity in Chicago Politics*. Urbana: University of Illinois Press.
Platt, Anthony M. 1991. *E. Franklin Frazier Reconsidered*. New Brunswick: Rutgers University Press.
Raboteau, Albert J. 1978. *Slave Religion*. New York: Oxford University Press.
Ricci, David M. 1984. *The Tragedy of Political Science*. New Haven: Yale University Press.
Rivlin, Benjamin, ed. *Ralph Bunche*. New York: Holmes and Meier.
Ross, B. Joyce. 1972. *J. E. Spingarn and the Rise of the NAACP*. New York: Atheneum.
Stuckey, Sterling, ed. 1972. *The Ideological Origins of Black Nationalism*. Boston: Beacon.
Toll, William. 1979. *The Resurgence of Race*. Philadelphia, Pa.: Temple University Press.
Turner, Ralph H., ed. 1967. *Robert E. Park*. Chicago: University of Chicago Press.
Van den Berghe, Pierre L. 1967. *Race and Racism*. New York: John Wiley & Sons.
Ware, Gilbert. 1984. *William Hastie*. New York: Oxford University Press.
Washington, Johnny. 1986. *Alain Locke and Philosophy*. Westport, Conn.: Greenwood.
Wilkins, Roy. 1984. *Standing Fast*. New York: Oxford University Press.
Williams, Verson J., Jr. 1989. *From A Castle To A Minority*. Westport, Conn.: Greenwood.
Wilson, James Q. 1960. *Negro Politics*. Glencoe: The Free Press.
Wolters, Raymond. 1970. *Negroes and the Great Depression*. Westport, Conn.: Greenwood.
Young, James O. 1973. *Black Writers of the Thirties*. Baton Rouge: Louisiana State University Press.

Organizational Character and Interest Group Strategies

Katherine A. Hinckley and Bette S. Hill

The University of Akron

It is customary to justify academic studies with the observation that inadequate work has been done in a particular area. This study is based on a contrarian view: In the area of interest group resources, too *much* work has been done. To put it more exactly, we believe that the strong research focus on group resources has led political scientists to neglect the more important role that nonresource organizational *characteristics* play in the scheme of things. While the importance of organizational characteristics has certainly been recognized theoretically, most actual research has tended to shift to resources and their tactical deployment. We think this has been a mistake, albeit an understandable one; for our basic argument is that it is organizational characteristics, rather than resources, that primarily determine the central strategic choices a group makes in the political world.

We will begin by attempting to distinguish between organizational characteristics and resources, and to discuss their relative places in the "pecking order" of interest group literature. We will then proceed to link these to the strategic decisions groups make, deriving as many links as possible from a propositional inventory of the major interest group literature, and adding some of our own. In the end, we wish to show that while some resources do affect some strategic decisions, by and large organizational characteristics assume much more importance.

Organizational Resources and Character

Ideally, we would like to distinguish between an organization's resources and its character by assigning "aggregate" characteristics to the former and "integral" characteristics to the latter. Thus, the number of members in the organization and their activism would be categorized as resources, as in fact they usually are in the literature; size and activism are a function of aggregated member characteristics.

But this approach, however tidy theoretically, quickly produces categorizations that are counterintuitive. Strictly speaking, organizational wealth, which is *always* treated as a resource, is not an aggregate characteristic as it does not derive from the level of wealth of its individual members (e.g., wealthy unions); and such "resources" as credibility and access plainly are not aggregative at all. The effect is to remove almost everything to the integral or "organizational character" category; and, while we want to demonstrate the relative importance of organizational character, we prefer not to do it by definitional fiat.

We therefore resort to a more commonsense, if less elegant, formulation, and simply define resources as items that can be employed or deployed in pursuit of the organization's goals. Under this formulation, "resources" would include the items shown in table 1; not surprisingly, they strongly resemble the list of resources Schlozman and Tierney investigated in their important 1986 study. The first four items, listed as tangible resources, constitute the central resource base for group action. Nonetheless, intangible resources, such as the prestige of leaders and members, technical expertise, and an appealing cause, are also of obvious importance. Prestige has been cited as an important resource at least as early as Truman (1951: 248–51); technical expertise has become increasingly important in a highly specialized, fragmented set of policy communities; and even the "market appeal" of the organization's goals can be put to use in a variety of ways.

Table 1
Group Resources

Tangible:
  Number of members
  Number of activist members
  Budget size
  Staff size
Intangible:
  Prestige (leaders and members)
  Technical policy expertise
  Appealing cause
  Wide circle of contacts
  Reputation for credibility and trustworthiness

We are somewhat less easy about including contacts and credibility in the list of resources. Much depends on phrasing. Schlozman and Tierney carefully avoid the term "access" in favor of "a wide circle of contacts" (1986: 104), but we think the difference is largely semantic; and access, as a major goal of interest groups, is uncomfortably close to the notion of success itself. Similarly, "credibility" is not 100 percent distinguishable from "legitimacy"; and for reasons we will see later, legitimacy is an important *organizational* characteristic. Assuming, however, that credibility refers primarily to performance reputation, we have included it along with contacts, despite some private reservations. (However, we have omitted "allies" from the Schlozman and Tierney listing. They are something over which the organization has very little control, and probably should be thought of as either part of the environment or the result of prior strategic and tactical choices.)

This is an impressive list, particularly with the addition of credibility, which was ranked first in importance by a large margin among Schlozman and Tierney's respondents. Money, of course, lies behind other characteristics, such as staff size and even technical expertise; in fact, Walker (1991) treated staff size as a surrogate for the less easily obtainable budget figures because the two are so highly correlated. Money, though it was lowest ranked by respondents in Schlozman and Tierney's list, ironically was *most* often cited as the resource the organization would "like to have more of" (1986: 114). Taken together, possession of these resources makes a strong *prima facie* explanation for many of a group's actions and much of its success.

Why do we argue then, that resources have been overemphasized? Basically for two reasons. First, it has proven very difficult to show the presumed relationships to organizational success empirically. Take money, for example. There almost surely is some monetary threshold below which a group cannot operate effectively on the national scene; one can hardly disagree with the axiom attributed to Sophie Tucker, "I've been rich and I've been poor, and believe me, honey, rich is better." Also, some kinds of actions (e.g., media advertising and campaign contributions) can hardly be undertaken *without* money. Yet the difficulty of showing any relationship between a group's wealth and its lobbying success is well known, even in the limited case of the effects of political action committee donations. The same problem arises with membership size; it is hard to show direct effects of a large membership. (In addition, maintaining the membership often eats up valuable cash resources which could be used for direct influence.) The problems are even greater when we come to less tangible and measurable qualities such as credibility or the appeal of one's cause.

Second, and more important, the list of resources in table 1 does not include a set of factors that are more related to the character of the organiza-

Table 2
Organizational Characteristics

Basic Categories:
  Type of interest: Associational/Institutional
Organizational Base:
  Source of funds: Member/Non-member
  Affiliates: Representatives/Individuals/Organizations/Mixed
  Incentives offered: Material/Solidary/Purposive
  Degree of heterogeneity
  Preferred style: Pragmatic/Ideological
  Retention rate (likelihood of exit)
  Presence of subunits
Decisional Structure:
  Decision flow: Top-down/Bottom-up
  Leadership focus: Internal/External
  Degree of cohesion
Political Status:
  Length of politicization: Nascent/Established
  Legitimacy

tion as organization, and that arguably have much more impact on the broad strategic decisions the group adopts. A tentative list of such characteristics is shown in table 2. Some of them will be quite familiar to interest group scholars, some less so; but all have significant potential value for explaining why groups behave politically as they do.

Type of Interest

The first category, or overall *type of interest*, confronts one of the major problems in interest group research—establishing a basic typology of groups that goes beyond the standard textbook listing of business, labor, civil rights, and so on. A number of types have been developed using dimensions we discuss below; but we think the most basic distinction is that made by Salisbury (1984), who noted the difference between associational and institutional interests, and the dominance in modern Washington of the latter type. However, we are not sure that Salisbury's definitional distinction between "voluntary associations of members and hierarchial structures which exercise authority over people within their jurisdiction" (1984: 67) is entirely satisfactory. Almond and Coleman defined institutional interest groups as those that were basically created to perform some other social or political functions, such as churches, legislatures, and bureaucracies, but yet may "articulate their own interests or represent the interests of groups in the society" (1960: 33). Associational groups, by contrast, were defined as explicitly representing the interests of a particular group (e.g., trade unions). Nonetheless, the Almond/Coleman and Salisbury definitions appear fairly close, and are therefore taken as a basic type distinction.

Organizational Base

The second set of variables incorporates many characteristics that have been used in developing other typologies; they all capture some element of the structural or resource base. For instance, we agree with Michael Hayes (1981) that much of a group's behavior may be a function of the way it has solved its basic resource problem—the way it obtains its funds. Though Hayes's typology appears not to have received a great deal of attention, we find quite compelling his argument that *funding sources* (rather than mere size) are central constraints on group choices. The source of funds dimension is also an important variable for Walker (1983), who discusses private and government patronage as major sources of support for many organizations.

The idea of *affiliates* as an organizational variable incorporates another idea explored by Walker. As he points out, some organizations are composed entirely of autonomous individuals, while others derive from members who join as part of their occupational duties and thus are really representatives of other organizations (Walker, 1991: 49). Still others, we might point out, are in fact composed entirely of other organizations (the AFL-CIO), and a final group includes a mixture of the different types. Each of the four may not be empirically distinct in behavior, but the categorization at least exhausts the possibilities.

We also think the mix of *incentives* offered for affiliating with an organization (material, solidary, and purposive) deserves the attention it has received in the literature. (See Clark and Wilson, 1961, for its early development.) St. Angelo has argued that these are motivations for membership, and hence do not apply to organizations "for which the concept of membership is meaningless," such as corporations (1989: 6). We disagree, however. If we think of organizational units or affiliates rather than members, as above, we can distinguish among incentives for affiliating with churches versus corporations just as we can distinguish among incentives for joining classic membership organizations. However, "professional" benefits, which King and Walker (1992) add to the typology, really do appear to apply only to voluntary associations; we have therefore omitted them as a category, though not without misgivings.

The same reasoning applies to three other affiliate-related organizational characteristics: *heterogeneity* of interests represented, *preferred style of action*, and *retention rate* (or likelihood of exit). *Heterogeneity*, for instance, distinguishes "umbrella" organizations such as the American Hospital Association, which represents a wide diversity of hospital types, from more specialized groups such as the for-profit hospitals in the Federation of American Health Systems. Organizations also differ significantly in the *retention rate* (retaining affiliates), and in the preferred *style* (pragmatic versus ideological) of those affiliates. Retention rate and style may apply most obviously to groups composed of autonomous individuals, but we think they may be relevant to other types of affiliate bases as well. Trade associations and other groups whose affiliates are organizations may be subject to retention rate problems, just as individual membership groups are; and certainly there are differences in organizational "culture" and style.

Finally, we have included from Walker the presence of *subunits* as a variable—"localized offices, chapters, headquarters, or other such organized bodies below the level of the central staff and headquarters" (1991: 112). Though this captures portions of both centralization and federated form, both of which tend to appear in the literature as decisional variables (Truman, 1963), we prefer the Walker formulation, which is neutral on its face as to decisional consequences.

Decisional Structure

This brings us to the third set of organizational variables, those related to the decisional structure of the organization. The central variable is, of course, the pattern of *decisional flow*; but here one encounters a variety of different formulations in the literature. Each captures some aspect of the elephant, but each also has problems that have prevented complete acceptance by scholars. Centralization versus decentralization tends to overlap with the existence of subunits, as noted above, while degree of internal democracy (Truman, 1963) and staff versus member focus (Hayes, 1981) become confused with the question of decision making versus responsiveness. Wilson's distinction between "caucus" and "primary" structures (1973: 217) is quite similar to Hayes's (1986) differentiation between organizations with face-to-face relationships among members versus those without; but both seem to apply to organizational networks rather than actual decision making. We therefore have adopted the more recently developed "top down" versus "bottom up" typology of decision making. Widely used in both the implementation and budgeting literatures (Linder & Peters, 1987), it evades some of the confusions of the other formulations, is at least as easily operationalized, and seems to us to reach the heart of the decisional calculus.

Are there any characteristics of the organizational leadership per se that might importantly affect political behavior? The common distinction between autocratic and democratic styles is rather too closely related to the flow of decision making; and it is hard to see exactly how Wilson's distinction between patrimonial and legal-rational administration (1973: 221) might translate into political action choices. However, the *focus* of the leaders—whether primarily internal or external—may constitute a significant variable. Some leaders appear primarily concerned with the internal development, operation, and maintenance of the organization (or their own place in it). Others, however, are more attuned to "larger" goals and matters beyond organizational boundaries, though doubtless this is a matter of degree rather than a strict dichotomy.

We are not aware that other writers have employed this leadership focus variable. It bears some resemblance to the re-election/power/policy typology of goals used to explain Congressional choices (Fenno, 1973), and also to the leadership/management distinction (Schuman & Olufs, 1988: chap. 7)—without the invidious implication that "true" leadership requires breadth of vision. But we think it better captures what everyone realizes intuitively—that the particular leadership focus often makes a significant difference in organizational choices.

The last of the decisional variables, *cohesion*, presents some problems; though it has a long history in the interest group literature (see Truman, 1963), it is very closely related to heterogeneity in terms of possible impact on behavior. Probably lack of cohesion is the product of heterogeneity, but the two are certainly not fully equivalent; lacking much specific guidance from the literature in the matter, we have chosen to include both.

Political Status

Finally, we have included a pair of characteristics related to the political status of the organization. One is simply the *length of politicization*—how long the group has been engaged in political activity; though it is not quite the same as Hayes's "nascent-established" distinction (1981: 77), it is close enough so that we feel comfortable combining them. A second is *legitimacy*, which Hayes actually incorporated into his "nascent/established" dimension. We earlier distinguished this from credibility as a resource, while noting their closeness. But what we mean by legitimacy in this context is acceptance *as a political actor*. From the point of view of some writers, such as Hayes, legitimacy is a critical survival problem, on a par with acquisition of resources; we prefer to think of it in terms of whether political activity is thought proper by outsiders and even by its own members. (For further elaboration and examples, see Campbell et al., 1960: 321–23.)

These considerations make it clear that some organizational characteristics may well underlie others, just as money may underlie many of a group's other resources. For instance, the type of incentives relied upon may affect retention rate, heterogeneity, preferred style of the members, and even the basic decisional flow. In fact, one could extract a great many hypotheses from the literature concerning the tendencies of the various characteristics to hang together, though we have been unable to do this in a single paper. Even without this, however, it should be evident that there has been a considerable amount of theoretical writing on the subject of organizational characteristics.

But then why has so little research focused on them, and so much on resources, as the determinants of political action? Three reasons spring to mind. First, resources are simply a good deal easier to define, operationalize, and work with than organizational characteristics; political scientists have not generally displayed much enthusiasm for plunging into the labyrinth of organization theory (Froman, 1967). Second, the American obsession with the power of money, amply documented by Sorauf (1988), may tend to skew our interests toward investigating that resource. Third, and perhaps most important, the deployment of resources is farther down the "chain" of group actions—more linked to immediate tactics and outcomes. We contend the broad strategies ultimately matter more; but this means we need to consider the distinction, and the links we are claiming.

Strategies, Tactics, and Linkages

The strategic choices we have in mind should be distinguished from tactical decisions. In common usage (for instance, in military terminology), "strategy" means the broad plan of attack, while "tactics" mean the ways that plan is carried out. Further consideration, however, leads one to think that the terms are really "nested" rather than dichotomous; that is, a particular "strategic" decision may be thought of as a "tactical" decision in the service of an even broader strategy, and so on up the line. This complicates matters, but not so much as to make the terms useless. No matter how the lines are drawn, some decisions clearly have broader implications than others, and some actions do clearly rest on a higher-order decision. (There may in fact be instances in which the cart leads the horse, and tactical preferences affect strategic decision; possession of a tactical unit may incline one to adjust strategy so as to use it. But generally one would expect decisions to flow the other way.)

Figure 1 shows a partial model of our argument, excluding, for simplicity's sake, within-category relationships and the complicated nesting of tactics. It is worth noting that the model indicates some indirect effect of both resources and characteristics on strategies through the reciprocal effects they have on each other; but in general the idea is that the resource-strategy link is comparatively weak. Equally important, the model posits that the social and political environment has significant and direct effects on *all* of the elements in the model; but we must defer discussion of those links until we have explicated the core strategies and their relationships to resources and characteristics. Thus, table 3 offers a tentative list of central strategic decisions a group must make, roughly in order of their precedence, while figure 2 presents in simple graphic form the resources and organizational characteristics that we believe affect the strategies (along with their relative importance as indicated by the width of the arrows).

Figure 1
General Model of Strategic Choice

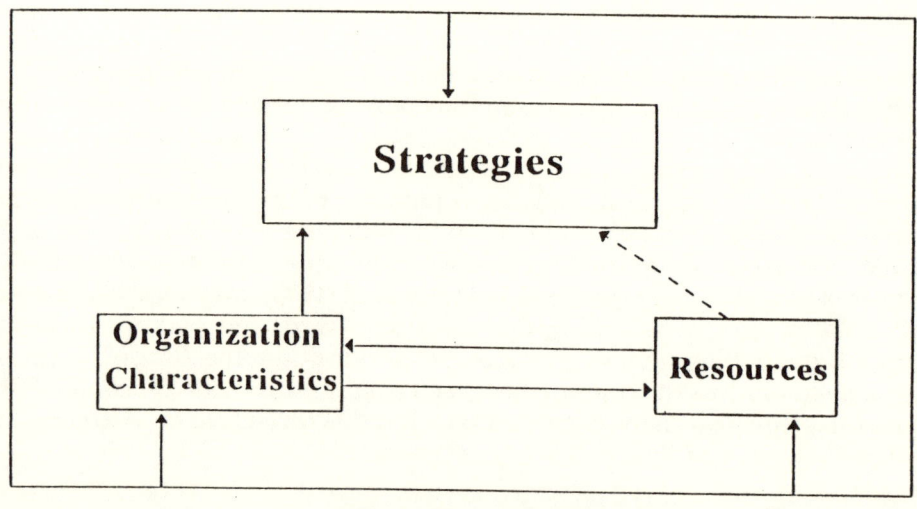

Strategies

Organization Characteristics

Resources

Environment

Figure 2
Effects on Strategy Choice

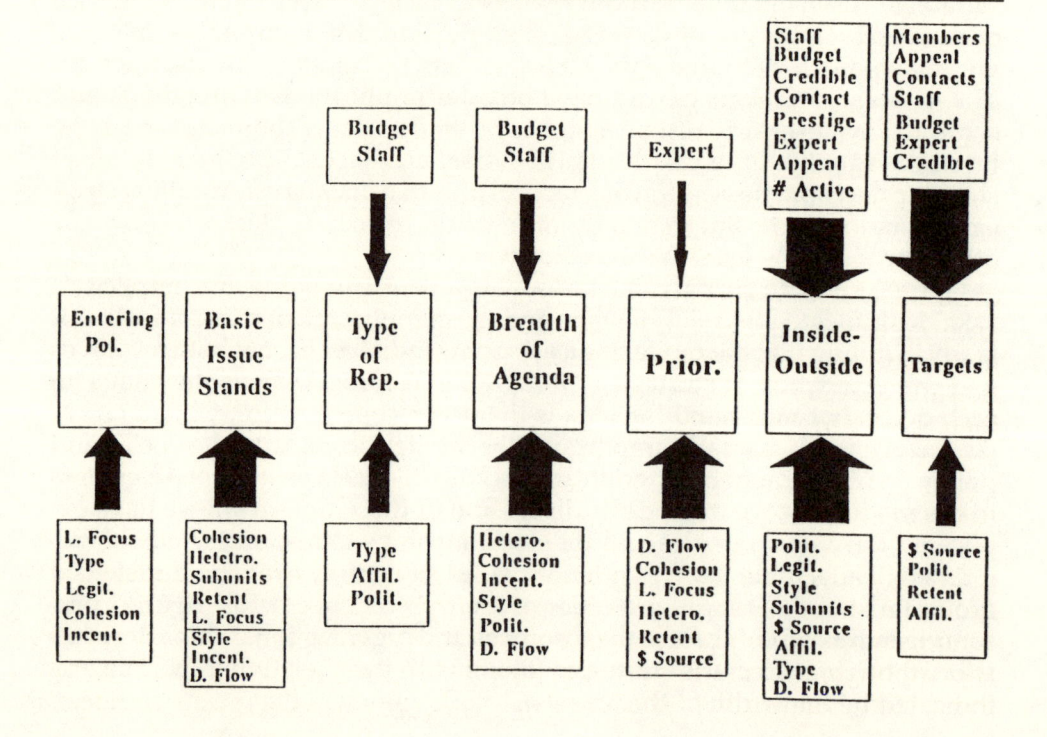

Entering Pol.	Basic Issue Stands	Type of Rep.	Breadth of Agenda	Prior.	Inside-Outside	Targets
		Budget Staff ↓	Budget Staff ↓	Expert ↓	Staff Budget Credible Contact Prestige Expert Appeal # Active ↓	Members Appeal Contacts Staff Budget Expert Credible ↓

L. Focus Type Legit. Cohesion Incent.	Cohesion Hetero. Subunits Retent L. Focus Style Incent. D. Flow	Type Affil. Polit.	Hetero. Cohesion Incent. Style Polit. D. Flow	D. Flow Cohesion L. Focus Hetero. Retent $ Source	Polit. Legit. Style Subunits $ Source Affil. Type D. Flow	$ Source Polit. Retent Affil.

Table 3
Important Strategic Decisions

Entering politics
Basic issue stances: Specificity and rigidity
Choosing a type of representation
Deciding on the breadth of the group's agenda
Setting priorities among items on the agenda
Choosing an "insider" versus "outsider" strategy
Selecting targets for action

Entering Politics

Whether to become involved in politics at all is the first decision, and by no means an obvious one. Five organizational variables—*leadership focus, type, legitimacy, cohesion, and incentives* for affiliation—seem especially likely to affect the decision on involvement. *Leadership focus* is clearly central. Some entrepreneurs start off with an external focus and form groups that are politically oriented at the outset (e.g., Common Cause). On the other hand, leaders preoccupied with internal goals and development may be slow to move to political action. Samuel Gompers's original reluctance to get the AFL involved in politics is an obvious case; a parallel, though less well known, example is the desire of Ethel Percy Andrus, the founder of the American Association of Retired Persons, to avoid political activity for the group.

Basic *type of interest* may also make a difference, most likely in conjunction with other variables. Salisbury (1984: 69) notes that institutional interests have several characteristics that may dispose them to enter politics—ample resources, less trouble with the "free rider" problem, and high exposure to the effects of public policy. Nonetheless, they may hesitate to enter the political arena for fear that their *legitimacy* as political actors will be called into question (e.g., churches, especially the less popular ones.) Or they may fear that politics will prove a threat to *cohesion*. The problem of cohesion in turn suggests that *incentives for affiliation* may well play a role in political involvement. Groups depending heavily on solidary benefits often choose not to become involved in politics because of the potentially divisive effects on that solidarity (Wilson, 1973: 43). Conversely, reliance on purposive benefits to draw members should be especially conducive to political action, while reliance on selective material benefits as a primary attractant is thought to result in political activity largely as a kind of "byproduct" subject to leader discretion and surplus revenues (Olson, 1965). The basic decision on involvement, then, is very much a function of organizational characteristics; resources are at best a secondary consideration.

Basic Issue Stances

Once the decision to enter politics has been made, the organization must decide its basic issue stances. At first glance, these decisions might be thought contingent on other decisions, or even tactical in nature. Further consideration, though, leads us to put them high on the strategy choice list. For one thing, basic issue stands really constitute a definition of the group's interest;

in fact, they may actually precede the decision to enter politics. Furthermore, we are not so much concerned with the exact content of the stands, which is not really comparable across groups, as we are with their *specificity* and *rigidity*. These characteristics manifest themselves early in the organization's political development, and are closely connected to the nature of the organization itself; indeed, in some instances they may be so closely connected as to not even be fully conscious decisions.

A variety of organizational characteristics appear likely to affect issue specificity and rigidity, all of them components of either the organizational base or decisional structure. Specificity is probably most affected by *cohesion* and the factors that may be related to it, such as *heterogeneity* and the *presence of subunits* (Truman, 1963: chap. 6); low cohesion is well known to make difficult the taking of any clear, specific stances at all. However, *retention rate* may also affect specificity; groups with a very high retention rate may be able to impose considerable specificity anyway without fear of loss. In addition, it seems probable that *leadership focus* also matters; an internally focused leadership will be relatively slow to clarify its political issue stands, just as it will be slow to enter politics in the first place.

Rigidity, on the other hand, is most likely to be affected by *style, incentives,* and *decisional flow*. Ideologically inclined affiliates and reliance on purposive incentives are fairly obvious correlates of a relatively rigid set of issue positions. The flow of decision making is somewhat less obvious, and indeed the effect of patterns of decisional control has been the subject of some debate. Nonetheless, there are several clear cases, such as the American Medical Association and the old International Typographical Union, in which bottom-up organization has tended to result in highly inflexible stances (Campion, 1984; Hill & Hinckley, 1991; Lipset, 1956). Again, however, resources seem to have little to do with the organization's basic issue stands.

Choosing a Type of Representation

A third strategic decision a group must make is the type of representative agent it will choose to influence government—externally hired or in-house. Though this might not appear a particularly significant distinction, Salisbury argues that externally hired agents tend to conduct representation on a more specialized, but also more persistent, basis. Collectively, at least, externally hired representation "surely must intensify the fragmenting, disaggregating tendencies in public policy so often alluded to" (1984: 75). In-house representation is more likely to be of a jack-of-all-trades sort, more subject to the whims of internal organization politics, and therefore weaker and less stable. Though it might lay claim to greater legitimacy than "hired guns" in areas of highly visible policy conflict, Salisbury points out that most policy decisions are *not* especially visible, giving the specialized external hires an implicit advantage.

Judging from Salisbury's work, *type of interest* seems to be a primary determinant of the type of representation chosen. Though much "representation" is by in-house employees, Salisbury shows that lawyers, mostly hired externally, comprised 35.6 percent of all Washington representatives in four broad policy areas, and that institutional interests were particularly inclined to this sort of representation (1984: 73–74). We suspect, however, that the nature of the organization's *affiliates* may also be useful predictors. Groups representing autonomous individuals may tend to rely on in-house staff, who are needed in any event for organizational and membership maintenance. At the opposite end of the spectrum, groups composed of other organizations may find it more convenient to hire externally. These variables appear further cross-cut by the *length of politicization*. For instance, institutional groups such as corporations or universities just embarking on political action may be particularly likely to hire their representatives externally and only later develop in-house representative capacity.

However, organizational characteristics are not the only factors that may affect choice of representative agents. Salisbury clearly notes that one reason institutional groups may hire externally is that they have the resources to do so—suggesting a connection with *budget* and *staff size*. We agree; groups on a shoestring budget will almost certainly have to rely on officers, volunteers, and a few staff doing a good bit of the job of representation. We also agree with his contention that this may well be a disadvantage for them in many policy areas.

Deciding Agenda Breadth

Another important decision for the organization involves the scope of issues it will act on—that is, the breadth of its agenda. On the face of it, this may appear simply a matter of resources *(budget and staff size)*; both Walker (1991: 105) and Wilson (1973: 210) indicate that more resources are likely to lead to broader goals.

But organizational factors are involved, too. Of these, the most important would appear to be related to the organizational base: *heterogeneity, cohesion, incentives, and style*. An "umbrella" organization with a highly heterogeneous membership and low cohesion may feel required to be active in a number of areas in order to accommodate all its members' demands (Browne, 1990, 1991); so, too, may groups with an ideologically inclined membership and those relying heavily on purposive incentives (Wilson, 1973: 315). Less heterogeneous (or less ideologically inclined) groups will probably find it profitable to concentrate more narrowly; Browne (1991), examining interest groups in the agricultural sector, found that nearly 84 percent of the groups were engaged in fewer than eight issues. Further, he suggests that they were more successful than the generalist organizations. This "niche-seeking" behavior, in which the organization tries to establish a stable identity for itself, and a stable policy product, closely resembles Wilson's description of a search for autonomy as a "prudent maintenance strategy" (1973: 263). This would be especially true for nascent organizations, which suggests that an additional variable, *length of politicization*, may be important.

It is also possible that *decision flow* can affect breadth of agenda; a "bottom-up" process might result in taking on a wider variety of issues. Whether this would have an independent effect once factors like heterogeneity and cohesion are controlled for, however, is certainly open to question. The literature in its current state does not make precedence and interrelationships among all these variables particularly clear.

Setting Priorities

The group's priorities are closely allied to the breadth of its agenda, but distinguishable nonetheless. Even a generalist organization with extensive resources cannot fight every battle; it must make choices. The process of setting priorities can be a painful one, as case studies going back to Bauer, Pool, and Dexter (1963) attest. If a group's "real" interests and basic stances are often hard to define, choosing among them is doubly so.

Here the most obvious determinants of strategic choice have to do with the decisional structure, for it is there that priorities are determined. *Decision flow, leadership focus,* and *cohesion* all are hypothesized to have significant effects.

A bottom-up *decision flow* can markedly affect the substance of priorities. Common Cause, which normally pursues "process" issues, set the MX missile as a top priority in 1982-85, largely to keep its most active members happy (Rothenberg, 1991). This in turn suggests that efforts to maintain or increase *cohesion* may also determine what issues a group chooses to emphasize; some priorities may be established largely to satisfy potential dissidents. *Leadership focus* will also certainly affect choice of group priorities, interacting with decision flow and degree of cohesion.

However, certain characteristics of the organizational base may also affect priorities, either directly or else indirectly through the decisional structure. The possible effects of *heterogeneity*, separately or in connection with cohesion, are clear here as in other contexts, though no empirical research has yet straightened out the relationship. *Retention rate* is surely also a factor in setting priorities. Regardless of whether the decision flow is top-down or bottom-up, an organization can hardly afford to ignore the loss of a significant number of affiliates, as the American Civil Liberties Union discovered in undertaking the defense of Nazis' right to march in Skokie, Ill. Even more central in this connection is the organization's primary *source of funds*. Walker (1983, 1991) stresses the importance of patronage from private donors, foundations and government in establishing and maintaining many citizen and nonprofit groups. It is reasonable to think that the preferences of these patrons would be reflected in organizational priorities, and indeed, Nownes and Cigler (1991) have found just that.

Finally, at least one item from our list of resources—the group's *expertise*— should be important in setting priorities. If expertise is increasingly important to group success, as many writers believe, then organizations should be inclined to emphasize those issues on which they can bring expert knowledge to bear.

So far we have delineated five primary strategic decisions. Judging from our survey of the interest group literature, each is importantly determined by a variety of organizational characteristics, but in only a limited fashion by resources. Now, however, we move to two types of strategic choices in which resources appear to play at least an equal role. Figure 2 shows the shift quite clearly. In line with our earlier contention that research has tended to emphasize resources and more tactically oriented choices, we also will start to see more empirical tests, most notably in Walker's posthumously completed volume (1991).

Inside Versus Outside Strategy

In undertaking substantive political action, groups must decide whether to pursue an "inside" or "outside" strategy—that is, whether to approach major policy-making institutions directly or try to reach them indirectly by mobilizing media, electorates, and public opinion. Though the two strategies are not mutually exclusive, since a group may use both, most likely one tends to dominate. Actual measurement of insider and outsider strategies tends to overlap with that of the final strategic decision, choice of targets (as in Walker, 1991); but conceptually, they are not equivalent. One could, for instance, approach Congress as a target using either an inside or an outside strategy. Furthermore, the determinants of target choices as opposed to inside-outside strategies appear somewhat different, as we will see.

A number of organizational characteristics appear to be related to inside-outside decisions. In our judgment, the most important are the group's *length of politicization* and its *legitimacy*. Hayes (1981) suggests that nascent groups will be especially inclined to follow more radical "outside" strategies, partly because they also tend to lack legitimacy. The experience of Greenpeace is instructive here. It relied almost entirely on well-publicized protest and direct action in its early years, but more recently has moved to direct Congressional lobbying as well.

Even having gained political experience and legitimacy, however, an organization may choose to continue an outside strategy because of the nature of its organizational base. *Affiliate style* almost surely plays a role, with a more ideological style creating pressure for outside strategies. The turmoil that rocked the American Agricultural Movement as its leaders tried to institutionalize (Cigler, 1991) and the tendency of the National Organization of Women to continue "outsider" protest activities are cases in point.

Walker's research shows still other relationships between organizational characteristics and strategy selection. The *presence of subunits* tends to result in the use of outside strategies regardless of other characteristics of the group (1991: 117). *Source of funds* is also a factor. Groups relying heavily on patronage tend to avoid inside strategies, though this does not necessarily mean they will opt for extensive use of outside strategies. The Walker research also shows that profit-based occupational groups are especially inclined to use inside strategies, whereas "citizen" groups are least inclined to do so, and groups with members from largely nonprofit organizations lie in between (1991: 117-19). This suggests that the *nature of affiliates* might be a factor in strategy selection, with organizations choosing outside strategies to the degree that their affiliates are composed of autonomous individuals. However, our affiliate variable is clearly different from Walker's typology, which, in any event, is based only on voluntary associations. It may be, then, that *type of interest* would be a better predictor. Salisbury's (1984) work discussed earlier indicates that institutional interests show a definite predilection for "going inside."

Finally, there is the possibility that organizations with bottom-up *decision flows* also tend to go for outside strategies, perhaps in interaction with style or presence of subunits. Unfortunately, there is a good deal of disagreement concerning whether staff-centered (top-down) or member-centered (bottom-up) groups tend to be more militant, and thus presumably more inclined to an outside strategy (Hayes, 1981; Wilson, 1973). Lacking any empirical resolution of the point, we include decision flow as a predictor, but with the proviso that it is not clear how the hypothesis should run.

The uncertainty surrounding several of these organizational variables strongly suggests that we might do well to consider the impact of *resource characteristics* on the inside-outside choice. In fact, a strong case can be made for almost all of them. Walker shows clearly that large *staff* (and therefore *budget*) *size* inclines groups to an inside strategy (1991: 113, 118). In addition, it is entirely reasonable to conclude that high *credibility*, wide *contacts*, affiliate *prestige*, and possession of technical *expertise* should push a group toward an inside strategy, while an *appealing cause* would be particularly useful for outside purposes. It is not clear that membership size would incline a group one way or the other, as many memberships, especially those of autonomous individuals, are purely of the "checkbook" variety. However, it may be that organizations with a large *number of activists* tend toward outside strategies, which give the activists something to do. We therefore include the number of activists as an influence on insider-outsider choice, though not the number of members per se.

Choosing Specific Targets

Finally, organizations must choose which policy-making institutions to approach. Though this choice nears the realm of tactical decisions, it still requires some rather global estimates of where the group's best chances lie, and therefore may be considered at least partly strategic. Of course, a group may choose more than one target, just as it may choose to pursue both inside and outside strategies. The matter is complicated a bit by the fact that choice of different targets may stem from different variables.

Some organizational characteristics do appear to affect these target decisions, though the evidence is a bit scanty. The Walker data show that reliance on patronage as a *source of funds* is negatively associated with use of the courts, possibly because many patrons are concerned about tax consequences or undue control by lawyers. On the other hand, older groups, presumably with greater *length of politicization*, are slightly more inclined to litigate (1991: 176–77).

It is also probable that *retention rate* is an important determinant of targets, especially for groups whose *affiliates* are autonomous individuals. The desire of the organization to retain old members and attract new ones may incline it to target "sexier" institutions like Congress rather than the less glamorous bureaucratic agencies. Several works indicate that much of what an organization does is as much focused on membership maintenance as it is on pursuit of policy goals. (See, for instance, Caldeira and Wright, 1990). This principle should apply to choice of target as well.

However, on balance it appears that resources matter more than organizational characteristics. As in the case of inside-outside strategy, most of the resource characteristics are implicated in at least some aspects of target choice. Large *membership size* and an *appealing cause* should make Congress a prime target, given its sensitivity to constituents; *contacts* are vital for both Congress and the bureaucracy; and the Walker data show a clear relationship between *staff/budget size* and the (very expensive) strategy of litigation (1991: 176–77). *Expertise* and *credibility* as "repeat players," to use judicial studies terminology, are relevant to all arenas.

Overall, our expanded propositional inventory of the sources of strategic choice shown in figure 2 tends to support our original thesis that organizational character is more important than resources. As one nears the tactical end of the spectrum, however, organizational characteristics tend to matter less, and resources matter more.

However, there are few clear indications of *which* organization or resource variables are more important. For resources, staff and budget size appear to be particularly critical, which fits well with the emphasis they receive in the literature. On the other hand, it is possible that the attractions of money as a variable have *produced* much more hypothesizing about it.

As for organizational characteristics, there is no obvious pattern at all. Organizational base characteristics show up most frequently, but that may be simply because we have listed more of them. Also, it should be remembered that there is a great deal of confusion and conflicting terminology in political science regarding these organizational variables, especially group types and decisional flows. The task of trying to sort them out with minimal overlap and maximum consistency has proved daunting enough; it would be doubly difficult to try to establish all the interconnections among them and thus discover which variables have primacy. Though this is a logical next step, we cannot accomplish it here.

...and the Environment

In devoting so much attention to showing the importance of organizational characteristics, we do not mean to imply that the environment for the groups is unimportant. Quite the contrary: It is a central influence on the character of the organizations *and* their resources, as well as directly on strategies and tactics.

One example of the way environment affects organizational character is the availability of funds other than membership dues. In all probability this has increased in recent decades, at least until the advent of the Reagan administration (Walker, 1983, 1991); and the increased availability in turn has made it easier for groups based on purposive incentives (hence especially subject to the free rider problem) to survive. At the same time, however, the relative growth of such groups was surely also fueled by the waves of affluence and desire for self-expression typical of the U.S. in the post-1960 period; it is not at all evident that similar growth took place in many other countries. In addition, some writers would argue that many Americans became more ideological in their style of thinking and acting, though this, of course, has been a matter of hot dispute in the voting literature. It is certain, however, that there was an expansion of political conflict; and Walker shows that organizations facing high levels of conflict in their environments tend to emphasize purposive benefits, even downplaying material ones (1991: 67, 96–97).

The environment also affects resources and their tactical deployment. As is implied in what we have just said about nonmember sources of revenue, this is partly a matter of availability; just as alternative funding has augmented the budget of many organizations and made them competitive, so the advent of direct mail and computer technology has given them new facilities for communication. But the influence of the environment is also partly a matter of the relative *value* of resources and their associated tactics. We strongly suspect that the value of different resources to groups varies both by time and place. Money is surely more important to groups in the United States, with its weak parties and candidate-centered election system, than it is in many other countries; but we would hazard a guess that it is in some ways less important now than it used to be, since so many groups possess reasonably sized budgets. If Schlozman and Tierney are correct, it has also become less vital for many purposes than technical expertise. With the increasing importance of television in politics, the value of an appealing cause for media and public opinion purposes has certainly grown.

In addition, though perhaps less obviously, the environment affects the value of particular strategies. The clearest case is the way that organizations have become politicized "by necessity" as government action has impinged on their vital interests, or given them opportunities to achieve cherished goals. The Walker research shows that a conflictual environment produces higher use of *both* the inside and outside strategies, that is, higher rates of political activity, period (1991: 111–19).

Almost as clear are the institutional factors that affect selection of targets. One example is the shift of conservative interest groups to the federal courts as more conservative judges have been appointed (Epstein, 1985). Another is the effect of tax and other legal provisions. Lobbying Congress, for instance, is constrained for many groups by their tax-deductible funding status under the Internal Revenue Code's Section 501(c)(3).

Still a third area of direct environmental impact on strategies is the "niche-seeking" behavior described earlier, which certainly has been occasioned by the growth of so many new competing groups, and by the incredible complexity of many issue areas today. One wonders whether it would even be **possible** in today's world to create umbrella organizations like the American Medical Association, the American Bar Association, or the American Farm Bureau Federation.

The environment, then, matters a great deal for what organized interests are like, and what they do. We have simply chosen to approach the subject from the angle of groups and their activities rather than from the side of the environment. From that angle, we can link the two by examining the way in which organizations *adapt* to their environment. Many of the organizational characteristics we have examined have real implications for adaptability in both the short and long terms.

Conclusions

Overall, we think a convincing argument can be made that the most central strategic decisions of a group are much more firmly embedded in its character as an organization than in the extent of its resources—though all three are highly subject to the nature of the political environment. Admittedly, much of what we have said is in the nature of hypotheses, as on many points not even the most basic data have been collected. Further, the lists of characteristics and strategies, though based on our best reading of the literature, are necessarily tentative in view of conflicting terminology and argument.

Thus, there is much to be straightened out theoretically as well as empirically. Nonetheless, we think there is very real utility in a thorough investigation of this area.

References

Almond, Gabriel A. and James S. Coleman, eds. 1960. *The Politics of the Developing Areas.* Princeton, N.J.: Princeton University Press.

Bauer, Raymond, Ithiel de Sola Pool, and Anthony Dexter. 1963. *American Business and Public Policy.* Chicago, Ill.: Aldine.

Browne, William. P. 1990. "Organized Interests and Their Issue Niches: A Search for Pluralism in a Policy Domain." *Journal of Politics,* 52: 477–509.

Browne, William P. 1991. "Issue Niches and the Limits of Interest Group Influence." In *Interest Group Politics,* 3rd ed., eds., Allan Cigler and Burdett Loomis. Washington, D.C.: CQ Press.

Caldeira, Gregory A., and John R. Wright. 1990. "Amici Curiae Before the Supreme Court: Who Participates, When, and How Much?" *Journal of Politics,* 52: 782–806.

Campbell, Angus, Philip Converse, Warren Miller, and Donald Stokes. 1960. *The American Voter.* New York: John Wiley & Sons, Inc.

Campion, Frank D. 1984. *The AMA and U.S. Health Policy Since 1940.* Chicago: Chicago Review Press.

Cigler, Allan J. 1991. "Organizational Maintenance and Political Activity on the 'Cheap': The American Agriculture Movement." In *Interest Group Politics,* 3rd ed., eds., Allan Cigler and Burdett Loomis. Washington, D.C.: CQ Press.

Clark, Peter B., and James Q. Wilson. 1961. "Incentive Systems: A Theory of Organization." *Administrative Science Quarterly,* 6: 219–66.

Epstein, Lee. 1985. *Conservatives in Court.* Knoxville, Tenn.: University of Tennessee Press.

Fenno, Richard. 1973. *Congressmen in Committees.* Boston: Little, Brown.

Froman, Lewis. 1967. "Organization Theory and the Explanation of Important Characteristics of Congress." *The American Political Science Review,* 62: 518–26.

Hayes, Michael T. 1981. *Lobbyists and Legislators.* New Brunswick, N.J.: Rutgers University Press.

Hayes, Michael T. 1986. "The New Group Universe." In *Interest Group Politics,* 2nd ed., eds., Allan J. Cigler and Burdett A. Loomis. Washington, D.C.: CQ Press.

Hill, Bette S., and Katherine A. Hinckley. 1991. "A Political Analysis of the Political Behavior of Health Interest Groups." In *Health Politics and Policy,* 2nd ed., eds., Theodor J. Litman and Leonard S. Robins. Albany, N.Y.: Delmar Publications.

King, David C., and Jack L. Walker. 1992. "The Provision of Benefits by Interest Groups in the United States." *Journal of Politics,* 54: 394–427.

Linder, Stephen H. and B. Guy Peters. 1987. "Policy Implementation: The Fallacies of Misplaced Prescriptions." *Policy Studies Review,* 6: 459–75.

Lipset, Seymour Martin, Martin Trow, and James Coleman. 1956. *Union Democracy.* Glencoe, Ill.: Free Press.

Nownes, Anthony J., and Allan J. Cigler. 1991. "The 'Other' Exchange: Group Entrepreneurs and Group Patrons." Paper for 1991 Southern Political Science Association, Tampa.

Olson, Mancur, Jr. 1965. *The Logic of Collective Action.* New York: Schocken Books.

Rothenberg, Lawrence S. 1991. "Agenda Setting at Common Cause." In *Interest Group Politics,* 3rd ed., eds., Allan Cigler and Burdett Loomis. Washington, D.C.: CQ Press.

St. Angelo, Douglas. 1989. "Typology Utilization in Interest Group Scholarship." Paper presented at Midwest Political Science Association Annual Meeting, 14 April 1989, Chicago, Ill.

Salisbury, Robert H. 1984. "Interest Representation: The Dominance of Institutions." *American Political Science Review*, 78: 64–76.

Schlozman, Kay L. and John T. Tierney. 1986. *Organized Interests and American Democracy*. New York: Harper & Row.

Schuman, David and Dick W. Olufs, III. 1988. *Public Administration in the United States*. Lexington, Mass.: D. C. Heath and Company.

Sorauf, Frank J. 1988. *Money in American Elections*. Glenview, Ill.: Scott, Foresman and Company.

Truman, David B. 1951. *The Governmental Process*. New York: Alfred A. Knopf.

Walker, Jack L., Jr. 1983. "The Origins and Maintenance of Interest Groups In America." *American Political Science Review*, 77: 390–406.

Walker, Jack L., Jr. 1991. *Mobilizing Interest Groups in America: Patrons, Professionals, and Social Movements*. Ann Arbor: University of Michigan Press.

Wilson, James Q. 1973. *Political Organizations*. New York: Basic Books, Inc.

Regimes, Party, and Federal Budgeting: Presidential Estimates, Appropriations, and Expenditures

Edward James Mullen

The University of Central Texas

Introduction

This chapter examines the effects both of partisanship and of regimes on budgetary spending patterns. Regime composition is indicated by the patterns of Republican or Democratic control of the elected institutions. If the President and the Congress are of the same party, then the regime is unified. If the President and the Congress are of different parties, then the regime is divided or mixed. The effect of regime is analyzed against whether the budget reflects partisan electoral competition, which has been the central question in much literature on the budgetary process. If partisan considerations do influence budget decision making, they will create detectable temporal patterns in budget decisions. Clearly, other forces affect budget decisions. War, the state of the economy, and external events all contribute to final decisions. In the midst of so many other forces, evidence of distinctive spending patterns gives great weight to the influence of regimes. While some contend that partisanship plays a role in budgetary decisions and economic policy, the salient characteristic determining policy may be neither party (Hibbs, 1977) nor administration (Beck, 1982), but "regime" (Ippolito, 1981; Malachowski et al., 1987; Beck 1984; Grier & Neiman, 1987; Kiewiet & McCubbins, 1985).

In order to make the present paper clear, we review the literature on partisan budgeting, describe the analytic examination of our date, state our own finding, and discuss the implication of regime composition effects.

---

* I gratefully acknowledge the support and critiques of Brian Roberts, Terry Sullivan, Matthew Holden, and an anonymous reviewer.

Partisan Budgeting: Literature Review

Research has uncovered distinguishable patterns of budget decision making that vary in regard to presidential budget estimates, to congressional appropriations, and to final government expenditures. First, some analysts report bargaining patterns in the president's budget estimates, as formulated in the Office of Management and Budget (OMB), the agency that peculiarly represents the President. There is some difference expected, depending on whether the budget is annual or is a multiyear budget. Those whose work is grounded in the "tradeoff" literature assume that the annual budget has a finite ceiling within which categories must compete for relative gain. Reductions in spending in one category compensate for increases in others, usually within each annual budget (Fischer & Kamlet, 1984; Berry & Lowery, 1990). Bargaining cycles are also reported in a different form in multiyear entitlement estimates and in the credit budget (Kamlet & Mowery, 1983, 1987). In the multiyear budgeting process, some argue, OMB trades increased budget authority in future years for agency acceptance of current year cuts. They suggest that this bargaining system supports interest groups following long-term strategies of steady growth while providing short-term targeted fiscal rewards.

As to appropriations, entitlements and defense appropriations are higher in election years (Kiewiet & McCubbins, 1985); interest group pressures create patterns in defense and in uncontrollable appropriations (Kamlet & Mowery, 1987). Nincic and Cusack (1979) find an inverse tradeoff between defense spending and aggregate private demand. This inverse relation supports long-term historical evidence provided by Kennedy (1989). They also report an electoral pattern in defense spending.

In expenditures, some researchers report short-term budget strategies designed to quickly reach a specifically targeted group of voters during election years. The strategies affect entitlement formulae and one-time laws that set patterns of spending for future cycles (Tufte, 1978).

In most of the budget activities described above, entitlement programs are the center of patterned activity. Since entitlements are "uncontrollable," yet have patterned outcomes, it may be that controllable spending is even more sensitive to electoral patterns. Multiyear appropriations are, Kanter suggested (1972), more susceptible to political manipulation. Agencies and interest groups show more concern about multiyear appropriations than single year outlays (Mowery, Kamlet, & Crecine, 1980). In addition, the electoral cycle influences spending decisions according to the type of electoral year: spending increases most in presidential years with incumbents running, then congressional election years, followed by presidential years with no incumbent running, and finally, nonelection years (Tufte).

In summary, studies find estimates, appropriations, and expenditures to follow the pattern of the electoral cycle. Certain years have more importance than others. Interest group politics encourage incumbents to structure entitlement spending to support re-election politics. Bargaining occurs within the executive branch, according to still other research, over current and future year spending estimates, between the branches, and between capital spending and transfers. Incumbents use parts of the budget to build electoral coalitions in patterns that conform to the electoral cycle. If decision makers use some parts of the budget to influence electoral coalitions, it appears logical to assume that they may use many other facets of the budget process also. Multiyear appropriations categories are more susceptible to political pressures than are single-year outlays. Therefore, multiyear, controllable expenditures should exhibit decision patterns that follow the electoral cycle.

However, is it not plausible that the electoral event that may affect budget outcomes is regime composition? For example, the period covered by Hibbs/Beck research included eight mixed and nine unitary regimes. The supposition is that the veto power inherent in bicameralism and divided government may produce patterns of greater spending accelerations in divided regimes. Institutional conflict over policy decisions appears, some researchers report, more muted in unified regimes. Some see the presidents' power enhanced when the dominant wing of the party (the presidential party) controls the White House and the Congress (Burns, 1963; Kemp, 1984). Presidents get better policy support from Congress (Peterson, 1990; Pfiffner, 1991; Oleszek, 1991). Members of Congress appear to support presidents of their own party more than presidents of the opposing party, although presidents attempt to avoid partisanship in dealing with Congress (Edwards, 1980; Sinclair, 1983; Keefe, 1991; Thurber, 1991).

Others find that the presidents' need for support from the opposing party and the decline of party-in-Congress argue for more cooperation between branches. Some report that mixed regimes provide evidence of greater policy changes and an expansive budget climate. (Cf. Lijphart, 1971; Shepsle & Weingast, 1981; Weingast, 1989 for explanations of legislative behavior. P. A. Beck, 1979; Browne & Rice, 1979; Ranney, 1983; Quirk, 1989; Beam, Conlon, & Wrightson, 1990.) Others theorize noncooperative behavior to be the norm, although usually in a zero-sum solution set. (Cf. Baron & Ferejohn, 1989, among others.) In a conflicting work, Mayhew (1991) reports no effective difference between divided and unified regimes in policy outcomes. However, no study yet examines whether the composition of the governing regimes influences the budget, and the objective of this paper is to give a better empirical test of the option.

Analytic Examination of Data: Measurement and Analysis

The budget is not a seamless work, but consists of unrelated programs and activities whose outcomes are decided by different forces. Partisan pressures may affect some programs but not others. Accordingly, the methodology investigates component parts of the budget. The components examined in this study are a mix of multi- and single-year appropriation categories.

Dependent variable. The dependent variable is the expenditures of the budget for some forty years (FY 1948–89). The expenditures are subdivided into categories that the United States Government calls "functions." These range from "Agriculture" to "Water transportation." (*The Budget of the United States*, e.g., pts. 6 and 7, *Budget* for FY 82, identifies functions that consist of predominantly multiyear or open-ended budget authority. See figure 1.)

To insure statistical continuity, the study examines only those functions that are continuous over the period 1948–91. This reduces the available func-

Figure 1
List of Functional Categories of Outlays in the Study

Function	Explanation
Agriculture	
Air transportation	Aviation and airports, but excluding space
Atomic energy	Shared by defense and natural resources functions
National defense	All DoD programs
Economic and technical development	International affairs: includes some military and economic assistance before 1954
Education	Elementary and higher education (501 and 502)
Executive direction/management	
Central fiscal operations	
Foreign information and exchange	
Conduct of foreign affairs	
Ground transportation	
Land/water resources	Combination of land and water conservation after 1971
Legislative functions	
Military assistance	
Natural resources	
Other natural resources	General surveys & administration
Postal	
Recreational resources	
Veterans income security	Pensions
Vets medical and other services	Veterans hospital and medical + other benefits; administration
Veterans'	Total benefits and services
Veterans readjustment benefits	Vet's education, training, rehabilitation
Water transportation	Combined merchant marine and navigation before 1957

Data in this table are taken from *The Historical Tables of the Budget* prepared by the Office of Management and Budget.

tions to twenty-three of the current fifty-one. They include most budget areas except entitlement programs. While this limits the research, it meshes with previous studies on the subject.

Unit of analysis. The unit of analysis is the rate of change between years for each function. The paper measures the rate of change in current dollars. The reason is that taking the first differential (rate of change) effectively transforms the raw data into a form that is equivalent between years and remedies the potential problems of serial correlation. When we focus on the analysis of changes, we eliminate the dominant, monotonic data patterns of steadily increasing current dollar amounts, and insure comparability of programs of different sizes (Padgett, 1980; Wonnacott & Wonnacott, 1984).

Independent variables. One independent variable in this model is the four-year presidential electoral cycle. While the election cycle may have little effect on regime activity, it may be that regime composition is an agent of change only in election years, or only in presidential elections. Because of this possible confounding effect, the study examines the impact of the electoral cycle separately and in conjunction with regime composition. The analysis compares presidential election-year spending with the other three years with some techniques; with others it analyzes each year separately. Most techniques also compare the effects of regimes and elections together. The model designates the years as:

- the presidential election year;
- the pre-election year (year before the presidential election year);
- the post-election year (the year following the presidential election);
- the congressional election year (off-year elections);

The second independent variable, as indicated, is regime composition and is defined by the patterns of Republican or Democratic control of the elected institutions. The model upon which we rely theorizes that multiyear spending follows regime composition more closely than single-year programs.

Unique statistical problems. Before we come to the substantive results, we present a short analysis of some important technical problems. Budgeting presents unique statistical problems and requires several analytic techniques to provide a composite picture of the data. Small samples, non-normal distributions, and wide variability suggest using more than one technique to describe the data (Padgett, 1980; Achen, 1982; Berry, 1986). The ratio-variable problem, combined with the effects of general incrementalism, may produce Type I errors, particularly with some regression models. Berry, in particular, cautions against accepting tests of statistical significance without substantively meaningful relationships. Achen (1982) warns against Type II errors, finding that the variability of small samples may cause rejection of substantive findings because of findings of statistical insignificance. He questions the utility of single regressions in summarizing a data set, particularly the overuse of measures of "goodness of fit" to describe the substantive parameters of social science quantitative investigations. Achen's central argument is that the assumptions required for regression analysis are simply implausible for realistic data in the social sciences. This criticism is especially important when examining budget data. Regression, the most commonly accepted technique used in political science analysis, may not be appropriate for examining budget data. Regression measures the tendency of data to regress toward an average from the extremes. Yet, this budget analysis theorizes that the annual averages diverge from one another according to the classification of years or regimes.

Time series linear regression is a nonfalsifiable method for distinguishing among decision models (Padgett, 1980). Padgett uses interval groupings of disaggregated budget data to escape the effect of statistical autoregression and hierarchical decision-making patterns.

Techniques employed. Regression analysis groups the data according to the relationship between the data points and the mean of the full sample. The unit of measurement is the dispersion of the dependent variables about the regression line. Analysis of variance (ANOVA) groups the data according to the classification of the independent variables. In ANOVA the unit of measurement is the pattern of data about the independent variables. The object of regression is to test the similarity of all data points, while that of analysis of variance is to test the equality (difference) of the sample means of the data sets. Spending may be more accurately described by comparing its means in the electoral years and regimes. Hence, the appropriate technique is two-way or multivariate analysis of variance.

The analysis in this paper also includes a variety of tests designed to compensate for limitations in the data caused by distribution, size, and composition. Two-way ANOVA compares group means and interactions between independent variables. Multivariate analysis of variance (MANOVA) examines the joint changes in groups of variables and compensates for the violations of normality experienced in ANOVA. Univariate T-tests compensate for the lack of homogeneity in variances among groups. Nonparametric tests analyze the data from a distributional perspective to compensate for the small sample sets and the violations of normality.

ANOVA determines the probability that the group means of dependent functions and subfunctions deviate from one another by chance alone. The groups are the selected electoral year versus the other three years for the first independent variable, and the composition of regime (unified or divided) for the second. The null hypothesis is that the group means of each independent variable are equal. The two-way ANOVA used here is useful because it analyzes the interactive effect of the independent variables.

ANOVA assumes that the variances of the groups are homogeneous for each dependent variable. Therefore, it measures the data using pooled variances and provides two-tailed estimates of the association. Another test, the T-test, does not make the assumption of homogeneity and measures the data using the separate variances of each group, providing one-tailed measures of association. The T-test therefore provides a more relaxed test of significance, although it cannot test the two-way interaction between the independent variables. Its utility in this analysis is in the comparison of group means while adjusting for the variability of the data. It compares individual function changes between a selected year and the other three years of the presidential election cycle, or between the two groups of regime composition. The sample sizes are relatively small ($n = 44$ for the range) for each variable, and the distribution is not normal. In addition, the variability of many samples is large, often exceeding the mean value. Since the t-value increases with a larger mean and smaller standard deviation, large variations in a small sample may hide even substantive differences between means.

MANOVA examine sets of dependent variables to determine if the individual functions change together according to the patterns of the grouping variables. A separate MANOVA examines each of the four electoral years with the independent variable: *Regime*. MANOVA have the advantage over simple ANOVA because MANOVA consider the effects of the predictors jointly. It partially compensates for the violations of assumptions of normality that are inherent in each budget function separately. The MANOVA assumption of normality requires a multivariate normal distribution that is easier to obtain than univariate normality with each single variable. In the following multivariate analyses, some departures from assumptions still exist, but at a substantially lower level than in univariate analysis. The variability in the data is of particular interest. Here MANOVA measure the differences in variability within, and between, groups in a pooled matrix that minimizes the impact of the variability of any single variable.

When data are non-normal and sample sizes are small, nonparametric tests of distribution are often appropriate. The Mann-Whitney nonparametric test examines the hypothesis that two samples have the same distributions. In this paper the distributions are the relative frequency (called ranks) of above- and below-average spending years in each group. The U statistic measures the relative frequency of the ranks of the two distributions. *Ceteris paribus*, the frequencies are equal, so the larger the U statistic, the greater the disparity of spending between the two groups. In this analysis the grouping variables are the electoral years and regime composition.

A second nonparametric test, Chi-square, compares the proportion of higher-than-average outlays between selected years and all other years; or between the two types of regimes. Each test compares the number of years that have above-average spending to those having below-average spending in a two-by-two contingency table. Because the contingency tables are based upon year-by-year analysis, they control for anomalous spending in any particular year.

Great variability in individual functions of the budget and the presence of exogenous forces produce non-normal distributions as a matter of course. For that reason, this paper accepts the results of the analysis as significant only if most tests reinforce them. This necessarily reduces the significant findings to a minimum, but provides more rigorous tests of the hypothesis.

Results of the Analysis

Regime composition influences some spending decisions. Temporal patterns that parallel regime composition exist in five of the twenty-three functions examined. The patterns are summarized here in verbal terms, due to lack of space, but the data are available in quantitative detail.

Defense and education spending follows regime patterns. Defense spending increases in unified regimes, especially in presidential election years. Education spending increases in unified regimes. Elections have little influence on these programs. Both the parametric and nonparametric analyses support these findings. This means that average spending is different between regime types, and that the patterns of change are evenly distributed between both types.

Foreign affairs, foreign information and exchange programs, and veterans spending also exhibit regime patterns. However, they do not show consistent evidence in both parametric and nonparametric tests. This indicates that spending is extremely variable in one regime type but more consistent in the other. It is possible, therefore, that the extreme variability during one regime type may skew the statistical results. Foreign affairs spending decreases markedly in presidential election years during unified regimes. The converse is true in divided regimes. Otherwise, there is little difference between regimes. This program's spending is a victim of election-year politics when it can be used as a political weapon. Foreign-aid spending is generally unpopular with Americans and, in a divided regime, partisans can make political capital out of this type of spending. In a unified regime it is less of a political issue and spending can rise without partisan comment. Foreign information and exchange programs are a subcomponent of foreign-affairs spending. The temporal patterns do not follow those of foreign affairs. This subcategory receives greater support in unified regimes than in divided regimes, except that it suffers the same decline as its parent function in presidential election years. This illustrates the value of investigating the budget in its details, and of doubting conclusions of studies drawn from examinations of the macrobudget. Veterans spending decreases in unified regimes. The electoral cycle, however, greatly influences this function. More than any other, this series of programs is on a roller coaster ride of electoral making. It exhibits wide swings—increasing in election years and falling rapidly in nonelection years. This argues that both elections and regimes affect veterans spending.

Seven other functions show the influence of the electoral cycle on their spending patterns. Each is particularly linked to one or more of the electoral years. However, regime composition does not appear to be a major influence in their temporal patterns (See Summary table).

Discussion

This section discusses theoretical reasons why regime composition affects spending, inferences that may be drawn from the analysis, and the importance of the debate on regime effects.

Why Regime Composition Affects Spending

The answer lies in the characteristics of partisan competition. For parties, cooperation in unified regimes and conflict in divided government is the normal dynamic in the competition for power. Programs lose their intrinsic merit and become tools or weapons in the election campaigns. Partisans support their own programs and attack their opponents using program spending as weapons. A football team creates an apt metaphor to describe partisan competition for spending whose four components are ownership, defense, offense, and sometimes special teams or circumstances.

1. *Like a team, each political party adopts or owns some programs and policies.* The interests of its voters, its campaign coalitions, and its interest-group supporters create arenas of concern for each party. In this sense, programs become as much symbol as substance; spending support for these programs becomes identified with the party.
2. *The party defends its programs to hold its coalition support.* Platforms and campaign promises show the support of party-peculiar programs in campaigns. During the budget process, the party will champion spending for its programs. In unified regimes, this support encompasses both branches and spending rises (for example, defense and education spending). Veter-

Summary Table
Summary of Analysis Results

EFFECT	ANOVA	MANOVA	T-TEST	NONPAR	NONPAR
	F	F	t	U	X²
Pres. Elec. Years		2.22*			
Atomic Energy	3.15*	3.15*	1.91**ø		
Foreign Affairs	3.21*				3.77*
Other Nat Resource	2.97*	3.00*	2.33***	106**	4.51**
Cong. Elec. Years		No Significant Functions			
Pre-Elec. Years		3.34**			
Military Assistance	5.35**	2.92*	1.71**ø	112*	4.78**
Natural Resources			−1.35*	109*	5.66**
Other Nat Resources	3.03*	2.12	1.46*	104**	9.36***
Postal	3.55*	5.04*	2.25***	107*	4.18**
Post-Elec. Years		5.31***			
Executive Direction			1.54*	114**	3.72*
Natural Resources		1.88	1.58*	112**	4.14**
Vets Medical Benefits				124*	4.19**
Regime		2.56**			
Defense	10.44***	5.67**	2.12**	130***	5.03**
Education	5.93**	5.65**	2.10**	149**	9.22***
Foreign Affairs	4.36**	4.82**			3.77*
For. Information & Exchange	5.36**	3.75*	1.73**		3.25*
Veterans	4.16**		−12.20**	121***	

*** p .01
** p .05
* p .10
ø=pooled variance

ans spending is a perverse example of this dynamic. In unified governments, veterans suffer low spending except in presidential election years. Then, veteran support is important to electoral success and spending rises. In divided regimes, veterans receive more support, perhaps because no party wants to be attacked as antiveteran by its opponents. This dynamic indicates that no party *owns* the veterans' issue, but both try to capitalize on it politically.

3. *Like a team on offense, in divided government each branch attacks the party programs of the opposition.* The programs lose substantive merit and become objects of attack, as in the case of foreign aid spending in presidential election years. The Foreign Affairs programs decline in presidential election years because foreign aid has historically been unpopular among Americans. If a unified regime increased foreign-aid spending in this

campaign, it would become a weapon used by the other party. In a divided regime, the parties share responsibility for the spending, and so it does not become a particularly sensitive issue. Spending in these presidential election years is normal. Except for presidential election years in unified regimes, foreign-aid spending is not a political issue and the spending patterns reflect that. Foreign Information and Exchange spending reflects the same dynamic in unified regime presidential election years. In other years of unified regimes it enjoys partisan support. In divided governments, the other party opposes it and spending remains low.

4. *Exogenous events, such as natural disasters or surprise wars (as in Kuwait), may occur to change the intended pattern of spending.* For this reason, some categories may not respond to regime pressures. "Iron triangles" may be so controlling that some categories become immune to changes in regime. The defenders of such categories have the power, it is sometimes reported, to resist change and to defend their prerogatives against president and Congress. Others, such as Legislative and Executive branch direction, follow the election cycle because the influx of new administrations causes spending jumps as they settle into office. Over time, interest groups have sometimes shifted political goals and parties, thus changing the historic pattern of regime effects. One such example may be the shift to the right by the business community in 1970s (Ferguson & Rogers, 1986). Such a change would hide regime patterns from statistical analysis. The existence of identifiable patterns in spite of the many special circumstances illustrates the strength of the relationships.

Inferences

What Inferences May be Drawn from this Analysis?

First, some federal spending results more from the political process than from some objective measures of need. Elections have significant importance to those most affected by regime composition. Whether the next president or the new Congress is Republican or Democratic can determine the level of spending for these programs. The findings support the work of others who report that institutional conflict over policy is reduced in unified regimes (Peterson, 1990; Pfiffner, 1991; Oleszek, 1991).

If the next election (1992) continues the trend of divided government, defense spending is likely to fall. Given today's international and budget realities, it will probably fall anyway, but regime composition may affect the degree of decline. The defense industry may be forced to choose between supporting a Democratic presidential candidate or several hundred Republican congressional candidates to restore regime unity. A similar choice faces education supporters. Given the renewed interest in this arena, a unified regime is more likely to increase funding for education. All but four of the last twenty-four years have been under divided government. Only one of those years has produced above-average spending on education, in spite of apparent need and political rhetoric. Those interested in education face the same electoral choices as those in defense. Yet, in divided government, education spending has often been the "bill-payer" for defense spending. That is, education, along with other social programs, has endured decreased spending when defense spending rose. Should these two disparate interest groups now join forces in the name of unified governance?

The irony of veterans spending is that it is another "bill-payer" for defense spending. Traditionally, veterans' groups have been major supporters for defense spending, yet the evidence is that this is counter to their own self-interest. While veterans spending in presidential election years is usually up in either regime configuration, it is in veterans' best interest to support a divided government in all other years. This again runs counter to the interest of defense spending. Finally, veterans spending is also a function of past wars. The aging of a large Vietnam veterans population, combined with generous legislated benefits, provided an increase in this spending under divided government. This singular pattern of events has declined during the 1980s and eventually may cancel out the spending differences between regimes.

A second inference may be drawn about the permanence of these relationships. As mentioned earlier, some programs such as veterans are related directly to outside events. Wars cause casualties who later need help and generate a large population of veterans whose political power grows with their numbers. The protracted Vietnam War created an immense veteran population that the shorter Korean War did not. As the number of war veterans declines, their political clout and spending will decrease.

Stephen Skowronek (1988) argues that there is a periodicity in political time. Because regimes are periodic, spending patterns are also. Defense spending is another example of periodicity. For example, brief spurts of defense spending during the Korean and Vietnam wars, and the rearming era, 1979–85, account for most increases in unified regimes. Defense spending has generally declined in other periods since World War II. The long-term trend is to reduce defense spending except for periodic times of high threat. Except for the early 1980s, the periods of high defense spending coincided with episodes of unified governance. If there is a trend in the various foreign-affairs programs, it is an increase in spending since the end of the Vietnam War. The U.S. has, perhaps, substituted diplomacy and technical assistance for direct military spending to some degree. While the rate of increase for foreign-affairs programs has accelerated much faster than defense spending, the dollar amounts are, of course, far apart.

These historical events create questions about whether the temporal patterns are actually products of regime composition or of circumstance. Statistically, there are significant spending differences between regime types. Are these accidents of history, or do different regimes produce policies that lead to these spending patterns? This paper adds one bit of statistical analysis to that body of work that sees periodic regularities in governance. However, a further intellectual issue should be joined. Because of the circumstances that clearly influence each statistically significant pattern, other researchers argue against the importance of regimes. David Mayhew, for instance, concludes that regimes make little difference (1991). He examines legislation and congressional investigations and finds policy uniformity among regimes. His conclusions are flawed for three reasons.

1. The central weakness of his argument is that he attempts to examine data numerically without using statistical inference. Although he does not explicitly examine budget data, Mayhew argues that in budgetary matters the president usually gets what he asks for. He offers no statistical evidence to support this contention, yet reports that deficits follow no temporal patterns. This is correct but does not sustain his point. By implication, his understanding of the budget is that of a seamless product wherein the deficit is the result of an ordered agreement. The deficit is a product of many separate decisions and is not a unified whole. Because budgets are a compilation from many sources, regimes have little to do with budget deficits. The level of inspection is too high from which to draw conclusions. In arguing from the macrolevel of deficits, Mayhew assumes that the budget is a unitary whole. However, each program is the product of a unique process made by many decision makers at different times. The culmination of the entire budget process is serendipitous and is unlikely to exhibit temporal patterns.
2. Mayhew's finding of "no difference" is flawed by his unit of measurement. His subjective selection of data excludes budget appropriations, including defense spending, although these are at the heart of congressional activity. Since much budget legislation draws bipartisan support, Mayhew avoids the complexity of the greater part of the legislative process—and insulates it from his calculations of regime effects.
3. He pays little attention to the asymmetric pattern of the data, thus slighting importance of omnibus bills in recent times, and ignores the bunching of data into a few administrations. Nearly 25 percent of the laws cited are in Nixon's administration. Should this weight divided government more heavily? Similarly, one-third of the investigations he cites occurred during the Truman administration. Fewer investigations occur in recent times, perhaps because of bipartisan agreement to suppress controversy. Recent major events seem to demand investigation—the savings and loan scandal, for one—and yet no committee or department investigated them before the 1988 elections. Similarly, the McCarthy hearings in the 1950s, which Mayhew cites as examples of investigations, had little to do with governance and much to do with the fortunes of a failing senator.

While the arguments against regime importance are flawed, historical circumstance challenges the supporting evidence. Neither side of the debate is conclusive. Ignoring budget laws that constitute the major part of legislative activity and avoiding the use of statistical inference weaken the force of Mayhew's conclusions. Examining the budget provides a more objective focus on regime influence but the possibility of historical accident cannot be overlooked.

Whether it is circumstance or regime composition that most influences policy is important for three reasons. First, reduction of conflict in unified regimes endangers the intended constitutional role of the checks and balances. Madison's intent was that the self-interested actions of each branch would check the abuse of power in the others. If unified regimes cooperate to obtain fiscal benefits, the safeguards of the Constitution no longer effectively constrain government. It weakens an important safeguard to liberty.

Second, if unified regimes cooperate, then the collaboration of interests may effectively shut out many citizens from government benefits. Conflict among constituencies is the essence of Madison's ultimate protection for the Republic. Many citizens may lose the benefits of a republican form of government when powerful groups influence both elected branches without the check of interbranch conflict.

Third, regime effects are important because of the electoral dynamics of a partisan system. The data, for example, appear to show that partisan effects in divided regimes work to change spending decisions in election years. Unified regimes smooth over many of those changes. Without the regime effect, the course of many policy decisions may be much different.

Regime effect, as revealed in this analysis, challenges the principal tenets of incrementalism. At the macrolevel, the budget does describe a slow process of small changes. However, the detailed programs exhibit wild fluctuations—sometimes as much as 45 percent in a year. Some functions *averaged* more than 30 percent change over a forty-five-year period. This fluidity shows how the process can create hope for those whose policy goals may be unfulfilled in any particular year. Lost ground can be recovered in the following year.

The policy implications are important. If regime composition makes little difference, then the system of checks and balances operates as intended. If partisanship does not govern policy, then other explanations must exist for election-year spending anomalies. If regimes matter, however, then the patterned behavior described in this analysis will show itself whenever we have divided government.

References

Achen, Christopher H. 1982. *Interpreting and Using Regression*. London: Sage Publications.

Baron, David and J. Ferejohn. 1987. "The Power to Propose." Quoted in Weingast, Beam, David R., Timothy J. Conlon, and Margaret T. Wrightson, 1990, "Solving the Riddle of Tax Reform: Party Competition and the Politics of Ideas." *Political Science Quarterly*, 105, 2: 193–217.

Beck, Nathaniel. 1982. "Parties, Administrations, and American Macroeconomic Outcomes." *American Political Science Review*, 76: 83–93.

_____. 1984. "Domestic Political Sources of American Monetary Policy: 1955–82." *The Journal of Politics*, 46: 786–817.

Beck, Paul Allen. 1979. "The Electoral Cycle and Patterns of American Politics." *British Journal of Political Science*, 9: 129–56.

Berry, William D. 1986. "Testing Budgetary Theories with Budgetary Data: Assessing the Risks." *American Journal of Political Science*, 30: 597–627.

Berry, William D. and David Lowery. 1990. "An Alternative Approach to Understanding Budgetary Trade-offs." *American Journal of Political Science*, 34, 3: 671–705.

Browne, Eric S. and Peter Rice. 1979. "A Bargaining Theory of Coalition Formation." *British Journal of Political Science*, 9: 67–87.

Burns, James M. 1963. *The Deadlock of Democracy*. Englewood Cliffs, N.J.: Prentice-Hall Inc.

Edwards III, George C. 1980. *Presidential Influence in Congress*. San Francisco: W. H. Freeman & Company.

Ferguson, Thomas and Joel Rogers. 1986. *Right Turn*. New York: Hill and Wang.

Fischer, George W. and Mark S. Kamlet. 1984. "Explaining Presidential Priorities: The Competing Aspirations Model of Macrobudgetary Decision Making." *American Political Science Review,* 78, 2: 356–71.

Grier, Kevin B. and Howard E. Neiman. 1987. "Deficits, Politics, and Money Growth." *Economic Inquiry,* XXV (April): 201–14.

Hibbs, Douglas A., Jr. 1977. "Political Parties and Macroeconomic Policy." *American Political Science Review,* 71: 1467–90.

Ippolito, Dennis. 1981. *Congressional Spending.* Ithaca: Cornell University Press.

Kamlet, Mark S. and David C. Mowery. 1983. "Budgetary Side Payments and GovernmentGrowth." *American Journal of Political Science,* 27, 4: 636–64.

———. 1987. "Influences on Executive and Congressional Budgetary Priorities, 1955-1981." *American Political Science Review,* 81, 1: 155–78.

Kanter, Arnold. 1972. "Congress and the Defense Budget: 1960–1970." *American Political Science Review,* 66, 1: 129–43.

Keefe, William J. 1991. *Parties, Politics, and Public Policy in America.* Washington, D.C.: CQ Press.

Kemp, Kathleen. 1984. "Industrial Structure, Party Composition, and the Sources of Regulation." In *The Political Economy,* ed., Thomas Ferguson and Joel Rogers. Armonk, N.Y.: M.E. Sharpe, Inc.

Kennedy, Paul. 1989. *The Rise and Fall of the Great Powers.* New York: Random House.

Kiewiet, D. Roderick and Mathew D. McCubbins. 1985. "Congressional Appropriations and the Electoral Connection." *The Journal of Politics,* 47: 59–81.

Lijphart, Arend. 1971. "Comparative Politics and the Comparative Method." *American Political Science Review,* 65: 682–93.

Lowi, Theodore J. and Benjamin Ginsberg. 1990. *American Government.* New York: Norton & Company.

Malachowski, James, Samuel Bookheimer, and David Lowery. 1987. "The Theory of the Budgetary Process in an Era of Changing Budgetary Roles." *American Politics Quarterly,* 15, 3: 325–54.

Mayhew, David R. 1991. *Divided We Govern.* New Haven: Yale University Press.

McCall, Robert B. 1980. *Fundamental Statistics for Psychology.* New York: Harcourt Brace Jovanovich.

Mowery, David C., Kamlet Mark S., and Crecine, John P. 1980. "Presidential Management of Budgetary and Fiscal Policymaking." *Political Science Quarterly,* 95, 3: 395–425.

Nincic, Miroslav and Thomas R. Cusack. 1979. "The Political Economy of US Military Spending." *Journal of Peace Research,* XVI (2): 101–15.

Oleszek, Walter J. 1991. "The Context of Congressional Policy Making." In *Divided Democracy,* ed., James A. Thurber. Washington, D.C.: CQ Press: 79–98.

Padgett, John F. 1980. "Bounded Rationality in Budgetary Research." *American Political Science Review,* 74, 2: 354–72.

Peterson, Mark A. 1990. *Legislating Together.* Cambridge: Harvard University Press.

Pfiffner, James P. 1991. "Divided Government and the Patterns of Governance." In *Divided Democracy,* ed., James A. Thurber. Washington, D.C.: CQ Press: 39–60.

Quirk, Paul J. 1989. "The Cooperative Resolution of Policy Conflict." *American Political Science Review,* 83, 3: 905–21.

Ranney, Austin. 1983. "The President and His Party." In *Both Ends of the Avenue,* ed., Anthony King. Washington, D.C.: American Enterprise Institute.

Shepsle, K. and Barry Weingast. 1981. "Political Preferences for the Pork Barrel: aGeneralization." *American Journal of Political Science,* 25: 96–111.

Sinclair, Barbara. 1983. *Majority Leadership in the U.S. House.* Baltimore, Md.: The Johns Hopkins University Press.

Skowronek, Stephen. 1988. "Presidential Leadership in Political Time." In *The Presidency and the Political System*, ed., Michael Nelson. Washington, D.C.: CQ Press: 115–60.

Thurber, James A., ed. 1991. "The Impact of Budget Reform on Governance." *Divided Democracy*. Washington, D.C.: CQ Press: 145–70.

Tufte, Edward R. 1978. *Political Control of the Economy*. Princeton: Princeton University Press.

Weingast, Barry R. 1989. "Floor Behavior in the U.S. Congress: Committee Power Under the Open Rule." *American Political Science Review*, 83, 3: 795–815.

Wonnacott, Thomas H. and Ronald J. Wonnacott. 1984. *Introductory Statistics for Business and Economics*. New York: John Wiley & Sons.

Data Sources

U.S. Office of Management and Budget, *The Budget of the United States*. Washington, D.C.: Government Printing Office, various years.

U.S. Office of Management and Budget, *Historical Tables, Budget of the United States*, various years. Washington, D.C.: Government Printing Office, 1987.

Ethics and Budgeting: Comment on an Integrity Model

Marjorie Lewis

University of Colorado-Denver

Introduction

On 30 June 1993 at the Denver School board's meeting to ratify their 1993-94 budget, one of the board members explained why she would not vote for the ratification of this budget. Her statement was, "The budget does not follow the mission statement." "What does she mean by that?" many would ask. The answer is grounded in a concept of ethics and the budgetary process. From an ethical perspective, the issue of integrity surfaces. Integrity is considered in the context of the correlation of budgeting decisions and the mission (goals and objectives of the organization). The budgetary practices of an entity represent its level of integrity.

For example, there are some people who alter their lifestyles (mission) to fit their budgets, and there are those who alter their budgets to fit their mission. In the initial case, the mission represents (follows) the budgets and in the latter case, the budget follows the mission. If the budget does not follow the mission, then the integrity is questionable. Integrity may be defined as an instance where the mission is optimal. An example is represented by the following scenario.

A citizen has identified herself as one who is committed to the liberation of the poor and underprivileged. This commitment is to supersede any other alternatives in her mission, including her comfort or pleasure. Her mission statement is an official and steady state condition, altered only through formal procedures. She has been absolutely convicted to provide a substantial amount of money for a charitable cause (to help the poor) by a certain date.

There are competing options which include (1) the purchasing of a larger home; (2) taking of a very expensive trip; or (3) doing nothing out of the ordinary (due to a lack of funds). Her response to the challenge to contribute the money to the charity would include two alternatives, yes or no. The "yes" response would represent an unconditional commitment to her mission. Any "no" response, regardless of the reason, would represent a conditional response to her stated mission.

Although the rationale for the negative responses provide many explanations, in cases when the mission has not been officially altered, the lack of a positive response to the mission represents a conditional commitment, placing the mission (goals and objectives) subject to other conditions. These conditional commitments represent situations where there exists a lack of integrity. The mission is not made complete or perfect. It is not optimized because it is subjected to constraints.

Among the conditions, as stated above, would be the lack of adequate funding. Its lack or degradation, in relation to the mission, imposes limitations on the mission, goals, and objectives. The mission is not made complete or optimized. Conceding to such limitations is representative of a lack of integrity.

The yes response, reflecting a level of integrity, would be manifested through alternatives in the budget constraints. If the money is not available, and the need is impending, the alternative to budget constraints might include expanding the sources of funding. Approaches to such alternatives are working extra jobs, taking out loans, seeking grants, as well as other legitimate and relatively immediate sources of funding.

Another approach to measuring integrity would be represented when alternatives to the mission are provided as options. In this case, the measure of integrity is a function of tailoring one's resources, particularly financial expenditures, to represent one's mission. A lack of integrity is manifested when an alternative is selected that is outside of the stated mission (goals or objectives).

This second case, representing a lack of integrity, is also identified as a reason for budget constraints. The following two quotes further crystalize this concept relating frugality to integrity. A preacher once stated, "The lack of resources is the result of a misuse of resources." Ben Franklin also provided similar insights through his quote, "A penny saved is a penny earned."

Motivation, as it relates to the budget and the mission, provides additional variables for assessing the integrity of an entity's mission relative to the budget. This factor is key in determining the correlation between the budget and the mission (unofficial or official).

This article offers an analytical model for evaluating the integrity of various entities as a function of correlations between an entity's budget and its mission. Additional analysis of the firm's motives provides contextual components essential in determining integrity.

Integrity is a function of an entity's correlation between (1) its mission, goals, and objectives and (2) its budgetary decisions. The analysis is enhanced through the assessment of goals and objectives as they relate to the proportional funding decision of the entity.

A model for analysis is presented and tested to assess the integrity of a nonprofit entity. The model includes the history, mission statement, and the budgetary process. The budgetary process includes the budgetary calendar, cycle, sources of funds, and uses of funds. The analysis of these factors categorize each budgetary component according to its relevance (direct or indirect), to the mission. Further analysis considers the relative proportions of the budgetary commitments, allowing for the tracking of budgeting priorities relative to the goals and objectives of the mission.

The results of the analysis are used to identify the level of integrity as measured by inconsistencies between the official mission of an organization and its budgetary activity. Applications of this model have included state and local public entities. Implications of the study point to accountability issues associated with the integrity of public entities.

The Rehnquist Court's 1990 and 1991 Terms: The Constitutional Politics of Federalism and its Consequences for Black Americans

Barbara L. Graham
Abraham L. Davis

University of Missouri—St. Louis
Morehouse College

In this article, we present an analysis of the major 1990 and 1991 Rehnquist Court decisions affecting racial and ethnic minorities in the following areas: voting rights, the discriminatory use of peremptory challenges, school desegregation in the secondary and higher education contexts, and habeas corpus law. The decisional propensities of the Rehnquist Court are examined against a federalism framework where a solid majority on the Court gives considerable weight to state sovereignty at the expense of limiting federal powers in the area of civil rights. We conclude in our analysis that the Supreme Court can no longer be viewed as the institution that will be consistently sensitive to the rights of victimized minorities.

Our study builds upon the Barker and Combs (1989) article which examined the major civil rights and liberties cases of the first term of the Rehnquist Court. Their analysis revealed that for the 1986–87 term, the Rehnquist Court did not produce the conservative revolution that many Court observers had expected. They correctly observed that this overall calculus could change depending on the influence of Rehnquist as chief justice and the behavior of individual justices such as Justice O'Connor. Since the publication of their article, we have witnessed the departure of the two most liberal justices on the Court, William Brennan and Thurgood Marshall. By 1992, the Reagan-Bush era had the opportunity to make six appointments to the high court. Consequently, the Rehnquist Court has continued to render conservative rulings, which make it very difficult for racial and ethnic minorities to realize the full promise of equality. These subsequent developments since the Barker and Combs study provide an opportunity to revisit the Rehnquist Court's quest for doctrines and votes in civil rights cases.

In some ways, the 1990 and 1991 Supreme Court terms should be considered as turning points for major shifts in civil rights policy. One Court observer noted a shift in the Court's solidified conservative posture during its 1992 term. A subgroup of conservative justices, Sandra Day O'Connor, Anthony Kennedy, and David Souter, appears to take a more cautious approach to deciding cases, especially those that may overturn precedents (Greenhouse, 1992a). Moreover, Justice Souter, who has been described as the Court's anchor among its conservative majority, did not hesitate to take on Justices Scalia and Rehnquist in areas involving school prayer and abortion (Greenhouse, 1992f). The Court's newest member, Justice Clarence Thomas, appears to fit comfortably with the extreme right Justices Rehnquist and Scalia. As evidenced in the cases analyzed in this article, however, the Court still appears to be in transition on some legal policy questions and the moderate conservative bloc does not always vote together. What is clear from our analysis of the 1990 and 1991 major decisions affecting the rights of racial and ethnic minorities is that the Court's solidified conservative policy stance has seriously questioned its contemporary role as protector and guardian of minority rights. Only major shifts in the current composition of the Court are likely to reverse this trend.

Historically, the struggle for equality before the U.S. Supreme Court has produced legal victories that have been consistently offset with legal defeats. According to this perspective, the struggle for equality has followed a win-lose cyclical pattern whereby blacks were being treated contrary to the policy directives of the Court. This resulted in their returning to the Supreme Court to regain rights that had been previously granted and thus made genuine progress painfully slow and incremental. This pattern emerged in a number of policy areas notwithstanding the victories that blacks were winning in the Supreme Court. Professor Derrick Bell has expressed the core of the problem facing blacks in these words:

> The common-held view of civil rights as a long, unbroken line of precedents resulting in slow but steady progress is reassuring. Encouragement though, while welcome, is not actuality. And too often, what is denominated progress has been a cyclical phenomenon in which legal rights are granted then lost, then gained again in response to economic and political developments...over which blacks exercise little or no control. (Bell, 1987: 3)

Professor Bell's insights suggest that an analysis of leading precedents in areas such as voting, school desegregation, employment, and the like, reveals that each litigation victory has been emptied because of subsequent losses. With respect to our analysis, it is virtually impossible to capture this cyclical phenomenon in our brief examination of the leading civil rights cases for only two terms. The present study is best viewed as a snapshot of a much broader and more complex pattern of wins and losses before the Supreme Court.

Our analysis does reveal a centrally important theme present in many Rehnquist Court decisions which have profound consequences for racial and ethnic minorities' quest to obtain equality before the Court—the Court's adherence to federalism as a mechanism for limiting the role of the federal government in safeguarding minority rights. Chief Justice Rehnquist, a longstanding articulator of state sovereignty jurisprudence, has strengthened his influence in various cases due to the addition of Justices Kennedy, O'Connor, and Souter to the Court. O'Brien's (1989) analysis reveals that the Rehnquist Court's deference to federalism goes beyond a mere respect for the diversity and independence of states. His analysis demonstrated that for the Rehnquist Court, federalism "is often a metaphor for states' sovereignty and restrictions on the federal government's powers, rather than appreciated as part of the political structure and processes created by the U.S. Constitution, which provides the basis for ongoing dialogue on the roles and responsibilities of federal and state governments in providing social services" (O'Brien, 1989: 411). The inherent danger of the state sovereignty approach to the Constitution is that it seriously undermines civil rights enforcement efforts in a number of policy areas affecting blacks. This implication of the philosophy of federalism is consistent with what scholars such as Walters (1983) have observed with respect to the Republican administrations of the Reagan-Bush era.

This article attempts to present an analysis of the leading civil rights cases decided by the Rehnquist Court during the 1990 and 1991 terms. We will examine four major policy areas of continuing significance for minorities: (1) voting rights; (2) the discriminatory use of peremptory challenges; (3) desegregation in the elementary, secondary, and higher education contexts; and (4) the use of habeas corpus petitions in challenging state criminal convictions. Our study reveals that the philosophy of federalism continues to be used to limit, narrow, and, in one area, overturn Warren Court precedents affecting the legal rights of minorities. In cases where federalism concerns are not directly addressed, such as in the areas of the discriminatory use of peremptory challenges, the Court has continued to incrementally rule in favor of minority rights.

The Rehnquist Court and Political Equality: The Elusive Quest for Third-Generation Voting Rights

Political equality is broadly defined in this article as a right to full and effective participation in the electoral process. Political equality incorporates both the right to vote and the right to have racial and ethnic minorities' votes count as much as those of whites. Historically, racial and ethnic minorities have experienced a pattern of exclusion in the electoral arena. Early schemes such as grandfather clauses, literacy tests, white primaries, poll taxes, and the racial gerrymander have undermined the concept of political equality in our constitutional democracy. First-generation voting rights litigation sought to remove these direct impediments to the basic right to vote since they resulted in the virtual exclusion of blacks from the electoral process. The Supreme Court's rejection of these unconstitutional barriers to the right to vote was a first step toward meaningful political participation for blacks. The Warren Court's commitment to the egalitarian principles underlying the Fourteenth and Fifteenth Amendments led to the formulation of the one-person, one-vote standard enunciated in *Reynolds* v. *Sims* (1964). In addition, the Voting Rights Act of 1965 and its subsequent extensions proved to be a powerful statutory weapon in eradicating voting discrimination despite early efforts to challenge its constitutionality (*South Carolina* v. *Katzenbach*, 1966).

After the passage of the Voting Rights Act, voting rights litigation shifted to the eradication of second-generation schemes such as at-large elections, which prevented minorities from casting meaningful votes in elections. The Burger Court grappled with the problem of establishing evidentiary standards in minority vote dilution cases during the 1970s and 1980s. It eventually required an overly burdensome standard of proof in *Mobile* v. *Bolden* (1980), where the Court held in a 6-3 ruling that a showing of discriminatory intent was necessary to prove minority vote dilution in at-large elections. In responding to the heavy criticism of the intent standard in *Bolden*, Congress was successful in statutorily overturning *Bolden* when it amended Section 2 of the Voting Rights Act in 1982 and established a results test. Subsections (a) and (b) of the amended Section 2 state:

> (a) No voting qualification or prerequisite to voting, or standard, practice, or procedure shall be imposed or applied by any State or political subdivision in a manner which results in a denial or abridgment of the right of any citizen of the United States to vote on account of race or color.
>
> (b) A violation of subsection (a) is established if, based on the totality of circumstances, it is shown that the political process leading to nomination or election in the State or political subdivision are not equally open to participation by members of a class of citizens protected by subsection (a) in that its members have less opportunity than other members of the electorate to participate in the political process and to elect representatives of their choice.

In the first case construing the amended Section 2, *Thornburg* v. *Gingles* (1986), the Court established a test that made it easier for minorities to challenge electoral schemes that diluted their votes. In writing for the plurality in *Thornburg*, Justice Brennan established that in minority vote dilution cases, it must be shown that (1) the minority group is significantly large and geographically compact to constitute a majority in a single-member district; (2) the group must show that it is politically cohesive; and (3) the minority group must be able to demonstrate that the white majority, as a whole, was sufficiently able—in the absence of special circumstances, such as the minority candidate running unopposed—to defeat the minority's preferred candidate.

Judicial Redistricting and Minority Vote Dilution

The judicial redistricting problem surfaced in the 1980s when minority plaintiffs alleged that the use of at-large and multimember judicial districts diluted their votes under the Voting Rights Act of 1965. The primary objectives of judicial redistricting litigation were to bring state judicial elections under the act's coverage and to increase the number of minority judges on the state bench. Lower federal court decisions produced mixed results in the determination of whether the Voting Rights Act covered state judicial elections. For example, in *Mallory* v. *Eyrich* (1988) and *Chisom* v. *Edwards* (1988), the Court of Appeals for the Sixth and Fifth Circuits, respectively, held that the at-large judicial elections in Cincinnati and Orleans Parish diluted minority voting strength in violation of Section 2. In contrast, in *League of United*

Latin American Citizens Council (LULAC) No. 4434 v. *Clements* (1990), the Fifth Circuit sitting *en banc* held that Section 2 did not apply to judicial elections. In 1991, however, one aspect of the judicial redistricting problem was resolved in favor of the minority plaintiffs when the Supreme Court held in three cases that Sections 2 and 5 of the Voting Rights Act applied to state judicial elections.

Clark v. *Roemer* (1991) addressed the problem of preclearance under Section 5 of the act. Section 5 requires covered states to obtain judicial or administrative preclearance before implementing new voting changes or practices from the U.S. District Court in the District of Columbia or the attorney general of the Department of Justice. In *Clark*, a unanimous Court held that the district court erred by (1) not enjoining elections for judgeships to which the attorney general interposed valid objections for certain Louisiana appellate, district, and family court judgeships and (2) in holding that the attorney general approved unprecleared voting changes when it precleared later voting changes. The Court's ruling in *Clark* is significant because it reaffirmed that Section 5 applies to judicial elections. Moreover, the Supreme Court gave covered states notice that they must be specific in identifying voting changes to be considered by the attorney general. Thus, *Clark* made it more difficult for covered states to subvert the objective of Section 5—to prevent voting changes that have a discriminatory purpose or effect—by failing to follow proper administrative preclearance submission procedures (Graham, 1992).

Black and Latino voters won another important voting rights victory from the Rehnquist Court under Section 2 of the Voting Rights Act in *Chisom* v. *Roemer* (1991) and *Houston Lawyers' Association* v. *Attorney General of Texas* (1991), in which the 6–3 majority ruled for the first time that state judicial elections for state supreme court justices and trial judges, respectively, are covered by Section 2. In *Chisom*, a class of black registered voters in Orleans Parish, Louisiana brought suit to challenge Louisiana's method of electing its state supreme court justices from the New Orleans area. Of the seven justices on the Louisiana Supreme Court, five were elected from five single-member supreme court districts and two were elected from one multimember supreme court district. The multimember district consisted of Orleans, St. Bernard, Plaquemines, and Jefferson Parishes. Orleans Parish contained about half the population and registered voters in that Supreme Court district. It should be noted that no black had ever been elected to the Louisiana Supreme Court from any of the Supreme Court districts. Since more than one-half of the registered voters of Orleans Parish were black and three-fourths of the other registered voters in the other three parishes were white, the black petitioners alleged that the method of electing two justices at-large from the New Orleans area impermissibly diluted minority voting strength in violation of Section 2 of the Voting Rights Act (*Chisom* v. *Roemer*, 1991: 2358).

Justice Stevens addressed three main contentions raised by Louisiana and the LULAC majority. First, the Supreme Court rejected the argument that two distinct types of protection for minority voters are present in the language of Section 2(b); that is, that it protects their "opportunity to participate in the political process" *and* their "opportunity to elect representatives of their choice." The respondents argued that the right to participate in the political process exists independently of the right to elect representatives of minorities' choice. Since Congress used the word "representatives," according to the respondents, then it intended to exclude judicial elections from the latter protection (the opportunity to elect representatives of their choice). Justice Stevens rejected such an incredible reading of Section 2(b). For Stevens, "Any abridgement of the opportunity of members of a protected class to participate in the political process inevitably impairs their ability to influence the outcome of an election.... The Statute does not create two separate and distinct rights" (*Chisom* v. *Roemer*, 1991: 2365). The majority concluded that Congress set up a unitary claim under Section 2 and that the word "representatives" did not place a limit on the coverage of the Voting Rights Act for judicial elections.

Next, respondents argued that since Congress used the word "representative" instead of "legislators" in the language of Section 2, it intended to exclude judicial elections from its coverage. Justice Stevens rejected this narrow interpretation of Section 2 in reasoning that the substitution of the word "representatives" indicated at the very least that Congress intended to cover more than legislative elections. For the Court, the correct interpretation of Section 2 is much broader,

> that the better reading of the word "representative" describes the winners of representative, popular elections. If executive officers, such as prosecutors, sheriffs, state attorneys general and state treasurers, can be considered "representatives" simply because they are chosen by popular elections, then the same reasoning should apply to elected judges. (*Chisom* v. *Roemer*, 1991: 2366)

The majority in *Chisom* also rejected the respondents' final contention that since the Supreme Court held in *Wells* v. *Edwards* (1973) that the one-person, one-vote standard does not apply to judicial elections, then judicial elections are entirely immune from vote dilution claims. For Justice Stevens, the *Wells* holding was based on a constitutional challenge under the equal protection clause of the Fourteenth Amendment and was not relevant to a correct interpretation of the Voting Rights Act. Nor does an analysis of the proper statutory standard under Section 2 rely on the one-person, one-vote standard (Graham, 1991).

Justice Scalia, joined by Chief Justice Rehnquist and Justice Kennedy, dissented. Justice Scalia's dissent turned primarily on rules of statutory interpretation and linguistic analysis. For Justice Scalia, an "ordinary" reading of Section 2 leads to the conclusion that the word "representatives" does not include judges. Justice Scalia also questioned how vote dilution claims could occur without the one-person, one-vote standard.

On the same day *Chisom* was decided, the Court addressed the issue of whether Section 2 applies to the election of trial judges in Texas. In *Houston Lawyers' Association* v. *Attorney General of Texas* (1991) and the companion case of *League of United Latin American Citizens* v. *Attorney General of Texas* (1991), Mexican-American and African-American petitioners challenged the at-large, countywide method of electing state district (trial) judges. Relying on the reasoning found in *Chisom*, the same 6–3 majority held that the election of trial judges is also covered by Section 2.

In ruling that the results test of the amended Section 2 of the Voting Rights Act applied to elected judges, the *Chisom* case is expected to diversify the state bench, especially in the South where most states use partisan and nonpartisan elections as the primary methods of selecting general jurisdiction judges. Not only does this decision broaden the terms "voting" and "vote" in the Voting Rights Act, it also paves the way for a more representative public policy on the state bench. Previous research has illustrated the problem of black underrepresentation on the state bench (Graham, 1990b) and an empirical study found that pre-*Chisom* judicial elections have been less successful in increasing black representation on state courts (Graham, 1990a). Although the Court did not address the issue of permissible remedies in redressing minority vote dilution in judicial election cases, the expansive interpretation of the Voting Rights Act removes a major barrier to hundreds of elected state court judgeships previously dominated by whites.

Chisom should be appropriately viewed as a successful attempt to bring state judicial elections under second-generation voting rights jurisprudence. Although the Court reached the proper result in *Chisom*, it can also be argued that a majority of the Court "simply disregarded the flawed reasoning of lower court judges who sought to differentiate judicial elections from other kinds of elections based on the 'function of the office' theory which had no support in the language or the legislative history of the Voting Rights Act of 1965 as amended" (Graham, 1992: 16). Lower court judges also based their rationale for excluding state judicial elections from the Act on the debate over the proper role of the judiciary. The formalistic view adopted by some lower courts that judges do not perform a representative function has been largely discredited by the legal realist movement of the 1930s. The conventional view of state and federal judges places them in a policymaking role.

Does the Voting Rights Act Protect the Right to Govern?

Voting rights scholars such as Guinier (1991a, 1991b) have criticized second-generation voting rights lawsuits that focus too much on simple representation and not enough on minority legislative influence. For Guinier (1992: 288), "Political equality requires both a standard for evaluating legislative influence and explicit mechanisms for overcoming inequality within the governing policymaking body." Consequently, third-generation voting rights litigation is expected to deal with the problem of legislative influence. Once second-generation lawsuits have succeeded in getting blacks elected to various positions in government, third-generation voting rights lawsuits focus on the ability of blacks to govern effectively. These lawsuits are designed to attack voting procedures and practices that hinder blacks from participating meaningfully in a governing body. The Supreme Court during its 1991 term expressed its unwillingness to consider third-generation lawsuits in *Presley v. Etowah County Commission* (1992). In the first major civil rights case since he joined the Court, Justice Clarence Thomas voted with the 6–3 majority in which the Rehnquist Court in *Presley* (1992: 832) declared that, "The Voting Rights Act is not an all-purpose antidiscrimination statute" and limited the scope of Section 5 of the Voting Rights Act.

In *Presley*, black commissioners won elections in 1986 to all-white Etowah and Russell County Commissions as a result of voting rights litigation (Southern Regional Council, 1992: 2). Because of the changes adopted in *Presley*, the black commissioners were not able to exercise the decisionmaking authority that had been traditionally associated with the office. In the Etowah case, the county commission was restructured in 1986 under a consent decree which required a six-member commission with each of the members elected by votes of a different district. Two new members were elected to the commission, one of whom was black (Commissioner Presley). In 1987, the commission passed a road supervision resolution that stripped the new commissioners' authority over road districts. A common fund resolution was passed that also stripped the commissioners' authority to determine how funds were to be allocated in their own districts. Prior to the 1986 consent decree, individual commissioners had control over spending priorities within the district. The Etowah commission did not seek preclearance of either resolution under the Voting Rights Act. The district court held that the road supervision resolution was subject to preclearance but not the commission fund resolution. Since no appeal was taken on the first ruling, only the common fund resolution was considered by the Supreme Court.

In the Russell County case, newly elected black commissioners Nathaniel Gosha and Ed Mack challenged the adoption of the unit system that abolished individual road districts and transferred responsibility for road operations to a county engineer appointed by the entire commission. Black appellants alleged that failure to preclear the unit system violated Section 5 of the Voting Rights Act. The legal issue before the Court in *Presley* was whether the changes in the decisionmaking authority of the elected members on two different county commissions were changes with respect to voting within the meaning of Section 5 of the Voting Rights Act.

In a 6–3 ruling, Justice Kennedy, writing for the majority, held that the common fund resolution in Etowah County and the adoption of the unit system in Russell County did not involve changes covered by the Voting Rights Act. Justice Kennedy reasoned that *Allen* v. *State Board of Elections* (1969) (the first time the Supreme Court construed Section 5) and its progeny established that changes subject to Section 5 preclearance only pertain to voting. The majority then formulated a new standard—that substantive or procedural changes must have a direct relation to voting and the election process. The Etowah and Russell County Commission changes, according to the Court, affected the distribution of power among officials and, thus, did not involve a new voting qualification or prerequisite to voting, or standard, practice or procedure with respect to voting. In its narrow interpretation of Section 5, the majority rejected the view that Section 5 covers changes "with respect to governance." Federalism was clearly the driving force behind Justice Kennedy's restrictive interpretation of the Voting Rights Act. For Justice Kennedy, the Etowah and Russell County changes were "routine" and that Congress did not intend to subject these changes to federal supervision. According to Justice Kennedy, "Were the rule otherwise, neither state nor local government could exercise power in a responsible manner within a federal system" (*Presley* v. *Etowah County Commission*, 1992: 831). The majority concluded its analysis on the impact of its ruling on federalism:

> If federalism is to operate as a practical system of governance and not a mere poetic ideal, the States must be allowed both predictability and efficiency in struc-

turing the governments. Constant minor adjustments in the allocation of power among state and local officials serve this elemental purpose. (*Presley* v. *Etowah County Commission*, 1992: 832)

In the dissenting opinion, Justice Stevens (joined by Justices White and Blackmun) argued that the changes in the reallocation of decisionmaking authority in an elective office, such as the Etowah and Russell County commission changes, were "at least in [their] most blatant form, [are] indistinguishable from, and just as unacceptable as, gerrymandering boundary lines or switching elections from a district to an at-large basis." (*Presley* v. *Etowah County Commission*, 1992: 838). For Justice Stevens, the Etowah County change was "an obvious response to the redistricting of the county that produced a majority black district from which a black commissioner was elected," and that the circumstances surrounding the adoption of such resolutions are suggestive of discrimination and should require Section 5 preclearance (ibid.).

The voting rights victory in *Chisom* was offset by the legal defeat in *Presley*, which has been characterized as "a very formal and shallow view of the right to vote" (Greenhouse, 1992g). As indicated earlier, this ruling not only undermines the enforcement of the Voting Rights Act, but it also signals that a solid majority of the Court is very unlikely to be sympathetic to third-generation lawsuits designed to attack procedures that undermine blacks' authority to govern in local jurisdictions. *Presley* may portend serious implications for future voting rights challenges under Section 5 since the decision may be an impetus to local governments that are determined to weaken blacks' influence in government. This posture reflects whites' acceptance of blacks' right to vote, but not their right to govern (Greenhouse, 1992d).

Jury Discrimination and the Use of Peremptory Challenges: The Rehnquist Court Responds

Racial discrimination in the composition and selection of juries has been a persistent problem in the United States. Jury discrimination against blacks heightened after the Civil War (Moore, 1988: 148). As early as 1875, Congress passed a law that prohibited racial discrimination in the selection of jurors (18 Stat. 336, Section 4). In 1968, Congress passed the Federal Jury Selection and Service Act, which prohibited discrimination in the selection of jurors for the federal judicial hierarchy (28 U.S.C. Section 1861). Title I of the 1968 Civil Rights Act makes it a crime to willfully interfere with any person serving as a petit juror in any court (18 U.S.C. Section 245[b][D]). The Sixth Amendment requirement that grants a person accused of crime the right to a speedy and public trial by an impartial jury has given rise to numerous challenges to the exclusion of racial and ethnic minorities from juries. The Supreme Court has decided a plethora of cases involving allegations of racial discrimination in the jury selection process. For example, in the second Scottsboro case, *Norris* v. *Alabama* (1935), Chief Justice Hughes held that the systematic and arbitrary exclusion of blacks from jury service violated the equal protection clause. Justice Black, in writing for the majority in *Smith* v. *Texas* (1940), declared that the selection of a mere five blacks from a total of 384 persons who served on the grand jury between 1931 and 1938 constituted an intentional exclusion of blacks from grand jury service in violation of the equal protection clause. *Smith* established the principle that jurors must reflect a cross-section of the community. One pernicious violation of the right to an impartial trial that has been considered by the contemporary Court deals with the use of peremptory challenges by prosecutors who attempt to exclude all blacks from a jury because they believe blacks will be sympathetic toward black defendants.

Two important cases were the precursors to the three decisions involving peremptory challenges that were rendered by the Supreme Court in 1991 and 1992. In the first case, *Swain* v. *Alabama* (1965), the Supreme Court was called upon to review the prosecutorial use of peremptory challenges to eliminate jurors without having to give a reason. In *Swain*, all blacks were peremptorily stricken from the jury pool by the prosecutor. Writing for the majority, Justice White observed that the use of peremptory challenges to strike all blacks did not constitute racial discrimination in violation of the equal protection clause unless it could be shown that the prosecutor engaged in this practice "in case after case, whatever the circumstances whatever the crime and whoever the defendant or the victim may be" (*Swain* v. *Alabama*, 1965: 223). He also noted that selecting jury panels within the context of an imperfect system is not equivalent to purposeful racial discrimination.

Twenty-one years later, the Court revisited the problem of the prosecutor's use of peremptory challenges and overruled *Swain* to the extent that it prohibited objections to the use of preemptories in a discriminatory fashion during the course of a specific trial. In *Batson* v. *Kentucky* (1986), the Court held that a prosecutor could not challenge the exclusion of potential jurors solely on account of race in a trial of a black defendant without violating the equal protection clause of the Fourteenth Amendment. Justice Powell contended that a defendant can prove purposeful discrimination by relying on the facts in his particular case concerning jury selection and that the burden then shifts to the prosecutor to show that the black jurors were not excluded for racial reasons. He also noted that the equal protection clause prohibits the prosecutor from challenging black jurors on the assumption that they will be unable to consider the case against a black man impartially. Justice Marshall concurred in the result, arguing that racial discrimination in the selection of jurors will not end until peremptory challenges are abolished. *Batson*, however, failed to address three questions: (1) whether a *Batson* claim was timely filed; (2) whether private litigants in a civil trial and criminal defendants can exercise their peremptory strikes in a racially discriminatory manner; and (3) whether the defendant and juror must be of the same race for a defendant to raise a *Batson* equal protection claim. In 1991 and 1992, the Rehnquist Court answered these questions in *Ford* v. *Georgia* (1991), *Powers* v. *Ohio* (1991), *Edmonson* v. *Leesville Concrete Company, Inc.* (1991), and *Georgia* v. *McCollum* (1992), which extended the *Batson* principle.

In *Ford* v. *Georgia*, a black man was indicted for the kidnap, rape, and murder of a white woman. Before the trial, Ford alleged that the county prosecutor had used peremptory challenges to exclude blacks from juries in those cases involving members of the opposite race and filed a motion to restrict their use on a racial basis. *Batson* was decided while Ford's first petition for certiorari was pending before the Supreme Court in 1986. The lower court denied his motion and he was convicted and sentenced to death. He moved for a new trial claiming that his Sixth Amendment right to an impartial jury had been violated. The Supreme Court held that Ford must be treated as having raised a cognizable *Batson* claim, "although he certainly failed to do it with the clarity that appropriate citations would have promoted" (*Ford v. Georgia*, 1991: 855). In writing for the majority, Justice Souter emphasized that, although Ford cited the Sixth Amendment rather than the Fourteenth Amendment in his new trial motion, the pretrial reference to a pattern of excluding blacks for jury service over extended periods of time constitutes an equal protection claim "on the evidentiary theory articulated in *Batson's* antecedent, *Swain*" (*Ford v. Georgia*, 1991: 855). He also pointed out that a defendant could make out a *prima facie* equal protection violation by examining prosecutorial use of peremptory challenges in the defendant's case, since *Batson* had dropped the *Swain* requirement of proving prior discrimination.

The Rehnquist Court declared in *Powers v. Ohio* that *Batson* applied not only to those cases in which the defendant and the jurors are of the same race, but also to those cases in which the excluded jurors and the defendant were not from the same race. In *Batson*, the defendant was black and alleged that the prosecutor violated his constitutional rights by excluding all blacks from the jury. In *Powers*, a white man who was convicted of murder had objected when the prosecutor used his first peremptory challenge to exclude a black venireperson for racial reasons. The prosecutor argued that *Batson* did not apply in this case because Powers was white. Writing for the majority, Justice Kennedy reasoned that a white defendant could object to the discriminatory exclusion of black jurors because such discrimination reflects negatively on the integrity and fairness of the judicial process. The Court also held that a criminal defendant has standing to raise an equal protection claim on behalf of the excluded jurors. Justice Scalia's dissent, joined by Chief Justice Rehnquist, turned primarily on contrasting interpretations of equal protection analysis in peremptory challenge cases. Justice Scalia also criticized the majority for using "its key to the jail-house door not to free the arguably innocent, but to threaten release upon society of the unquestionably guilty" (*Powers v. Ohio*, 1991: 1381). He stated, "Today's supposed blow against racism, while enormously self-satisfying, is unmeasured and misdirected. If for any reason the State is unable to reconvict Powers for the double murder at issue here, later victims may pay the price for our extravagance" (*Powers v. Ohio*, 1991: 1382).

In *Edmonson v. Leesville Concrete Company, Inc.*, the Rehnquist Court ruled that *Batson* applied not only to criminal cases, but also to civil cases in which peremptory challenges are used to exclude jurors on the basis of race. This case involved a black construction worker, Edmonson, who sued a concrete company for a job-site injury. Leesville used two of its three peremptory challenges to exclude prospective black jurors. Justice Kennedy, speaking for a 6–3 majority, declared that a private litigant in a civil case violates the equal protection clause when peremptory challenges are used to exclude jurors on a racial bias. He also emphasized that the injury caused by a discriminatory peremptory challenge becomes even more serious because it is allowed to happen with governmental permission. Summing up, he observed, "The selection of jurors represents a unique governmental function delegated to private litigants by the government and attributable to the government for purposes of invoking constitutional protections against discrimination by reason of race" (*Edmonson v. Leesville Concrete Company, Inc.*, 1991: 2086). Thus, the majority reasoned that state action exists when governmental authority dominates the exercise of peremptory challenges. For Justice O'Connor, writing for the dissenters, the practice in *Edmonson* did not constitute state action, for it is the litigant, not the government, who exercises peremptory challenges. Furthermore, she argued that since peremptories are not used to select jurors, but only to exclude them, they are not part of the traditional governmental function of determining jury selection (*Edmonson v. Leesville Concrete Company, Inc.*, 1991: 2092–93).

In contrast, the Court in *Hernandez v. New York* refused to extend *Batson* to prosecutors' use of peremptory challenges to exclude Hispanics from a jury. In *Hernandez*, several Hispanic jurors were excluded by the prosecutor because he felt that their spanish-language proficiency would adversely affect their ability to accept the translator as the final arbiter of the spanish-speaking witnesses. Writing for the majority, Justice Kennedy argued that race-based discrimination was not present in this case since the prosecutor had presented a race-neutral explanation for his peremptory strikes. Thus, the trial court had not committed an error in deciding to believe the prosecutor's reasons. Justice O'Connor, joined by Justice Scalia, concurred in the judgment but argued that only race-based discrimination and not language-based governmental decisions that result in a disproportionate impact is appropriate for equal protection analysis. Justice Steven's dissent (joined by Justices Blackmun and Marshall) argued that "the Court therefore errs when it concludes that a defendant's *Batson* challenge fails whenever the prosecutor advances a nonpretextual justification that is not facially discriminatory" (*Hernandez v. New York*, 1991: 1875).

In *Georgia v. McCollum*, the Rehnquist Court had to decide whether a criminal defendant is prohibited by the Constitution from practicing racial discrimination in using his or her peremptory challenges. Relying on the *Edmonson* rationale, Justice Blackmun, writing for the 7–2 majority, held that (1) public confidence is undermined where a defendant, assisted by racially discriminatory peremptory strikes, obtains an acquittal; (2) that state action is present in the case; (3) the state has standing to challenge a defendant's discriminatory use of peremptory challenges; and (4) a prohibition against the discriminatory exercise of peremptory challenges does not violate a criminal defendant's constitutional rights. In a concurring opinion, Justice Clarence Thomas agreed with the majority that this case was governed by the *Edmonson* decision. However, he felt that this decision protects jurors and provided defendants with fewer avenues to protect themselves. He also argued forcefully that this decision would lead to a point of no return because eventually the Court would have to decide if black defendants may use peremptories to strike white jurors or use them on the basis of sex. Justices O'Connor and Scalia were the two dissenters. Justice Scalia contended that the *Edmonson* case had been wrongly decided. He also argued that the majority had simply used the Constitution to "destroy ages-old right of criminal defendants to exercise peremptory challenges as they wish, to secure a jury that they consider fair" (*Georgia v. McCollum*, 1992: 2365).

A majority of the Rehnquist Court has supported a chain of opinions that culminated incrementally in the eradication of the infamous practice of selecting juries on the basis of race. However, some jury observers argue that many blacks are still excluded from juries, leaving juries disproportionately white (Levine, 1992: 191). Despite the safeguards established in *Batson* and its progeny, the very nature of peremptory challenges undermines the core values underlying the Sixth and Fourteenth Amendments. Thus, abolishing peremptory challenges altogether would democratize the jury selection process. Justice Marshall articulated this position in his concurring opinion in *Batson* v. *Kentucky* (1986). For Marshall, "Even if all parties approach the Court's mandate with the best of conscious intentions, that mandate requires them to confront and overcome their own racism on all levels—a challenge I doubt all of them can meet" (*Batson* v. *Kentucky*, 1986: 106).

Erasing the Legacy of Segregated Education: The Struggle Continues

To fully appreciate the landmark desegregation decisions that were rendered by the Rehnquist Court in 1991 and 1992 it is important to examine the nature of the issues that had to be resolved following *Brown* v. *Board of Education* (1955) . Dismantling a dual school system occupied a great deal of the Supreme Court's time during the first twenty years. Desegregating the public schools following *Brown* v. *Board of Education* (1954) has proved to be as difficult as the United Nation's role of enforcing international law among nations. Rosenberg (1991: 52) observed, "The statistics from the Southern states are truly amazing. For ten years, 1954–64, virtually *nothing happened*." According to his analysis, from 1964–72 desegregation increased due to Congress and the executive branch becoming more assertive; not by actions of the Supreme Court. Hochschild (1984) argues that there would have been very little reduction in public school racial isolation had it not been for the courts, which are capable of producing perceptible social change (see also Glick, 1988: 353–55). Despite the significant increase in desegregation between 1964–1972, there was still a great deal of official disobedience of the *Brown* mandate and footdragging because whites did not perceive desegregated schools to be in their best interest. Urofsky (1991: 204) has pointed out that a Florida poll indicated that only one in seven police officers would be genuinely committed to enforcing attendance at desegregated schools.

In the 1970s, the Supreme Court grappled with the problem of school desegregation in the following contexts: *de jure* versus *de facto* segregation in northern cities (*Keyes* v. *School District No. 1*, 1973), whether multidistrict remedies were permissible where *de jure* segregation existed in only one of the districts (*Milliken* v. *Bradley*, 1974), and whether a systemwide remedy was appropriate upon a finding of school boards intentionally operating a dual school system (*Dayton Board of Education* v. *Brinkman*, 1979; *Columbus Board of Education* v. *Penick*, 1979). In the early 1980s, the Supreme Court had to determine whether antibusing measures violated the equal protection clause (*Washington* v. *Seattle School District No. 1*, 1982; *Crawford* v. *Los Angeles Board of Education*, 1982).

A number of districts sought an end to federal court supervision because they believed that they were in compliance with *Brown*, (1954). In *Pasadena*

City Board of Education v. *Spangler,* (1976), the Court had to decide if federal court supervision could be terminated where a previously desegregated school system had become resegregated due to the movement of people in and out of the school system. The lower court found *de jure* segregation in the Pasadena public schools in 1970 and ordered that they desegregate so there would be no school "with a majority of any minority students." The Court retained jurisdiction until full compliance was accomplished. Population movements undermined the "no majority of any minority" mandate and school officials requested a modification of the requirement in 1974. The district court judge declared that his 1970 order would remain effective at least during his lifetime and, therefore, refused to grant the school officials' request. Justice Rehnquist, writing for the majority, declared that the district court had exceeded its authority in enforcing its order and that school officials are not required to make yearly adjustments to fulfill the "no majority of any minority" mandate once the segregative practices were eliminated by the appropriate school officials. The normal movement of people in and out of the city obviously changed the demographics and such movements could not be attributed to official segregative actions. Justice Marshall, joined by Justice Brennan, dissented. They believed that the refusal of the district court to modify the "no majority of any minority" provision was not erroneous since the dual school system had not been eliminated. This case made it crystal clear that school boards would not be expected to make adjustments of zone lines in perpetuity due to normal changes in residential patterns. This precedent establishes the significance of two cases that were decided by the Rehnquist Court in 1991 and 1992, respectively, that dealt with the termination of desegregation decrees in the nation's elementary and secondary schools.

School Desegregation and the Termination of Federal Court Supervision: A Retreat from *Brown?*

Fifteen years after the *Pasadena* case was decided, the Rehnquist Court revisited the question of whether there were time limits to a federal court's supervision of a desegregation decree. In *Board of Education of Oklahoma City Public Schools* v. *Dowell* (1991), the district court, upon a finding that previous efforts to eliminate *de jure* segregation had not been successful, imposed a school desegregation plan on the Board of Education in 1972 that involved systemwide busing. The plan resulted in substantial public school integration and the Court ordered an end to its jurisdiction in 1977 by pointing out that the plan had been implemented and that there was no reason to believe that the Board would undertake any actions to undermine it. The district court denied the respondent's motion to reopen the case, but the Court of Appeals reversed and held that a desegregation decree can remain in effect until a school district is able to show "grievous wrong evoked by new and unforseen conditions" (*Board of Education of Oklahoma City Public Schools* v. *Dowell*, 1991: 635). Writing for a 5–3 majority (Justice Souter did not participate), Chief Justice Rehnquist declared that desegregation decrees were intended to operate temporarily to remedy past discrimination. Otherwise, a school district would be condemned "to judicial tutelage for the indefinite future" or "in perpetuity." He also established that: (1) after school districts have complied in good faith with a decree for a reasonable time period; (2) the evidence indicates that they are not likely to return to their former ways and; (3) the vestiges of past discrimination have been eliminated to the extent practicable, dissolution of a decree is appropriate.

Justice Marshall was joined in his dissent by Justices Blackmun and Stevens. He argued forcefully that the decree had not been achieved because one-race schools could have been avoided. For him, the majority opinion had failed to adequately examine Oklahoma's history of vigorously resisting desegregation. He concluded his opinion in language that is strictly Marshallian, "In its concern to spare local school boards the 'Draconian' fate of 'indefinite' 'judicial tutelage'...the majority risks subordination of the constitutional rights of Afro-American children to the interest of school board autonomy" (*Board of Education of Oklahoma City Public Schools v. Dowell*, 1991: 647).

The problem in *Dowell* was that the Supreme Court's decision did not clarify its good-faith standard in providing guidance to district courts in their determination of whether formerly segregated school districts should be released from desegregation decrees. *Freeman v. Pitts* (1992) gave the Supreme Court the opportunity to clarify its ruling in *Dowell*. *Freeman* raised the question whether a district court can relinquish supervision over those aspects of a school system which are in compliance with a judicial desegregation decree in some respects but remains in noncompliance in other respects. The DeKalb County school system had been under the supervision of a U.S. District Court in Georgia since 1969 and filed a motion for final dismissal in 1986. The district court in its order relinquished remedial control in four categories in which unitary status had been achieved but retained judicial tutelage over two categories (faculty assignments and resource allocation) due to the fact that the school district was not in full compliance. The Court of Appeals for the Eleventh Circuit reversed the holding of the district court. Judge Hatchett, writing for the court, contended that the Board could not avoid its constitutional obligation by pinpointing demographic shifts that occurred prior to the achievement of a unitary school system. He also argued that unitary status is not achieved until the school system has maintained racial equality for a minimum of three years in all six categories. In a 8–0 ruling (Justice Thomas took no part in the consideration of this case), the Rehnquist Court reversed the Court of Appeals holding. Relying on the *Pasadena* case, it held in *Freeman v. Pitts* that a district court may relinquish supervisory authority of a school district in incremental stages before achieving full compliance in all aspects of school operations. Justice Kennedy believed that this approach would allow a district court and the school district involved to concentrate their resources to those areas in which full compliance had not been achieved. For him, the return of local autonomy to school authorities where justified is an integral part of our national tradition.

Mixed views persist on the question of whether the *Dowell* and *Pitts* rulings signal a retreat from *Brown* (1954). In commenting on the *Pitts* ruling, William Taylor, a Washington Lawyer who has handled several school desegregation cases, was quoted as saying, "I do think this is a retreat from *Brown v. Board of Education* and the decisions that gave it content. This retreat is so shrouded in ambiguity that its going to be very difficult for lower courts who are faced with similar petitions to know how to handle them" (Chira,

1992a: A17). Other observers such as David Tatel, director of the Office of Civil Rights under the Carter Administration, viewed both rulings as not producing the dramatic changes in school desegregation law and that the decisions largely reiterate earlier Supreme Court doctrines. Unquestionably, the Rehnquist Court's deference to state sovereignty has actively led to the removal of federal court supervision from state and local institutions. These desegregation rulings pave the way toward local autonomy after operating under federal court supervision for decades. In addition, these rulings did not provide clear guidelines to lower courts in determining how long court-ordered desegregation must continue (Greenhouse, 1992e; Chira, 1992a). These decisions will likely encourage whites who resist desegregation efforts to play a central role in affecting the demographic changes that will ensure the resegregation of the nation's public schools. Moreover, the principles established by *Brown* (1954) will become more symbolic with each passing day since private individual choices with racial overtones unlike state action fail to raise a serious constitutional issue.

Desegregation in the Higher Education Context

Public colleges and universities, like elementary and secondary schools, desegregated very slowly before 1964. Following the enactment of the Civil Rights Act of 1964, there was an increase in the number of black Americans attending predominantly white southern universities, but genuine progress was still painfully slow. This was even true following the decision that was rendered in the case of *Adams v. Richardson* (1973). Several civil rights organizations complained to the Department of Health, Education, and Welfare (HEW) that the public colleges and universities in ten states had failed to desegregate. The Legal Defense Fund of the NAACP initiated suit against HEW which alleged that it had not acted to enforce Title VI of the Civil Rights Act of 1964. U.S. District Court Judge John Pratt held that HEW must commence enforcement proceedings against all institutions that had not complied with Title VI. The district court's order was affirmed by the District of Columbia's Court of Appeals. Silver and Dennis (1990) found that *Adams* states progress in the areas of recruitment, promotion, and retention of black faculty mixed and their analysis showed little optimism for positive change.

The concerted efforts of Congress, the executive branch, and the courts did not result in more than token progress in desegregating public colleges and universities in the South (Rosenberg, 1991: 104-5). Racism, which encouraged deliberate footdragging and a lack of genuine commitment to enforce the *Adams* decision, was the major culprit. The Court had the opportunity to rule in numerous desegregation cases following *Brown* (1954), but had never addressed the issue in the higher education context. Thirty-eight years following *Brown* (1954), it addressed the issue of *de jure* segregation at the university level in the case of *United States v. Fordice* (1992).

Thirty years following *Brown* (1954), Mississippi maintained five universities that whites attended, for the most part, and three universities that were almost 100 percent black. Initially, the parties agreed to solve the problem voluntarily. However, by 1987, it had become very clear that both sides had failed to agree that the appropriate action had been taken to dismantle

Mississippi's *de jure* segregated system. The district court declared that the defendants had taken steps to dismantle their *de jure* segregated system and the Court of Appeals agreed and held that the defendants had implemented race-neutral policies that afforded students the freedom to attend the college or university of their choice. The Supreme Court reversed the holding of the appeals court and contended that a seemingly race-neutral policy does not necessarily cure a constitutional violation. Justice White, writing for an 8–1 majority (Justice Scalia concurred in the judgment in part and dissented in part), examined four policies (admissions standards, duplication of programs, institutional mission assignments, and the continued operation of all eight universities) and concluded that they were the relics of the state's prior *de jure* system of higher education. He also emphasized the Court's rejection of the plaintiffs' request to upgrade the three predominantly black institutions since they are for all of the state's citizens and cannot remain exclusive "black enclaves by private choice." For Justice White, "The Equal Protection Clause is offended by 'sophisticated as well as simple-minded modes of discrimination'" (*United States v. Fordice*, 1992: 2736). Justice Scalia dissented to the part of the judgment that required previously segregated universities to demonstrate that they were complying with the *Brown* (1954) mandate because he felt that this requirement had no "proper application" to institutions of higher learning and provided inadequate guidance to the states.

Fordice is illustrative of the difficulty of dismantling *de jure* segregation at the university level without vigorous political support. Black Americans' quest for educational opportunities in the nation's public colleges and universities had met with very limited success and the struggle is far from over despite the *Fordice* ruling. The full implications of *Fordice* are unknown since the case was sent back to the lower courts for reexamination in light of the Court's ruling (Greenhouse, 1992b). Like the *Dowell* and *Pitts* rulings, the Rehnquist Court failed to "spell out the steps states must take to eliminate segregation, [and] whether it was necessary to funnel more money to traditionally underfinanced black universities, saying that lower courts must decide" (Chira, 1992b: A10). Chira (1992b) also noted that some blacks at historically black colleges feared that these institutions would eventually be robbed of their missions and that enrollments at black colleges would fall. Rosenburg's (1991: 106) observation that "Courts can matter, but only sometimes, and only under limited conditions" must be taken very seriously.

Restrictions on Federal *Habeas Corpus* Petitions: The Rehnquist Court's Aggressive Policy Agenda

One legal policy area where the Rehnquist Court has been especially activist is *habeas corpus* jurisprudence. A post-conviction procedure, *habeas corpus* petitions permit prisoners to challenge on constitutional grounds whether they have been illegally detained. Originally, *habeas corpus* was regarded as an extraordinary method to challenge unlawful detention. However, the Warren Court precedents, *Fay v. Noia* (1963) and *Townsend v. Sain* (1963) transformed the nature of *habeas corpus* law, essentially making it easier for state prisoners to challenge their state court convictions in federal courts. In particular, *habeas* petitions allow death-row inmates the opportunity to raise constitutional claims that often result in delay of their executions. Rehnquist Court *habeas corpus* rulings in 1991 and 1992 signal a strong willingness to limit this important route of federal court appeals for state prisoners.

Limiting Subsequent *Habeas Corpus* Petitions: Expediting the Execution of Death-Row Inmates

In 1991, the Rehnquist Court in several rulings paved the way for expediting executions of death-row inmates by removing procedural barriers and limiting opportunities for appealing death sentences. For example, in *Mississippi* v. *Turner* (1991), the state requested a thirty-day extension in order to file a petition for a writ of *certiorari* in order to appeal an overturning of a death sentence by the Mississippi Supreme Court. The state argued that because of state budget cuts, which resulted in reduced appellate staff, an extension was necessary. Justice Scalia, in his capacity as Circuit Justice newly assigned to the Fifth Circuit, denied the state's request in finding that a reduction in staff was not "good cause shown" that was necessary to grant an extension under the Supreme Court Rules. He wrote, "Like any other litigant, the State of Mississippi must choose between hiring more attorneys and taking fewer appeals. Its budget allocations cannot...alter this Court's filing requirements" (*Mississippi* v. *Turner,* 1991: 1032). In another request for extension to file a petition for *certiorari* cases, Justice Scalia, writing as Circuit Justice, announced his policy position on this issue in *Madden* v. *Texas* (1991): "Extending the period in which to file a petition for a writ of certiorari to a point after an established execution date is either futile or will disrupt the state's orderly administration of justice." He went on to say that it was possible that as Circuit Justice for the Fifth Circuit, his views were "more restrictive of extensions than what the Fifth Circuit bar has been accustomed to," and that he would "not grant extensions in similar circumstances again" (*Madden* v. *Texas,* 1991: 905).

In *McCleskey* v. *Zant* (1991), a solid majority emerged in a landmark case involving the abuse of *habeas corpus* petitions in capital sentencing cases. In 1978, Warren McCleskey was convicted of murdering an off-duty police officer during an armed robbery. Upon receiving the death sentence, McCleskey appealed the sentence and also filed petitions for *habeas corpus* relief in state and federal court over a ten-year period. Following unsuccessful appeals to the U.S. Supreme Court, McCleskey filed his first unsuccessful state *habeas* petition in January 1981. Three claims were raised among the twenty-three challenges to his murder conviction and death sentence involving testimony by a prosecution witness, Evans. In one of the three claims, McCleskey alleged that Evans was deliberately placed in the adjoining cell in order to elicit incriminating statements that were later used without the assistance of counsel in violation of *Massiah* v. *United States* (1964). In December 1981, McCleskey filed his first federal *habeas* petition, but failed to present the *Massiah* claim. Following another unsuccessful state *habeas corpus* action in 1987, McCleskey filed a second federal *habeas* petition, which included the *Massiah* challenge to the prosecution's witness testimony. The District Court granted *habeas* relief, holding that McCleskey did not deliberately abandon the *Massiah* claim after raising it in the first state *habeas* petition, thus rejecting the state's argument that McCleskey's assertion of a *Massiah* claim for the first time in the second federal *habeas corpus* action constituted an abuse of the writ of *habeas corpus*. The District Court determined that when McCleskey filed the first federal *habeas* petition, he did not know about a twenty-one-page document consisting of Evans's incriminating testimony. The Court of Appeals for the Eleventh Circuit reversed, holding that the district court abused its discretion by failure to dismiss McCleskey's *Massiah* claim as abuse of the writ of *habeas corpus*. In a 6–3 decision written by Justice Kennedy, the Court held that failure to raise the *Massiah* claim constituted abuse of the writ of *habeas corpus*. The Court then established a new standard that will make it more difficult for valid constitutional claims to be heard in *habeas corpus* petitions.

Under the previous standard, "inexcusable neglect," a petitioner could abuse the writ by "raising a claim in subsequent petitions that he could have raised in his first, regardless of whether the failure to raise it earlier stemmed from a deliberate choice" (*McCleskey* v. *Zant*, 1991: 1468). Justice Kennedy was clearly more concerned with conserving judicial resources when he examined the costs associated with filing subsequent *habeas* petitions. The new cause and prejudice standard devised by the Court in *McCleskey* sharply restricts the ability of state prisoners to file more than one *habeas corpus* petition. According to the Court, this new standard "should curtail the abusive petitions that in recent years have threatened to undermine the integrity of the habeas corpus process" (*McCleskey* v. *Zant*, 1991: 1471).

When the Court applied the cause and prejudice standard to McCleskey's failure to raise the *Massiah* claim in the first *habeas* petition, it found that McCleskey failed to show cause, which required some external impediment such as governmental interference, to have prevented him from raising the claim. Since the abuse of writ doctrine examines the petitioner's conduct, according to Justice Kennedy, the "petitioners must conduct a reasonable and diligent investigation aimed at including all relevant claims and grounds for relief in the first federal habeas petition" (*McCleskey* v. *Zant*, 1991: 1472). For the majority, ignorance about the prosecution witness' testimony did not prevent McCleskey from raising the *Massiah* claim in the first federal petition and will not excuse his failure to do so since McCleskey knew about the conversations with the prosecution's witness at the trial. The Court thus ruled that McCleskey abused the writ under the cause and prejudice standard.

In a sharp dissent written by Justice Marshall, who was joined by Justices Blackmun and Stevens, the majority was accused of engaging in "judicial activism" and departing "drastically from the norms that inform the proper judicial function" when it ignored precedents that established the "good faith" standard in determining whether abuses of the writ had occurred. Furthermore, Justice Marshall referred to the majority as a "backup legislature for the reconsideration of failed attempts to amend existing statutes" when it established a new standard contrary to Congress' intent (*McCleskey* v. *Zant*, 1991: 1482).

Since the *McCleskey* ruling will make it more difficult to file more than one *habeas corpus* petition, state prisoners will have the incentive to file all possible claims, even frivolous ones, in the first *habeas corpus* petition. Under this likely scenario, meritorious claims may not receive proper consideration in the federal courts. Since studies of *habeas corpus* petitions show that most prisoners file their own claims without the assistance of counsel, it will be exceedingly difficult under the tougher *McCleskey* standard to submit the all-inclusive petition the first time, given the complexity of *habeas corpus* law. Even those prisoners represented by counsel, such as those in death-penalty cases, will find the requirement cumbersome. Valid constitutional claims are likely to go unvindicated because of the *McCleskey* ruling. Without such protection in capital punishment cases, the criminal defendant may ultimately be deprived of his life. This indeed was the final outcome of McCleskey's thirteen-year odyssey through the courts which ended on 25 September 1991 when he was put to death in Georgia's electric chair (Harris & Curriden, 1991).

Limiting Habeas Corpus *Petitions in Cases of Attorney Neglect*

In 1992, the Rehnquist Court went even further in limiting *habeas corpus* petitions in those cases where a prisoner's attorney failed to properly present the critical facts of the cases in a state court appeal. Cuban immigrant Jose Tomayo-Reyes, who spoke no English, pleaded no contest to first-degree manslaughter. Later, he brought a collateral attack on the plea in state court, alleging that his plea was invalid because he thought he was agreeing to be tried for manslaughter. The state courts rejected Tomayo-Reyes' contention in their finding that he was properly served by his trial interpreter and defense attorney. Tomayo-Reyes then sought a writ of *habeas corpus* in federal district court, contending that the material facts concerning the translation were not adequately developed at the state court hearing under *Townsend* v. *Sain* (1963). He also sought a federal evidentiary hearing on whether his no contest plea was unconstitutional. The district court held that the failure to develop the critical facts relevant to his federal claims was attributable to inexcusable attorney neglect and that no evidentiary hearing was required. The Court of Appeals for the Ninth Circuit held that *Townsend* v. *Sain* (1963) and *Fay* v. *Noia* (1963) required an evidentiary hearing in the district court because his counsel's negligence in failing to develop the facts did not constitute a deliberate bypass of the state courts. Under *Townsend*, a prisoner would have to forfeit his right to a *habeas corpus* appeal if the crucial facts of the case were not properly developed in a state court appeal either on purpose or because of attorney neglect. The issue in *Keeney* v. *Tomayo-Reyes* (1992) was whether the deliberate bypass standard is the correct one for excusing a *habeas* petitioner's failure to develop a material fact in state court proceedings.

In writing for the 5–4 majority, Justice White determined that in light of recent *habeas corpus* decisions, *Townsend* must be overruled. Relying on the cause and prejudice standard established in *McCleskey* v. *Zant* (1991), Justice White found no distinction in the *McCleskey* case, which involved failing to properly assert a federal claim in court, and the present case, which involved failing to properly develop a claim in state court. Justice White then gave five reasons why the cause and prejudice standard should apply in cases like this: (1) it contributes to the finality of convictions; (2) it advances the principle of comity by allowing state courts the opportunity to correct their own errors first; (3) it serves the interest of judicial economy by not duplicating factfinding in federal court; (4) it adheres to the principle of exhaustion of state court remedies before obtaining federal habeas relief; and (5) it advances uniformity in the law of *habeas corpus*.

Although Justices O'Connor and Kennedy joined the majority in *McCleskey*, they broke ranks with the majority in *Keeney*. Justice O'Connor, writing for the dissenters, argued that the majority "has changed the law of habeas corpus in a fundamental way by effectively overruling cases decided long before *Townsend v. Sain* (1963)" (*Keeney* v. *Tomayo-Reyes*, 1992: 1721). She rejected the majority's transformation of the question of whether a federal court will consider a claim raised on *habeas* to one whether the court should hold an evidentiary hearing once it decides to consider the claim. For O'Connor, the Court's ruling cannot be reconciled with Section 2254(d)(3), in which Congress established a procedural framework based on the *Townsend* ruling. On this point, she stated, "While we may deprive portions of our own opinions of any effect, we generally may not, of course, do the same with portions of statutes" (*Keeney* v. *Tomayo-Reyes*, 1992: 1727).

In response to the large number of applications for *habeas corpus* review in the federal courts, the Rehnquist Court has sharply curtailed the availability of federal *habeas* review in the cases discussed in this section. Deference to the principle of comity—state court sovereignty over its laws and judicial decisions—is the driving force behind these rulings. A solid majority of the Rehnquist Court views state courts as the most appropriate forums in resolving these criminal cases. As Greenhouse (1992h: A15) pointed out:

> It is beyond debate that habeas corpus is a particular target of the Court under Chief Justice William H. Rehnquist. While the Court is taking fewer cases and issuing fewer decisions than it has for decades, it has reached out to add habeas corpus cases to its docket, and has made clear in this as in no other area its displeasure with the way modern law had developed.

Criminal defendants, many of them members of racial and ethnic minority groups, will have a very important avenue of appeals severely limited by the Rehnquist Court's *habeas corpus* jurisprudence.

Conclusion

This analysis of the most significant Rehnquist Court decisions affecting racial and ethnic minorities for the 1990 and 1991 terms has shown that the struggle for equality can be characterized as tenuous at best. With the exception of the discriminatory use of peremptory challenges, the Rehnquist Court has not developed a consistent set of judicial principles for black litigants in the remaining areas that have been examined. The transformation of the Court from its role as guardian of minority rights is disturbing and black Americans must understand that it can no longer be viewed as the institution that will be consistently sensitive to the rights of victimized minorities. Legal victories such as *Chisom* are consistently offset with legal defeats such as *Presley*. This win-lose-win cyclical pattern and the deference given to state sovereignty on several civil rights issues discussed in this article suggest that the Rehnquist Court will most likely continue this trend. Given the current direction of the Court, black Americans might have to seriously consider developing some creative alternative strategies to litigation in their continuing quest for equality.

References

Applebome, Peter. 1992. "In Alabama, Blacks Battle for the Authority to Govern." *The New York Times* (31 January): A8.

Barker, Twiley W. and Michael W. Combs. 1989. "Civil Rights and Liberties in the First Term of the Rehnquist Court: The Quest for Doctrines and Votes." *National Political Science Review* 1: 31–57.

Bell, Derrick A., Jr. "Victims as Heroes: A Minority Perspective on Constitutional Law." A Paper Presented at the Smithsonian Institution's International Symposium on Constitutional Roots, Rights, and Responsibilities, 21 May 1987, Washington, D.C.

Chira, Susan. 1992a. "Ambiguity Remains After Decision." *The New York Times* (1 April): A17.

_____. 1992b. "Ruling May Force Changes at Southern Colleges." *The New York Times* (27 June): A10.

Glick, Henry. 1988. *Courts, Politics and Justice*, 2nd ed. New York: McGraw-Hill Book Company.

Graham, Barbara L. 1990a. "Do Judicial Selection Systems Matter? A Study of Black Representation on State Courts." *American Politics Quarterly* 18: 316–36.

_____. 1990b. "Judicial Recruitment and Racial Diversity on State Courts: An Overview." *Judicature* 74: 28–34.

_____. 1991. "Federal Court Policymaking and Political Equality: An Analysis of Judicial Redistricting." *Western Political Quarterly* 44: 101–17.

_____. "The Political Significance of Judicial Redistricting for Racial Diversity on State Courts." A Paper Presented at the 1992 Meeting of the American Political Science Association, September 3–6, 1992, Chicago.

Greenhouse, Linda. 1992a. "Changed Path for Court?" *The New York Times* (26 June): A1.

_____. 1992b. "Court, 8–1, Faults Mississippi on Bias in College System." *The New York Times* (28 January): A1.

_____. 1992c. "High Court Votes to Further Limit Prisoner Appeals." *The New York Times* (5 May): A1.

_____. 1992d. "In Alabama, Blacks Battle for the Authority to Govern." *The New York Times* (31 January): A8.

_____. 1992e. "Justices Relax Court Supervision of Schools in Desegregation Case." *The New York Times* (1 April): A1.

_____. 1992f. "Souter: Unlikely Anchor at Court's Center." *The New York Times* (3 July): A1.

_____. 1992g. "Supreme Court Decision Limits Scope of '65 Voting Rights Act." *The New York Times* (28 January): A1.

_____. 1992h. "A Window on the Court." *The New York Times* (6 June): A1.

Guinier, Lani. 1991a. "No Two Seats: The Elusive Quest for Political Equality." *Virginia Law Review*, 77: 1413–514.

_____. 1991b. "The Triumph of Tokenism: The Voting Rights Act and the Theory of Black Electoral Success." *Michigan Law Review*, 89: 1077–154.

_____. 1992. "Voting Rights and Democratic Theory: Where do We Go From Here?" In *Controversies in Minority Voting: The Voting Rights Act in Perspective*, ed., Bernard Grofman and Chandler Davidson. Washington, D.C.: The Brookings Institution.

Harris, Lyle, V. and Mark Curriden. 1991. "McCleskey is Executed for '78 Killing." *The Atlanta Journal/Constitution*: September 25, 1991, p. 1, col. 4.

Hochschild, Jennifer. 1984. *The New American Dilemma: Liberal Democracy and School Desegregation*. New York: Yale University Press.

Levine, James P. 1992. *Juries and Politics*. Pacific Grove, California: Brooks/Cole Publishing Company.

Moore, Lloyd E. 1988. *Jury: Tool of Kinds, Palladium of Liberty*. Cincinnati, Ohio: Anderson Publishing Co.
O'Brien, David M. 1989. "Federalism as a Metaphor in the Constitutional Politics of Public Administration." *Public Administration Review*, 49: 411–19.
Rosenberg, Gerald. 1991. *The Hollow Hope: Can Courts Bring About Social Change?* Chicago: The University of Chicago Press.
Southern Regional Council. 1992. "Supreme Court: Enough Justice?" *Voting Rights Review* (Winter): 1–3.
Silver, Joseph Sr. and Rodney Dennis. 1990. "The Politics of Desegregation in Higher Education: Analysis of Adams States Progress." *National Political Science Review* 2: 110–28.
Walters, Ronald W. (1983). "Federalism, 'Civil Rights' and Black Progress." *Black Law Journal* 8: 220–34.
Urofsky, Melvin. 1991. *The Continuity of Change*. California: Wadsworth Publishing Company.

Cases

Adams v. Richardson, 356 F. Supp. 1159 (1973); affirmed *per curiam*, 480 F.2d 1159 (1973)
Allen v. State Board of Elections, 393 U.S. 544 (1969)
Batson v. Kentucky, 476 U.S. 79 (1986)
Board of Education of Oklahoma City Public Schools v. Dowell, 111 S.Ct. 1454 (1991)
Brown v. Board of Education, 347 U.S. 483 (1954)
Brown v. Board of Education, 349 U.S. 294 (1955)
Chisom v. Edwards, 839 F. 2d 1056 (5th Cir. 1988), *cert. denied Roemer v. Chisom*, 109 S.Ct. 390 (1988)
Chisom v. Roemer, 111 S.Ct. 2376 (1991)
Clark v. Roemer, 111 S.Ct. 2096 (1991)
Columbus Board of Education v. Pennick, 443 U.S. 449 (1979)
Crawford v. Los Angeles Board of Education, 458 U.S. 527 (1982)
Dayton Board of Education v. Brinkman, 443 U.S. 526 (1979)
Edmonson v. Leesville Concrete Company, Inc., 111 S.Ct. 2077 (1991)
Fay v. Noia, 372 U.S. 391 (1963)
Freeman v. Pitts, 112 S.Ct. 1430 (1992)
Ford v. Georgia, 111 S.Ct. 850 (1991)
Georgia v. McCollum, 112 S.Ct. 2348 (1992)
Hernandez v. New York, 111 S.Ct. 1859 (1991)
Houston Lawyers' Association v. Attorney General of Texas, 111 S.Ct. 2376 (1991)
Keeney v. Tamayo-Reyes, 112 S.Ct. 1715 (1992)
Keyes v. School District No. 1, 413 U.S. 189 (1973)
League of United Latin American Citizens v. Attorney General of Texas, 111 S.Ct. 2376 (1991)
League of United Latin American Council No. 4434 v. Clements, 914 F.2d. 260 (1990)
Madden v. Texas, 111 S.Ct. 902 (1991)
Mallory v. Eyrich, 839 F.2d 275 (6th Cir. 1988)
McCleskey v. Kemp, 481 U.S. 279 (1987)
McCleskey v. Zant, 111 S.Ct. 1454 (1991)
Massiah v. United States, 377 U.S. 201 (1964)
Milliken v. Bradley, 418 U.S. 717 (1974)
Mississippi v. Turner, 111 S.Ct. 1032 (1991)
Mobile v. Bolden, 446 U.S. 55 (1980)
Norris v. Alabama, 294 U.S. 587 (1935)
Pasadena City Board of Education v. Spangler, 427 U.S. 424 (1976)

Powers v. Ohio, 111 S.Ct. 1364 (1991)
Presley v. Etowah County Commission, 112 S.Ct. 820 (1992)
Reynolds v. Sims, 377 U.S. 533 (1964)
Smith v. Texas, 311 U.S. 128 (1940)
South Carolina v. Katzenbach, 383 U.S. 301 (1966)
Swain v. Alabama, 380 U.S. 202 (1965)
Thornburg v. Gingles, 478 U.S. 30 (1986)
Townsend v. Sain, 372 U.S. 293 (1963)
United States v. Fordice, 112 S.Ct. 2727 (1992)
United States v. Roemer, 111 S.Ct. 2354 (1991)
Washington v. Seattle School District No. I, 458 U.S. 457 (1982)
Wells v. Edwards, 409 U.S. 1095 (1973)

Agenda and Roll-Call Responsiveness to Black Interests: A Longitudinal Analysis of the Alabama Senate*

Mary Herring

Wayne State University

Are elected representatives responsive to their constituents? This question is the subject of popular debate (hence the current movement toward term limitations) as well as academic concern. The predominant method of assessing responsiveness has relied on calculating congruence between legislative voting behavior and measures of constituency preference, usually as indicated by demographic characteristics of the district. With regard to responsiveness to African-American constituents, this research stream has shown that the reenfranchisement of southern blacks led to a substantial change in the responsiveness of elected representatives. Before passage of the Voting Rights Act, there was a negative relationship between the percentage of blacks in a constituency and legislative support for issues of importance to blacks; now we find either no relationship (Feagin, 1972; Black, 1978; Bullock, 1981; Whitby, 1985), a curvilinear one (Bullock & MacManus, 1981), or a relationship that is positive for certain issue areas (Herring, 1990).

Although useful in many ways, there are also problems with this approach. There is, for instance, no control for the type of bill that makes it to the stage of a recorded vote; instead most research has depended on the bills that a legislature considers at a given time. Yet, representation is seriously impaired if legislative elites succeed in keeping issues of importance to constituents out of the realm of serious consideration. An agenda that is attentive to constituency groups is a necessary (although not sufficient) precondition for representing constituents' interests.

---

* A previous version of this paper was delivered at the Annual Meeting of the American Political Science Association, San Francisco, September 1990. This research was supported in part by a grant from the College of Urban, Labor, and Metropolitan Affairs, Wayne State University.

Indeed, one problematical aspect of the democratic process is that elites may act to restrict serious discussion of issues which are contrary to their interests (Cobb & Elder, 1983). Bachrach and Baratz (1970) call this the "restrictive face of power" and "non-decisionmaking" is their term for the process of keeping important issues from public discussion. Nondecisions are a difficult problem to assess since, by definition, what is kept off an agenda is not there to study. However, the enfranchisement of a substantial number of voters in the South provides the opportunity to study what was kept off of the agenda by means of comparing legislative agendas in the South prior to the Voting Rights Act to those considered in the South after blacks began to regain voting power in the late 1960s.

The South provides a particularly good setting to test for changes in political agendas because the role of political elites there is well documented (e.g., Key, 1949; Dolbeare & Hammond, 1972; Kousser, 1974). Part of the effort to prevent black political participation was based on the desire of business and planter elites to keep government services, and hence taxes, at a minimum. The inclusion of a significant number of poor persons in the electorate might force elected representatives to pay attention to the economic concerns of these people. The potential constituencies for redistributive services were (and are) black voters as well as low-income whites. In the days of white supremacy these questions were kept at a minimum by excluding African Americans from the electorate and by refocusing the attention of poor whites onto questions of race. Thus, one might expect that with the sources of support for increased government services being largely neutralized by the divide-and-conquer strategy of "bourbons," business leaders, planters, and other southern elites, that the legislative agenda would reflect the lack of interest in expanding redistributive programs. At the same time, with the need to continue to divert the attention of poor whites away from economic issues, there might be a fair number of bills which have a racial component and, because blacks were almost completely disfranchised, there would be no incentive to mute the racist element of such bills.

An overtime analysis of the shifts in legislative agendas is important because it allows an examination of changes in the ability of elites to restrict the issues that receive serious deliberation. Moreover, changes in the relationship of legislator responsiveness to black constituents may be more pronounced if these changes are accompanied by a more responsive legislative agenda.

This paper examines political agenda change in the context of the Alabama state senate. Alabama is selected because, with its reputation of resistance to black demands, it provides a stringent test of the effect of the Voting Rights Act. Senate rather than house votes are chosen because constituency characteristics are very difficult to obtain for state house districts, which rarely conform to census subdivisions. Senate sessions meeting in 1961, 1971, 1981, and 1991 are analyzed with regard to (1) the content of the legislative agenda and (2) the roll-call voting behavior of legislators in light of the characteristics of the constituents they represent.

Examining the Content of the Legislative Agenda

Data and Methods

We begin by examining the legislative agenda, where "agenda" is operationally defined as all roll-call votes on which at least 10 percent of the voting members dissent from the majority position.[1] Bills that survive to the point of a recorded vote have overcome a variety of hurdles in subcommittee and committee deliberations, and many important issue concerns may be filtered out of the legislative process before this stage. Thus, to say that an issue is on the legislative agenda only if it receives a recorded vote is a more demanding requirement than defining all bills introduced to be a part of the legislative agenda.

Four time periods are analyzed in order to examine change in the agenda. The 1961 session shows the agenda as it was before the Voting Rights Act effectively reenfranchised Southern blacks and before the Supreme Court mandated state legislative reapportionment on the one-person, one-vote model. The 1971 session allows an assessment of the agenda at a point where there are still many inertial forces to overcome. For instance, there may still be many "Old South" legislators—who received their political socialization during the days prior to black voting power and who may have been particularly resistant to black issue demands—holding legislative office and, quite possibly, in positions of legislative leadership. By 1981, and certainly by 1991, most of these should have retired from legislative life. If black voting indeed produces pressures for legislative responsiveness, it should be reflected in the nature of the bills reaching the status of a recorded vote.

The roll-call analysis is based on the procedure developed by Clausen (1973; Clausen & Cheney, 1970) and used by others (particularly Sinclair, 1982) to examine issue dimensions in the U.S. Congress. The Clausen procedure first assigns roll calls to broad issue categories or domains. A "civil liberties" domain deals with equal treatment for all citizens as well as questions of criminal procedure. Also included in this category are all bills dealing with issues of criminal and civil justice.

A "social welfare" domain involves bills aimed at a "direct intercession of the government on behalf of the individual" (Clausen & Cheney, 1970: 141) and includes education, minimum wages and working conditions, and traditional "relief benefits (Clausen, 1973: 48). A third domain, "government management of the economy," deals with less direct interventions in the economy. It includes all legislation

> concerned with the government ownership and regulation of economic enterprises, government spending on public works as opposed to incentives to private business to maintain and restore the economy, private vs. public development of natural resources, regulation of business activities, distribution of the tax burden, conservation, setting of interest rates, and balancing the budget. (Clausen, 1973: 47)

Two of Clausen's categories are not used because they are unsuitable for a study of state legislative agendas. The "foreign affairs" domain is clearly inappropriate in the state setting; similarly, "farm policy" is a very small part of state legislative business. However, states deal with some issues that do not fall into any of these categories. Some examples are bills that would define a "city," authorize local zoning ordinances, redistrict Congressional and state legislative districts, change the rules of order and procedure for the legislature, create a legislative fiscal budget office, change the length of legislative sessions, and determine the election structure for incorporation of contiguous territory by municipalities. To deal with this difference between the state and national legislatures, I created a residual domain, called "state business," in order to reflect the sorts of issues that states, rather than the national government, are likely to handle.

The purpose of assigning bills to a domain based on their issue content is to make it possible to make across-time comparisons; procedures such as factor or cluster analysis alone applied to all roll calls in a session too often reveal clusters for which a substantive interpretation is strained. However, within domains, roll calls are factor analyzed to illustrate the various "dimensions" that occur within broad issue areas.

Clausen finds that there is a change in agenda when a new dimension appears in a domain, and when that new dimension appears in several Congresses. Since this study is a "snapshot" of a legislature at three different time points and not a study of consecutive legislative sessions, Clausen's definition of agenda change cannot be used. Moreover, this study is concerned with the effect of the Voting Rights Act on agenda change. Therefore, within each domain, I have identified the issue dimension that is the "most racial" in nature. This is done by correlating the senators' factor scores on each dimension with the percentage of blacks in the senator's district. For the sessions of 1961, 1971, and 1981, and on the civil liberties domain of the 1991 session, the first factor in the initial solution was also the most racial factor. In the discussion below, the dimensions are compared according to the content of the roll calls with "significant" loadings.[2]

Findings

The differences between the most racial dimension on the civil liberties domain in 1961 and that of 1991 is illustrative of the difference thirty years can make. (See table 1.) In 1961, twelve of the sixteen votes are characterized by attempts to restrict the franchise. For instance, there were seven votes on a proposal to change residency requirements for voter registration, dominated by amendments that would extend the residency requirement from one year in the state to two years, with various restrictions on time in county and precinct. Another amendment would have made it necessary for the potential voter to have paid the poll tax for the current year and two years preceding. Three of the four remaining roll calls loading on this dimension also deal with elections in some form: one bill sets forth the conditions for regulation of primary elections (the precise regulations could not be determined from the Senate journal), direct election of the president and vice president of the U.S., and a bill to amend the Alabama constitution so that apportionment of the state house and senate would be required at regular intervals.

Table 1
Issue Content of Roll Calls Loading on Predominant Factor, Civil Liberties Domain

1961 (Eigenvalue=6.21)

Create a state board of examiners for voter registration. (3)*
Prohibit use of voting machines in primary and run-off elections for U.S. House, Senate. (2)
Change residency and poll tax requirements for voter registration. (7)
Regulate primary elections. (1)

Petition Congress to provide for direct popular election of president and vice president.(1)
Amend Alabama constitution to set frequency of apportionment of state house and senate. (1)
Time restriction on paternity suits. (1)

1971 (Eigenvalue=9.68)

Ratify 26th Amendment to U.S. Constitution enfranchising 18-year-olds. (1)
Provide assistance for disabled voters in municipal elections. (2)
Abolish State Sovereignty Commission. (1)
Give Public Service Commission power of peace officers. (1)
Full-time deputy D.A. for 9th Judicial Circuit. (2)
Additional appropriation to Department of Public Safety. (3)

Rules of procedure for trials at law and equity. (2)
Study Alabama prison system. (1)
Size of juries, vote requirement for conviction. (2)
Abolish position and jurisdiction of Justice of Peace. (2)
Change allowable grounds for divorce to irretrievable breakdown and incompatibility. (5)

1981 (Eigenvalue=4.20)

Revise death penalty statutes. (4)
Fund youth detention center. (1)
Prohibit workers covered by Workers Compensation from suing co-employers for injury compensation. (3)

Authorize city clerks to act as voting registrars. (3)
Power of attorney to survive incompetency, to actual death of principle. (1)
Give National Guard police power. (1)

1991 (Eigenvalue=4.17)

Provisions re: incentive time for prisoners (1)
Judicial retirement provisions (2)
Liability of performers for audience injuries (1)

Appropriations for Attorney General (1)
Appropriations for Judicial Department (1)
Increase service charge on worthless checks (1)

*The number of roll calls taken on a bill, including procedural votes and amendments, is noted in parentheses.

Election issues appear on the 1971 agenda as well, but not ones which are detectably targeted at hurting the prospects of potential black voters. There was one roll call on ratification of the Twenty-Sixth Amendment, giving the vote to eighteen-year-olds, and two others requiring that assistance be given in municipal elections to disabled voters. A bill to abolish the State Sovereignty Commission also loaded on this dimension, along with roll calls on

Table 2
Issue Content of Roll Calls Loading on Predominant Factors, Government Management Domain

1961 (Eigenvalue=3.19)

Regulation of engineering and land surveying. (2)*
Use of oil/gas fund to make improvements to Alabama Oil and Gas Building. (2)
Funding for Agricultural and Industrial Commission. (1)
Boat registration fees. (2)
Create cattle commission to promote cattle industry. (1)

1971 (Eigenvalue=55.6)

Property tax rates and assessment practices. (48)
Tax on leased personal property. (6)
Alcohol license tax. (4)
Permit fee and regulation of petroleum products. (8)
Motor fuel tax rate. (4)
Motor vehicle license and registration tax. (5)
Driver license fee. (1)
Motor vehicle license for JCs. (1)
Utilities license tax. (8)
Utilities services tax. (2)
Utilities property assessment, for purpose of determining rate levels. (2)
Franchise tax on domestic corporations. (8)
Highway bond issue. (6)
Highway Department Appropriation. (2)
Investigation of utility rate hike requests. (2)
Decrease funding for capital expenses for certain counties. (1)
Regulate sewage treatment plants. (3)
Create water pollution control commission. (1)
Create air pollution control commission. (1)
Fund furnace/foundry commission. (1)
Maximum allowable finance charge on loans and credit purchases. (8)
Regulate ambulance service. (1)
Allow cooperative ventures between dairy operators and suppliers. (2)
Require warning devices on heavy equipment. (1)
Allow counties to prohibit liquor sales in unincorporated areas. (1)
Legalize possession of small quantities of liquor in all counties. (2)
Appropriation to truck weighing stations. (2)
Regulate publication rates for legal notices. (1)
Oppose placement of Alabama in Eastern Time Zone. (1)

---

the various elements of the justice system, including issues of who has police powers, funding for the Department of Public Safety, and the workings of the court and prison systems.

If in 1971 elections-oriented bills were not aimed at harming black interests, by 1981 the one roll call concerning the vote was an attempt to expand voting opportunities by authorizing city clerks to act as voting registrars. Again, criminal justice issues surfaced, including four votes to provide the death penalty for capital offenses. In 1991, none of the bills were concerned with voting rights. Rather, criminal justice issues, such as incentive time for prisoners and funding of the judiciary, predominated.

Table 2 (continued)
Issue Content of Roll Calls Loading on Predominant Factors, Government Management Domain

1981 (Eigenvalue=17.1)

Current use value tax of property. (4)	Qualifications for bank investigators. (1)
Permit fees. (1)	Deceptive Trade Practice Act. (4)
Tax on alcohol beverage license. (3)	Cosmetology and barber licensing. (3)
Tobacco tax rates. (1)	Exempt not-for-profits from usury laws.(2)
Sales tax on motor vehicles. (1)	
Bond issue for public facilities. (6)	Exempt Highway Finance Comm. from usury laws. (1)
Create reserve fund to be administered by Treasurer. (1)	Create Alabama Municipal Electric Authority. (3)
Oil and gas revenue funds earmarked for public works and infrastructure. (8)	Regulate fireworks sales. (1)
	Require smoke detectors in hotels. (1)
Distribution of public utility gas funds.	Regulate petroleum vendors. (1)
Create trust for offshore oil revenue. (10)	Day care center licensing. (1)
Appropriations for government operating expenses. (4)	Debt limitations on public utilities. (1)
	Establish conditions for use of eminent domain. (1)

1991 (Eigenvalue=2.86)

Auto registration fees. (1)	Mobile home registration fee. (1)
Gasoline and diesel inspection fees. (2)	Transfer funds from Econ. Dev. to Public Safety. (2)
Bond issue for industrial access roads. (2)	Expand counties included in Jefferson Co.
Unfair and deceptive practices. (1)	
Creation of a public gas authority. (2)	Convention Bureau (1)

*The number of roll calls taken on a bill, including procedural votes and amendments, is noted in parentheses.

The issue content in the government management domain and the social welfare domain also exhibits a substantial change. As reported in table 2, the number of votes and bills that load on the dominant racial factor for government management issues varies from 8 votes involving 5 bills in 1961, to 134 roll calls on 29 different bills in 1971, and back down to 62 votes involving 23 bills in 1981, with only 11 votes on 8 bills in 1991. Both the content of the government management legislation and the greater number of bills in 1971 and 1981 are consistent with the demands of society for a more activist government, while the 1991 session may reflect the limitations under which the states labor in the 1990s. In 1961 the roll calls dealt mainly with government assistance to industry, for example, promotion of the cattle industry or funding an agricultural and industrial commission. In 1971 there is a continuation of effort to assist agriculture, as seen by the votes to allow cooperation between the farmers and distributors of dairy products. However, there are also bills which are aimed more at assisting the consumer than helping business: setting maximum finance charges, regulating ambulance services, and requiring warning devices on heavy equipment. Similarly, pollution control

Table 3
Issue Content of Roll Calls Loading on Predominant Factors, Social Welfare Domain

1961 (Eigenvalue=4.32)

Disqualification for unemployment benefits. (4)*
Fund archaeology museum at University of Alabama. (3)
Fund veterans, disabled veterans groups. (1)

Authorize municipalities to fund public health clinics. (1)

1971 (Eigenvalue=15.24)

Appropriations for free texts in public schools. (7)
Operating expenses for public schools. (21)
Bond issue for public schools. (1)
Decrease public school funding, certain counties. (2)
Capital outlay appropriations, public schools. (4)

Create Health Study Commission. (2)
Mental Health appropriations. (2)
Bond issue for medical education and mental health programs. (1)
Fund fire-fighter pension program. (1)

1981 (Eigenvalue=10.6)

Create Mental Health Finance Authority. (14)
Create Mental Health Board. (5)
Authorize prenatal education programs. (1)
Debt assistance for Gadsden State Junior College. (1)

Education appropriation. (4)
Permit local control of portion of state appropriation to public schools. (1)

1991 (Eigenvalue=5.67)

Education Reform Act. (7)
Appropriations for various vocational and technical colleges and programs. (5)

Create Public Health Insurance Board. (1)

*The number of roll calls taken on a bill, including procedural votes and amendments, is noted in parentheses.

issues surface with votes on various water and air quality measures. The most noticeable change in 1971, though, is the number of initiatives dealing with revenue raising: over 100 votes were taken on various proposals regarding taxes, fees, and bond issuance. Both the 1981 and the 1991 agendas looks similar to the agenda for 1971. Consumer protection legislation and revenue-raising issues predominate.

On the social welfare domain, again the 1961 agenda appears much more limited than subsequent agendas. The main issues in 1961 were the conditions under which individuals could be disqualified for unemployment benefits and funding an archaeology museum at the University of Alabama. In

Table 4
Issue Content of Roll Calls Loading on Predominant Factors, State Business Domain

1961 (Eigenvalue=5.61)

Reapportionment of Congressional districts. (8)*	Reconvene in special session. (5)

1971 (Eigenvalue=17.9)

General rules of procedure. (12)	Increase legislative salaries. (1)
Extend time for introduction of budget document. (1)	Increase salary for capitol security guards. (1)
Change conference committee rules. (1)	Provide retirement pay for governors. (2)
Create a legislative fiscal office. (4)	Responsibilities of Chief Justice. (1)
Create a senate fiscal office. (6)	Delete appropriation, state armory commission. (1)
Create space for legislators' offices. (1)	Give municipal corporations authority to enact and enforce ordinances. (1)
Code of ethics for state elected officials. (1)	Allow referenda on wet/dry status of counties. (1)
Length of special sessions. (1)	Define "city." (1)
Days per week senate must meet in current session. (1)	Provide Code in state offices. (1)
Increase salaries for Clerk of House and Secretary of Senate. (1)	Allow referenda on wet/dry status of counties. (1)
Increase salary for Capitol security guards. (1)	

1981 (Eigenvalue=9.83)

Reapportionment of state legislative districts (10).	Regulate corporate contributions to PACs. (2)
Increase population requirement for municipal annexation of contiguous land. (2)	Regulate corporate contributions directly to political campaigns. (3)
Revise Sunset Law. (1)	Regulate PAC contributions to political campaigns. (1)
Change sick leave policy for Merit employees. (1)	Code of ethics for state elected officials, including financial disclosure statement. (1)
Prohibit state revenues from being used for buildings which will profit an individual or firm. (1)	Set meeting days of senate. (2)
Local referenda on prohibition of alcoholic beverages in state parks. (1)	

1991 (Eigenvaoue=10.28)

Establish a legislative compensation commission. (1)	Develop state-wide emergency medical system. (1)
Referendum on horse racing (1)	Vanity plates for Purple Heart recipients. (1)
Bond issue for Correctional Finance Authority. (1)	Retirement plans for state officials. (2)

*The number of roll calls taken on a bill, including procedural votes and amendments, is noted in parentheses.

1971, 1981, and 1991, education issues predominate, mainly through votes on the amount of appropriation for public schools and vocational-technical training. Also surfacing in the latter sessions were health issues, especially those concerning mental health.

The dominant factor in the state business domain exemplifies both the similarity and the change of a thirty-year interval. In both 1961 and 1981, legislative redistricting overwhelms other state business concerns, although in 1961 the issue was Congressional reapportionment while in 1981 legislators had to contend with drawing the lines for their own legislative districts. In 1961, moreover, only reapportionment, and whether there should be a special session to resolve the redistricting issue, appear on the dominant racial factor. In 1981 on the other hand, there was a host of "good government" concerns such as the regulation of political action committees and campaign contributions and the creation of a legislative review commission. The 1971 session stands out as one concerned with providing the conditions for legislative professionalization. This is consistent with Stanley's (1975) study of the 1971 Alabama senate, which documents the legislature's drive to increase its independence from the governor. The 1991 session also included a vote on legislative compensation, but otherwise is a collection of seemingly unrelated topics.

Overall, the 1961 agenda stands out as the least representative of the concerns of African Americans and less affluent whites. The civil liberties agenda was dominated by attempts to hinder the exercise of the right to vote, while the agendas for government management of the economy, social welfare, and state business were limited both in the scope of bills considered and in their content. By 1981 and 1991 the civil liberties dimension tended to deal with criminal justice concerns rather than voting rights, the government management domain included consumer protection legislation, the welfare domain was dominated by votes on education and health, and the state business domain had expanded from a consideration of only redistricting to one that included a broader array of questions. Clearly, the content of the agenda has changed. The least responsive agenda occured in 1961, well before the passage of the Voting Rights Act. This suggests that the reenfranchisement of blacks was at least partly responsible for the change in the legislative agenda.

Examining Congruence with Constituency Characteristics

Data and Methods

Even if an agenda reflects the issue concerns of an electorate, representation is hindered if legislators fail to support bills that address constituency demands. In this section, two characteristics of the constituency are assessed for their impact on legislative roll-call behavior.

Black voting strength. The black proportion of the district's population is used to judge the impact of the electorate's racial composition on legislative roll-call voting. In the latter sessions the percentage of blacks is a surrogate for the potential contribution African-American voters could make to a winning coalition. A more accurate indicator would be the percentage of the registered voters that are black, or of the voting age population, but neither of these data are available over the entire period of the study. However, Stern (1982) reports a high correlation between the percentage of the population that is black and the percentage of registered voters that are black (r = .82). Moreover, using the percentage of blacks in the general population (rather than of registered voters) allows an assessment of the relationship between legislators' roll-call behavior and the black population in the session prior to federal guarantees of voting rights.[3]

Urbanization. It is thought that people who live in cities have different opinions and attitudes than people who live in small towns and rural areas. Consequently, legislators' roll-call voting behavior ought to be influenced by the urban characteristics of their constituencies. There is evidence that legislators who represent urban constituencies tend to be supportive of the liberal position on civil rights (Nye, 1991), on redistributive issues (Herring, 1990), and on legislative support for a wide spectrum of issues that are of interest to blacks (Brooks 1982; Bullock, 1981; Feagin, 1972). On the other hand, Herring (1990) found no significant relationship between urbanization and state legislative support for bills with an obvious racial component. Thus, depending on the type of issue under consideration, urban constituencies might have very different effects.

Urbanization is measured as the size of the largest place in the district according to the U.S. Census Bureau for the count taken immediately prior to the session (e.g., the 1970 count for the session that met in 1971). It was not possible to calculate the more typical measurement of urbanization—percent urban—for the post-1961 sessions because districts were not contiguous with county or county subdivision lines.[4]

Measures of black voting strength and urbanization are entered into Ordinary Least Squares regression models. Dependent variables consist of factor scores from the predominant racial factor in the various domains. The signs have been adjusted so that positive coefficients indicate voting behavior that is relatively more liberal on civil liberties and social welfare, more interventionist on government management of the economy, and more reformist on state business. The results are presented in table 5.

Findings

There is no consistent pattern for the effect of urbanization on roll-call voting. Within issue areas, there are large changes in the magnitude of the coefficient, and even the direction of the relationship often differs from one session to the next. This lack of consistency may be due to our inability to differentiate truly urban constituencies from ones that are suburban. The migration of middle-class whites to the suburbs, along with districting arrangements that reflect the increased voting power of suburbanites, make it important to operationally define urban in a more discriminating manner than is possible with these data.

The effect of the percentage of blacks in the constituency is much less ambiguous. On civil liberties and social welfare issues in particular, the impact of the reenfranchisement of southern blacks is clear. The percentage of blacks had a significant negative influence on support for civil liberties in 1961 and 1971. This was expected for the pre-Voting Rights session of 1961

Table 5
Influence of Constituency Characteristics on Roll-Call Voting, Alabama State Senate

Domain	Year	Intercept	Pct. Black	Size	Adj. R²	Hier. F@
Civil Liberties	1961	0.475	−0.002*** (3.608)	0.007*** (3.635)	.43	—
	1971	−0.409	−0.029** (2.786)	−0.005*** (3.752)	.34	—
	1981	−0.525	0.013 (1.309)	0.002 (1.506)	.09	12.99***
	1991	0.371	0.021** (2.753)	−0.002 (1.360)	.14	3.58+
Social Welfare	1961	1.018	−0.029*** (4.891)	0.001 (0.078)	.39	—
	1971	−0.553	−0.000 (0.002)	−0.005*** (4.562)	.36	—
	1981	−0.512	0.017+ (1.719)	0.001 (0.608)	.06	.84
	1991	−0.510	0.015+ (1.827)	0.001 (0.766)	.09	.94
Government Management of the Economy	1961	−0.334	0.013+ (1.810)	0.003 (1.434)	.10	—
	1971	−0.421	−0.011 (1.611)	0.007*** (9.229)	.71	—
	1981	−0.676	0.010 (1.220)	0.005*** (3.538)	.31	.00
	1991	−0.207	0.024+ (1.831)	−0.005* (2.652)	.21	2.74
State Business	1961	−0.373	0.002 (0.327)	0.002*** (3.935)	.28	—
	1971	−0.295	−0.101 (1.108)	0.006*** (5.422)	.45	—
	1981	0.507	−0.005 (0.603)	−0.004** (2.896)	.20	1.90
	1991	−0.642	0.023** (3.077)	0.002 (0.187)	.22	3.34+

Entries are unstandardized coefficients, with the absolute value of t printed in parentheses.
@ F of difference between model which includes Race of Legislator and model which excludes it. + $p<.10$ * $p<.05$ ** $p<.01$ *** $p<.001$

when the Black Belt was the most conservative area of the state. While these counties had a majority of blacks, few African Americans were allowed to vote. This gave the whites of the Black Belt—who were concerned with keeping a potential black political majority in its place—an exaggerated influence on political outcomes. The negative relationship between the percentage of blacks and civil liberties support held in 1971, perhaps because there had not been enough time for increases in black voting strength to be felt. By 1981, the sign is positive though nonsignificant, while in 1991 there is a statistically significant, positive coefficient for the percentage of blacks. The pattern on social welfare issues is similar to the one for civil liberties. The percentage of blacks has a strong negative impact in 1961, in 1971 the influence of the percentage of blacks is insignificant, and by 1981 there is a modest positive relationship that is sustained in 1991. For both of these dimensions, the pattern is one of a gradual rise in responsiveness.

The percentage of blacks has a positive impact on voting for government management of the economy issues in 1961. Since most of the bills that loaded on this dimension deal with government assistance to agriculture and industry, caution should be taken in interpreting this as an indicator of responsiveness to blacks. The coefficients are small and nonsignificant in 1971 and 1981, but for 1991 the coefficient doubles in magnitude and approaches standard significance levels. For state business, there are no significant relationships until 1991.

It appears that the consequences of the racial composition of the constituency have changed substantially over the thirty years covered by this study. This trend is especially clear for civil liberties and social welfare issues, but it is also evident in the government management and state business dimensions. Is this improvement in responsiveness due to the election of African-American senators by the few senate districts that have a majority of blacks? There are enough black senators in the 1981 and 1991 sessions to allow a test for the effect of legislator's race on roll-call scores. However, the high degree of collinearity between the percentage of blacks and the race of the legislator ($r = .84$ in 1991) makes parameter estimates unreliable. Therefore, testing for the effect of legislator's race is done by examining the extent to which adding the race variable to the model increases the explained variance. The last column in table 5 indicates the hierarchical F statistic for the difference between the unadjusted R^2 values of the full model, which includes a variable for legislator's race, and the restricted model, which does not.

In only one case is the effect of legislator's race indisputable. On the 1981 civil liberties dimension, African-American senators had very different levels of support for these bills than did their white counterparts. Yet, on the 1991 civil liberties dimension, the effect of race is much less clear: the difference in explained variance is significant only if one is willing to accept the findings at the .10 level. Examination of the content of these dimensions suggests why the legislator's race is so important in 1981. Although in both years questions of criminal justice predominated, the 1981 agenda included issues such as the death penalty which were more salient and probably received more press coverage than the more mundane matters considered in the 1991 session. Moreover, given the racial composition of death row, it is reasonable to assume that the capital punishment debate in Alabama has a strong racial component. Using Kingdon's (1981) terminology, on issues that are both highly visible and tinged with questions of race, legislators may be particularly reluctant to create a "string of votes" which they would have to explain to their white constituents.

This may also explain why there is no significant effect of legislator's race on social welfare and government management issues, and only a marginal effect on the 1991 state business dimension. While the bills that load on these dimensions are often important to the well-being of constituents, the more technical and regulatory nature of these bills makes them less visible, and less likely to be seen as favoring the interests of blacks or whites. Under these circumstances, white senators who represent districts with sizable black minorities are free to support legislation that directly or indirectly assists their black constituents without having to explain their votes to the white majority. Thus, with the exception of civil liberties votes in 1981, and possibly the 1991 civil liberties and state business dimensions, the positive relationships between The racial composition of the district and voting scores are not simply the result of majority black electorates selecting African-American representatives. Rather, white legislators also appear to respond positively to increases in black voting strength, provided the issues are of relatively low visibility in the constituency.

Conclusion

Overtime examination of the bills that are contested in the roll-call stage allows an assessment of agenda change, and hence, the restrictive face of power. This analysis of four sessions of the Alabama legislature suggests that there has been a transformation in the agenda, which is most clearly seen in the civil liberties domain. The 1961 civil liberties dimension reflected the political era in which it occurred. Not only were race and voting rights highly charged issues, but with blacks still not politically empowered, there was no reason to disguise attempts to further the extent of disfranchisement. By 1981, and again in 1991, the civil liberties domain was dominated by issues which might be considered "standard" for the states: criminal penalties and the regulation of standing to sue. If the agenda was not demonstrably favorable to African Americans, neither was it an overtly antiblack agenda.

Of course, with only one state to examine, cause and effect cannot be unambiguously inferred. Some agenda change is always to be expected, and war-on-poverty-type mandates from the federal government surely affected the content of legislative agendas to some degree. However, analysis of congruence between constituency characteristics and legislative roll-call behavior bolsters our confidence that increases in black voting have altered representational behavior. The impact of the percentage of blacks on both civil liberties and welfare issues is strong and negative in the early sessions, becomes much weaker and nonsignificant in the interim sessions, then becomes positive and significant in the most recent sessions. This pattern of an overtime increase in responsiveness, gradual though it may be, indicates a profound change in the role of African Americans in southern politics.

This study has also addressed the question of whether improvements in responsiveness are due primarily to the election of African-American senators. Of the eight instances in which it was possible to test for the effects of legislator's race (the four dimensions each in 1981 and 1991), only once—for the 1981 civil liberties dimension—was there clear evidence that this was the case. It appears that white legislators who represent districts with black minorities are willing to respond to black constituents, provided that in doing so they do not alienate white voters. This is more likely to happen on issues of lower saliency which have no obvious racial component. For the more controversial issues, it may be that black interests are represented only when African Americans constitute an electoral majority.

Black voting does make a difference, both in the content of the legislative agenda and in the roll-call voting behavior of elected representatives. Moreover, except on high-visibility issues, the effect of black voting power is often evident in the roll-call votes of white as well as African-American legislators.

Two cautionary notes are in order, though. First, roll-call votes are only a small part of legislative activity and a legislator's race may be more important in determining behavior that occurs prior to floor roll calls, such as bill introduction and committee work. Miller's (1990) study of the North Carolina Legislative Black Caucus, for instance, illustrates how a black delegation can affect the legislative agenda. Second, this is a study of the effect of constituency characteristics on the most racial issue dimensions; in each session and for each issue area, there are other dimensions for which the percentage of blacks has a much smaller relationship. Thus, the coefficients in table 5 represent the maximum effect of the percentage of blacks in each session. Still, when one considers both the direction of the change in coefficients and the fact that the content of the agenda has become less overtly hostile to black interests, it is clear that the representation of African Americans in Alabama has improved, especially when contrasted with the total absence of representation prior to the Voting Rights Act.

Notes

1. Roll-call votes are coded as follows: 1 = yes; 2 = pair or announced yes; 3 = absent or abstained; 4 = paired or announced no; 5 = no.
2. A roll call is considered to load on a common factor if its correlation with the factors is greater than the standard deviation of all loadings on all factors. This is the default for the FLAG option on the SAS factor procedure. A factor is retained for solution if its eigenvalue, or characteristic root, is greater than or equal to one. The eigenvalue measures the usefulness of a factor in simplifying a set of variables; eigenvalues below one indicate that the factor does not appreciably simplify the set of roll calls studied.
3. Because the definition of census tracts and count subdivisions changes from one census count to the next, it was not possible to use the most recent census to calculate the percentage of blacks. Therefore, for each session, I used the census count from ten years before.
4. I tried two other measures of urbanization: a dummy for whether the district was entirely within a Standard Metropolitan Statistical Area (SMSA), and another for whether the district was partly within an SMSA. The entire-SMSA variable was better at explaining variance than was the part-SMSA variable, but size of largest place was almost always better than either of the SMSA variables. For the 1960 session, where districts consist of whole counties, I calculated percent urban. The Pearson's r correlation of percent urban with size of largest place was greater than .90.

References

Bachrach, Peter and Morton Baratz. 1970. *Poverty and Power*. New York: Oxford University Press.

Black, Merle. 1978. "Racial Composition of Congressional Districts and Support for Federal Voting Rights in the American South." *Social Science Quarterly*, 59: 435–50.

Brooks, Gary H. 1982. "Black Political Mobilization and White Legislative Behavior." In *Contemporary Southern Political Attitudes and Behavior*, ed., Laurence W. Moreland, Tod A. Baker, and Robert E. Steed. New York: Praeger.

Bullock, Charles S., III. 1981. "Congressional Voting and the Mobilization of a Black Electorate in the South." *Journal of Politics*, 43: 662–82.

Bullock, Charles S., III and Susan A. MacManus. 1981. "Policy Responsiveness to the Black Electorate." *American Politics Quarterly*, 9: 357–68.

Clausen, Aage R. 1973. *How Congressmen Decide: A Policy Focus.* New York: St. Martin's Press.

Clausen, Aage R. and Richard B. Cheney. 1970. "A Comparative Analysis of Senate House Voting on Economic and Welfare Policy: 1953–1964." *American Political Science Review*, 64 (1): 138–52.

Cobb, Roger W. and Charles D. Elder. 1983. *Participation in American Politics: The Dynamics of Agenda-Building*, 2nd ed. Baltimore, Md.: Johns Hopkins University Press.

Dolbeare, Kenneth M. and Phillip E. Hammond. 1972. "Inertia at Midway: Supreme Court Decisions and Local Response," *Journal of Legal Education*.

Feagin, Joseph R. 1972. "Civil Rights Voting by Southern Congressmen." *Journal of Politics*, 34: 484–99.

Kingdon, John W. 1981. *Congressmen's Voting Decisions*, 2nd ed. New York: Harper and Row.

Herring, Mary. 1990. "Responsiveness to Black Constituents in Three Deep South State Legislatures." *Journal of Politics*, 52: 740–58.

Key, V. O. 1949. *Southern Politics in State and Nation.* New York: Knopf.

Kousser, J. Morgan. 1974. *The Shaping of Southern Politics: Suffrage Restrictions and the Establishment of the One-Party South, 1810–1910.* New Haven, Conn.: Yale University Press.

Miller, Cheryl M. 1990. "Agenda-Setting by State Legislative Black Caucuses: Policy Priorities and Factors of Success," *Policy Studies Review*, 9:339-54.

Nye, Mary Alice. 1991. "The U.S. Senate and Civil Rights Roll-Call Votes." *Western Political Quarterly* 44:971-86.

Sinclair, Barbara. 1982. *Congressional Realignment 1925–1978.* Austin: University of Texas Press.

Stanley, Harold W. 1975. *State vs. Governor, Alabama 1971: Referents for Opposition in a One-Party Legislature.* University: University of Alabama Press.

Stern, Mark. 1982. "Assessing the Impact of the 1965 Voting Rights Act." In *Contemporary Southern Political Attitudes and Behavior*, ed., Laurence W. Moreland, Tod A. Baker, and Robert E. Steed. New York: Praeger.

Welch, Susan. and Eric H. Carlson. 1973. "The Impact of Party on Voting Behavior in a Nonpartisan Legislature." *American Political Science Review*, 72: 854–67.

Whitby, Kenny J. 1985. "Effects of the Interaction Between Race and Urbanization on Votes of Southern Congressmen." *Legislative Studies Quarterly*, 10: 505–17.

Race, Abortion, and Judicial Retention: The Case of Florida Supreme Court Justice Leander Shaw

Susan A. MacManus
Lawrence Morehouse

University of South Florida, Tampa

> "The people want a fair and just legal system and [today] they said they don't want any single-issue group toppling that system.... The system has vindicated itself [today]. This was the acid test, my opponents gave it their best shot—bringing in societal fears and playing fast and loose with the truth—and the people saw through it."[1]
> —Chief Justice Leander Shaw, eve of his second successful retention election, 8 November 1990.

Leander Shaw became Florida's second black state supreme court justice on 10 January 1983.[2] Since his initial appointment by then-governor Bob Graham, he has survived two retention elections. In Justice Shaw's first retention election in 1984, 71.9 percent of the electors voted to retain him in office. His second retention election, November 1990, was not as consensual. Only 59.6 percent voted to retain him on the court—the closest retention vote since the state began using retention elections for the supreme court in 1980.[3] The election has been described by one analyst as "the hardest fought retention election in memory for a Supreme Court justice" (McKinnon, 1991b).

At the heart of the controversy was Justice Shaw's authorship of a majority opinion in a controversial abortion case. The court, by a 4–3 majority, ruled unconstitutional a statute requiring unmarried females under eighteen years of age to get written consent from a parent or guardian before obtaining an abortion (*In re: T.W.*, October 1989). The court also agreed that the Florida Constitution guaranteed women the right to an abortion in the first trimester of pregnancy under the constitution's privacy provisions.[4]

While Justice Shaw's stance on abortion was the major focus of the anti-retention campaign against him, there is some postelection evidence to suggest that racism may also have played a role. A white female supreme court justice, Rosemary Barkett, up for retention in 1992, was the also the target of a vigorous antiretention campaign, primarily for her rulings on abortion. Yet she still received a more positive retention vote (61 percent) than did Shaw in 1990 (Dyckman, 1992).

The Spread of Antiretention Campaigns

In 1986, California's voters ousted three justices from the state supreme court. In the heat of the campaign, some observers predicted that "unseating [the Justices] would touch off a rash of attacks on Supreme Court justices in other states" (Horning, 1992:12a). The prediction quickly came true in Florida where Justice Shaw was the focus of the attack (and then Justice Barkett). Both the Florida and California votes are indicative of the increasing politicization of judicial retention votes and have challenged the old adage that "Judicial elections rarely feature the colorful candidates, controversial issues, and spirited campaigns" that characterize other major federal and state offices (Dubois, 1979b: 867).

The 1990 retention vote for Justice Shaw affords us the unique opportunity to study the "interactive effects" of race and ideologically-based, single-issue voting at the state supreme court level. Such scenarios are likely to emerge in other states as a consequence of growing minority populations, an increase in the number of minorities serving on state supreme courts, and the U.S. Supreme Court's turn back of authority over abortion to the states.[5]

Previous Research: Correlates of Judicial Retention

Judicial retention rates are generally high. A 1978 study showed that in all states holding retention elections, voters rejected only 2.7 percent of the incumbent candidates. The authors found that the average vote in favor of retention exceeded 70 percent (Griffin & Horan, 1979).

Another study of judicial retention rates between 1972 and 1978 indicated that only 1.6 percent were rejected (Carbon, 1980). Yet another study by Hall and Aspin (1987) of retention rates in ten states over a twenty-year period (1964–1984) found that only 1.2 percent of the major trial court judges up for retention were defeated. While the Hall and Aspin study observed the mean affirmative vote to be 77.2 percent over the twenty-year period (1964–1984), they recognized a decline in the positive vote for retention. The downward trend was best explained by a general decline in the public's political trust.

A relatively recent analysis of judicial elections in California from 1849–1986 also indicated that the percent voting "yes" for judges has steadily declined. The author (Uelmen, 1988: 343) concluded by stating, "The prospect of increasing vulnerability at the polls is part of every justice's future."

Common Support Patterns

Typically, studies have shown that "yes" votes are remarkably similar for state supreme court justices. To some, this is evidence that votes are cast more for the judicial system than for the individual justices (Morris, 1989: 193). In their postelection survey of Wyoming voters, Griffin and Horan (1983) found that more than eight out of ten voters reported identical decisions on the two supreme court justices up for a retention vote in 1980. Hall and Aspin (1987) observed a similar phenomenon. Judges running in the same district tended to end up with similar affirmative vote percentages. There also was a high level of consistency in the percentages cast for retention regardless of whether it was in a presidential or midterm election year (Hall & Aspin, 1987).

Correlates of "No" Votes

Judicial retention votes have been found to be correlated with a number of factors. Early studies discovered "No" votes to be associated with evidence transmitted to the voters about a judge's incompetence or unethical conduct, either on the bench, or in his/her personal life (cf. American Judicature Society, 1973; Carbon, 1980).

Perhaps a signal of things to come, Carbon's 1980 study identified yet another reason for "no" votes—the public's perception that judges either were "too lenient, permissive, or liberal" or "had rendered controversial decisions" (1980: 224, 226; see also Griffin & Horan, 1982: 97).[6] Analysts generally attribute the 1986 defeat of three California Supreme Court justices—Bird, Grodin, and Reynoso—to the general perception among voters that they were too soft on criminals (Grodin, 1987; Wold & Culver, 1987; Thompson, 1988). At the heart of the anti-Shaw vote in Florida in 1990 was the perception that he was too liberal, as evidenced by his abortion ruling (Citizens for a Responsible Judiciary, 1990).

Other studies have tested the relationship between various political and socioeconomic characteristics of voters and the direction of their retention votes. A Wyoming study found little relationship between age, sex, education, or income and the direction of a voter's ballot on retention (Griffin & Horan, 1982: 98).

The Wyoming study also observed little relationship between a voter's self-professed political ideology and his/her vote for retention. The authors speculated that the weak linkage was due to the fact that the issues were not highly visible nor defined in liberal-conservative terms (Griffin & Horan, 1982: 95). Such was not the situation in the case of Leander Shaw's second retention vote setting.

Perhaps even more intriguing is the failure of early studies to focus on the issue of either the voter's or the judge's race or ethnicity. This dimension is especially important in Florida where blacks now make up nearly 14 percent of the state's population, but few blacks serve as judges in the state judiciary system.

In an increasingly media-dominated age, some scholars have suggested that the media, especially newspapers, might influence the outcome of retention votes, although "evidence concerning their influence seems inconclusive" (Griffin & Horan, 1979: 83). In their study of Wyoming voters, 17.3 percent of the voters surveyed indicated that the media (newspapers, radio, television) were important sources of information in their decision to vote for or against retention (Griffin & Horan, 1979: 85). Even so, the study found no significant difference in the support/opposition patterns of those reporting they had information about the record and qualifications of a judge and those with no information about the judge. In regard to Florida, it is interesting to note that the authors speculated that informational levels are generally higher in less-populous states like Wyoming (1982: 100), where it is easier to know a justice's record.

A later Wyoming post-election survey focused exclusively on voters' recollections of their retention votes for two state supreme court justices. The survey found that 34 percent of the population had heard about the justices because of decisions made by the court, while 29.5 percent reported that they had gotten information about the justices through news stories or editorials in the media. Only 10.3 percent reported that they had heard or seen bar poll results (Griffin & Horan, 1983: 72). Ironically, the study found that voters with the greatest amount of information were most likely to vote against retention. "No" voters were most likely to vote in that manner because of a judge's bad job performance, long period of service on the bench, the retention system itself, or negative personal knowledge of the candidates (Griffin & Horan, 1983: 75).

Carbon's study of judicial retention elections across the U.S. between 1972–1978 found an even closer relationship between "No" votes and the media. She found that 58 percent of the judges who were defeated in judicial retention elections were the subject of negative editorials in one or more newspapers (Carbon, 1980: 231). Only 12 percent had received an endorsement. Carbon found that judges were most likely to receive negative editorial comments if they had been accused of improper judicial conduct. The content of their rulings was far less likely to be the source of negative editorials.

Carbon's study concluded that negative retention votes were highest where all three of these conditions were present: negative bar polls, negative editorials, and organized bar or public campaigns against a particular judge (1980: 232). However, in the 1990 Florida Bar Merit Retention preference poll, 92 percent of the lawyers responding were of the opinion that Chief Justice Shaw "should be retained." In addition, all twelve former Supreme Court justices—including nine who served as Chief Justice—publicly endorsed Shaw, as did virtually all of the state's major metropolitan newspapers.[7] Thus, in the case of Justice Shaw, only one condition was present in any sort of magnitude—a public campaign against him organized by pro-life groups and joined by individuals who opposed his positions on several criminal cases.[8]

Negative Campaign Tactics and Outlets

Negative political campaigning is now a widely used technique, even in judicial races, as evidenced in the recent experiences in California and Florida. According to Johnson-Cartee and Copeland (1991), negative advertisements usually reflect one of two tactics—berating a candidate's position on critical issues or exposing flaws in a candidate's character. In the case of Leander Shaw, his opponents took the first approach—challenging his stands on critical cases before the Florida Supreme Court. Interestingly, Shaw's supporters chose to emphasize the positive dimensions of his character.

Studies of negative advertising and campaigning have found that the receptiveness of the individual is dependent, in part, on his/her socioeconomic background, the nature of the campaign (issue versus character), and the modes of delivery. For example, negative campaigns focusing on issues are more likely to be viewed as a "fair" approach than those focusing on the candidate's character (Garramone, 1985; Johnson-Cartee & Copeland, 1991). Poorly educated, low-income, and female voters are more likely than well-educated voters to respond positively to negative advertisements about a candidate's character (Johnson-Cartee & Copeland, 1991). Conversely, well-educated people are more likely to respond positively to negative campaigns with an issue-stance focus.

Studies of the 1986 California State Supreme Court retention elections credit negative television ads with the defeat of three of the six justices up for retention (Grodin, 1987; Wold & Culver, 1987). A heavily financed coalition comprised of Republicans, Crime Victims for Court Reform, a coalition of state and local prosecutors (the Prosecutors' Working Group), and many law enforcement organizations helped defeat these justices through a successfully orchestrated media-based campaign. Typically, however, in low-visibility campaigns, television is less often used than other outlets, primarily because it is much more expensive, although it is most effective in reaching large, undifferentiated audiences (Johnson-Cartee & Copeland, 1991).

In contrast, radio tends to be used for particularly strident attacks, because radio audiences do not perceive radio ads to be as harsh or as unfair as television ads, which add visual effects. Newspapers are primarily used to reach individuals who are more politically knowledgeable and more likely to vote. Direct mail is most effective in low-visibility races and in influencing "late deciders" (Johnson-Cartee & Copeland, 1991). But late deciders often are less prone to vote positively on referenda or retention votes—and more likely to decide not to vote at all on bottom-of-the-ballot issues.

At any rate, Shaw's opponents, due to limited resources that prohibited an extensive broad-based television, radio, or newspaper campaign, had no choice but to rely on direct mail campaigning, thereby giving the edge to Shaw, who was able to use television, radio, and newspaper advertisements.[9] (Shaw's detractors raised approximately $3,000–$4,000, as compared to the $300,000 raised by Shaw. Thus, his opponents were left to rely more on direct mail and flyer techniques.) Opposition efforts were led by newly formed Tallahassee-based political action committee known as Citizens for a Responsible Judiciary, along with The Florida Right to Life Political Action Committee, and the Florida Chapter for the American Way.[10] These groups heavily targeted church groups through direct mail efforts and, to a lesser extent, appearances on Christian radio stations. There is evidence to suggest that reliance on direct mail techniques vis-à-vis television may have not have been such a big disadvantage as such approaches have been found to be effective in low-visibility elections, such as judicial races (Swinyard & Coney, 1978; Hofstetter & Buss, 1980; Hofstetter & Zukin, 1979; Patterson & McClure, 1976).

Another intriguing media-related question is whether Shaw's campaign approach (targeting the heavily populated metropolitan areas) minimized rolloff (nonvoting) in those areas. Typically rolloff is very high in low-visibility elections.

Correlates of Rolloff

A number of studies have examined the correlates of rolloff. Rolloff, or dropoff, is the tendency for voters to vote for high-visibility offices at the top of the ballot, such as President or Governor, but not for contests or issues lower on the ballot (e.g., Supreme Court retention races).

The public's interest in judicial retention races is generally low; for many, these races simply are not "salient" (cf. American Judicature Society, 1973; Johnson, Shaefer, & McKnight, 1978; Dubois, 1979a,b; Griffin & Horan, 1979; 1982; 1983; Carbon, 1980; Hall & Aspin, 1987). The tendency to vote for top positions on a ballot such as governor or president, but not on judicial retention races, is common. Hall and Aspin's (1987: 347) study found that over a twenty-year period, at least one-third of the voters typically passed up the opportunity to vote in retention elections.

It is frequently presumed that rolloff is higher among less-educated voters. Dubois (1979b) studied voter turnout in elections held for justices of state courts of last resort in twenty-five nonsouthern states from 1948-1974. Among states using merit retention elections, rolloff averaged 40.2 percent in presidential election years and 36.1 percent in mid-term years. Dubois concluded that "Voting in nonpartisan or merit retention elections may demand an extraordinary and unrealistic amount of attention and information from the average individual" (1979b: 886). In such situations, voters must get their voting cues from a variety of sources, including name familiarity or "more dubious voting guides such as the sex [and race] of a candidate, the use of an eye-catching nickname, or even the relative position of competing candidates on the ballot" (Dubois, 1979a).

A Texas study initially hypothesized that those most likely to vote in judicial elections in general are "those who are more psychologically involved in the election," "recall receiving more about the election," "are aware of a controversy surrounding the election," "have had experiences with actors or institutions in the judicial process," and are "middle-aged, white, middle-class, and/or male" (Johnson, Shaefer, & McKnight, 1978). Interestingly, the study found no relationship between socioeconomic variables and likelihood of voting in judicial contests. The most significant determinant of the likelihood of voting in a judicial contest was information obtained from legal sources. More importantly for our study, the ability of voters to recall the names of judicial candidates was greater among those who were more aware of the controversy surrounding a Texas state supreme court race. Rolloff is reduced when there is controversy and extensive media coverage surrounding a retention vote. The greater the controversy and media coverage, the higher the proportion of "no" votes and the lower the rolloff or dropoff (Johnson, Shaefer, & McKnight, 1978).

Rolloff is typically more characteristic of minority voters, except "when the issue to be decided...is racially salient or divisive" (Vanderleeuw & Engstrom, 1987: 1082). There is evidence to suggest that for blacks, the Shaw race in Florida was more racially salient than racially divisive. The presence of a black on the state's highest court made Chief Justice Shaw's retention vote "racially salient" for blacks. On the other hand, there was little evidence to show that Shaw had done anything to merit him being perceived as a "racially-divisive" supreme court justice. His abortion opinion certainly could not be characterized as such. While surveys have shown that blacks are slightly more anti-abortion than whites, these differences are not substantial (cf. Hall & Ferree, 1986; Risley, 1990; *The American Enterprise*, 1991a). In summary, studies of the determinants of rolloff have been less conclusive than studies of the determinants of affirmative retention votes.

The Study

We begin by examining the fourteen Florida Supreme Court retention votes that have occurred since the inception of retention elections in 1980. We compare Justice Shaw's affirmative vote and the rolloff in the number of votes cast in his election with affirmative and rolloff vote percentages for the other justices.

We hypothesize that:

H_1: Justice Shaw's affirmative vote in 1990 was lower than the affirmative vote in each of the other thirteen retention elections, including his own in 1986.

H_2: The rolloff vote for Shaw's 1990 retention election was lower than the rolloff vote in each of the other thirteen retention elections, including his own in 1986.

Using Florida's sixty-seven counties as the units of analysis, we test the validity of various demographic and socioeconomic variables as determinants of (1) Shaw's affirmative vote (percent voting to retain him) and (2) voter rolloff in the Shaw 1990 retention election.

Hypotheses: Determinants of Affirmative Vote for Shaw

Based on previous research, we hypothesize that:

H_3: The larger the county, the higher the percentage of "yes" vote to retain Shaw.

Shaw's campaign *for* retention much more heavily utilized television, radio, and newspaper ads in the state's large metropolitan areas than his opponents' campaign against him. Plus, with the exception of the *Orlando Sentinel* (which was neutral), all the state's major metropolitan daily newspapers endorsed Shaw's retention. As previous research has suggested, negative votes are more likely in smaller jurisdictions where negative information about a judge can be more easily transferred. Thus, we expect a positive relationship between votes to retain Shaw and population size.

H_4: The higher the proportion of black registered voters, the higher the percentage of positive votes for Shaw.

Justice Shaw is one of the state's most visible black leaders. His race was clearly articulated in most newspaper stories prior to the election. The State NAACP chapter issued an alert on his election to each of its local chapters. In addition, a news service specializing in minority political and economic news, The Gantt Report, made an exception to its usual no-endorsement policy and endorsed Shaw in a news release (Gantt, 1990).

There is little evidence to suggest that support for Shaw among blacks would be substantially negated by his stance on abortion. A national survey taken in November 1990 found very little difference between blacks and whites in their attitudes toward abortion. Only 16 percent of the blacks and 14 percent of the whites surveyed said abortion should be illegal under all circumstances. In fact, abortion was a less-salient issue among blacks than whites. Only 9 percent of the blacks surveyed identified it as an issue that mattered the most to them, compared to 15 percent of the whites surveyed (*The American Enterprise*, 1991b: 92). A survey limited to Democratic voters in the 1988 Super Tuesday presidential primary in Tallahassee, Florida also found that only 8 percent of the blacks surveyed and 9 percent of the whites surveyed strongly agreed with the statement that "There should be a constitutional amendment to prohibit abortion" (Risley, 1990: 23).

H_5: The higher the proportion of females in the population, the higher the percentage of positive votes for Shaw.

A national public opinion survey taken on 6 November 1990 showed that, when asked to identify issues that matter the most to them, nearly three times as many women identified abortion as men (19 percent and 7 percent, respectively). Nonetheless, men and women differ little in their general attitudes about the legality of abortion. Most support it, at least under some circumstances. Only 15 percent of the women and 14 percent of the men surveyed said that abortion should be illegal in all circumstances (*The American Enterprise*, 1991b: 93).

H_6: The higher the proportion of registered Republican voters, the lower the "Yes" vote to retain Justice Shaw.

National surveys indicate that a slightly higher proportion of Republicans than Democrats oppose abortion. For example, a CBS News/*New York Times* poll taken in September 1989, found that 42 percent of the Democrats but only 39 percent of the Republicans surveyed believe that "abortion should be legal as it is now" (*The American Enterprise*, 1990: 95).

There is one factor, namely education, that might reverse the direction of the hypothesized relationship between Republicans and support for Chief Justice Shaw's retention. A much larger proportion of Republicans have a college education. Previous research has found that people with higher educations are more likely to support candidates of a different race/ethnicity. Individuals with higher educations also are far less opposed to abortion than those with only some high-school education. For example, among those with postgraduate education, only 9 percent believe abortion should be illegal in all situations compared to 23 percent of those with only some high-school education (*The American Enterprise*, 1991: 93).

H_6: The larger the percent of the vote for Martinez (R) for Governor, the smaller the percent of "yes" votes to retain Justice Shaw.

The incumbent Republican Governor, Bob Martinez, had called a special session on abortion in Fall, 1989. The session came close on the heels of the U.S. Supreme Court's *Webster* v. *Reproductive Health Services* ruling in 1989, effectively turning back authority over abortion to the states. Because of Martinez's strong pro-life position, one might expect a stronger negative correlation between the percentage of votes for Martinez for Governor (1990) and an affirmative vote for Shaw's retention than between the percentage of registered Republicans in a county and that county's vote to retain Justice Shaw.

H_7: The greater the proportion of persons over 65 years of age, the larger the affirmative vote for Justice Shaw's retention.

Somewhat surprisingly, previous research has found that older whites are more pro-choice than older Blacks or younger whites (Hall and Ferree, 1986). Hall and Ferree speculate that "older whites, but not older Blacks, have more experience with illegal abortion and resist return to the danger and social stigma of that period" (1986: 206). In the case of Florida, whites comprise the greatest proportion of the over 65 population and women comprise a larger proportion of this population than men.

Hypotheses: Determinants of Rolloff in the Shaw Retention Election

H_8: The higher the proportion of registered Republican voters, the lower the rolloff.

Alternatively,

H_9: The higher the proportion of registered Republican voters, the higher the rolloff.

H_{10}: The higher the proportion of the population over 65 years of age, the higher the rolloff.

According to previous research, rolloff is greatest among the less-educated, less-informed voters. A higher proportion of Democrats are less-educated than Republicans; thus, we would predict H_8.
On the other hand, some literature on rolloff suggests that rolloff is higher when voters are unfamiliar with a system or a candidate. A high proportion of Republicans in Florida are newly arrived and may choose to bypass retention elections, thereby giving credence to H_9. A high proportion of the newly arrived Republicans are also over 65, thereby lending support to H_{10}.

H_{11}: The larger the population, the greater the rolloff.

Alternatively,

H_{12}: The larger the population, the lower the rolloff.

Past studies have suggested that the larger the population, the more difficult it is to get information about a candidate or issue, thus H_{10}. On the other hand, it may be easier to gain information about state-wide races in larger jurisdictions where media coverage is greater, especially of controversial contests, such as Shaw's retention.

H_{13}: The larger the population growth rate, the greater the rolloff.

Alternatively,

H_{14}: The larger the population growth rate, the lower the rolloff.

Where population growth is most extreme, one might expect voters to be less likely to vote in retention elections merely because of being less-informed about the retention system or the individual judges being voted upon. However, again, media coverage may be better, and the socioeconomic profile of newcomers may be more activist than expected.

H_{15}: Rolloff is lower where media coverage is highest.

We have already shown that media coverage (all mediums) was highest in the state's major metropolitan (largest) counties. The ads and editorials clearly informed the voters that the retention vote was somewhat controversial (although they urged them to vote "yes"). As previously noted, rolloff is lowest when the contest or issue is controversial, although it also tends to be lower among voters with negative opinions about a justice up for a retention vote. Our tests of these hypotheses should give us insight into judicial retention patterns we can expect in the next decade, especially in large, heterogeneous states like Florida.

Findings

No Florida Supreme Court Justice has ever been defeated in a retention vote since the inception of the retention system in 1980. In the fourteen retention votes, the average affirmative percentage was 71.2 percent, consistent with national patterns previously cited. (See table 1.) The average rolloff for all fourteen votes was 26.3 percent, slightly lower than the percent ob-

Table 1
Retention of Florida Supreme Court Justices: A Decade of Evidence

Florida Supreme Court Justice Race	Year	% Affirmative Vote					
		1980	1982	1984	1986	1988	1990
SHAW, LEANDER J., JR.*	1993			71.9			59.6
Barkett, Rosemary (W)*	1985				76.8		
McDonald, Parker Lee (W)*	1979	71.4			76.1		
Overton, Ben (W)*	1974	71.1			76.3		
Grimes, Stephen H. (W)*	1987					74.6	
Kogan, Gerald (w)*	1987					73.3	
Harding, Major B. (W)*[1]	1991						
Adkins, James C. (W)	1969	70.6			Ret[2]		
					Res		
Alderman, James E. (W)	1978	70.7			1985		
Boyd, Joe (W)	1969	61.9			Ret[2]		
			Res				
England, Arthur J. (W)	1974	71.2	1981				
Ehrlich, Raymond (W)	1981			71.8			Ret

*Currently on the bench.
[1] Harding took his position on January 1991 and will not have a retention vote until November 1992.
[2] Mandatory retirement age is seventy.

Table 2
Rolloff in Vote for Florida Supreme Court Justices: A Decade of Evidence

Florida Supreme Court Justice Race	% Rolloff[2]					
	1980	1982	1984	1986	1988	1990
SHAW, LEANDER J., JR.*			–25.8			–13.0
Barkett, Rosemary (W)*				–19.7		
McDonald, Parker Lee (W)*	–33.4			–22.2		
Overton, Ben (W)*	–33.0			–23.1		
Grimes, Stephen H. (W)*					–22.3	
Kogan, Gerald (W)*					–25.1	
Harding, Major B. (W)*[1]						
Adkins, James C. (W)	–30.0			Ret Res		
Alderman, James E. (W)	–31.6			1985		
Boyd, Joe (W)	–31.5			Ret		
England, Arthur J. (W)	–33.0	Res 1981				
Ehrlich, Raymond (W)				–24.3		Ret

* Currently on the bench.
[1] Harding took his position on January 1991 and will not have a retention vote until November 1992.
[2] Rolloff is the percentage of drop in the number of electors voting for the top ballot position (President 1980, 1984, 1988; Governor, 1982, 1986, 1990) and the number voting in each supreme court justice retention election.

served elsewhere (around 33 percent). Rolloff has also declined over time as has had the highest percentage of positive votes since 1986. (See table 2.)

Our examination of Chief Justice Shaw's retention votes shows that his 1990 retention vote was the closest in history and the closest in a decade. (Justice Boyd received only a 61.9 percent affirmative vote in 1980.[11]) Our data also confirm that the rolloff vote in Shaw's 1990 retention election was the lowest in Florida's history. This supports the general contention that rolloff rates decline in controversial retention elections, which Shaw's certainly was.

Correlates of the "Yes" Votes for Shaw

Many of our hypotheses are challenged by the results of our bivariate analyses. (See table 3.) First, the proportion of black voters in a county is not significantly related to the percentage of "yes" vote for Shaw. Second, we find a significant positive (not negative) relationship between the percentage of Republican registrants in a county and the county's vote to retain Shaw. Without 1990 education data, we cannot prove our initial concern about the interactive effects of party and education, but these results suggest that it is the case that newly arrived Republicans are more liberal than commonly perceived.[12] The negative relationship between the vote for Martinez for governor and the percentage of "Yes" votes for Shaw, although not statistically significant, also lends credence to this theory.

Table 3
Correlates of Affirmative Votes for Justice Shaw's Retention on the Florida Supreme Court, 1990

Variables	
% Black registered voters, 1990	.03
% Republican registered voters, 1990	.58***
% Female populations, 1990	.27*
% Population of 65, 1990	.33**
% Vote for Rep. Gov. Martinez, 1990	–.14
% Population, 1990	.59***
% Population growth, 1987–1990	.18

* = significant at .05; ** = .01; *** = .001

The Martinez vote reflects much more than the sheer proportion of Republican registrants. (The correlation between the percentage of votes for Martinez and the percentage of Republican registrants was only .48.) It appears that a sizeable proportion of the Martinez voters were Democrats, a disproportionately larger number of whom were most likely strong right-to-life (single-issue) advocates.

Unexpectedly, population growth rate had no significant relationship to the percentage of votes to retain Shaw, nor was it in the negative direction we had anticipated. Again, the positive relationship may be an artifact of heavier media coverage in fast-growing areas. It may also be that the newly arrived residents are somewhat more liberal in their racial views and ideological positions. Some earlier research has suggested this is the case (cf. Sly, Serow, & Calhoun, 1989).

Consistent with our expectations, population size is positively related (r = .59) with the affirmative vote for Shaw. An important element of this is undoubtedly the media campaign (television, newspaper, radio) Shaw's proponents were able to mount in the state's large metropolitan areas. Our hypotheses regarding the expected positive relationship between the size of the female and elderly populations and the percentage of affirmative vote for Shaw's retention were also confirmed. The larger the female population, the more positive the vote for Shaw (r = .27). Similarly, the larger the elderly population, the more positive the vote for Shaw (r = .33).

Multivariate Analysis of Affirmative Retention Vote

A multivariate model incorporating seven independent variables explains 65 percent of the variance in the vote for Shaw's retention. (See table 5.) Each of these variables (percentage of black registered voters; Republican registrants; female population; population 65 years of age or older and percentage of the votes for Bob Martinez, Republican candidate for governor; 1990 population; and population growth rate, 1987–1990) has a theoretical basis for inclusion in multivariate model since all of these phenomena co-exist on election day.[13] There is no multicollinearity problem. None of the independent variables are highly correlated with any of the others.[14]

Table 4
Correlates of Rolloff Vote in Justice Shaw's Retention Election, 1990

Variables	
% Black registered voters, 1990	.13
% Republican registered voters, 1990	−.23*
% Female population, 1990	−.07
% Population over 65, 1990	−.21*
% Vote for Rep. Gov. Matrinez, 1990	.09
% Population, 1990	−.07
% Population growth rate, 1987–1990	−.22*

* = significant at .05 level; ** = .01; *** = .001.

Table 5
Multivariate Models for Percentage of Affirmative Retention Votes for Chief Justice Shaw, 1990 and Percentage of Rolloff Votes in the Election

1. *Percentage Affirmative Vote for Shaw's Retention*
SHAW = 53.8 + .282 PCTBKVOT* + .38 REPUBLIC*** − .402 MARTINEZ**
               (.086)   (.059)   (.105)
+ .027 female − .015 OVER65 + .0000059 POPULAT* + .019 growth
  (.181)   (.118)   (.0000023)   (.071)
R^2 = .69   Adjusted R^2 = .65

2. *Percentage of Rolloff Vote in Shaw Retention Vote Election*
ROLLOFF = −12.9 − .358 PCTBKVOT − .267 REPUBLIC − .129 MARTINEZ
                   (.121)   (268)   (.266)
+ .762* SHAW + .293 FEMALE − .306 OVER65 − .000009 POPULAT
  (.295)   (.409)   (.268)   (.000005)
− .184 GROWTH
  (.161)
R^2 = .21
Adjusted R^2 = .10

***p <.001; **p < .01; *p < .05. Standard errors in parentheses
SHAW = % Affirmative vote for Shaw's retention
PVTBKVOT = % Black registered voters, 1990
REPUBLIC = % Republican registered voters, 1990
MARTINEZ = % Vote for Republican Bob Martinez for Governor
FEMALE = % Female population, est. 1990
OVER65 = % Population over 65 years of age, est. 1990
POPULAT = % 1990 population
GROWTH = % Growth in population 1987–1990
ROLLOFF = % Fewer votes cast in Shaw retention election that for top position on ballot (Pres.; Gov.)

Our results, shown in table 5, indicate that Chief Justice Shaw's retention vote was most heavily influenced by the size of the black electorate, the size of the Republican electorate, the size of the vote for Bob Martinez for Governor, and population size. Generally, Shaw's support came from populous counties with sizeable black and Republican constituencies— that is, large, heterogeneous counties where electronic and print media advertising for Shaw was heaviest. Opposition to Shaw's retention was more common in smaller counties, with larger proportions of conservative white voters (who voted more heavily for Martinez for Governor). It is among this constituency that Shaw's abortion ruling, and race, may have been viewed with the most contempt.

Correlates of Rolloff in the Shaw Retention Vote

The results of our bivariate analysis challenge most of our hypotheses about the correlates of rolloff. (See table 4.) Rolloff was significantly lower where the proportion of Republican voters was higher, the proportion of voters over 65 was higher, and where the population growth rate between 1987 and 1990 was higher. This is further evidence that Florida's newly arrived voters do not participate in judicial retention elections at rates below longer-term residents. This confirms what Sly, Serow, and Calhoun (1989) found about political participation rates of newcomers—they exceed those of natives. Heavier and more diverse media coverage in the high-growth areas to which they are relocating may make it easier to become informed about Florida politics more quickly.

Our correlational analysis found that other variables (percentage of black registrants, female population, population size) were not significantly related to rolloff. This is consistent with earlier studies showing little relationship between socioeconomic factors and participation in judicial retention races.

Multivariate Analysis of Rolloff

Our model of the rolloff in the Shaw retention race is not nearly as explanatory as our multivariate model of the affirmative vote for Shaw. (See table 5.) Our eight-variable model (which adds the percentage of affirmative vote for Shaw to our seven-variable model) explains a mere 10 percent of the variance in rolloff. Only the percentage of "yes" votes for Shaw's retention turns out to be a significant predictor. As expected, rolloff is higher where Shaw got the most positive votes.

It is possible that aggregate data cannot explain rolloff as well as survey data gleaned from exit polls or post-election surveys. It is through such surveys that factors such as ballot format, ballot confusion, and more idiosyncratic features of a voter's rationale for not voting can be explored in more depth.

Conclusion

Floridians' affirmative votes for the retention of its state supreme court justices have followed national patterns, for the most part. Since the inception of Supreme Court retention elections in 1980, no Supreme Court justice has been defeated; the average affirmative vote across fourteen retention elections has been 71.2 percent. Only twice have justices failed to get at least a 70 percent affirmative retention vote (Boyd in 1980—61.9 percent; Shaw in 1990—59.6 percent). Boyd's relatively low rate of retention votes was a product of personal problems that caused the public to question his mental competency.

Shaw's low rate was perceived by most analysts to be a product of a controversial pro-abortion ruling; a few saw it as a racially motivated vote.

Our analysis showed that Shaw's heaviest support came from heavily populated areas with sizeable black and Republican constituencies (i.e., heterogeneous areas). His greatest opposition came from smaller counties, with more white conservative voters. Our study also suggests that newcomers to Florida (older, white Republicans) are more liberal in their views on racial and ideological issues, like abortion, than generally perceived. Our findings on the determinants of rolloff were considerably less informative. Nonetheless, the results are consistent with earlier research showing little connection between rolloff and voter socioeconomic characteristics. On a more positive note, rolloff is declining in the state, meaning more voters are choosing to exercise a voice in judicial retention decisions. From the perspective of justices, however, our study, along with those of recent retention votes in California, leads one to conclude that judicial retention votes are becoming more politicized, and personalized. It is likely that margins of victory (percentage of affirmative votes) will continue to decline in the 1990s.

Significance of the Findings

The recent decline in affirmative retention vote percentages across the U.S. and the rise of negative campaigning against state supreme court justices on the basis of past judicial rulings (California—crime-related matters; Florida—abortion-related rulings) threaten the very tenets of judicial retention elections. Papier (1987: 754–56) reviewed the advantages of retention systems. He noted that they are supposed to "remove the need for political campaigns by incumbent judges by allowing judges to concentrate on their judicial duties without the distraction of campaigning for reelection;" "eliminat[e] the expense of a political campaign"; "remove political factors from the process of judicial selection"; and mean that "judges no longer feel 'obligated' to a specific interest group since judicial selection [is] based only upon considerations of professional qualifications and competence."

This study of the retention experiences of black Supreme Court Justice Leander Shaw of Florida adds to the growing literature showing that, regardless of the method of choosing judges, politics can play a key role. The age-old debate over the relative importance of judicial independence and judicial accountability persists. Our study suggests that in the decade of the 1990s, the debate may take on new meaning. The focus of inquiry will shift to empirical examinations of the degree to which race/ethnicity and ideology (single-issue politics) help or hinder the accountability and independence of the judiciary—or even define the concepts themselves.

Notes

1. See Brennan (1991: B1, B10).
2. The first black to serve on the Florida Supreme Court was Joseph W. Hatchett, Jr., of Jacksonville who was appointed by Governor Askew in 1975. He resigned in 1979 to become Florida's first black federal judge. Justice Hatchett never went through a retention vote. Prior to his appointment to the Florida

Supreme Court, Justice Shaw served as Duval County Assistant Public Defender; Assistant State Attorney; Judge, Industrial Relations Commission; Judge-First District Court of Appeals (Morris, 1989:190).
3. Florida Supreme Court justices serve six-year terms. In 1976 the state constitution was amended to provide for a Missouri-Plan-type method of selecting justices of the state supreme court and judges of the District Court of Appeals. The Judicial Nominating Commission submits a list of three nominees to the Governor, who then makes the appointment. The justice serves one year, then must face a retention vote at the next state election. At that time, the justice's name is placed before the electorate, which is posed with the question of whether the justice should be retained and given a full six-year term. The first retention election for state supreme court justices was held in 1980, when six justices were on a retention ballot (Morris, 1989: 191–92).
4. In 1989, in *In re: T.W.*, the supreme court of the State of Florida declared unconstitutional section 390.001(4)(a) of a Florida statute that required parental consent before a minor could get an abortion. The court ruled that this restraint violated the minor's right to privacy guaranteed by the Florida Constitution under a 1980 Florida Amendment. The 1980 Amendment stated: "Right of Privacy—Every natural person has the right to be let along and free from governmental intrusion into his private life except as otherwise noted herein." The court inferred that the right to an abortion existed pursuant to this statute, although the Amendment does not explicitly confer such a right. In its ruling, the Florida Supreme Court effectively accorded greater protection to the rights of minors than has the U.S. Supreme Court.
5. *Webster* v. *Reproductive Health Services* (1989).
6. Carbon (1980: 227) identified controversial decisions involving the constitutionality of a public improvements ordinance, obscenity, fluoridation of water, construction of a high school, a countywide tax reassessment, and sexual assault. Other have identified controversial decisions interpreted as favoring criminals over victims.
7. Shaw was endorsed by the *Miami Herald, Jacksonville Times-Union, St. Petersburg Times, Tampa Tribune, Tallahassee Democrat, The Daytona Times, and the Ft. Lauderdale Sun Sentinel.*
8. Although the *In re: T.W.* case (1989) involving parental consent for abortion was the most controversial ruling made by Shaw, four other cases were cited by Citizens for a Responsible Judiciary as examples of the unacceptable decisions of Chief Justice Shaw—*Haliburton* v. *State, Cox* v. *State, Bostick* v. *State,* and *Riley* v. *State*. In each, his rulings were judged as too liberal and more protective of the accused's rights than of the victim's rights.
9. Shaw used television, radio, and newspaper outlets for his retention campaign (All World Consultants, 1990). He ran two Fox network television ads (2 and 4 November), six television sports per day 29 October–5 November between 12:00 P.M. and 12:00 A.M. on all cable networks (rotating between ESPN, CNN, USA) in Tallahassee, Pensacola, Tampa, St. Petersburg, Ft. Myers-Naples, Jacksonville, Orlando, West Palm Beach, Miami, and Ft. Lauderdale. Shaw also ran sixty radio spots between 1–6 November on radio stations in Miami (two), Tampa, St. Petersburg, Jacksonville, and Orlando. He ran 278 spots between 31 October and 6 November on *five* Tallahassee radio stations alone. He also ran 1/4-page newspaper ads in sixteen of the state's newspapers (mostly in large newspapers, but also in some smaller ones in areas with large black concentrations). These appeared at least once between 18 October and 5 November.
10. Citizens for a Responsible Judiciary was formed in 1990 by Stephen Zeller and Timothy J. Warfel after the Florida Supreme Court unanimously removed a

convicted murderer from death row in December 1989 on the grounds that there was insufficient evidence to convict. (The victim was Zeller's brother.) This PAC was designed as an umbrella organization combining interests of "parents, victims of crime, families of those victims, law enforcement officers, attorneys, prosecutors, former jurors, and citizens in general who are concerned about the direction that certain members of the Florida Supreme Court are taking" (Citizens for a Responsible Judiciary, 1990; Judd, 1990). The group raised roughly $3000–$4000, which it primarily used for direct mail efforts. The Florida Right to Life Political Action Committee, with a membership of 60,000–100,000, did not orchestrate a heavy campaign against Shaw but did call a few press conferences in larger cities, sent out flyers to chapters, and developed a position paper against Shaw. The Florida Chapter for the American Way spent little money but campaigned through appearances of its director on fifty Christian radio stations over a two-month period. This group also issued 35,000 postcards, primarily to church groups.

11. Boyd was ordered by an impeachment committee to undergo a mental competency exam, which he passed.
12. The largest stream of Republican newcomers have been suburbanites from the Midwest (and to a lesser extent, from the Northeast) who are generally more educated and more liberal than long-time southern Republicans. (See Morgan, 1990; Osinski, 1990.)
13. The presence of each of these phenomena on election day is the reason for their inclusion in the multivariate models even though some did not turn out to be statistically significantly related to the Shaw retention vote in the bivariate analyses (percentage of black registrants; percentage of votes for Martinez; percentage of population growth 1987–1990). Multivariate models more appropriate for explaining which "combination" of conditions yielded a more favorable retention vote for Justice Shaw.
14. The highest correlations are between the percentage of Republican registrants and the percentage of the population over sixty-five ($r = .58$) and between the percentage of Republican registrants and percentage of black registrants ($r = .53$).

References

All World Consultants. 1990. "Media Schedule for Leander Shaw Campaign." Tallahassee, Fla.: All World Consultants.

American Enterprise Institute (1990). "Public Opinion and Demographic Report." *The American Enterprise*, 1 (November/December): 95.

American Enterprise Institute (1991a). "Public Opinion and Demographic Report." *The American Enterprise*, 2 (January/February): 92–93.

American Enterprise Institute (1991b). "Public Opinion and Demographic Report." *The American Enterprise*, 2 (September/October): 84.

American Judicature Society. 1973. "Merit Retention Elections in 1972." *Judicature*, 56 (January): 252–61.

Anonymous. 1986. "Insulating Incumbent Judges From the Vicissitudes of the Political Arena: Retention Elections as a Viable Alternative." *Fordham Urban Law Journal*, 15 (1986/87): 743–66.

Anonymous. 1990. "An Independent Frame of Mind." *The American Enterprise*, (November/December): 95.

Anonymous. 1991. "Comparing Whites, Blacks and Hispanics." *The American Enterprise*, (January/February): 92.

Anonymous. 1991. "Revamping Flawed System of Choosing Florida's Judges." Editorial, *The Tampa Tribune*, (7 March).

Brennan, Tom. 1990. "Chief Justice Heads Toward Another Term." *The Tampa Tribune*, (7 November): 1, 10B.
Carbon, Susan B. 1980. "Judicial Retention Elections: Are They Serving Their Intended Purpose?" *Judicature*, 64 (November): 211-33.
Citizens for a Responsible Judiciary. 1990. *Organization Handbook*. Tallahassee, Fla.: Citizens for a Responsible Judiciary.
Devlin, L.P. 1983. "Contrast in Presidential Campaign Commercials in 1980." *Political Communication Review*, 7: 1-38.
Dubois, Philip L. 1979a. "The Significance of Voting Cues in State Supreme Court Elections." *Law and Society Review*, 13 (Spring): 759-79.
_____. 1979b. "Voter Turnout in State Judicial Elections." *Journal of Politics*, 41 (August): 865-67.
Dyckman, Martin. 1992. "The Folly of Electing Judges." *St. Petersburg Times*, (29 November): 3D.
The Florida Bar. 1990. "Statewide Judicial Poll." Memorandum to 1990 Merit Retention Candidates (21 August).
Gantt, Lucius. 1990. "The Gantt Report: Economic and Political News for Minorities." Tallahassee, Fla.: Lucius Gantt.
Garramone, Gina M. 1984. "Voter Response to Negative Political Ads." *Journalism Quarterly*, 61: 250-9.
_____. 1985. "Effects of Negative Political Advertising: The Roles of Sponsor and Rebuttal." *Journal of Broadcasting & Electronic Media*, 29 (Spring): 147-59.
Griffin, Kenyon N. and Michael J. Horan. 1979. "Merit Retention Elections: What Influences the Voters?" *Judicature*, 63 (August): 78-88.
_____. 1982. "Judicial Retention Election Decisions: A Search For Correlates." *The Social Science Journal*, 19 (October): 93-101.
_____. 1983. "Patterns of Voting Behavior in Judicial Retention Elections for Supreme Court Justices in Wyoming," *Judicature*, 67 (August): 68-77.
Grodin, J.R. 1987. "Judicial Elections: The California Experience." *Judicature*, 70 (April/May): 365-69.
Hall, Elaine J. and Myra Marx Ferree. 1986. "Race Differences in Abortion Attitudes." *Public Opinion Quarterly*, 50 (Summer): 193-207.
Hall, W.K. and L.T. Aspin. 1987. "What Twenty Years of **Judicial Retention** Elections Have Told Us." *Judicature*, 70 (April/May): 340-47.
Hofstetter, C. Richard and Terry F. Buss. 1980. "Politics and Last Minute Political Television." *Western Political Quarterly*, 33 (March): 24-37.
Hofstetter, C. Richard and Cliff Zukin. 1979. "TV Network News and Advertising in the Nixon and McGovern Campaigns." *Journalism Quarterly*, 56: 106-52.
Horning, Jay. 1992. "Once-Controversial Calif. Justice Leaves Politics by the Wayside." *St. Petersburg Times*, (6 December): 12A.
Jenkins, William. 1977. "Retention Elections: Who Wins When No One Loses." *Judicature*, 61 (August): 79-86.
Johnson, Charles A., Roger C. Schaefer, and R. Neal McKnight. 1978. "The Salience of Judicial Candidates and Elections." *Social Science Quarterly*, 59 (September): 371-78.
Johnson-Cartee, Karen S. and Gary A. Copeland. 1991. *Negative Political Advertising*. Hillsdale, N.Y.: Lawrence Erlbaum Associates.
Judd, Alan. 1990. "Victim's Brother Leads Drive to Get Chief Justice Ousted." *Sarasota Herald-Tribune*, (11 September): 6B.
Kuzins, R. 1986. "Looking Beyond Retention Elections." *California Law*, 6 (October): 30 ff.
McKinnon, John D. 1991a. "Chiles Picks Court Justice." *St. Petersburg Times*, (23 January).

_____. 1991b. "Shaw Strives to be a Justice For All." *St. Petersburg Times*, (4 March): pp. 1, 3D.
Morgan, Lucy. 1990. "Florida's Republicans Are Building Strength." *St. Petersburg Times*, (15 April): 7B.
Morris, Allen. 1989. *The Florida Handbook 1989–1990*. Tallahassee, Fla.: The Peninsular Publishing Company.
Osinski, Bill. 1990. "The GOP Army: Retirees Moving Into Florida Have Turned It Into a Republican Base." *The Tampa Tribune*, (20 March): 4–5F.
Overton, B.F. 1988/89. "Trial Judges and Political Elections: A Time for Re-Evaluation." *University of Florida Journal of Law and Public Policy*, (2): 9.
Parker, Suzanne L. 1990. *The Florida Annual Policy Survey*. Tallahassee, Fla.: Survey Research Laboratory, Policy Sciences Program, Florida State University.
Patterson, T.E. and R.D. McClure 1976. "Television and the Less Interested Voter: The Costs of an Informed Electorate." *The Annals of the American Academy of Political and Social Science*, 425: 88–97.
Resnick, Rosalind. 1990. "This Court's a Backwater No More: The Florida Supreme Court is Expanding the Right of Privacy Beyond Federal Limits." *The National Law Journal*, 12 (28 May): 1, 30.
Risley, Allen J. 1990. "Race Differences in Democratic Voters: A Look at Super Tuesday Voters in Tallahassee, Florida." *Florida Public Opinion*, 5 (Winter): 20–6.
Sly, David F., William J. Serow, and Shannon Calhoun. 1989. "Migration and the Political Process in Florida." *Florida Public Opinion*, 4 (Winter): 8–11.
Stookey, John D. and George Watson. 1980. "Merit Retention Elections: Can the Bar Influence Voters?" *Judicature*, 64 (November): 234–41.
Surlin, Stuart H. and Thomas F. Gordon. 1977. "How Values Affect Attitudes Toward Direct Reference Political Advertising." *Journalism Quarterly*, 54: 89.
Swinyard, W. R. and K.A. Coney. 1978. "Promotional Effects on High-Versus Low-Involvement Electorates." *Journal of Consumer Research*, 5: 41–8.
Thompson, R.S. 1988. "Judicial Retention Elections and Judicial Method: A Retrospective on the California Retention Election of 1986." *Southern California Law Review*, 61 (1988): 2007–64.
Uelmen, G.F. 1988. "California Judicial Retention Elections: Essay—Supreme Court Retention Elections in California." *Santa Clara Law Review*, (Spring): 333.
Vanderleeuw, James M. and Richard L. Engstrom. 1987. "Race, Referendums, and Roll-Off." *Journal of Politics*, 49 (November): 1081–92.
Watson, Richard A. and Rondal G. Downing. 1969. *The Politics of the Bench and Bar: Judicial Selection Under the Missouri Nonpartisan Court Plan*. New York: John Wiley & Sons.
Wold, J.T. and J.H. Culver. 1987. "The Defeat of the California Justices: The Campaign, the Electorate, and the Issue of Judicial Accountability." *Judicature*, (April/May): 348v4,33 55.

Mayoral Politics Chicago Style: The Rise and Fall of a Multiethnic Coalition, 1983–1989

Paul Kleppner

Office for Social Policy Research
Northern Illinois University

In April 1983, Harold Washington was elected Mayor of Chicago. Following a bitter campaign that attracted attention from the national media, Washington defeated his Republican opponent by 48,321 votes (out of 1.28 million cast) to become the first African American to serve as the city's chief executive. Six years later, in April 1989, Richard M. Daley was elected Mayor of Chicago, handily defeating African-American candidates in both the Democratic primary and the general election. With Daley's election, Chicago joined Cleveland as the only major cities in the country in which a restoration of white control over the executive followed a period of African-American empowerment. Moreover, Chicago is the only large city in the county with an African-American population of 35 percent or more that does not have a member of that community as its chief executive.

Initial victories typically come only after a city's African-American community reaches threshold (around 35 to 40 percent) of the voting age population (VAP), which is sufficient to provide a solid electoral base for subsequent efforts. Moreover, the white-black differences in age structures, migration, and mortality rates tend to mean that the African-American share of the eligible VAP increased at later elections. Third, initial efforts usually involve broad drives to register and turn out voters. Finally, these initial campaigns usually evoke a backlash that endows the effort with even greater meaning within the African-American community, converting it from a campaign for public office into a crusade for racial equity. Under such conditions, elections engage the interest and evoke higher-than-usual levels of participation and cohesiveness within the African-American community (Nelson & Meranto, 1977; Browning, Marshall, & Tabb, 1990.)

These conditions characterized Chicago during the election of Congressman Harold Washington to the office of mayor. Race was the factor dominating vote choices in April 1983; *most* of Washington's votes came from African-American citizens. It is important to note that he needed votes from other groups in order to win. A coalition by which he won was created. Yet, less than two years after Washington's death by heart attack, and but six years after Washington's initial election, Richard M. Daley became the city's mayor, defeating the coalition that elected Harold Washington. The coalition is in disarray. The task here is to deal with the questions of how this happened and what its occurrence suggests about the process of constructing and maintaining biracial or otherwise multiethnic coalitions in U.S. cities. This, in turn, requires initially that we describe the components of Washington's 1983 coalition, the degree to which the coalition held together, whether it broadened in Washington's re-election effort four years later, and what happened to the coalition after Washington's death. With these essential descriptions in hand, we can turn to the larger tasks of explaining why things happened as they did and what this implies for the future of biracial or otherwise multiethnic coalitions.

The Social Basis of the Washington Coalitions

Coalitions across racial and ethnic lines do not arise simply because the "objective conditions" are in place. Their emergence requires a developing cohesiveness within the African-American community and then the building of links to potential allies outside that community (Sonenshein, 1990: 203). Moreover, once they have been constructed, such coalitions do not maintain themselves automatically. Later events can lead to conflicts of interest among previously cooperating groups, fracturing the unity and reducing the effectiveness of the original coalition.

Building what became Washington's coalition (African Americans, Latinos, and some Asians and whites) began well before the 1983 election season. Jane Byrne owed her upset victory in the 1979 mayoral election to reactions by African-American voters. In the 1979 Democratic mayoral primary, Michael Bilandic polled majorities among whites, Latinos, and "others," while Byrne received 59.3 percent of the African-American vote. Turnout among African Americans was low, however (only 32.3 percent), and Byrne and Bilandic divided the white vote almost evenly—50.6 percent for Bilandic and 49.3 percent for Byrne. (For a detailed discussion of the 1979 election, see Kleppner, 1985: 103–17.) But Byrne did not effectively consolidate this African-American support once in office. To the contrary, within the first year of her administration, in handling a school funding crisis and appointing a new superintendent of schools, as well as in dealing with strikes initiated by the Chicago Transit Authority union and the Chicago Teachers Union, Byrne seemed to rebuff African-American interests and sensitivities. Thereafter, a series of policy conflicts embroiled the Byrne Administration in virtually continuous battle with the African-American community.

Some of these conflicts were highly focused and involved well-publicized events or decisions by the city council over health care facilities, representation for African Americans on the school board and the public housing authority, Byrne's efforts to reduce the number of wards in which they made up majorities, and the elimination of an African-American alderman who had refused to vote to confirm her nominations of two opponents of school integration to the board of education (Alkalimat & Gills, 1984: 68–77; and Kleppner, 1985: 140–43.)

There were also less-sharply focused (and consequently, less-well-publicized) bases of conflict between the Byrne administration and the city's African Americans. Community leaders continuously voiced complaints that the city's hiring and contracting practices were discriminatory, that Byrne's apparent quiescence—alone among mayors of big cities—to Reagonomic cutbacks in federal and state assistance during a time of recession was intolerable, and that 80 percent of the mayor's allocation of federal funds for urban and community development was used to support the city's central business district and agencies based inside it. Moreover, Byrne frequently "reprogrammed" even the small share of funds devoted to housing and neighborhood redevelopment, using them instead to meet other needs (including some aimed at boosting her campaign efforts).

These struggles around seemingly isolated and discrete issues provided African-American leaders with opportunities to develop cohesiveness within their own community while building links between themselves and activists from the white and Latino communities. Activists came together, forging networks and developing a consensus that defined both the problem (Byrne and the Democratic machine) and the solution (a reform candidate) (Alkalimat & Gills, 1984: 82). This protest and organizational activity in 1981 and 1982 created the basis for Harold Washington's biracial coalition at the electoral level in early 1983. Washington's candidacy capitalized on the cohesiveness that had earlier been forged among leaders within the African-American community and on the links that had been built with white and Latino activists. This broad, grassroots organizational base spearheaded the highly successful drive to register new voters in September and early October 1982 (Kleppner, 1985: 144–50), provided precinct workers and poll watchers during the primary and general elections, and ultimately generated votes for Washington. The unity that had been developed among African-American activists in their battles against Byrne had its counterpart among African-American voters. The publicity surrounding those conflicts no doubt heightened and focused public awareness, accounting for the sag in Byrne's popularity among African-American poll respondents. When Washington convincingly demonstrated his viability as a candidate, as he did in four televised debates in January 1983, he ignited the African-American community. His campaign took on the dimensions of a crusade. Only a handful of African-American officeholders, along with a few West Side ministers, remained obedient to the machine.

Links had been built with white and Latino activists, though not sufficient to produce a similar payoff in votes to the same degree. The effort to move beyond the leadership connections, to mobilize a broader biracial coalition of voters, collided with the city's history. Decades of racial conflict over housing, schools, and job opportunities left in its wake only bitterness and vivid memories. By evoking those memories, Washington's candidacy solidified responses on both sides of the city's racial divide. Among African Americans, his candidacy sparked enthusiasm and virtually unanimous support. Among the city's white voters, the prospect of an African American as the city's chief executive aroused a fearfulness that led most of them to cross the political divide and vote for a white Republican. The trust, the goodwill, needed to bridge the racial chasm and to build a broader biracial coalition was simply lacking. Trust is essential to developing coalitions (Hinckley, 1981: 72–73). Democratic party leaders and officeholders, by abandoning Washington (some even supported his opponent), legitimized and encouraged the "white flight" from their party's nominee.

Social workers, municipal employees, and health care professionals, who had been involved in battles against the Byrne Administration, formed the core of Washington's white voting support. Lower- and middle-income whites, especially those who were not college graduates, rejected his candidacy. Despite common interests derived from shared economic standing, differences in racial outlooks continued to divide the city's whites from its African-Americans. This conflict blocked access to potential allies who shared interests, thus limiting the size of the biracial coalition that could be mobilized in 1983 (Sonenshein, 1990: 206.)

The Shape of Washington's 1983 Voting Coalition

Chicago had not elected a Republican mayor for sixty-six years, since the last victory of William Hale ("Big Bill") Thompson in 1927. In 1983, however, despite having won the Democratic primary, Washington barely eked out a victory in the general election over Bernard Epton, a former Republican state legislator who was otherwise virtually unknown to the city's electorate. The election was extremely close because the city's white Democrats did not rally behind the winner of their party's primary, as they had four years earlier when Jane Byrne had upset the organization's candidate and the incumbent acting mayor, Michael Bilandic. Washington won the April election because African-American turnout was very high—68.1 percent of the group's VAP. Moreover, as John Deardourff (Epton's campaign manager) put it, he got all of their votes "except for the accidents" (quoted in the *Chicago Sun-Times*, 10 April 1983.) White turnout was also unusually high—68.2 percent of the group's VAP.

Confronted with a choice in 1983 between supporting an *African-American* Democrat and a *white* Republican, 80 percent of the city's white Democratic voters opted to cross party lines and ballot for a candidate of their own race; 90 percent of the city's white Republicans and 77 percent of its white independents also voted for Epton. Of all the white respondents, 50.8 percent identified themselves as Democrats and another 34.4 percent referred to themselves as independents (WMAQ-TV [NBC] exit poll.)

The vote for mayor broke along racial lines. Given Chicago's residential patterns, the geographic distribution of the vote in April 1983 had a distinctive shape, as map 1 shows. Washington carried the South and West Side wards of the city, the areas with high proportions of African-American residents; in fact, he carried all of the city's nineteen predominantly black wards. He lost all seventeen predominantly white wards by wide margins. Epton carried the white redoubts on the Southwest and Northwest sides of Chicago. Washington carried three other wards that did not have African-American majorities among their VAPs. Two of these (wards 22 and 31) had Latino majorities. The third (ward 1) had an African-American plurality of 48 percent, with an additional 13 percent Latino.

Map 1
Distribution of Washington's Support: General Election, 1983

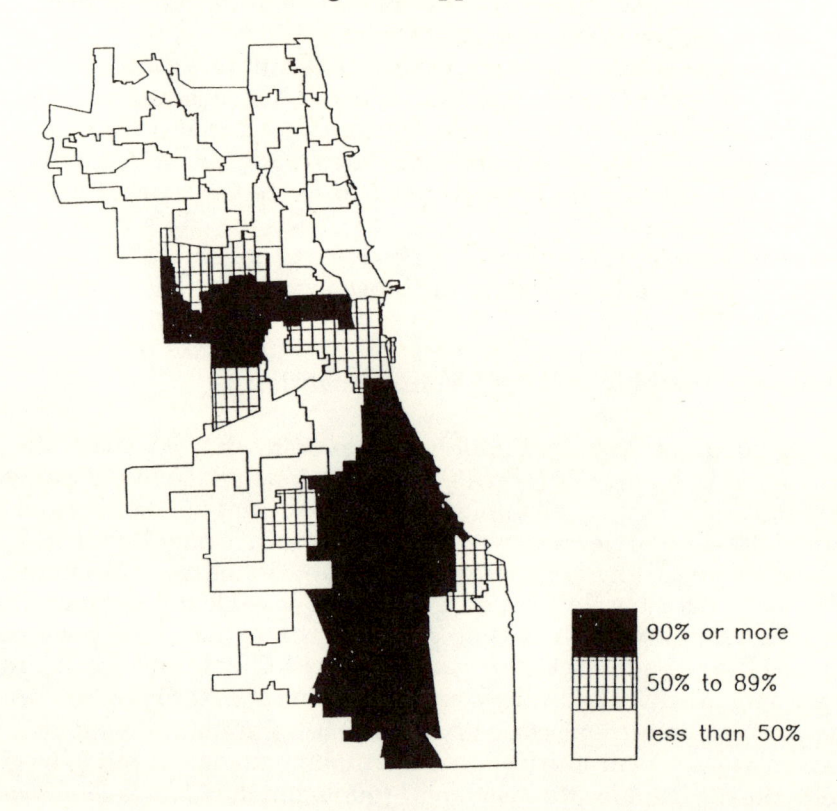

90% or more
50% to 89%
less than 50%

Washington also ran a competitive race, polling between 43 and 47 percent of the vote, in several northern Lakefront wards: 42, 46, 48, and 49. As conventionally used by the media and politicians in Chicago, the term "Lakefront wards" refers to the six wards north of the Loop that border Lake Michigan: wards 42, 43, 44, 46, 48, and 49. These wards are also often described as being "liberal" politically, primarily because of their past opposition to machine candidates. Moreover, the population mix in these wards is considerably more heterogeneous than in most other wards. The Lakefront wards, though Epton finally carried all of them, were battlegrounds. Washington did much better there than in any other wards with white majorities.

Washington attracted the support of only 12.3 percent of the whites who voted in April 1983, but he polled strong majorities among the Latinos (82.3 percent) and the varied Asian groups (62.6 percent) casting ballots in the mayoral election. Although the *number* of votes Washington received from each of these three other groups was small compared with his African-Ameri-

Figure 1
Composition of Washington's Voting Coalition: General Election, 1983

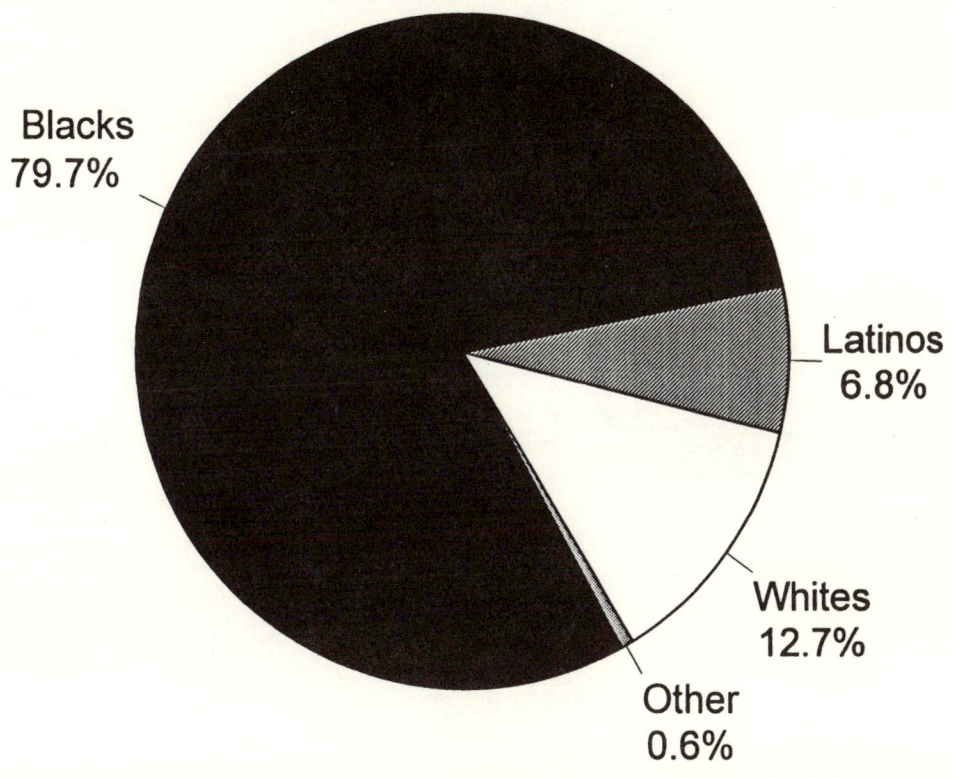

Blacks 79.7%
Latinos 6.8%
Whites 12.7%
Other 0.6%

can base, together they were vital to his victory. Figure 1 graphically depicts the components of Washington's winning coalition, showing the proportion of his total vote that came from each of the city's identifiable voter groups.[1]

Nearly eight out of every ten votes Washington received came from African-American voters, whereas only slightly more than one out of ten came from whites. To assess the significance of these numbers, it is necessary to note that at the time of the election, whites comprised 52.9 percent of the city's registered voters, and African Americans only 41.0 percent. Thus, compared with their citywide percentage of the registered electorate, African Americans were "overrepresented" in Washington's coalition by 38.7 percentage points, and whites were "underrepresented" by 40.2 percentage points.[2]

The distinctiveness of Washington's voting coalition can be underscored if we compare it with those of his running mates for citywide office. Walter Kozubowski, the incumbent city clerk, and Cecil Partee, the incumbent city treasurer, also ran against Republican opponents in the April 1983 election. Each of these officeholders had originally been slated by the Democratic organization and had faced no serious primary challenge. Kozubowski won reelection by polling 84.0 percent of the city's vote, including 95.2 percent of the vote cast by African Americans; Partee, an African American and an organization stalwart, polled 80.7 percent of the citywide vote, and 64.3 percent of the vote cast by whites. These margins of victory and vote divisions were more nearly typical of the outcomes of partisan contests in Chicago

Figure 2
Voting Coalitions of Democratic Candidates for Clerk and Treasurer: General Election, 1983

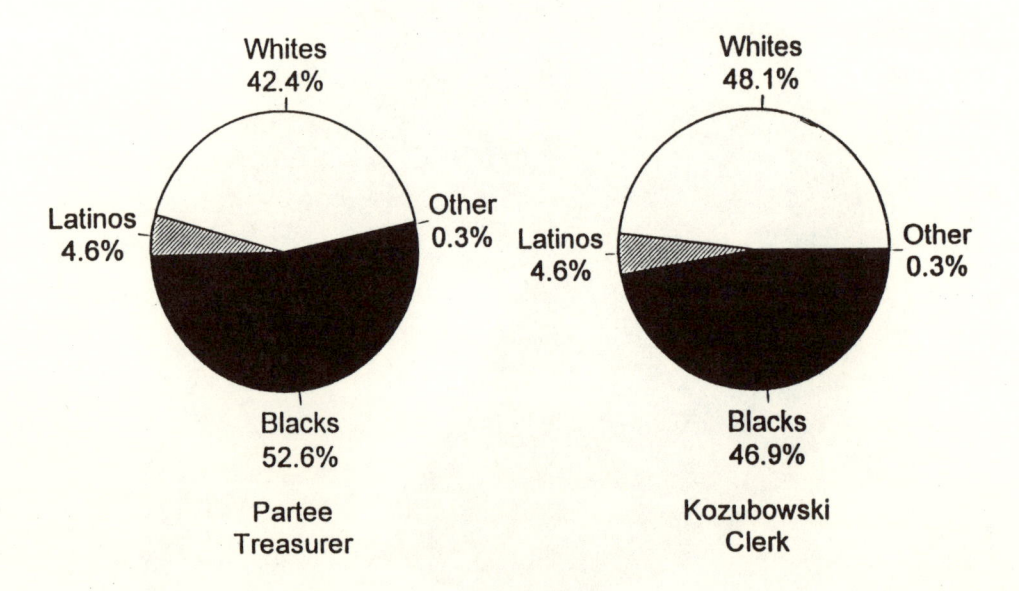

Partee — Treasurer
- Whites 42.4%
- Latinos 4.6%
- Other 0.3%
- Blacks 52.6%

Kozubowski — Clerk
- Whites 48.1%
- Latinos 4.6%
- Other 0.3%
- Blacks 46.9%

than Washington's narrow victory over Epton. Figure 2 shows the components of the voting coalitions of both Kozubowski and Partee. Compared with the composition of the city's registered electorate, neither of these coalitions exhibited the large indexes of over- and under-representation that marked Washington's coalition.[3] (The largest disparity was in Partee's coalition. African Americans comprised 11.6 percentage points more of his coalition than they did of the registered electorate.)

The behavior of the city's white voters mainly produced these differences among the three coalitions. Ticket-splitting, widespread in the April 1983 election, was neither even nor random. It was particularly high in the city's predominantly white wards. In the six wards where whites made up 85 percent or more of the VAP, over 98 percent of Kozubowski's supporters, and 96 percent of Partee's, crossed party lines and voted for a Republican for mayor. In the eleven wards where whites comprised from 50 to 84 percent of the VAP, the cross-over rates were lower but still arresting: 59 percent of Kozubowski's voters and 45 percent of Partee's chose Epton over Washington. In contrast, in the comparable groups of African-American wards, virtually all of Kozubowski's and Partee's voters cast their ballots for Washington.[4] As a result, and as figure 3 shows, African Americans were only slightly less likely to vote for Partee and Kozubowski than they were for Washington. Kozubowski, while receiving the lowest vote total of the three among African Americans, polled only 62,716 fewer votes than Wash-

Figure 3
Votes for City Candidates by Racial Groups: General Election, 1983

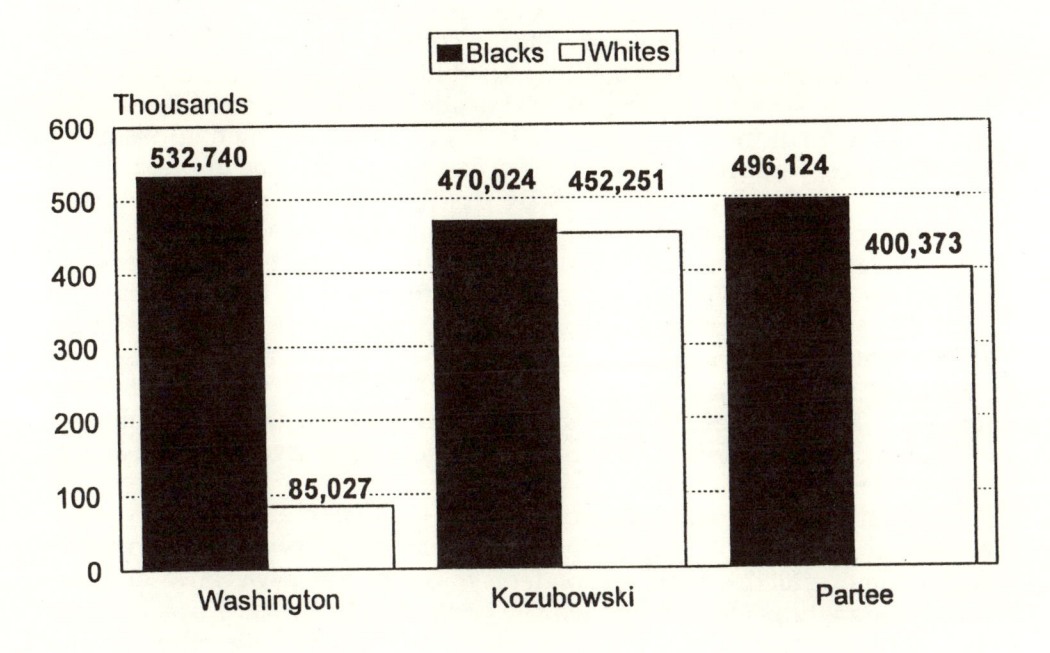

■ Blacks □ Whites

Thousands

- Washington: Blacks 532,740; Whites 85,027
- Kozubowski: Blacks 470,024; Whites 452,251
- Partee: Blacks 496,124; Whites 400,373

Table 1
Support for Washington Among White Voters: General Election, 1983

	Unadjusted Percentage	Adjusted Percentage*	Partial Beta	(N)
Education			.32	
Not HS Grad	9.6	9.1		(114)
HS Grad	11.7	12.3		(298)
Some College	11.5	13.6		(303)
College Grad	25.7	25.0		(171)
Grad School	50.8	47.3		(179)
Ideology			.27	
Liberal	39.0	35.3		(356)
Moderate	12.3	14.3		(431)
Conservative	8.6	10.1		(278)
Religion			.10	
Protestant	25.0	24.7		(275)
Catholic	16.2	18.0		(674)
Jewish	30.6	19.1		(88)
None	43.4	37.3		(23)

*Each variable controlled for the effects of the other variables and for age, income, party identification, and sex.

ington. In contrast, Partee received the support of 81,878 fewer white voters than Kozubowski, and Washington polled dramatically fewer votes (397,224 fewer) from whites than the Democratic candidate for city clerk.

White support for Washington came mainly from the Lakefront wards and the Hyde Park-University of Chicago community (ward 5).[5] It seemed likely that well-educated and self-identified liberals in these areas would be the white voters most likely to vote for Washington. To explore this possibility and to sort out the confounding effects of a series of potentially significant variables, Multiple Classification Analysis (MCA) was applied to the responses to the WMAQ-TV (NBC) exit poll. MCA produces the counterfactual pattern that would have obtained if supporters and opponents of Washington had had the same distribution on each of the other variables in the equation. For this analysis, only the responses from whites were used, and they were controlled for the effects of age, education, ideology, income, party identification, religion, and sex. Only two variables proved to have a statistically significant effect (at the .001 level): education and ideology. Table 1 reproduces the results for these two variables and for religion, which reached the criterion level of significance in some comparable analyses for later years.

The analysis confirms that among whites education and ideology were the best predictors of voting support for Washington. While Washington's support among all the white respondents to this exit poll was only 20.2 percent, among whites classifying themselves as liberals it was 15.1 percentage points higher, and among whites who had attended graduate school it was 27.1 percentage points higher.

In summary, in April 1983 Washington's candidacy enlisted the support of a somewhat diverse coalition of voters. African Americans were energized by his candidacy to turn out at record rates and to give him virtually monolithic support. To this large African-American base, Washington added strong majorities of the Latinos and Asians who voted, and a small but important segment of white voters. The latter were mainly whites living in the Hyde Park-University of Chicago community and the northern Lakefront wards, and they were whites who had some postgraduate education and identified themselves as liberals.

The Persistence of Washington's Voting Coalition

Washington's voting coalition did not disintegrate once he took office. At least in its broad outlines, it remained essentially intact, accounting for his triumphs in the 1987 primary and general elections.

Washington's first term was both tumultuous and eventful. Even before he took office, his opponents on the city council were in the process of organizing themselves into a voting bloc. With Alderman Edward R. Vrdolyak (ward 10) acting as both coach and cheerleader, a solid group of twenty-nine white aldermen lined up to oppose every significant action and appointment proposed by Mayor Washington.

The "Vrdolyak 29," with four exceptions, represented wards whose populations were collectively about 70 percent white and gave Washington only about 26 percent of their total vote in April 1983. The members of the "Washington 21," also with four exceptions, represented wards whose populations were about 72 percent African American and which registered 86 percent voting support for Washington.[6] Lacking the votes to put its own program into place, but with the mayor's veto preventing the opposition from enacting the measures it preferred, the Washington administration appeared to be paralyzed. The ongoing and often acrimonious conflict between the "Vrdolyak 29" and the "Washington 21," locally dubbed "Council Wars" (Kleppner, 1985: 242–49), led outsiders to depict Chicago as "Beirut on the Lake" (*Crain's Chicago Business*, 20 February 1984; and the *Wall Street Journal*, 6 August 1984).

As he daily battled his council foes, Washington found his public image under assault because of the biggest corruption scandal in Chicago politics since the 1972–74 revelations that rocked Richard J. Daley's administration. In "Operation Incubator," a 1985–86 undercover investigation by federal authorities, four of Washington's supporters in the city council were implicated in the scandal. His corporation counsel and chief of staff, as well as the two top officials in the city's revenue department, were forced to resign in its wake. Though independent investigations exonerated Washington personally, his image as a reformer, a champion of clean and honest government, was damaged (Holli & Green, 1989: 19–26; 158–59).

Ironically, Operation Incubator became public knowledge just as the federal district court was ending the stalemate between Washington and his enemies in the city council. In late December 1985, U.S. District Court Judge Charles R. Norgle accepted a settlement to the long legal dispute over the post-1980 reapportionment of the city council. The ruling added more African-American voters to wards 15, 18, and 37, and changed the boundaries of wards 22, 25, 26, and 31 to increase the number of Latino voters. In a separate ruling, Judge Norgle ordered special aldermanic elections to be held in the seven wards that gained new minority populations. The special elections were held in the spring of 1986 and produced a net swing of four seats in the city council, giving each bloc twenty-five votes. Interpreting the procedures of the council to allow the mayor to cast a vote to break ties, Washington gained effective control over the city government as a result of the remap elections (*Ketchum* v. *Byrne*; *Ketchum* v. *City Council of City of Chicago, Ill.* See Holli & Green, 1989: 27–36, for a discussion of the special elections and their significance.)

Washington had no sooner gained this control, however, when his opponents devised one more obstacle to his re-election. They hit upon the scheme of changing the election laws to provide for a nonpartisan election of the mayor. The plan provided for a two-stage election process. In the first stage, all candidates would run without party labels. If none secured a majority of the vote cast, then the two leading candidates would face each other in the second stage of the process. To secure the adoption of this process, Washington's opponents organized a petition campaign to put the question on the ballot at the November 1986 general election.

Richard M. Daley and his strategists were the driving force behind this nonpartisan election scheme. According to their assessment, Washington had won the 1983 primary only because the white vote split so evenly between Daley and Jane Byrne, who was then the incumbent mayor. To avoid a repeat performance, it was necessary to force Washington into a one-on-one contest. The problem for Daley was that Jane Byrne had already declared her candidacy in the summer of 1985, and there was no way that she could be driven from the contest. Under the existing rules, Daley could not enter the Democratic primary without running the risk of being seen as a "spoiler" who was only dividing the white vote and thus guaranteeing Washington's re-election. By changing the rules, however, Daley could enter a free-for-all primary, expecting to beat Byrne and face Washington in a one-on-one run-off election (Holli & Green, 1989: 37–43)

The effort to secure voter approval for a nonpartisan election of Chicago's mayor was ultimately unsuccessful. Washington's supporters on the city council took advantage of a state law limiting the number of referenda that could appear on the ballot at any election. By acting quickly to approve placing three nonbinding referenda on the November 1986 ballot, Washington's council majority killed the chance for a vote on the nonpartisan scheme. Daley's forces took their argument into court, while at the same time continuing to collect signatures to qualify their referendum for the November ballot. When the petitions were submitted, however, challengers discovered numerous irregularities in the signatures, calling into question whether there were even enough valid signatures to qualify. The Illinois Supreme Court ended the intense struggle in early fall when it ruled that the city council's action properly preempted the nonpartisan referendum and that the petitions submitted on behalf of the referendum were "totally defective" in any case.

It was within the context of these developments that Washington stood for reelection in early 1987. After much posturing about bypassing the primary and running in the general election as an independent, thus assuring himself of two white opponents, Washington chose to file for the Democratic primary. His opponent in that contest was Jane Byrne, the former mayor, whose early announcement had effectively prevented other white challengers from entering the February battle. While Byrne was Washington's only significant opponent in the Democratic primary, other aspirants were waiting to face him in the general election. Edward Vrdolyak, although chairman of the Democratic Central Committee of Cook County, decided to run for mayor on the Solidarity label. Thomas Hynes, the assessor of Cook County, announced his plans to run for mayor as the candidate of his newly created Chicago First party. The Republicans had set up a blue-ribbon committee that selected Donald Haider as that party's candidate. Bernard Epton originally contested Haider's designation and planned to run in the Republican primary. He proved unable to collect an adequate number of signatures on his filing petition and withdrew. Technically, Vrdolyak had to run in the Solidarity primary, but there was only nominal opposition and his victory was a foregone conclusion. Two days before the general election, Hynes dropped out of the mayoral race, explaining to a crowd of supporters that "I love Chicago enough not to be mayor."

Washington won both rounds of the 1987 battle, polling 53.4 percent of the vote in the primary and 53.7 percent in the general election. Both were comfortable victories, and both the outcomes and Washington's shares of the vote in the two contests were predicted fairly accurately by most pre-election polls. Some commentaries after the elections expressed "surprise" at the closeness of the final outcomes, since Washington's margin over his

**Map 2
Distribution of Washington's Support: Primary Election, 1987**

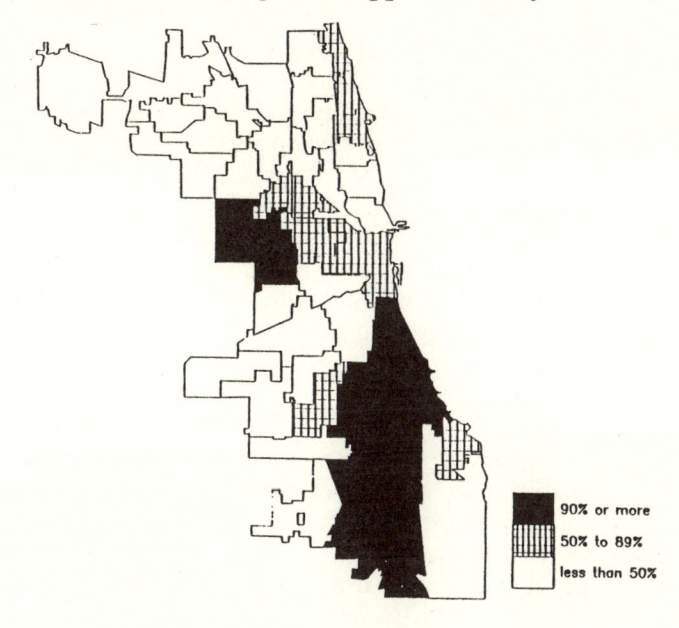

**Map 3
Distribution of Washington's Support: General Election, 1987**

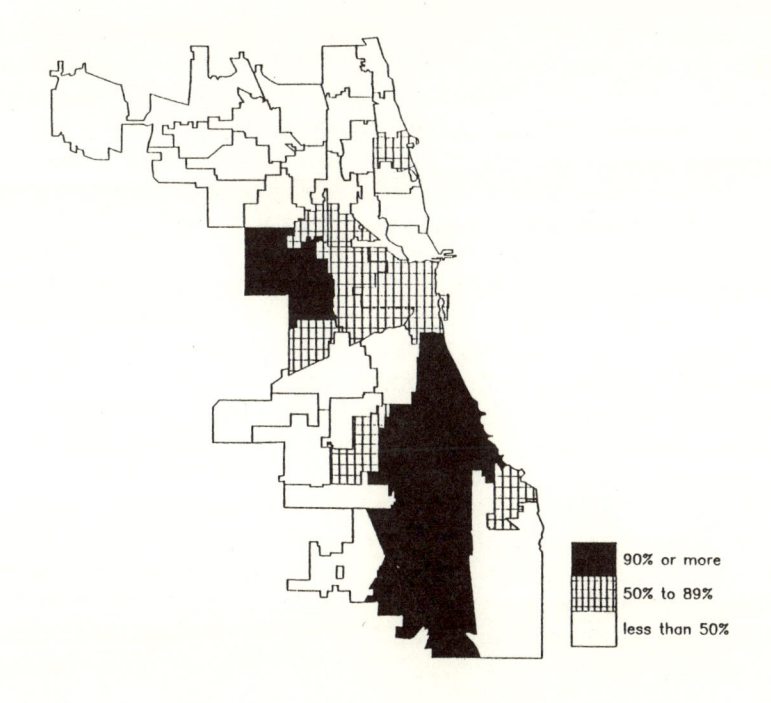

nearest opponent in the preelection polls had been much larger. These commentaries simply overlooked the fact that the "undecided" vote in pre-election polls tends overwhelmingly to break against the incumbent. Moreover, in biracial contests, undecided white voters tend overwhelmingly to vote for white candidates. On both counts, informed commentators should have expected virtually all of the pre-election "undecided" vote to have gone against Washington. If they had made that assumption, and looked primarily at Washington's absolute percentages in the polls, they would have expected reasonably close outcomes in each contest, with Washington winning with roughly 52 percent of the total vote.

Unlike 1983, then, there was something of an aura of inevitability surrounding the Washington candidacy. The tone of the election campaigns was generally civil, lacking the frenzy, intensity, and open displays of racial antagonism evident four years earlier.

This is not to say that racial conflict was absent; only that it was not expressed as openly as it had been in 1983. In the intervening years, "good government" groups, appalled by the racial hostility expressed in the 1983 contest, set up a committee to monitor campaign practices—the Committee on Decent and Unbiased Campaign Tactics (CONDUCT). The committee formally reprimanded candidates and/or their supporters when they engaged in what it judged to be racial attacks or displays of racial insensitivity. But the 1987 elections did not differ from the 1983 general election in the social character and shape of the voting coalitions. Geographically, Washington's support in the 1987 elections was concentrated pretty much where it had been four years earlier—in the African-American wards on the city's South and West Sides (see maps 2 and 3). In the 1987 primary, Washington added four wards to the twenty-two that he had carried in April 1983: ward 26, one of the wards that had picked up more Latino voters as a result of the remap decision, and wards 46, 48, and 49, all on the Lakefront and in all of which he had run reasonably competitive races in 1983, getting between 40 and 49 percent of the vote. In the 1987 general election, he carried these twenty-six wards and added one more, ward 25, another ward whose Latino population had been increased as a result of the remap decision. Washington barely polled a majority in ward 25 (50.8 percent), and he fell below 50 percent in wards 48 and 49, carrying them with 48.5 and 47.1 percent, respectively, due to the three-way split in the vote.

Washington's improved showing in the Lakefront wards is sometimes cited to support the impression popularized by the Chicago media that he did much better among white voters in 1987 than he had in 1983. That impression assumes that Washington's strongest support in the Lakefront wards was among white voters, an assumption that was incorrect in both 1983 and 1987. Against Epton, Washington polled about 26 percent of the white vote in the six Lakefront wards; against Byrne that figure rose to 31 percent, but then it fell back to only 23 percent in the general election. Vrdolyak, Washington's prime antagonist on the council, captured 59 percent of the white vote in these allegedly "liberal" bastions. In both 1983 and 1987, Washington's strongest support in this six-ward area came from its nonwhite voters—African Americans, Latinos, and Asians, all of whom gave him strong majorities of their vote.

Table 2
Turnout of Voting Support for Washington
by Racial/Ethnic Group, 1983 and 1987

	1983 General		1987 Primary		1987 General	
	Turnout	% Wash.	Turnout	% Wash.	Turnout	% Wash.
White	66.6	12.3	58.4	13.7	58.7	11.7
Black	67.7	99.7	55.9	99.5	58.5	99.3
Hispanic	31.1	82.3	25.2	69.2	23.1	83.5
Other	22.4	62.6	26.1	72.9	25.0	78.4
Total City	63.2	51.8	53.2	53.4	54.1	53.7

How then is it possible to explain Washington's improved performance in the Lakefront wards between 1983 and 1987? Two factors account for this. First, while turnout both among whites and African Americans on the Lakefront fell from their 1983 peaks, African-American turnout remained slightly higher than white turnout. Even more significant, the white share of the total VAP in the Lakefront wards dropped by five percentage points between 1983 and 1987, from 76 percent to 71 percent.

The data in table 2 allow us to compare the levels of Washington's support among the city's major racial and ethnic categories. The lower turnout rates

Figure 4
Composition of Washington's Voting Coalition:
Primary and General Elections, 1987

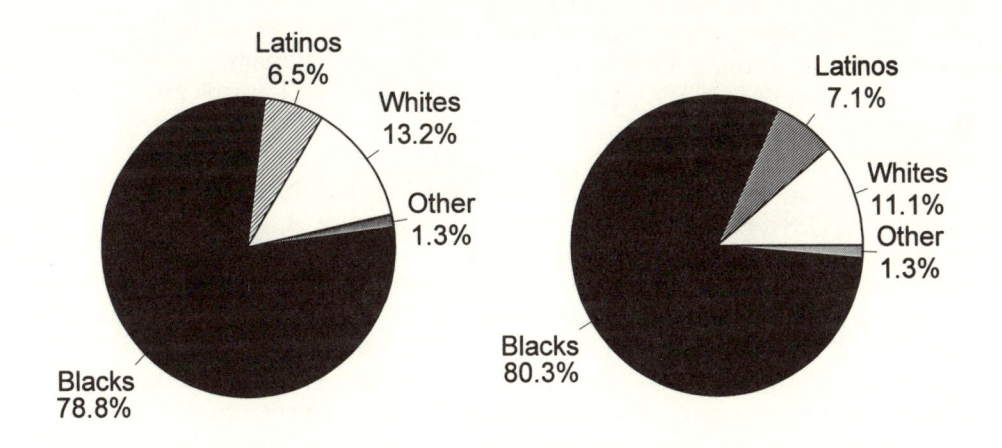

Primary: Blacks 78.8%, Latinos 6.5%, Whites 13.2%, Other 1.3%

General: Blacks 80.3%, Latinos 7.1%, Whites 11.1%, Other 1.3%

Figure 5
Composition of Voting Coalitions of Democratic Candidates for Clerk and Treasurer: General Election, 1987

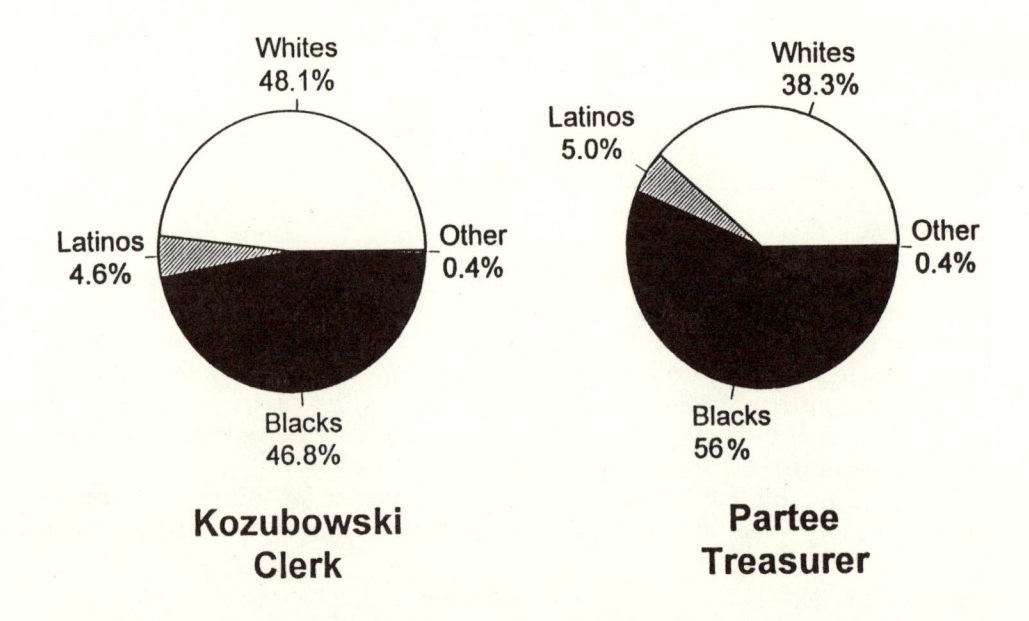

Kozubowski
Clerk

- Whites 48.1%
- Other 0.4%
- Blacks 46.8%
- Latinos 4.6%

Partee
Treasurer

- Whites 38.3%
- Latinos 5.0%
- Other 0.4%
- Blacks 56%

that marked the 1987 elections, compared with the 1983 general election, testify to a general drop in intensity level. African-American turnout dropped slightly more than white turnout, but the differences were not great. African-American voters delivered virtually all of their ballots to Washington, as they had in his epic battle against Epton in 1983. And Latinos and "others" (mostly Asian) gave him solid majorities of their votes. His showing among whites, however, was generally disappointing, principally because it was not much different than it had been four years earlier. Indeed, because white turnout was lower, Washington actually received fewer votes from whites in February or April 1987 than he had in the general election in 1983. In April 1983 Washington received about 85,027 votes from whites in Chicago. In the February 1987 primary he polled about 77,946 votes from whites, and that number fell further to 66,988 in the April 1987 general election. These figures are derived from regression equations applied to precinct-level voting and census data. (See note 6, above, for an outline of the procedures.)

The composition of Washington's voting coalitions in February and April 1987 did not differ very much from April 1983 (figure 4). In all three cases, nearly eight-tenths of his vote came from African Americans, with only slightly more than one-tenth coming from white voters. Thus, as they had been four years earlier, whites were greatly "underrepresented" and African Americans "overrepresented" in Washington's voting coalition. Whites were "underrepresented" in the primary coalition by 38.4 percentage points and by 40.7 percentage points in the general election. The corresponding indica-

Figure 6
Votes for City Candidates by Racial Groups: General Election, 1987

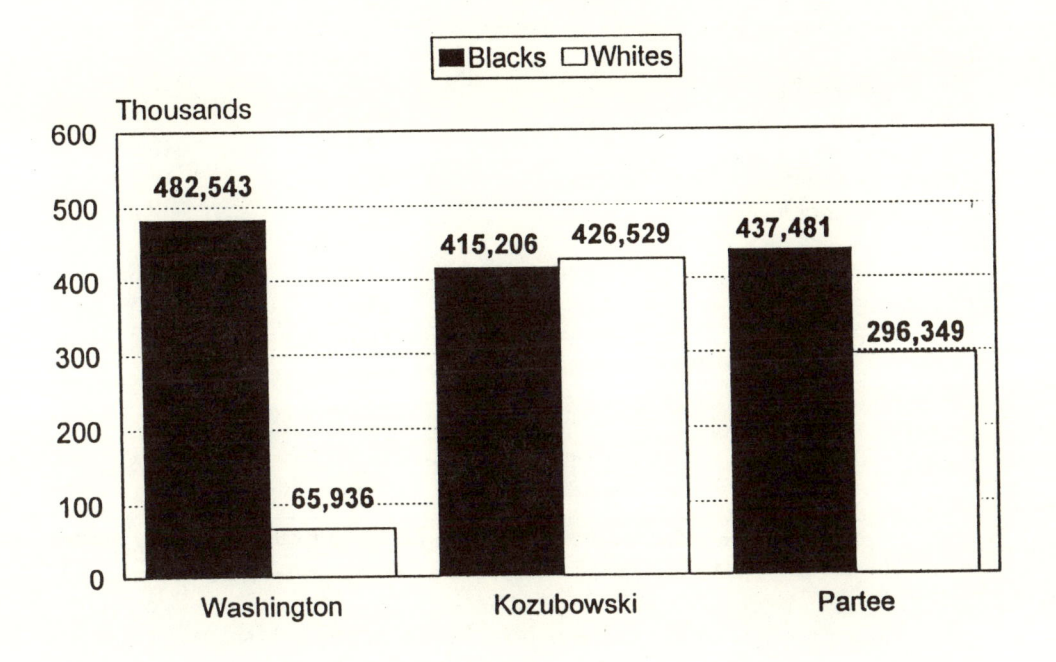

■ Blacks □ Whites

Thousands

- Washington: 482,543 (Blacks); 65,936 (Whites)
- Kozubowski: 415,206 (Blacks); 426,529 (Whites)
- Partee: 437,481 (Blacks); 296,349 (Whites)

tors of "overrepresentation" for African Americans were 37.2 and 38.9 percentage points, respectively. For the 1987 primary, whites made up 51.6 percent of the city's registered electorate, and African Americans 41.6 percent. The figures for the general election were whites, 51.8 percent and African Americans, 41.4 percent.

The distinctiveness of Washington's voting coalitions is apparent when they are compared with those of his running mates in the 1987 general election (figure 5). Walter Kozubowki and Cecil Partee were again the Democratic candidates for city clerk and city treasurer, respectively. Again, both ran well ahead of Washington, with Kozubowski polling 85.3 percent of the vote and Partee 79.3 percent. Unlike Washington's support, the vote for these offices did not divide along racial lines: Kozubowski received 96.3 percent of the African-American vote and Partee 61.4 percent of the white vote. As a result, their voting coalitions again failed to show anything like the large indexes of over- and underrepresentation that marked Washington's.

The pattern of ticket splitting that occurred in the 1987 general election was very much like that in 1983. In the wards in which whites comprised 85 percent or more of the VAP, about 96 percent of Kozubowski's supporters and 92 percent of Partee's voted against Washington. In the wards where whites made up from 50 to 84 percent of the VAP, the crossover rates were again lower: 56 percent of Kozubowski's voters and only 22 percent of Partee's supporters marked their ballots for a candidate other than the incumbent Democratic mayor.

Table 3
Support for Washington Among White Voters: 1983 and 1987*

	General 1983	Primary 1987	General 1987
Education			
No HS Graduate	9.1	10.3	17.7
HS Graduate	12.3	14.3	8.4
Some College	13.6	18.5	10.6
College Graduate	25.0	22.5	15.6
Graduate School	47.3	34.7	30.0
Ideology			
Liberal	35.3	29.6	27.8
Moderate	14.3	15.8	10.3
Conservative	10.1	11.4	9.2
Religion			
Protestant	24.7	29.0	20.2
Catholic	18.0	17.7	8.8
Jewish	19.1	24.0	30.6
None	37.3	24.1	33.1

*Entries are percentage controlled for the effects of the other variables and for age, income, party identification, and sex.

The consequence was the same as it had been in 1983. African Americans were about as likely to vote for the mayor's ticket mates as they were for him (figure 6). But white voters continued to resist casting their ballots for an African-American chief executive, even though they were willing to vote for his Democratic ticket mates. Thus, Kozubowski polled only 67,337 fewer votes among African Americans than Washington, but Washington received 359,541 fewer white votes than Kozubowski. It may be symptomatic of the city's increased racial polarization that Partee received 127,180 fewer votes from whites than Kozubowski did in 1987, while he had lagged only 81,878 votes behind in 1983.

As had been the case in 1983, in both the primary and general elections of 1987 Washington ran better among whites in the Lakefront wards and in Hyde Park-University of Chicago community (ward 5) than he did elsewhere. In 1983 Washington received the support of 56.5 percent of the white voters in ward 5. In the 1987 primary the percentage among whites there rose to 76.0, and then fell again to 61.1 percent in the general election. Of course, whites comprised less than a quarter of the total VAP of ward 5 in 1983 and 1987. This again suggests that Washington did better among whites who were well educated and ideologically liberal than among other white voters. To explore this possibility, the MCA executed for the 1983 election was replicated for the 1987 primary and general elections, and table 3 presents those results as well as repeating the data from the 1983 general election to facilitate comparisons. The exit polls for the 1983 general and 1987 primary were conducted for WMAQ-TV (NBC), and the exit poll for the 1987 general election was conducted for WBBM-TV (CBS). The valid number of cases used in each of the MCA's: 1983 general, N = 1,065; 1987 primary, N = 997; 1987 general, N = 1,202.

These results confirm the general hunch. While Washington's support among white respondents to the WMAQ-TV (NBC) primary exit poll was only 20.3 percent, 29.6 percent of the liberals and 34.7 percent of those who had some postgraduate education supported him. However, these were lower levels of support than he had received from both of these categories four years earlier. These declines were somewhat offset by the fact that in the 1987 primary, unlike 1983, religion operated as a significant predictor of support for Washington among whites, as he gained about five percentage points among both Protestant and Jewish voters. For the 1987 primary, the partial betas were: ideology, .20; education, .18; and religion, .14. These were the only three variables that were statistically significant at the .001 level.

Although showing still another slight decline, in the general election white liberals and those who had gone to graduate school again gave Washington more support than most other whites. In that respect, the profile of Washington's support remained basically unchanged. But there was some shift in the pattern of support among religious groups. Support among white Protestants and Catholics declined compared with either the 1987 primary or the 1983 general election, while support among Jewish voters increased. Support among voters with no religion also increased between the 1987 primary and general elections, although even during the latter it remained below the level for April 1983. The difficulty in making observations about this category lies in the fact that the number of cases was very small in 1983 (N = 23) and in the primary exit poll in 1987 (N = 12). In the exit poll for the 1987 general election, the category had ninety cases. For the 1987 general election, the partial betas were: religion, .24; ideology, .23; and education, .22. Again, these were the only three variables that were statistically significant at the .001 level.

In summary, Washington's coalitions in 1987 remained roughly what had emerged initially in April 1983. He enjoyed virtually unanimous support among African Americans, strong majority support among Latinos and "others," but only a thin sliver of support among whites. His white support was mainly concentrated among well-educated and liberal voters and, by the 1987 general election, among Jewish voters. While four years in office hadn't done much to broaden his coalition, the intensity levels seem to have been dampened while support among his African-American base solidified.

When Washington was re-elected in April 1987, an "era of good feelings" seemed to have begun in city politics. Washington had polled majorities in both the primary and general elections, defeating well-known white candidates in each. The outcomes of the aldermanic elections guaranteed that the mayor could enlist twenty-five votes on most issues, assuring him at worst of being able to cast the tie-breaking vote. Moreover, the chief strategist of the opposition, and the mayor's leading tormentor, Edward Vrdolyak (ward 10), had not sought re-election to the city council, so the opposition lacked the creative and determined leadership it had had since 1983. Without Vrdolyak to hold them in line, some of the mayor's sharpest critics among the aldermen now pledged their cooperation. "Council Wars," the battle between the mayor and an implacable opposition on the council, seemed to have come to an end.

There was yet another indicator that politics in Chicago and Cook County might have entered its "kinder and gentler" phase. In early November 1987

Washington and George Dunne, who replaced Vrdolyak when the latter resigned as chairman of the Democratic Central Committee of Cook County, cooperated to put together what the mayor characterized as a "dream ticket" for the county offices that were to be contested in the 1988 election. The party slated Richard M. Daley, a representative of the Irish community, for reelection as state's attorney; Aurelia Pucinski, a Polish representative and daughter of one of the mayor's more outspoken foes on the city council, for county clerk; and Carol Mosley Braun, a representative of the African American community, for recorder of deeds. This sort of ethnic and racial mixture seemed to signify the ascendancy of a politics of inclusion, in contrast to the politics of racial polarization that had marked the preceding four years.

Whether or not these signs of "good feelings" would have persisted may be conjectured. Conflict with the council may very well have been renewed over the mayor's budget proposals for 1988. Opposition to the "dream ticket" would certainly have appeared on both sides of the city's racial divide even had Washington lived to campaign actively on its behalf. But we shall never know what might have been.

Washington's Coalition after Washington

Washington's passing removed the central and dominating figure from the city's political stage, opening the way for larger roles to be played by otherwise minor actors. The death of Harold Washington, on 25 November 1987, set in motion a series of events that culminated in the outcomes of the special primary and general elections in 1989.

The Succession Struggle

The mayor's unwavering and virtually unanimous support among African-American voters had served to hold in line several African-American aldermen who felt more comfortable pursuing machine objectives than they did reform goals. With Washington gone, these conflicts and long-standing fissures among black leaders quickly resurfaced. Even before the official announcement of Washington's death, several of the African Americans loyal to the machine were planning for the succession (Dodd & Lipinski, 1987: 1; Rivlin, 1987: 25–29.)

Since the city council was legally obliged to select the acting mayor from among its own members, those who wanted to control the succession concentrated on lining up the necessary twenty-six votes. Among the members of the council were seventeen African-American aldermen, four Latinos, seven independent whites representing the Lakefront wards and Hyde Park, and twenty-two other white aldermen who had routinely opposed Washington during his first term and who were generally loyal to one or another of the machine factions. Building a coalition of twenty-six votes from among such a membership was no small or simple task.

Among the African-American aldermen, three major contenders quickly emerged. Alderman Danny Davis (ward 29) was a Washington loyalist and enjoyed the support of many of the community activists and was endorsed by Lu Palmer's Black Independent Precinct Organization. Alderman Timothy Evans (ward 4) had served as Washington's floor leader in the council and as chairman of the powerful budget committee that had been created in May 1986 when the mayor gained control over the council. Alderman Eugene Sawyer (ward 6), a long-time machine stalwart and early supporter of Washington's election in 1983, was supported by the African Americans loyal to the machine. Unable to enlist much support among the aldermen, Davis withdrew his candidacy and supported Evans.

An eleven-hour council meeting on the night of 1-2 December culminated in the election of Alderman Sawyer at 4:01 a.m., 2 December. All of the local stations telecast the council's proceedings that night, and an estimated three quarters of the Chicago viewing audience watched events unfold. They witnessed a tumultuous scene, with thousands of Evans's backers jamming La Salle Street and even crowding into the lobby of City Hall itself. They chanted "No deals, no deals," to remind of their opposition to any sellout of Washington's reform efforts. At other points they chanted "Uncle Tom Sawyer, Uncle Tom Sawyer," depicting the alderman as willing to compromise the interests of African Americans to win white support for his mayoral bid (Cose & Ihejirika, 1987.)

The demonstrations weakened Sawyer's resolve, nearly leading him to postpone the vote. They did not change the final outcome. Sawyer was selected acting mayor, but with the votes of only five African-American aldermen, including himself. The other African Americans voting for Sawyer were: Marlene Carter (ward 15); Anna Langford (ward 16); William Henry (ward 24); and Sheneather Butler (ward 27). One African-American alderman, Lemuel Austin (ward 34) was not present at the council meeting and did not vote. Twenty-four white aldermen voted for Sawyer. Eleven of the other twelve African-American aldermen voted for Evans, as did all four of the Latinos. Four white aldermen also cast their ballots for Evans, while the white aldermen voting for Evans were: Lawrence Bloom (ward 5); Edwin Eisendrath (ward 43); Helen Schiller (ward 46); and David Orr (ward 49), who also served as interim mayor and chaired the council session at which Sawyer was selected acting mayor. One white alderman, Patrick Huels from Richard M. Daley's eleventh ward, was present and abstained.

Sawyer's Travail and Daley's Victory

The circumstances under which Sawyer became acting mayor shaped his administration. He could not count on the support of the Washington loyalists on the council, nor even from the white aldermen whose votes selected him. To many African-American citizens of Chicago, he was the choice of the white aldermen to succeed Washington and not that of the African-American community. He was an acting mayor without a solid constituency, and with little realistic hope of developing one. Sawyer's prospects became even poorer once the court decided that a special election was to be held in 1989 to fill the remainder of Washington's four-year term.

The 1989 special election provided the occasion for the next stage of the conflict within the African-American community. With Sawyer deciding to run for the Democratic nomination for mayor in the February primary, Evans chose to bypass the primary and run in the general election under the label of a new organization, the Harold Washington party. This tactic allowed Evans to avoid having his candidacy divide the African-American vote in the primary, a circumstance which clearly would lead to a victory by a contender who was not African American. But while not a candidate for the Democratic nomination himself, Evans refrained from endorsing Sawyer.

With Evans bypassing the primary, Alderman Lawrence Bloom entered that contest as the standard bearer of the reformers. Bloom hoped to appeal to Lakefront whites concerned with good government, as well as to Latinos and Asians who sought inclusion in city government, and to those African Americans not reconciled to Sawyer. But Bloom's candidacy never aroused the enthusiasm he had expected and never became a focal point for those who hoped to revive the Washington coalition.

Alderman Edward Burke (ward 14) publicly considered running for the Democratic nomination but decided instead to support Richard M. Daley. There had really never been any doubt but that Daley would enter the race. He had run successfully for re-election as state's attorney in November 1988, refusing during that campaign to say whether he would serve out the term for which he was running or would seek the mayoralty. The fact that Daley hired David Axelrod, a highly regarded political consultant, to run his re-election campaign against an unknown Republican challenger was widely interpreted as an indication that he was using the contest for state's attorney simply as a warm up for the main event, the race for mayor. When Daley formally entered the mayoral race, he instantly became "the great white hope."

Daley defeated Acting Mayor Sawyer by 101,647 in the February primary, becoming as a result the Democratic nominee for mayor. He won 55.3 percent of the vote cast, 11.6 percentage points more than Sawyer. Six weeks later, Daley triumphed in the second part of the battle, the general election. The April contest was a three-way affair, with Evans using the Harold Washington label and Edward Vrdolyak running as the Republican nominee. Vrdolyak formally switched his allegiance to the Republican party in 1987 after he had run unsuccessfully in the general election for mayor against Washington under the Solidarity party label. When he ran against the Democratic nominee in April 1987, Vrdolyak was still formally the chairman of the Democratic Central Committee of Cook County. Vrdolyak won the Republican nomination for mayor in the 1989 primary as the result of a write-in campaign. Against these two opponents, Daley won 53.9 percent of the vote, 12.8 percentage points more than Evans, his closest challenger. Moreover, he outpolled Evans by 133,596 votes, an even larger edge than his margin of 101,647 over Sawyer in the primary. Vrdolyak polled only 35,964 votes, or 3.4 percent of the total. Daley even carried Vrdolyak's ward, the tenth, with 46.5 percent of the vote. Vrdolyak received only 25.3 percent in ward 10, which put him in *third* place, 2.8 percentage points behind Evans. We can begin to get a sense of what shaped the outcomes of these contests by examining the rates of mobilization and candidate support by racial and ethnic groups.

As has generally been the case in Chicago, a higher proportion of whites of voting age than African Americans were registered for both the primary and general elections (table 4). The gap was 12.7 percentage points in the primary and 12.3 in the general. More significantly, however, *there was an even larger difference in the turnout percentages.* Measured as a percentage of

Table 4
Mobilization in Special Mayoral Elections: February and April 1989*

	Primary % Registered	Primary % Turnout	General % Registered	General % Turnout
White	85.8	54.7	86.1	62.6
Black	73.1	36.8	73.8	43.7
Hispanic	34.1	11.6	35.2	16.0
Other	23.3	16.3	22.1	21.8
City Total	73.0	41.3	73.6	48.3

*Percentages of voting age population (VAP)

each group's eligible VAP, white turnout was 17.9 percentage points higher than African-American turnout in the primary and 18.9 percentage points greater in the general election.

In other words, the city's white electorate seems to have been aroused and enthusiastic, while its African-American electorate lagged well behind the turnout rates that it had achieved in the mayoral elections of 1983 and 1987. The following comparisons summarize the point. White turnout in the 1989 general election was only 5 percentage points lower than white turnout in the 1983 general election, when all commentators pointed to a broadly diffused sense of fear and frenzy that gripped and mobilized the white community at the prospect of the election of the city's first African-American mayor. In contrast, African-American turnout in April 1989 was more than 24 *percentage points below* its April 1983 level. African-American turnout in the 1989 primary was 19.1 percentage points lower than it had been in the 1987 primary, and in the 1989 general election, was 14.8 percentage points below the level it reached in the 1987 general election. In contrast, white turnout in the 1989 general election was 3.9 percentage points *higher* than it had been in the 1987 general election.

The data in table 5 tell the second part of the story of the 1989 elections. In both of these contests, nearly nine out of every ten whites voted for Daley, while better than nine out of every ten African Americans voted against him. The African-American community was not as highly mobilized as it had been in either 1983 or 1987, but the collective behavior of those casting votes was nearly as cohesive as it had been in those earlier mayoral contests. The white

Table 5
Candidate Support in Special Mayoral Elections: February and April 1989*

	Primary Daley	Primary Sawyer	General Daley	General Evans	General Vrodolyak
White	89.3	9.7	88.2	6.4	5.3
Black	1.7	97.3	3.6	95.3	1.0
Hispanic	49.1	49.6	52.4	46.0	1.4
Other	37.5	61.3	35.8	62.8	1.2
City Total	55.3	43.7	53.9	41.1	3.4

*Percentages of total vote cast

community, on the other hand, reacted more cohesively in 1989 than it had in either April 1983 or in the mayoral primary and general elections in 1987.

In summary, Daley won the 1989 primary and general elections by comfortable margins because of the combined effect of two factors. First, white turnout remained high and white voters exhibited even more cohesiveness in their voting choice than they had in earlier biracial contests for mayor. Second, while African-American *voters* displayed only slightly less cohesiveness than they had in 1983 and 1987, turnout among African Americans lagged well below the levels of those earlier years.

Figure 7
Composition of Daley's Voting Coalitions:
Primary and General Elections, 1989

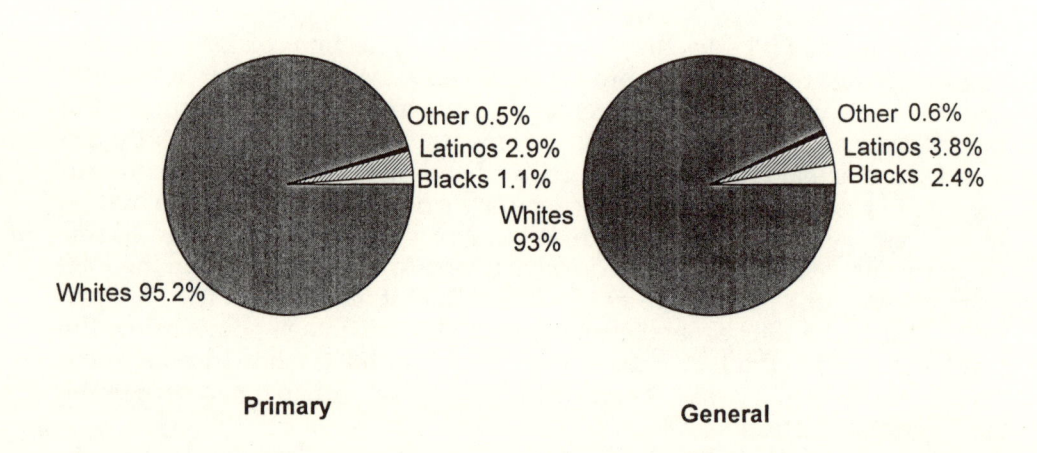

Primary:
- Whites 95.2%
- Other 0.5%
- Latinos 2.9%
- Blacks 1.1%

General:
- Whites 93%
- Other 0.6%
- Latinos 3.8%
- Blacks 2.4%

As a result of the sharp racial polarization in voting choices, Daley's victories depended to an extraordinary degree on white voting support (Figure 7). His total vote in both the primary and general elections depended more exclusively on whites than Washington's had on African Americans in either 1983 or 1987. Indeed, it is nearly a misnomer to refer to Daley's voting "coalition," since 95 percent of his vote in the primary, and 93 percent in the general election, came from white voters. In earlier elections Daley's voting coalition had not been so exclusively white. In his first general election for state's attorney in 1980, for example, he ran against a Republican incumbent, Bernard Carey, who himself had been elected with considerable African-American voting support. Yet, in that election, 38.5 percent of Daley's vote in Chicago came from African Americans, while 55.4 percent came from whites. Even in his 1988 reelection against a virtually unknown Republican chal-

Table 6
Support for Black Candidates among White Voters:
Primary and General Election, 1989*

	Primary % Sawyer	General % Evans
Education		
Not HS Graduate	0.0	1.5
HS Graduate	3.0	3.4
Some College	8.2	8.5
College Graduate	7.8	12.6
Graduate School	20.4	16.4
Ideology		
Liberal	14.1	15.6
Moderate	6.6	6.0
Conservative	5.5	4.8
Religion		
Protestant	10.5	7.4
Catholic	7.2	5.7
Jewish	3.7	8.0
None	11.0	22.0

*Entries are percentages controlled for the effects of the other variables and for age, income, party identification, and sex.

lenger, 30.0 percent of Daley's vote in Chicago came from African Americans and 64.3 percent from whites. Since whites made up only about 52 percent of Chicago's registered electorate, they were overrepresented in Daley's voting base by 42.9 percentage points in the primary and by 40.9 percentage points in the general election. African Americans, on the other hand, were underrepresented by 40.2 percentage points in the primary and 39.0 percentage points in the general election.

Sawyer and Evans each carried the same nineteen wards, those with majorities of African Americans in their VAPs. Otherwise, they ran competitive races in very few wards. Sawyer polled between 40 and 49 percent only in wards 1, 10, and 18, while Evans reached that mark only in wards 1 and 18. Such a result was not surprising in view of how little white support either attracted citywide and the low turnout rates among Chicago's nonwhite voting groups.

The results in the six Lakefront wards reveal what happened to Washington's coalition. Although he did not win any of these wards in 1983, Washington had been competitive there, polling 42.1 percent of the vote against Epton. Four years later, he carried three Lakefront wards against Byrne, while attracting 46.2 percent of the primary vote in the six-ward group. In the three-way general election, his vote dropped to 41.8 percent, compared with Vrdolyak's 45.2 percent, but Washington still carried three of six Lakefront wards. In 1989 Daley handily carried all six Lakefront wards in both the primary and the general elections. In the February battle, Daley outpolled Sawyer 69.5 percent to 29.1 percent; and in the general election, he beat Evans by 73.3 percent to 22.4 percent.

Daley owed his Lakefront victories to the area's white voters. Their turnout was much higher than that of the area's African Americans, by 13.5 percentage points in the primary and by 15.4 percentage points in the general election. While African-American voters on the Lakefront gave overwhelming support to Sawyer and Evans, white voters gave almost equally high percentages to Daley. Among white Lakefront voters, Daley polled 82.3 percent in the primary and 87.4 percent in the general election. While Washington had never carried the white vote on the Lakefront, he had pulled about a quarter of it. That fraction, combined with his solid support among African Americans, Latinos, and "others," enabled him to run competitively in the area. Neither Sawyer nor Evans was able to reach even that threshold share of support among the white electorate in the Lakefront wards.

Their weakness among Lakefront whites suggests that Sawyer and Evans also failed to attract as much support as Washington had among white liberals and those who had some postgraduate education. The MCA results for the 1989 elections confirm that suspicion (see table 6). Table 7 uses exit polls conducted for WBBM-TV (CBS). The number of valid cases for white respondents was 957 in the primary and 960 in the general election. In the primary the partial betas were: education, .23; ideology, .12; and religion, .08. Of the seven variables used in the MCA, only the ideology and education betas were significant at the .001 level. For the general election, the partial betas: education, .18; religion, .17; and ideology, .16. These three partial betas were the only ones significant at .001.

While it was still true that liberal and well-educated whites gave these African-American candidates more voting support than other whites, the level of that support was only about half as much as it had been in Washington's elections. Moreover, notice that while support declined across all religious categories, the drop between the 1987 general and the 1989 primary was especially sharp among Jewish voters.

In summary, the 1989 elections reveal three dimensions of change in Washington's voting coalition. First, and most important, there was a demobilization of a significant proportion of the African-American community. This was essential to Daley's victories, and avoiding any statement or action that ignited the African-American electorate and raised its turnout was a vital ingredient of his pre-election strategy. Second, at least half of the liberal and well-educated white voters who supported Washington opted not to vote for African-American candidates in the 1989 elections. Neither Sawyer nor Evans was able, as Washington had been, to capture the imaginations and the voting support of this segment of the white electorate. Third, unlike Washington, Sawyer and Evans were unable to poll solid majorities among Chicago's Latino voters. The so-called black-brown coalition that was a feature of Washington's successful campaigns simply could not withstand the powerful pressures aimed at fracturing it.

The Rise and Fall of a Multiethnic Coalition

What happened in Chicago between 1983 and 1989 illustrates both the possibilities and problems involved in constructing and maintaining multiethnic coalitions. Nothing happened following Washington's first election to make it possible to broaden the original coalition. To the contrary, the pitched battle between Washington and his organized opposition in the city council maintained the battle lines that had been formed initially during Byrne's administration. These conflicts over integration issues occurred in the 1960s and 1970s and had been sharply redrawn in April 1983. Washington occasionally reached out to allay white anxieties, meeting with community leaders to listen to concerns about public housing sites in their neighborhoods and indicating support for a scheme designed to protect housing values in racially changing areas. The mayor's opponents worked even more vigorously to keep white fears alive, especially among Jewish voters. Alderman Vrdolyak, for example, led the effort to associate Washington with black Muslim leader Louis Farrakhan's anti-Semitic diatribes. After the 1986 elections, Vrdolyak incorrectly charged that the incumbent Democratic sheriff, Richard Elrod, who is Jewish, lost his reelection bid because African-American voters failed to support him.[7]

Washington's effort to spread calm, and Vrdolyak's effort to spread alarm, each had only marginal impact. "Council Wars" overpowered all other cues and strengthened the perception of continuing racial conflict. Washington carried wards 1, 15, 22, and 37, whose alderman had voted with the Vrdolyak bloc; and he lost wards 42, 43, 48, and 49, whose aldermen opposed the Vrdolyak group. Overt racial division at the aldermanic level simply encouraged voters of both races to view the conflict as a continuation of the struggle for cultural dominance. Washington and Vrdolyak both reinforced that perception, through their actions and statements, both to keep pressure on their aldermanic allies and to reinforce the resolve of their grassroots supporters.

Thus, it was no surprise that the battle alignments of 1983 remained in place four years later. The groups that had opposed the election of an African-American as mayor in 1983 also did so in 1987, and to about the same extent. The groups that supported an African-American as mayor in 1983 supported the same aim in 1987. Chicago remained a city *politically* divided along racial lines because it had been for so long—and still was—divided along racial lines economically and socially. The memories of past battles over integration issues remained alive, cutting across party lines, organizing political blocs, shaping mass reactions, and constraining efforts to enlarge the city's fledgling biracial coalition.

The network of activists and community organizations that had played so vital a role in the drive to register African-American voters and to elect a reform candidate as mayor remained in place during Washington's administration. Indeed, these grassroots community groups came to function as replacements for the Democratic party organization in wards where the party was either hostile or indifferent to the success of Washington's administration. They also benefitted from the mayor's decision to emphasize neighborhood development over large-scale construction projects in the downtown area (Holli & Green, 1989: 140–41). Community development funds, earlier used to underwrite showplace projects in the Loop, were redirected to the neighborhoods, mainly through this standing network of activist organizations. This was one of the major items of contention in the mayor's annual budget battle with his city council opposition. The details and resolution can be followed in local newspaper reports during November and December of each year, when the mayor's budget was presented to the council and debated there.

The community groups once again found themselves on the outside. A long-time Democratic loyalist, Sawyer depended on the party organization, not community groups and their leaders. Besides, Sawyer did not share the reform agenda of the grassroots groups that had labored in behalf of Washington and his administration. As a result, Sawyer's administration reduced the flow of community development funds to the neighborhoods, cutting off community organizations and undermining their vitality. Deprived of funding and functions, these groups played no role in Sawyer's plans for the city or for his own re-election. Since their staffs had been cut and morale lowered, they were less able to perform effectively in any case.

Moreover, the Cokely incident in the spring of 1988 worked to undermine the network of connections that had been built between African-American and white social activists. Steve Cokely had been a city employee since 1985, working for then-Alderman Eugene Sawyer and Alderman Marion Humes (although the latter fired him for denouncing Columbus Day as a "racist" holiday). When Sawyer became acting mayor, Cokely became a mayoral aide whose main activities seemed to focus on defending Sawyer to African Americans who felt he was betraying "the Washington legacy." In any case, Cokely was a self-styled nationalist whose anti-white, anti-Semitic conspiracy theories—including one that Jewish doctors had infected African-American children with AIDS—were reasonably well known in circles both inside and outside City Hall (McCullom, 1988: 3–5,7).

On 1 May the *Chicago Tribune* broke the story of acting Mayor Sawyer's knowledge of Cokely's statements. Many white politicians, including former Alderman Vrdolyak and Alderman Edward Burke, called for Cokely's firing. So did the city's two downtown daily newspapers. Most African-American leaders hesitated. The Reverend B. Herbert Martin, an African American and Sawyer's nominee to head the city's Commission on Human Relations, was even quoted as saying that there was "a ring of truth" in Cokely's remarks and that Cokely should not be fired. (Martin later claimed that he had been misquoted. See McCullom, 1988: 3.)

However, it was Sawyer's action—or, rather, the lack of it—that drew most attention and criticism. After the story first broke, Cokely issued a formal apology, while Sawyer said he was "moving aggressively" on the matter. By 3 May, still unsure of how the African-American community viewed the matter, Sawyer continued to hesitate, saying he had no plans to fire Cokely. On the following day, Sawyer met with Cokely for over two hours, but was unable to convince Cokely to resign or bring himself to fire him. Finally, after news of Martin's alleged remark, and as public pressure continued to mount, on 5 May Sawyer announced his decision to fire Cokely.

Sawyer's initial inaction reflected his lack of a solid constituency, his uncertainly about how major segments of the African-American community would react if he fired Cokely in response to public pressure. His behavior throughout the five-day period projected an image of indecisiveness, an incapacity to act and a willingness to allow himself and the city to become bogged down by what was itself a minor event.

The most important aspect of the incident, however, was its impact on the biracial coalition that had propelled Washington into office. The Cokely affair, and the hesitancy of Sawyer and other African-American spokespersons to respond, strained relations with the Jewish community and with liberal whites more generally. This served to raise doubts, rekindle suspicions, undermine goodwill, and weaken the links that had been built among white and African-American liberal activists.

It is plausible to believe that, had Cokely's actions come to light while Washington was mayor, the mayoral reaction would have been different. Sure of his standing within his own community, Washington could have taken a moral stance, denouncing and firing Cokely without delay. Sawyer, however, lacked Washington's stature and knowledge of his own community, so he delayed, needing time and information to assess the politics of the situation. But in this instance the moral stance was also the politically astute one, since it would have eased tensions with Jewish leaders and prevented further damage to the city's fragile multiethnic coalition.

By the time of the special mayoral elections in 1989, the conditions that had prevailed in 1983, and that had made Washington's election possible, no longer prevailed. Social and political divisions split the African-American community, as reformers battled party regulars. The Sawyer-Evans conflict, while itself only a symptom of these deeper and persisting fissures, projected mixed and conflicting cues to grassroots voters. These worked to dampen enthusiasm and depress turnout. Lacking the widespread and dependable basis of support among African Americans that Washington had enjoyed, both Sawyer and Evans had to work to spark interest and enlist support. Thus, they had no opportunity, even if they had had the inclination and the resources, to repair the damage that had been done in the interim to links with activist groups outside their community.

As his father before him, Richard M. Daley's hold on the mayor's office depends on two factors: high turnout and cohesive support among the city's white ethnics, and continuing internal conflict and low turnout among African-American voters. His interest, objectively speaking, is not in building a biracial coalition, as the city's major media pretend, but in maintaining virtually monolithic white ethnic support and preventing the reemergence of the conditions that made Washington's coalition possible.

References

Alkalimat, Abdul and Doug Gills. 1984. "Black Power vs. Racism: Harold Washington Becomes Mayor." In *The New Black Vote: Politics and Power in Four American Cities*, ed., Rod Bush. San Francisco, Calif.: Synthesis Publications. 68–77.

Browning, Rufus P., Dale Rogers Marshall, and David H. Tabb, eds. 1990. *Racial Politics in American Cities*. New York: Longman.

Cose, Larry and Maudlyne Ihejirika. 1987. "2,500 to 5,000 Stage Rally for Evans, against Sawyer." *Chicago Sun-Times*, (2 December).

Dodd, R. Bruce and Ann Marie Lipinski. 1987. "The Making of the Mayor." *Chicago Tribune*, (6 December).

Holden, John. 1986. "Integrating the Bungalow Belts: Can Guaranteed Home Equity Take the Worry Out of Being Too Close?" *The Reader* (Chicago), (20 March): 3, 36.

Holli, Melvin G. and Paul M. Green. 1989. *Bashing Chicago Traditions: Harold Washington's Last Campaign*. Grand Rapids, Mich.: William B. Eerdmans Publishing Company. 19–26; 158–59.

Hough, Hugh. 1984. "'Ethnic Mistrust' of Mayor Told." *Chicago Sun-Times*, (1 February).

Kleppner, Paul. 1985. *Chicago Divided: The Making of a Black Mayor*. DeKalb: Northern Illinois University Press.

McCullom, Rod. 1988."The Cokely Affair: A Crisis that Didn't Have to Happen." *The Chicago Reporter* 17 (June): 3–5, 7.

Nelson, William E., Jr. and Philip J. Meranto. 1977. *Electing Black Mayors: Political Action in the Black Community*. Columbus: Ohio State University Press.

Rivlin, Gary. 1987. "Seven Wretched Days." *The Chicago Reader,* (25 December): 1; 25–29.

Sonenshein, Raphael J. 1990. "Biracial Coalitions in Big Cities: Why They Succeed, Why They Fail." In Rufus P. Browning, Dale Rogers Marshall, and David H. Tabb, eds., *Racial Politics in American Cities*. New York: Longman. 203.

Ziemba, Stanley. 1983. "Mayor Plans No Housing 'Stampede.'" *Chicago Tribune*, (17 April).

Cases

Ketchum v. Byrne, 740 F2d 1398 (1984)
Ketchum v. City Council of City of Chicago, Ill., 630 F. Supp. 551 (N.D. Ill., 1985)

Notes

1. Regression procedures were applied to precinct-level voting and census data to estimate the proportions of white, African-American, Latino, and "other" VAP for each of the candidates, as well as the proportions not voting in the election. For each group, the appropriate proportions were then applied to the estimated size of its VAP in 1983 to produce the number of votes it cast for each candidate. It is then a simple matter to sum across groups for each candidate and calculate the proportion of the resulting total attributable to each component. For an explanation of the steps involved in the calculation of the regression estimates, see Kleppner, 1985, 267-8; Kleppner and Taylor, 1988 (September); Appendix, 1–15; Kleppner et al., 1990.
2. Using the same criterion, Latinos were "overrepresented" in Washington's voting coalition by 1.2 percentage points and the groups comprising the "other" category (mostly Asians) by 0.2 percentage points.
3. For the procedures used to arrive at these figures, see note 1.
4. Regression equations were used with precinct-level data within each of these ward groups to develop these estimates of crossover rates.
5. Washington received 56.5 percent of the vote from whites who cast ballots in ward 5. However, there were only 11,179 whites of voting age in the ward, which amounted to 24.3 percent of its total VAP.
6. Washington carried wards 1, 15, 22, and 37, whose aldermen voted with the Vrdolyak bloc; and he lost wards 42, 43, 48, and 49, whose aldermen opposed the Vrdolyak group.
7. Stanley Ziemba. 1983. "Mayor Plans No Housing 'Stampede.'" *Chicago Tribune,* (17 April); Hugh Hough. 1984. "'Ethnic Mistrust' of Mayor Told." *Chicago Sun-Times,* (1 February); John Holden. 1986. "Integrating the Bungalow Belts: Can Guaranteed Home Equity Take the Worry Out of Being Too Close?" *The Reader* (Chicago), (20 March): 3, 36; Holli & Green. 1989. *Bashing Chicago's Traditions,* 146. In the 1986 sheriff's contest, African-American voters cast 89.7 percent of their ballots for Elrod, while the city's white voters gave him only 43.2 percent. In the city's white ethnic redoubts, Elrod ran even more poorly, polling only 32.4 percent from whites on the northwest side and 42.8 percent from whites on the southwest side.

Party Sorting at the Local Level in South Carolina

Robert P. Steed
Laurence W. Moreland
Tod A. Baker

The Citadel—The Military College of South Carolina

Introduction

Over the past four decades, southern politics has been substantially transformed. While this transformation has been multifaceted, one of the most obvious and most important components is the development of two-party competition in what was previously the nation's most solidly one-party region. This dramatic change has included the growth of Republican organizations in practically all southern states, increased Republican registration and identification within the southern electorate, a higher number of Republican candidates and contested elections throughout the region, a significant alteration of the Democratic party coalition (especially with the fuller entry of blacks into the political arena), and, especially at the presidential election level, significant increases in Republican votes and electoral victories (with some noticeable improvements for Republican fortunes in down-ticket elections, too) (Havard, 1972; Bartley & Graham, 1975: chaps. 4, 7–8; Seagull, 1975; Bass & DeVries, 1976; Black & Black, 1987: chaps. 11–14; Lamis, 1984: 3–43; Havard, 1986; Stanley, 1986; Steed, Moreland, & Baker, 1986; Brodsky, 1988; Stanley & Castle, 1988; Van Wingen & Valentine, 1988; Steed, 1990; Sturrock, 1990.)

The majority of the research on partisan transformations in the South deals with data on such matters as party switching among voters, split-ticket voting, electoral outcomes and trends, and the effects of migration and generational replacement on voting patterns. (See, for example, Havard, 1972; Seagull, 1975; Bass & DeVries, 1976; Beck, 1977; Campbell, 1977a; Campbell, 1977b; Prysby, 1980; Hadley & Howell, 1980; Beck & Lopatto, 1982; Steed, Moreland, & Baker, 1986; Steed, Moreland, and Baker, 1994; and Carmines &

Stanley, 1990.) Paying attention to the party-in-the-electorate is, of course, important, but an understanding of party change requires drawing attention as well to the other components of the party structure. While analyses of data on southern party activists, most notably state party convention delegates, have demonstrated the utility of exploring partisan realignment within this context (Abramowitz, 1981; Abramowitz, McGlennon, & Rapoport, 1982; Moreland, Steed, & Baker, 1988; Nesbit, 1988; Baker, Hadley, Steed, & Moreland, 1990), there are far fewer studies of party activists than of the electorate. Indeed, almost no efforts have been made to examine southern party change with data on local party officials in the region, which is surprising in light of the widely accepted notion that party activists at the local level are one of the key components of the party organizational apparatus (e.g., Eldersveld, 1964; Sorauf & Beck, 1988: 79–80) and in light of the rather large literature on local party leaders. (See the summary in Bowman, Hulbary, & Kelley, 1990.)

A major exception to this general lack of attention to local party activists as a window to exploring southern party change is the ground-breaking, statewide survey of party precinct officers in Florida conducted in the mid-1980s by Lewis Bowman, William Hulbary, and Anne Kelley. In particular, their analysis of party sorting—a two-way movement of party activists between the parties in an effort "to reduce ideological and personal dissonances by reassessing where they belong politically"—demonstrates that Florida's two major parties' local organizations have undergone a substantial coalitional realignment in recent years (Bowman, Hulbary, & Kelley, 1990). They show that party switchers in Florida have tended strongly to move into the party that is most congruent ideologically with their personal preferences. This, in turn, makes the two parties more distinctive and more capable of offering voters in the state more clear-cut, policy-relevant political choices. Moreover, this party sorting has moved the Florida party system more in line with the national party system.

This analysis is limited to one state, and Bowman and his coauthors make no claim that the state is representative of other southern states, but it is suggestive of similar changes which may be occurring in other parts of the region as well. It is also consistent with Charles Prysby's conclusions on party switchers among delegates to state party conventions in six southern states in 1984 (Prysby, 1990). A finding that the patterns of party sorting among Florida's local party officials are present in other southern states, as Prysby's broader analysis suggests, would do much to clarify the nature of party change in the region and would complement nicely the wealth of data coming from public opinion surveys and electoral studies.

This chapter seeks to build on the work of Bowman and his colleagues by examining similar data gathered through a survey of party precinct officers in South Carolina. To facilitate comparisons between the two states, the discussion will be organized according to the framework utilized in their analysis of party sorting in Florida. This will enable us to expand that analysis to include a Deep South state which differs from Florida socially, demographically, culturally, and politically. Of course, Florida is not a typical southern state, and Bowman, Hulbary, and Kelly make no claim that it is; the conclusions suggested in their research may, indeed, be unique to that state. However, if we find similar patterns of party change in another, quite different state, our confidence in generalizing from those findings will be strengthened, and our understanding of the southern party system will be improved. If the patterns in the two states are significantly different, we shall have a better perspective on the limits of each case study as an indicator of southern party change.

While no claim is made that South Carolina is any more typical of other southern states than Florida, its recent political history demonstrates a number of the general patterns found in the region. Up to the end of World War II, South Carolina clearly demonstrated the political characteristics associated with V. O. Key's description of the traditional southern political system: one-party politics, low voter turnout, a high percentage of blacks in the population (but not in the electorate), white demagogues willing to utilize the race issue for their benefit, and malapportioned state legislatures (Key, 1949). The Republican party was virtually nonexistent as Democrats controlled the state's electoral system at all levels.

In the years since the end of World War II, however, South Carolina politics, along with the politics of the other states in the region, changed dramatically (Moreland, Steed, & Baker, 1983; Fowler, 1966; Moore, 1983; Moreland, Steed, & Baker, 1986.) The economic and social changes associated with increased urbanization, economic development, the pressures of the civil rights movement, and population diversification resulting from people moving into the state were accompanied by a decline in racist rhetoric on the part of candidates and public officials, an enlarged and eventually integrated electorate, a reduction of the political influence of rural areas, and an increasingly competitive two-party political system. As early as the presidential elections of 1952 and 1956, the Democratic vote diminished, and by the mid 1960s the Republican party had established itself as a political force in the state which could no longer be ignored, especially at the level of presidential elections. Since 1964 the Republicans have come to dominate the state's presidential politics, winning six of the seven elections held during this period, and they have shown increasing strength in state and local politics as well. Highly publicized defections of former Democrats such as Senator Strom Thurmond in 1964, efforts to build a state party organization, and success in recruiting more attractive candidates all contributed to changing the competitive status of the party. While the Democratic party is still dominant at the state and local levels, holding clear majorities in both houses of the state legislature and in local offices, the Republican party is no longer a doormat. Currently, the governor, the senior senator, and one-half of the state's congressional delegation, along with a scattering of other state and local officials, are Republicans.

Arguably the most significant change has come in the increased involvement of African-Americans in the state's electoral and party systems. This has been especially important in the Democratic party, where blacks have come to hold a number of official party positions and on occasion (e.g., 1988) have constituted a majority of the delegates at the state party convention.

Some organizational changes have paralleled this electoral change. Gone are the days when neither party had much more than a skeletal organization—the Democrats, because they did not need effective and active organization to retain control of South Carolina's political system and the Republicans, because their numbing electoral weakness made organizational effort meaningless. At least on paper, both parties now have tangible organizations. State headquarters have been established, each with an executive director, and they are operable on a continuing basis, not just during the weeks around a major election. Both parties regularly organize county committees throughout the state, and all counties have at least limited precinct organizations. Precinct organizational meetings are coordinated by the state parties, and efforts are made to maintain up-to-date records of such meetings (although in reality these efforts have resulted in only spotty success).

Of course, the existence of a paper organization is not a guarantee of an active or effective party apparatus. It is further evidence, however, of the partisan change that has taken place in the Palmetto State, and it is against this background of recent partisan change that our data on party precinct officials should be understood.

The Study

The data utilized in this paper are from a survey of Democratic and Republican party precinct officials in South Carolina. Three waves of questionnaires, essentially identical to the questionnaire used by Bowman, Hulbary, and Kelley in their Florida precinct officials survey, were mailed to a sample of precinct officers drawn at random from master lists supplied by the parties' state headquarters. The sample was drawn on a county-by-county basis through a skip-interval technique, which alternately selected either the precinct president or the precinct executive committee-person from every fourth organized party precinct. Since the Democrats had more organized precincts than the Republicans, the Democratic sample was larger ($N = 563$) than the Republican sample ($N = 467$). Although the survey was conducted during the summer and fall of 1986, the lists were of people holding their official positions during 1984. While many thus selected as part of the sample were no longer party officials at the time of the survey (inasmuch as the 1986 precinct reorganizations had already taken place and the lists of officers changed accordingly), we decided to use the 1984 lists so that the South Carolina data could ultimately be merged with the Florida data, or at least be used to build on the Florida data along the lines of this paper; therefore, we urged the respondents to complete the questionnaire even if they were no longer a party officer at the time of the survey. This undoubtedly reduced the response rate, but we felt that the cost in a lower response rate would be more than offset by the opportunity to combine the datasets from the two states. Even under these conditions, the response rate for the Republican officials was 51 percent and the response rate for the Democratic officials was 41 percent. These return rates represent 231 completed questionnaires for the Democrats and 239 completed questionnaires for the Republicans.

Two basic sources of changes in party support levels and in the composition of party coalitions in the South can be identified. First, change may occur as new voters and new political activists enter the electorate as a result of recent enfranchisement, movement into the region, or young people reaching voting age (Black & Black, 1987: chap. 11; Beck, 1977; Campbell, 1977b;

Prysby, 1990). Second, change may occur as a result of conversion or switching party loyalties, the process that Bowman, Hulbary, and Kelley label party sorting. In the analysis that follows, we shall concentrate on conversion among precinct officers as an agent of southern party change. The discussion is guided by such basic questions as: What is the nature of party sorting in South Carolina? How much party sorting has recently occurred at the grassroots level in the state? What are the variations in the backgrounds, ideologies, and issue positions of those who have switched parties and those who have not? Finally, what are the larger implications of these data for the future of the southern party system?

Findings

Stability and change. Following the categorizations used by Bowman, Hulbary, and Kelley, we are interested in comparing Democrats and Republicans, subdividing each party into stable partisans (those who have always been affiliated with their present party) and party changers (those who have switched their party affiliations in the past).

Slightly over one-tenth of the South Carolina precinct officers surveyed report they have changed party affiliation. (See table 1.) While this proportion is lower than that in Florida, where over 20 percent of the precinct officers are party changers, it is distributed between the parties in roughly the same way with Republicans picking up converts at a slightly better than 2:1 ratio over the Democrats (70 percent to 30 percent). Among Republicans, 19 percent indicate former affiliation with the Democratic party, a rather sharp contrast with the approximately 8 percent of former Republicans in the Democratic ranks. Even though the total number of party changers is fairly small,

Table 1
Stable Partisans and Party-changers Among South Carolina
Grass Roots Party Officials in 1984

	Percent of subgroup	Percent sample	N
Stable partisans*			
Stable Democrats (always Democrat)	52	45	213
Stable Republicans (always Republican)	48	42	196
Subtotal—Stable partisans	100	87	409
Party-changers**			
Former Republicans (now Democrats)	30	4	18
Former Democrats (now Republicans)	70	9	43
Subtotal—Party-changers	100	13	61
Total Sample	100		470

*Those who report never having previously "been affiliated" with any other political party; they were always either Democrats or Republicans, whichever they are now.
**Change constitutes reporting having previously "been affiliated" with the major party opposite to their current affiliation.
Source: South Carolina Precinct Committeepersons Survey, 1986.

Table 2
Profile of Stable Partisans and Party Changers: Social and Demographic Characteristics (in percent)

	Democrats Stable Demo.	Democrats Former Repub.	Republicans Former Demo.	Republicans Stable Repub.	Total
Age (in years)					
Younger (18–39)	23	44	9	27	24
Middle-aged (40–59)	38	33	49	40	40
Older (60 and above)	38	22	42	33	36
(N)	(205)	(18)	(43)	(188)	(454)
Race					
White	88	100	98	98	94
Black	12	0	2	2	6
(N)	(197)	(17)	(43)	(180)	(437)
Gender					
Female	29	22	26	30	29
Male	71	78	74	70	71
(N)	(198)	(18)	(43)	(183)	(442)
Religion					
Protestant	92	89	93	94	93
Catholic	4	6	5	4	4
Jewish	0	0	0	0	0
Other	4	6	2	2	3
(N)	(202)	(18)	(41)	(186)	(447)
Education completed					
Grade school	4	0	2	1	2
High school	30	0	14	15	21
Some college	20	33	30	27	25
College (Bachelor)	16	17	30	28	22
Graduate Degree	30	50	23	29	30
(N)	(203)	(18)	(43)	(188)	(452)
Family income					
Less than $25,000	31	28	21	27	26
$25,000–$39,999	34	50	42	28	34
$40,000 and above	35	22	37	45	39
(N)	(191)	(18)	(38)	(180)	(427)
Occupation					
Professional/technical	24	33	28	22	24
Manager/administrator	6	11	0	2	4
Sales	7	6	5	8	7
Clerical	10	11	14	27	17
Blue-collar	17	28	9	7	13
Service	5	0	2	2	3
Retired					
labor force	32	11	42	32	32
(N)	(205)	(18)	(43)	(188)	(454)

Source: South Carolina Precinct Committeepersons Survey, 1986.

they are sufficiently numerous, especially within the local Republican organizations, to constitute an important potential source of change among local party activists in South Carolina.

The backgrounds of stable partisans and party changers. The growth of Republicanism in the South has been connected in large part with that party's association with relatively conservative ideological and issue orientations. Black and Black (1987), Carmines and Stanley (1990), Green and Guth (1990), Baker, Steed, and Moreland (1982), Steed, Moreland, and Baker (1990), and numerous others have demonstrated this connection from a variety of perspectives. In light of this, a reasonable expectation is that the parties are likely to have different appeals to different social groups. For example, we could expect the Republican party in South Carolina to be more appealing to such groups as whites, males, business and professional groups, and suburbanites than the Democratic party; such groups would be expected to be more heavily represented among former Democrats turned Republican as well.

These expectations are only partially supported by the data reported in table 2. A comparison of party switchers reveals that former Democrats and former Republicans are virtually undifferentiated with regard to race (almost all of each group are white), gender (similar majorities are male), and religion (all are overwhelmingly Protestant). The key differences are on age, education, and income. The former Republicans are considerably younger in the aggregate than the former Democrats, they are somewhat better educated, and they tend to be slightly less affluent, a condition probably related to their youth. There are also some differences in the patterns of occupations of the two groups of party changers with the former Republicans having higher proportions of managers, administrators, and blue collar workers and the former Democrats having a significantly higher proportion of retirees (the other occupation categories reveal few interparty differences among the party switchers).

Not only do the party changers differ in some respects from each other, they also differ in a number of ways from the stable partisans in the parties to which they have switched. For example, the former Republicans, in addition to being considerably younger than the former Democrats, are also somewhat younger as a group than the stable Democrats; thus, they constitute an infusion of younger blood into the ranks of local Democratic officers in the state (although this is tempered by their small numbers). Conversely, the former Democrats contribute toward increasing the overall age of local Republican activists in South Carolina. Similarly, with regard to occupation, the newcomers in each party differ from their fellow activists. For the Republicans, the major variations are that the party switchers are somewhat more likely to be employed in professional/technical jobs, less likely to be clerical workers, and more likely to be retired. Among local Democratic officials, larger percentages of the party changers are in the professional/technical, manager/administrator, and blue collar categories, and a much smaller percentage are retired. While the two groups of Republicans demonstrate almost no differences on the other background variables in table 2, the Democrats demonstrate a bit more heterogeneity; in comparison with the stable Democrats, the former Republicans are somewhat more likely to be white, male, well educated, and less affluent.

Table 3
Profile of Stable Partisans and Party Changers by Residential Characteristics
(in percent)

	Democrats Stable Demo.	Democrats Former Repub.	Republicans Former Demo.	Republicans Stable Repub.	Total
Length of time lived in county					
1–15 years	18	11	28	42	29
16–25 years	12	33	26	21	18
26 years or more	70	56	46	37	53
(N)	(205)	(18)	(43)	(188)	(454)
Where respondent grew up					
Solid South*	89	100	77	67	79
(South Carolina)	(80)	(89)	(63)	(46)	(65)
(Other South)	(9)	(11)	(14)	(21)	(14)
Non-South	11	0	23	33	21
(N)	(205)	(18)	(43)	(188)	(454)

*Border states are included in Non-South region, not in the Solid South.
Source: South Carolina Precinct Committeepersons Survey, 1986.

Local officials in both parties tend to be relatively long-term residents of their present home counties; majorities of each aggregate have lived there for at least fifteen years. (See table 3.) However, larger percentages of each group of Republicans have moved into their home counties within the past fifteen years than either group of Democrats. Not only are the Republicans relative residential newcomers, the stable Republicans are more likely to be newcomers than the former Democrats who have switched to the Republican party. Similarly, within the Democratic party the stable Democrats are slightly more likely to have moved into their current home counties within the past fifteen years than the former Republicans.

The Republicans are also more likely than the Democrats to have grown up outside the South, although a clear majority are natives of the region. (See table 3.) Among party switchers, the Democrats are more likely than the Republicans to be from the South in general (100 percent to 77 percent) and from South Carolina in particular (89 percent to 63 percent). These former Republicans are also a bit more likely to be southern and South Carolinian than the stable Democrats, although these differences are not as large as the interparty ones. The data on the Republicans is even more interesting, suggesting as it does that the South Carolina Republican party has begun to attract more long-time southerners and more native South Carolinians; whereas less than half of the stable Republicans are from South Carolina (underscoring the importance of population movement into the state as a factor contributing to the development of the party), almost two-thirds of the former Democrats are from South Carolina. When this is coupled with the first set of data in table 3 showing former Democrats to be generally longer-term residents in their current home counties, there is some indication that the Republican party's recent organizational development is based increasingly on its appeal to South Carolinians. While this may be offset slightly by the existence of a similar pattern among the two groups of Democrats, that pattern is not so pronounced inasmuch as the stable Democrats are overwhelmingly southerners from South Carolina; in short, the Democrats who switched from the Republican party do not change the past residential composition of the local party organizations in nearly the same way as the Republicans who switched from the Democratic party.

Political ideology and issues. Other studies of political activists in the South have demonstrated that one of the clearest indications of partisan realignment in the region is the evidence that the two parties are attracting people with sharply contrasting ideological and issue positions (Moreland, Steed, & Baker, 1988; Green & Guth, 1990; Moreland, 1990; Abramowitz, McGlennon, & Rapoport, 1982.) Mirroring similar patterns emerging within the electorate (e.g., Carmines & Stanley, 1990; Black & Black, 1987), Bowman and his colleagues (1990) found strong evidence of this type of policy-oriented sorting taking place among Florida's local party precinct officials. It is not at all surprising, then, that the data on South Carolina party precinct officers show the same general pattern.

As indicated in table 4, which reports responses on an ideological self-placement scale, Republican activists are considerably more conservative than Democratic activists. Approximately nine-tenths of each group of Republicans identify themselves in this manner as compared to less than half of the Democrats. The Democrats, on the other hand, are much more likely to call themselves moderates or liberals; roughly one-third of the Democrats place themselves in the liberal category as compared to only about 5 percent of the Republicans.

Among the Democrats, the party switchers are a more conservative group than the stable Democrats (50 percent to 32 percent), but they are much less conservative than Republicans in the state. Not only have the former Republicans switched to a party with which they are more ideologically in tune, so have the former Democrats who have switched to the Republican party. Indeed, for the Republicans, the party switchers are virtually identi-

Table 4
Profile of Stable Partisans and Party Changers by Self-Identified Ideology
(in percent)

Ideology	Democrats Stable Demo.	Democrats Former Repub.	Republicans Former Demo.	Republicans Stable Repub.	Total
Very liberal	6	6	5	1	4
Liberal	27	22	0	1	13
Moderate	35	22	5	9	21
Conservative	27	33	71	52	42
Very conservative	5	17	20	37	20
(N)	(194)	(18)	(41)	(182)	(435)

Source: South Carolina Precinct Committeepersons Survey, 1984.

cal to the stable Republicans in their highly conservative aggregate ideological orientations.

The ideological polarization of the two parties suggested in table 4 is further supported by the pattern of responses on a series of specific issues reported in table 5. On each of the fifteen issues listed, the Republican activists are significantly more conservative than the Democratic activists, as they tend generally to favor efforts to limit government economic regulation while supporting government policies to strengthen the military, stop abortion, and balance the budget. In fact, the only issue with less than a 10 percent gap between the parties concerns support for an amendment to prohibit abor-

Table 5
Stable Partisans and Party Changers by Views on Issues:
Percent Favoring or Strongly Favoring Each Issue

Issues	Democrats Stable Demo.	Democrats Former Repub.	Republicans Former Demo.	Republicans Stable Repub.	Total
Social Welfare					
Cuts in domestic spending	55	57	93	96	76
Support national health insurance	58	56	19	20	38
Govt. aid to help unemployment	57	56	14	15	34
Govt. job guarantees	58	67	15	27	41
Federal aid to education	42	50	7	10	25
Govt. aid for low-cost health care	74	78	28	30	51
Social/Religious Issues					
Affirmative action	67	59	25	25	45
Antiabortion amend.	48	50	56	56	52
ERA	79	61	35	26	52
Cons. Rel. Organs.	25	39	55	65	45
Government Intervention					
Rapid development of nuclear power	36	50	72	77	57
Leave electric power to private sector	54	44	86	83	69
Foreign Policy					
Defense spending increase	34	44	83	82	60
Military intervention in Lebanon	35	44	83	85	61
Domestic Budget					
Amend. to balance national budget	69	76	90	92	81

Source: South Carolina Precinct Committeeperson Survey, 1986.

tion except when the mother's life is in danger; almost all the other issues have gaps exceeding 30 percent! As with general ideological self-placement, the two groups of Republicans are much closer across these issues than the two groups of Democrats, but in each party the partisan switchers have moved in a direction which brings their issue positions closer to their fellow precinct officers. This is especially true for the Republicans, both groups of which display very similar views on practically all issues listed; on only three issues—government job guarantees, the Equal Rights Amendment, and feelings toward conservative religious organizations—do the aggregate differences approach as much as 10 percent. While the Democrats are less homogeneous, the former Republicans' issue positions are generally more compatible with the stable Democrats than with the Republicans. On five issues, the differences between the two groups of Democrats are 10 percent or more (reaching as much as 18 percent on the ERA), with the former Republicans being more conservative than the stable Democrats on four of these issues. In short, there is clear evidence of party sorting on ideologies and issues at the local level in South Carolina. Those precinct officials who have switched parties have moved to reduce dissonance and, in the process, have contributed to the continuing transformation of the state's party system.

Conclusion

The composite profile presented in table 6 provides a summary that illustrates the nature of partisan transformation among South Carolina precinct activists. Although the data do not differ on all points considered, they do suggest that a process of party sorting at the local level is taking place in the state.

The most revealing information on socioeconomic backgrounds relates to the increased attraction of the Republican party in South Carolina to older Democrats who have lived in the state for fairly long periods of time and who are more likely than the stable Republicans to be from South Carolina (or from the South in general). This indicates that the Republican party is relying less than before on in-migrants who brought their partisanship with them upon moving to the South and on younger voters who have recently become active. To the extent that this continues or becomes more widespread, the southern Republican party's development will be accelerated, freed as it would be from the limits of growth dependent on population movement into the region and/or on generational replacement.

The most interesting and indisputable evidence of party sorting among South Carolina's precinct officials is, of course, the data on ideology and issues. The recent division of the southern party system into a conservative Republican party and a moderate/liberal Democratic party is demonstrated clearly and consistently in these data. Moreover, not only are the parties' activists sharply differentiated on both their ideologies and their issue positions, those switching parties have consistently moved in directions compatible with their perspectives, thus reinforcing and sharpening these partisan divisions.

While the particulars differ in some ways, these findings are quite consistent with the conclusions of Bowman, Hulbary, and Kelley (1990) in their

Table 6
Composite Profile of Stable Partisans and Party Changers

Characteristics	Democrats Stable Demo.	Democrats Former Repub.	Republicans Former Demo.	Republicans Stable Repub.
Social background				
Age	mid-age	younger	oldest	mid-age
Race	white (12% black, 9/10 of blacks)	white	white	white
Gender	males greatly overrepresented	males greatly overrepresented	males greatly overrepresented	males greatly overrepresented
Religion	Protestant	Protestant	Protestant	Protestant
SES background				
Education	relatively low/medium	highest	medium	medium
Income	medium to high	medium	medium	high (almost 1/2 $40,000+)
Occupation	prof./tech, blue-collar and high retired	high prof./tech and high blue-collar	high prof.tech and high retired	high retired, clerical and prof.tech
Residential				
Length of time in county	longest	long	medium	shortest
Where "grew up" in U.S. disproportionately from:	S.C. and the South	S.C. and the South	S.C. and the South	the South and S.C.
Ideology and Issues				
Ideological self-id	most liberal	moderate to liberal	very conservative	very conservative
Views on issues:				
Social welfare	slightly liberal	slightly liberal	very conservative	very conservative
Social issues	liberal	slightly liberal	conservative	conservative
Government	moderate intervention	moderate (mixed)	very conservative	very conservative
Domestic budget	conservative	conservative	very conservative	very conservative
Foreign policy	liberal	slightly liberal	very conservative	very conservative

Source: South Carolina Precinct Committeeperson Survey, 1986.

research on local party officials in Florida; of Abramowitz (1981) in his study of county party chairs in the South; of Moreland (1990), Steed, Moreland, and Baker (1990), and Prysby (1990) in their respective examinations of state convention delegates in the South; and of Abramowitz, McGlennon, and Rapoport (1982) in their research on state convention delegates in Virginia. They show that the development of two-party electoral competition in South Carolina (and in the South) is being accompanied by parallel developments within the ranks of party activists at various levels in the party organizational structure. Furthermore, and perhaps more significantly, the data on local party officials in Florida and South Carolina suggest that an end to the traditional southern Republican electoral weakness below the presidential level may come sooner than many expect. The historical problems of developing strong tickets and voter support in state and local elections (Black & Black, 1987: chap. 13; Bullock, 1988; Duncan, 1989; Scher & Heyman, 1988; Sutton, 1990; Sturrock, 1990) may be alleviated by the type of party sorting at the local level that is taking place, at least in two rather different southern states. Indeed, the existence of such similar patterns of party sorting in two quite different states, combined with the conclusions of other recent studies of other party activists in various parts of the South, suggests strongly that these patterns are not strictly casebound.

Party sorting among local party activists, combined with changes related to greater involvement of blacks and in-migrants into the region, can be expected to facilitate a more policy-relevant politics for down-ticket elections. In the same way that presidential contests in the South took on new meaning (with radically different outcomes) as southern voters came to see identifiable differences between the national parties, we can speculate that state and local elections in the region will also be affected as the parties become more clearly different at those levels. While such a partisan differentiation depends on the actions of many in addition to party officials, and indeed may be muted intentionally by candidates (especially Democratic ones), who see the path to victory to be in the "political straddle" (Black & Black, 1987), the contribution of precinct activists to such a development should not be discounted.

References

Abramowitz, Alan I. "Party Leadership, Realignment, and the Nationalization of Southern Politics." Paper presented at the 1981 Annual Meeting of the Southern Political Science Association, Memphis, Tennessee.

Abramowitz, Alan I., John McGlennon, and Ronald Rapoport. 1982. "Presidential Activists and the Nationalization of Party Politics in Virginia." In *Contemporary Southern Political Attitudes and Behavior*, ed., Laurence W. Moreland, Tod A. Baker, and Robert P. Steed. New York: Praeger.

Baker, Tod A., Charles D. Hadley, Robert P. Steed, and Laurence W. Moreland. 1990. *Political Parties in the Southern States: Party Activists and Party Coalitions*. New York: Praeger.

Baker, Tod A., Robert P. Steed, and Laurence W. Moreland. 1982. "Southern Distinctiveness and the Emergence of Party Competition: The Case of a Deep South State." In *Contemporary Southern Political Attitudes and Behavior*, ed., Laurence W. Moreland, Tod A. Baker, and Robert P. Steed. New York: Praeger.

Bartley, Numan V., and Hugh D. Graham. 1975. *Southern Politics and the Second Reconstruction*. Baltimore, Md.: Johns Hopkins University Press.

Bass, Jack, and Walter DeVries. 1976. *The Transformation of Southern Politics: Social Change and Political Consequence Since 1945*. New York: Basic Books.

Beck, Paul Allen. 1977. "Partisan Dealignment in the Postwar South." *American Political Science Review*, 71: 477–96.

Beck, Paul Allen, and Paul Lopatto. 1982. "The End of Southern Distinctiveness." In *Contemporary Southern Political Attitudes and Behavior*, ed., Laurence W. Moreland, Tod A. Baker, and Robert P. Steed. New York: Praeger.

Black, Earl, and Merle Black. 1987. *Politics and Society in the South*. Cambridge, Mass.: Harvard University Press.

Bowman, Lewis, William E. Hulbary, and Anne E. Kelley. 1990. "Party Sorting at the Grass Roots: Stable Partisans and Party-Changers Among Florida's Precinct Officials." In *The Disappearing South? Studies in Reqional Change and Continuity*, ed., Robert P. Steed, Laurence W. Moreland, and Tod A. Baker. Tuscaloosa: University of Alabama Press.

Brodsky, David M. 1988. "The Dynamics of Recent Southern Politics." In *The South's New Politics: Realignment and Dealignment*, ed., Robert H. Swansbrough and David M. Brodsky. Columbia: University of South Carolina Press.

Bullock, Charles S., III. 1988. "Creeping Realignment in the South." In *The South's New Politics: Realignment and Dealignment*, ed., Robert H. Swansbrough and David M. Brodsky. Columbia: University of South Carolina Press.

Campbell, Bruce A. 1977a. "Change in the Southern Electorate." *American Journal of Political Science*, 21: 37–64.

———. 1977b. "Patterns of Change in the Partisan Loyalties of Native Southerners, 1952–1972." *Journal of Politics*, 39: 730–61.

Carmines, Edward G., and Harold W. Stanley. 1990. "Ideological Realignment in the Contemporary South: Where Have All the Conservatives Gone?" In *The Disappearing South? Studies in Regional Change and Continuity*, ed., Robert P. Steed, Laurence W. Moreland, and Tod A. Baker. Tuscaloosa: University of Alabama Press.

Duncan, Phil. 1989. "For GOP Down South, Challenges Remain." *Congressional Quarterly Weekly Report*, 47: 2522.

Eldersveld, Samuel J. 1964. *Political Parties: A Behavioral Analysis*. Chicago, Ill.: Rand McNally.

Fowler, Donald L. 1966. *Presidential Voting in South Carolina, 1948–1964*. Columbia: Bureau of Governmental Research and Service, University of South Carolina.

Green, John C., and James L. Guth. 1990. "The Transformation of Southern Political Elites: Regionalism among Party and PAC Contributors." In *The Disappearing South? Studies in Regional Change and Continuity*, ed., Robert P. Steed, Laurence W. Moreland, and Tod A. Baker. Tuscaloosa: University of Alabama Press.

Hadley, Charles D., and Susan E. Howell. 1980. "The Southern Split Ticket Voter, 1952–76: Republican Conversion or Democratic Decline?" In *Party Politics in the South*, ed., Robert P. Steed, Laurence W. Moreland, and Tod A. Baker. New York: Praeger.

Havard, William C. 1986. "Southern Politics: A Prelude to Presidential Politics in 1984." In *The 1984 Presidential Election in the South: Patterns of Southern Party Politics*, ed., Robert P. Steed, Laurence W. Moreland, and Tod A. Baker. New York: Praeger.

———. 1972. *The Changing Politics of the South*. Baton Rouge: Louisiana State University Press.

Key, V. O., Jr. 1949. *Southern Politics in State and Nation*. New York: Alfred A. Knopf.

Lamis, Alexander P. 1984. *The Two-Party South*. New York: Oxford University Press.

Moore, William V. 1983. "Parties and Electoral Politics in South Carolina." In *Government in the Palmetto State*, ed., Luther F. Carter and David S. Mann. Columbia: Bureau of Government Research and Service, University of South Carolina.

Moreland, Laurence W. 1990. "The Impact of Immigration on the Composition of Party Coalitions." In *Political Parties in the Southern States: Party Activists in Partisan Coalitions*, ed., Tod A. Baker, Charles D. Hadley, Robert P. Steed, and Laurence W. Moreland. New York: Praeger.

Moreland, Laurence W., Robert P. Steed, and Tod A. Baker. 1988. "Ideology, Issues, and Realignment Among Southern Party Activists." In *The South's New Politics: Realignment and Dealignment*, ed., Robert H. Swansbrough and David M. Brodsky. Columbia: University of South Carolina Press.

_____. 1986. "South Carolina." In *The 1984 Presidential Election in the South: Patterns of Southern Party Politics*, ed., Robert P. Steed, Laurence W. Moreland, and Tod A. Baker. New York: Praeger.

_____. 1983. "Regionalism in South Carolina Politics." In *Government in the Palmetto State*, ed., Luther F. Carter and David S. Mann. Columbia: Bureau of Government Research and Service, University of South Carolina.

Nesbit, Dorothy Davidson. 1988. "Changing Partisanship Among Southern Party Activists." *Journal of Politics*, 50: 322–34.

Prysby, Charles L. 1990. "Realignment Among Southern Political Party Activists." In *Political Parties in the Southern States: Party Activists and Party Coalitions*, ed., Tod A. Baker, Charles D. Hadley, Robert P. Steed, and Laurence W. Moreland. New York: Praeger.

_____. 1980. "Electoral Behavior in the U.S. South: Recent and Emerging Trends." In *Party Politics in the South*, ed., Robert P. Steed, Laurence W. Moreland, and Tod A. Baker. New York: Praeger.

Scher, Richard, and Warren Heyman. "The Limits of Southern Republicanism." Paper presented at the Sixth Citadel Symposium on Southern Politics, March 13, 1988, Charleston, South Carolina.

Seagull, Louis M. 1975. *Southern Republicanism*. New York: John Wiley & Sons.

Sorauf, Frank J., and Paul Allen Beck. 1988. *Party Politics in America*, 6th ed. Glenview, Ill.: Scott, Foresman/Little Brown.

Stanley, Harold W. 1986. "The 1984 Presidential Election in the South: Race and Realignment." In *The 1984 Presidential Election in the South: Patterns of Southern Party Politics*, ed., Robert P. Steed, Laurence W. Moreland, and Tod A. Baker. New York: Praeger.

Stanley, Harold W., and David S. Castle. 1988. "Partisan Changes in the South: Making Sense of Scholarly Dissonance." In *The South's New Politics: Realignment and Dealignment*, ed., Robert H. Swansbrough and David M. Brodsky. Columbia: University of South Carolina Press.

Steed, Robert P. 1990. "Party Reform, the Nationalization of American Politics, and Party Change in the South." In *Political Parties in the Southern States: Party Activists in Party Coalitions*, ed., Tod A. Baker, Charles D. Hadley, Robert P. Steed, and Laurence W. Moreland. New York: Praeger.

Steed, Robert P., Laurence W. Moreland, and Tod A. Baker. 1990. "Searching for the Mind of the South in the Second Reconstruction." In *The Disappearing South? Studies in Regional Change and Continuity*, ed., Robert P. Steed, Laurence W. Moreland, and Tod A. Baker. Tuscaloosa: University of Alabama Press.

_____, eds. 1986. *The 1984 Presidential Election in the South: Patterns of Southern Party Politics*. New York: Praeger.

_____, eds. 1994. *The 1992 Presidential Election in the South: Current Patterns of Southern Party and Electoral Politics*. Westport, Conn.: Praeger.

Sturrock, David E. "The Quiet Frontier: Recent Developments in Southern Down-Ticket Politics." Paper presented at the Seventh Citadel Symposium on Southern Politics, March 8, 1990 Charleston, South Carolina.

Sutton, David. 1990. "The Contemporary Electoral Order in American Politics and the Fate of the GOP in Dixie." Paper presented at the Seventh Citadel Symposium on Southern Politics, March 8, 1990, Charleston, South Carolina.

Van Wingen, John, and David Valentine. 1988. "Partisan Politics: A One-and-a-Half, No-Party Politics." In *Contemporary Southern Politics*, ed., James F. Lea. Baton Rouge: Louisiana State University Press.

Boston's Mandela Referendum: Urban Nationalism and Economic Dependence

Nancy Haggard-Gilson

University of San Diego

In 1986 and again in the fall of 1988, portions of Boston's electorate were asked to vote on a referendum proposing municipal incorporation of the city's black neighborhoods into a new entity called Mandela. The Mandela Referendum was a radical, "urban nationalist" solution to Boston's longstanding racial problems. The new city of Mandela, intentionally tied to the anti-apartheid movement by its name, was to be carved from seven neighborhoods, the largest section of which is known as Greater Roxbury. Proponents drew the boundaries of Mandela by demarcating those precincts that showed at least 50 percent voter support for Mel King, the black candidate in the 1983 mayoral election. In all, Mandela would have taken 12.5 square miles and 22 percent of Boston's population, including 95 percent of its black residents (see map). The Mandela area has a total population of 150,000, of whom 74 percent are black, 16 percent are white, and 10 percent are Hispanic, Asian, or other. Despite this multiethnic, multiracial makeup, however, both supporters and opponents spoke of Mandela as a black city, an opportunity to achieve black empowerment and autonomy through home rule.

In 1986, the referendum was placed on ballots in both the Mandela area as well as neighborhoods with contiguous boundaries, appearing in 141 of Boston's 252 precincts. The inclusion of voters outside the proposed new city meant that over one-half of those deciding on the issue were white. Given Boston's past history with racial politics, many believed that the referendum could very well carry on the strength of racist votes favoring separatism and segregation. Such was not the case. In this first outing, the referendum was defeated 57 percent to 20 percent, with a 23 percent abstention rate in a remarkably uniform vote across all precincts. (See table 1.)

In the fall of 1988, Mandela was again on the ballot, this time in 97 precincts. It was defeated with a 40 percent negative vote, 22 percent affirmative, and 37 percent abstention rate. It won eight precincts, but these successes were less the result of increased interest in municipal incorporation than the

Proposed Boundaries of Mandela

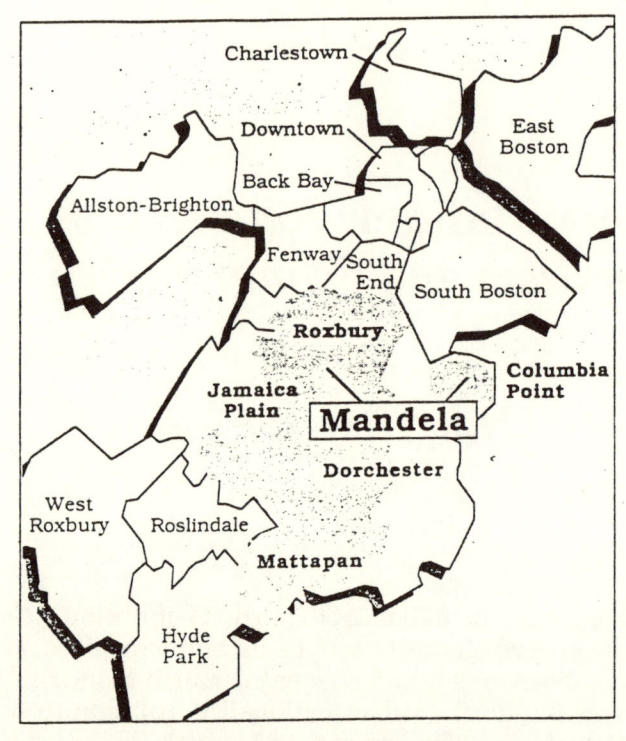

Source: Andrew Jones, Greater Roxbury Incorporation Project

result of a 1987 redistricting that replaced split districts with racially homogeneous ones. When the vote is compared with that of 1986, either overall or by pairing the outcome in particular neighborhoods, the opposition was relatively constant across both elections.

The fight over the Mandela initiative is interesting because it raises a number of questions about the state and concerns of black urban politics in the United States. The ballot initiative provided the opportunity to debate the circumstances under which racial and ethnic minorities choose to establish political autonomy. It is a widely shared idea that political control is the necessary first step to solving the economic problems of poor communities in metropolitan areas, whether or not they are in the majority. "The hope" is, as Orfield and Ashkinaze have said in reference to Atlanta, "that black political and educational leaders would be able to make large moves toward racial equality simply by devising policies and practices reflecting their understanding of the background and needs of black people" (1991: 14). The same sentiments have been voiced in election campaigns in Detroit, Washington, D.C., Newark, Philadelphia, and Chicago. In cities in which a black mayor is not likely, such as Boston or East Palo Alto, California (the other recent attempt at secession), the alternative is incorporation as an independent municipality. The vote against the Mandela initiative goes against the grain of this conventional wisdom. This paper attempts to explain this outcome.

Table 1
Vote for the Mandela Referendum by Neighborhood, 1986

Neighborhood	Percentage of Precincts Voting*		Racial Composition of Neighborhood			Vote (%)		
			White	Black	Other	Yes	No	Blank
Central	100%	(9/9)	78%	1%	21%	19%	51%	30%
Back Bay/ Beacon Hill	12.5	(1/8)	94	1	5	20	50	30
South End	100	(9/9)	40	25	35	22	55	23
Fenway/ Kenmore	80	(8/10)	65	34	1	20	57	23
So. Boston	12.5	(2/16)	96	0	4	22	41	37
Roxbury	100	(25/25)	8	78	14	20	56	14
Parker Hill/ Jamaica Plain	76.1	(16/21)	53	17	30	22	58	20
N. Dorchester	43.3	(10/23)	58	26	16	17	61	22
S. Dorchester	100	(33/33)	75	18	7	20	60	20
Roslindale	46.6	(7/15)	97	1	2	21	56	23
Hyde Park	18.1	(2/11)	88	7	5	17	64	19
Mattapan	89.5	(17/19)	11	81	8	18	62	20

Source and Notes: Calculated from the *U.S. Census*, 1980; Boston Elections Commision, *Ward and Precinct Voting*, November 1986.
*Fraction indicates the number of precincts voting on Mandela out of the total for the neighborhood.
**There are two precincts for which there was no racial data: Columbia Point, ward 13, precinct 3; and, Savin Hill, ward 13, precinct 10. The vote in these precincts, however, refelcted that of the neighborhoods reported above.

The battle over Mandela thoroughly reviewed the debates about the potential for black control. They took place along two tracks: between white elites and blacks, and within the black community, itself. The mayor of Boston, Raymond Flynn, posed his opposition primarily in terms of the economic viability of Mandela, charging that the residents of Roxbury would be made dangerously vulnerable if their ties to the downtown business boom were severed. The economic growth that began in the late 1970s leapfrogged the Mandela area, moving from the city center to the nearly all white suburbs. Roxbury, to the extent that it benefitted, did so in large part as a result of municipal mandate. Flynn's predecessor, Kevin White, established a policy of set asides and linkage programs to channel revenue and development contracts to the minority communities. Flynn himself used downtown business taxes to subsidize loses in federal payments for social programs. Supporters of the incorporation initiative acknowledged the benefits of linkage programs and demanded that business hold to their commitments even though they were formally bound only to the city of Boston. Drafters of the initiative believed that the force of their moral argument would win out.

The debate was subtly different in the African-American community. It confronted the relative importance of self-government and political autonomy versus the likelihood of economic expansion. Sponsors of the referendum

Table 2
Overall Vote for the Mandela Referendum in 1986 and 1988

	1986	(141 precincts)	1988	(97 precincts)
Yes	12,110	(20%)	11,643	(22%)
No	35,273	(57%)	21,262	(40%)
Blank	14,205	(23%)	19,659	(37%)
Total	61,588		52,559	

Comparison of Vote for Mandela Referendum in 1986 and 1988 In Precincts Unchanged by 1987 Redistricting

	1986	(95 precincts)	1988	(95 precincts)
Yes	7,000	(20%)	11,216	(22%)
No	20,939	(59%)	20,298	(40%)
Blank	7,778	(22%)	18,941	(38%)
Total	35,717		50,455*	

Source and Note: Boston Election Commission, 1986 and 1988.
*Higher turnout for the 1988 election is most likely due to the presidential election.

framed their arguments in nationalist terms. Praising the community's ability in the past to successfully organize and press its interests, they insisted that single-issue politics, such as education, was no longer sufficient; "movement" politics had to be transformed into autonomy and formal control. Black opponents of the referendum, however, pointed to changes in Boston in the last decade and argued that there was a clear trend toward inclusion and expanded participation: increased representation on the City Council and School Committee, and the growth in influence of top black businesses and professionals. They agreed with Flynn that Roxbury could not survive outside the economic structure of Boston, and insisted that demographic changes suggested the possibility of increasing strength in coalitional politics.

Community debate made it clear that residents in the proposed Mandela area were acutely aware of the economic dependence of both the neighborhoods of Greater Roxbury and black business on downtown growth and the city government. They also knew that school and neighborhood segregation, critical factors in the lack of economic growth, had not declined in the last twenty years. The community gave vocal support to the Mandela proponents' contention about persistent racism in Boston, but questioned whether minority control of Roxbury-based resources could more effectively reduce income and service disparities. The consistency of the vote across both the poor and middle-class neighborhoods suggests that the black community as a whole agreed that political empowerment was not the solution to its problems. The community, already economically vulnerable, recognized that improvements in Roxbury would require access to private and public resources that lay not only beyond the reach of Mandela, but also, increasingly, outside the municipal boundaries of Boston itself. As Orfield and Ashkenaze, and Clarence Stone have shown in their studies on Atlanta, economic and political power has shifted to the suburbs, thus, placing a premium on political coalitions that straddle the city limits.

The Mayor's Case and the Economic Reality of Roxbury

Raymond Flynn ran for mayoral office in 1983 on a platform emphasizing his intention to protect the integrity of neighborhoods while also expanding the political community. He called himself an "urban populist." It was a conscious strategy to distance himself from both former mayor Kevin White's elitist image and his own association with the antibusing factions of the 1970s. Flynn wanted to erase the fears of displacement in the old, ethnic working-class neighborhoods while also assuring everyone of their right to participate in Boston's part of the "Massachusetts Miracle." Though he won the election, his antidesegregation past followed him, causing him to lose 95 percent of the black vote to Mel King. In his bid for re-election in 1987, when there was no viable black candidate, Flynn gathered overwhelming support from all the neighborhoods of Boston, including Roxbury. The city continues to be plagued by racial tensions: a loud, sometimes violent fight in 1989 over integration of public housing in the Irish neighborhoods, the 1990 firing of the black superintendent of schools by the white majority of the school board, a recent study detailing discriminatory mortgage lending and neighborhood redlining, and substantial evidence of bias in the police department in both its personnel policies and the manner in which it treats suspects and victims of crimes. Nonetheless, Flynn is secure in public office.

The central point of contention between supporters of the referendum and Mayor Flynn was the economic feasibility of Mandela and, by extension, the economic well-being of Greater Roxbury. Of particular concern were the provision of services, including education, and the control of development that appeared to threaten displacement of the minority population. Boston's record on these two issues, like most cities of its age and demographics and with similar industrial histories, is not particularly good.

City Development and Displacement

Following the pattern of most of the older American cities, Boston experienced a decline in its industrial base between World War II and the early 1960s. The city lost more than one-half of its 112,000 manufacturing jobs between 1947 and 1975. At the same time, suburbanization increased as electronics companies and other high-tech industries located in the Route 128 "beltway" area outside the city, drawing white skilled workers and professionals. Between 1954 and 1963, 400 new plants were built along Route 128, creating a 22 percent increase in suburban employment. At the same time, Boston's city center declined. However, discrimination in suburban housing, the particular skill demands of the new industries, and declining costs in the urban areas made the inner city a draw for minorities, especially blacks. Boston's fiscal problems were not solved by the influx of new residents, though. With the disappearance of manufacturing industries, blacks lost a traditional source of urban jobs. Metropolitan employment declined by 8 percent. As demographic and economic changes converged, extraordinary deterioration set in; in the decades following World War II, Boston's total real estate valuation declined by 28 percent.[1]

In the mid-1970s, the economy of Boston began to turn around. Heavy industries were replaced with service industries that located their corporate headquarters in the old downtown. Professionals were encouraged to move back by the lure of employment and low housing costs. One of the first neighborhoods to be affected was Boston's South End, an area adjacent to the city center. In 1960, the South End population was 40 percent black, highly ethnic, and among the poorest and most overcrowded in the city. A large number of its residents lived in rooming houses that were typical of the neighborhood. When gentrification came, little planning went into controlling displacement. The South End traded 5,250 low-rent units for 4,100 priced at the market rate.[2] Though some subsidized housing was eventually provided, poor black residents were pushed into the already overcrowded Roxbury or out of the city entirely.[3] As Boston became one of the most expensive housing markets in the country, it also became one of the most segregated.

As Boston's economic expansion continued into the 1980s, affecting one neighborhood after the other, Roxbury became a likely area of development. Relative to the rest of the real estate market, Roxbury housing stock was still affordable to middle and upper-middle class individuals interested in gentrification and speculation. Moreover, most of the available land for new building was in the Mandela area and much of it, bought and slated for urban renewal projects, was owned by the city of Boston. The mayor's office encouraged commercial and middle-income housing developments, selling parcels at below-market rates. In the early years of the boom, it appeared to many to be a rational economic strategy for attracting revenue. The city needed new businesses and a stable professional climate. There was no question, however, that the immediate economic needs of the poorer neighborhoods would have to wait until a dependable revenue flow was established.

Clearly, then, one of the logical points of contention in the fight over the referendum was whether Roxbury would be better served by stronger controls on development than the city was willing to pursue. Mandela supporters advocated a number of devices to protect Roxbury: speculation taxes, mandated construction of low-income housing, community approval of all development projects, and rules regarding minority equity in contracting and subcontracting. Flynn argued against all but the last of these as too restrictive. He defended city-wide policies that limited the costs of business growth, but which would result in strengthening Roxbury's economic base. The mayor made it clear that he preferred employment and business expansion over strong, public control of development. He held up as models of economic inclusion the Parcel-to-Parcel Linkage and Jobs Residency policies.

Boston Jobs Residency and Parcel-To-Parcel Linkage Programs

In 1979, then mayor Kevin White issued an executive order mandating employment quotas for Boston residents on all construction projects funded by the city or using city-administered public funds. The order stipulated that the work force of affected firms must be 50 percent Boston residents, 25 percent minority (the city is 38 percent minority), and ten percent women. The policy went immediately into affect, despite litigation by unions. When the case reached the United States Supreme Court in 1983, a majority ruled against the union claim of "reverse discrimination." In order to give the executive order more force, the city council passed a city ordinance and, in September 1983, the Jobs Residency Program became law. In 1984, an Office of Municipal Affirmative Action Officer was created and given the responsibility of monitoring compliance.[4] Whereas the residency program was designed to aid Boston-based business and labor, the parcel linkage policy was intended to protect against displacement by using commercial developments to finance middle- and low-income, mixed public/private housing. Since much of the available property in the city was owned by the Boston Redevelopment Authority (BRA), purchased in the 1960s with urban renewal funds, the mayor's office was given some measure of control over growth. Until recently, the parcels were bid on and developed with limited attention to the fit between the immediate needs of the neighborhood and the intended use of the new buildings. Middle- and upper-income housing side-by-side with high-density shopping areas having shown the highest investment return became the developments of choice. Then, as evidence began to mount of severe overcrowding in poor neighborhoods, the mayor's office paired parcels of city-owned land, requiring the building of low- and middle-income housing as a prerequisite to the approval of major developments.

The linkage policy served other community interests as well. It was expected that developers would utilize minority architects and contractors in the neighborhood of the building sites. In one of the first linkage projects, 25 percent of $409 million in contracts went to minority contractors; in another, minorities were awarded 30 percent of a $400 million project to convert subsidized projects into mixed private/subsidized middle- and low-income housing. As one black contractor explained, "the black investment [capability] is minuscule compared to what Roxbury needs" and the city's commercial developers were looking for black business partners for mandated joint ventures.[5]

Though well designed, the jobs and linkage programs have often fallen victim to local politics and prejudice. One of the first major projects to fall under the linkage plan involved a large, highly desirable piece of land surrounding a newly constructed subway and bus station in one of Roxbury's smaller and poorer neighborhoods. The city negotiated a development, secured minority hiring and contracting, and promised community participation in determining the commercial use of the space. The Greater Roxbury Neighborhood Association (GRNA) sought facilities for community activities. Instead, the BRA planned a commercial development, intended as an extension of downtown business interests, and argued that it would provide jobs to local residents. The Roxbury activists believed, however, that new employees would more likely commute in, given the convenience of the new subway station. More important, however, was the city's failure to follow through on the heart of the linkage policy: the provision of affordable housing in the neighborhood containing the commercial development. Instead of building in Roxbury, the BRA chose a parcel in far-away Chinatown for the construction of mandated low-income housing.

The implementation of the Jobs Residency Program has had some positive results. In those instances when job sites were closely monitored by community activists, such as at the "Tent City" housing development in the South End, employment levels were met or exceeded. More generally, though, the city has not been aggressive in oversight. The major craft unions have been the greatest offenders of program circumvention. Their tactics vary from "checker-boarding," the shifting of blacks from one job to another to give the impression of greater numbers, to exclusion from apprenticeship programs and late calls for union jobs.[6] The hiring stipulation also mandates hiring for commercial occupants of completed developments. As shown in a study of Copley Place, a commercial center with a Neiman-Marcus, two major hotels, and several smaller, up-market concerns, hiring was uneven and focused on lower-paying jobs in maintenance, housekeeping, and food service.[7] Similar to Orfield and Ashkinaze's findings on the Atlanta airport project, Boston's jobs program aided a few black entrepreneurs, but has had no long-term affect on the economic base of the city's poorest neighborhood[8] (Orfield and Ashkinaze, 1991: 54–55).

The success or failure of the linkage and residency programs may be a moot point in light of the 1989 Supreme Court decision invalidating set asides in Richmond, Virginia. At the time, however, the mayor and his critics had considerably different opinions about what could be achieved and how extensively the city could shape business practices. First of all, by law, the Residency Program could be applied only to publicly funded or publicly administered projects or 10 percent of Boston construction jobs. Flynn promised to try to secure a similar agreement on private development, but warned against souring the investment climate. By the mid-1980s, growth was beginning to slow and Boston was suffering corporate defections to the "sun belt." Flynn was being forced to balance a number of problems; voter-mandated property tax caps, the withdrawal of federal block grants, and state fiscal trouble left him to make up Boston's revenue needs from new taxes on business. In at least one instance the city's fiscal problems left business in a strong bargaining position. When Flynn threatened to impose a tax on service industries in 1991, such as architectural and legal firms, many began making plans to leave the city. Flynn was subsequently forced to withdraw the proposal.

Most of the critics of the implementation of the Jobs Residency Program disagreed with the mayor's assessment of how far business could be pushed to support equity. Maynard Jackson's strong-armed negotiations over the construction of the Atlanta Airport were often cited. Boston's "Tent City" housing development served as similar evidence. In either case, however, the results are necessarily limited given current legal realities. Cities, in attempting to balance the interests of business and the economic needs of its poor neighborhoods, do not have easy choices. Increasingly, it is becoming certain that the economic system of metropolitan areas cannot be controlled by a single local unit.

Poverty and Service Provision in Roxbury

The second issue that stirred debate between the mayor and supporters of Mandela was the provision of city services. Roxbury had higher crime, infant mortality, and poverty rates and fewer individuals able to afford health insurance than other neighborhoods in the city. For Mandela supporters, the question was not whether the city would continue to provide municipal and emergency services, but why, at a time when the rest of Boston was doing better, conditions in Roxbury were continuing to deteriorate.

No one disputed Roxbury's neediness. According to BRA figures, while unemployment went down among whites from 5 to 3 percent between 1980 and 1985, it went up among blacks from 9 to 12 percent. Blacks were four times as likely to be unemployed. The disparity was a result of the fact that the vast majority of the newly created jobs were in employment areas, such as suburban high-tech industries or high visibility private sector firms, often closed to blacks because of transportation problems, skill deficits, and discrimination.[9]

Income statistics for Boston's black community reflect the unemployment problem. A 1985 study of Roxbury, produced for the BRA, painted a depressing picture of the neighborhood.[10] According to the study, the median household income in Roxbury in 1980 was $9,305, as compared to the Boston median of $12,530 and the metropolitan median of $18,000. However, because the prevalence of extended families means that Roxbury tends to have larger households, the per capita income of its residents was $4,515, only 69 percent of Boston's $6,555. The more telling figures were those on Roxbury's poverty level. In 1980, 29 percent of all Roxbury residents fell below the poverty line, compared to 20 percent of all Bostonians and 12 percent of U.S. residents. The result was a public assistance level of 34 percent, more than twice the Boston average.

By 1984-1985, conditions had improved in Roxbury, but only at the margins. According to the BRA, white households were twice as likely as black households to be earning $35,000 a year. On the other hand, 61 percent of black households earned less than $20,000 a year, compared to 43 percent of white households. In 1987, the median income among blacks in Roxbury was $14,300, compared to $37,809 for all Massachusetts families.[11] If the larger size of Roxbury households is factored in, the gap in per capita terms is even larger.[12]

The story of housing and education was every bit as grim as that of employment and income. As the property market soared and condominium conversions outnumbered housing starts, the housing crisis for minorities reached a peak. Blacks made up 5 percent or less of Boston's suburban population. Boston, with one-fifth of the metropolitan population, had two-thirds of the area's minority population.[13] What this meant, of course, is that black families were located in the tightest housing market in the area.

On top of the problem of housing costs was a shortage of subsidized housing and, as a 1989 District Court ruling states, discrimination in the housing that comes available.[14] In Roxbury, 80 percent of residents are renters, 73 percent of whom live in subsidized housing.[15] Waiting lists for apartments were often several years long.[16] During the 1970s and 1980s, the Boston NAACP claims, more than one thousand black families were passed over for units in projects in Charlestown and South Boston that were over 90 percent white. An attempt to integrate in 1989 failed when the two families placed in the public housing units left after repeated harassment and violence. Only in 1991 were the NAACP, the City of Boston, and the Department of Housing and Urban Development able to come to an out-of-court settlement about programs for instituting integration.

Since the busing violence of the 1970s, Boston's schools have been on a steady decline. Though blacks make up less than 30 percent of the city's population, they are 70 percent of the students in public schools. In 1985, only 66 percent of blacks in Boston were high school graduates and only 15 percent had college degrees. For whites, the numbers were 83 percent and 32 percent, respectively. Moreover, many black men and women who earn college degrees in Boston leave for friendlier employment markets. Those who watch education closely argue that the causes of the deterioration are both complex and deep seated. However, at least in the beginning, racism played a large part. When white parents moved their children to private schools to avoid integration in 1973–1974, inner-city schools began to die of neglect.

Finally, Roxbury residents are highly dependent on social services funded in part from Boston revenue. Blacks account for 50 percent of the in-patient care at Boston City Hospital. The School Committee, hoping to increase student retention, has provided day care and parenting classes for the school-age mothers who account for 20 percent of Roxbury births.

The Mandela Budget

Financial viability thus became the linchpin of the referendum battle between the mayor and Mandela supporters. Both sides produced hypothetical budgets that, in the end, were so wildly divergent as to make them suspect. The Flynn administration claimed that Mandela's municipal expenses would total $450 million with an annual revenue of only $320 million, leaving a first-year deficit of $130 million. The calculation was based on the assumption that the Greater Roxbury area received 25 percent of Boston's fiscal expenditures, but accounted for only 8 percent of revenues. The discrepancy was the result of the low return on Roxbury's residential tax base, the absence of a commercial tax base, and the neighborhood's high "misery index"; the need for basic health care, remedial education, and housing subsidies can not be funded by Roxbury revenue.

The budget produced by the group organized to support Mandela, the Greater Roxbury Incorporation Project (GRIP), was radically different from the city's. GRIP put together a composite budget, comparing Boston expenditures and revenues with those of cities roughly equivalent in size to Mandela's 150,000 population. Contrary to administration figures, the GRIP budget stated that the new city would have an income of $129.30 million, with liabilities of only $121.66 million. Rather than the deficit predicted by the mayor's office, Mandela would finish its first year with a surplus of $7.64 million.

Balancing what is known about Roxbury's assets, including tax revenues and development income, against the immediate needs of its population, it seems certain that GRIP predictions were wildly optimistic. First, the GRIP budget included in its revenues the profits from a one-time sale of undeveloped Boston-owned property and city parking garages, properties Mandela would first have to purchase. Second, in making comparisons with other cities, the GRIP budget assumed that size was the critical variable in determining Mandela's revenues and spending. It did not consider other factors, such as the comparability of the business base, housing stock, demand on emergency services, or income distribution. Finally, the Greater Roxbury area accounts for only 7 percent of Boston's tax levy, yet its demand on city coffers is almost three times that amount. Boston finances the difference by taxing downtown businesses at a higher rate than residential property and by adding an excise tax on hotel rooms and aircraft fuel. Experts outside the mayor's office estimated that Mandela would have to raise residential property taxes by 61 percent and commercial and industrial property taxes by 44 percent in order to make up the annual operating deficit. With no industrial base, the City of Mandela would be forced to ask those already financially constrained—small neighborhood businesses—to carry tax increases .

Opposition in the Black Community

While the Flynn administration focused on defeating the incorporation movement with questions about the budget and business climate, opposition in the black community posed larger questions about integration and nationalism. One group of Mandela's black critics was joined under the banner "Campaign for ONE Boston." Never did this coalition of church and business leaders suggest that Boston had managed to solve its racial problems. Indeed, the "ONE" in its name was an acronym for Organization for *New* Equality. Some in the group even suggested that the fight over Mandela created a positive challenge to the city to move on its publicly expressed convictions. Nonetheless, the campaign criticized what it understood as GRIP's central premise—that blacks in Boston had given up on traditional integration and would flourish only under their own management.

The Reverend Charles Stith, pastor of the Union United Methodist Church and founder of the campaign, argued that Boston had become committed to inclusion under the administration of Ray Flynn. To support this claim, Stith pointed to changes in the rules governing city council and school board elections as indicative of white receptivity to integration. Nationalism, as either an organizing strategy or intended outcome, was passé. The outcome of these rule changes, however, like the linkage and residency policies, is not easily characterized.

City-Wide Elections

Even though the black population of Boston is small, it has played a role in politics for several decades. Massachusetts was the first state to seat blacks in its legislature and, in the 1940s, Governor James Michael Curley thought them important enough to be courted at election time. But also in that decade, powerful white politicians moved to stanch the influence of the minority community. When, in 1949, a black man named Laurence Banks was elected to the city council, the remaining twenty-one members tried to prevent him from taking his seat. Unable to do that, they moved to change city elections from district to at-large seats. The school committee underwent an identical restructuring. Neither of the at-large institutions excluded blacks entirely; in 1979, a black man with an Irish name, John O'Bryant, won a seat on the school committee and, in 1967, Tom Atkins was elected to the council.[17] However, the size of the two bodies neutralized the representation of black interests.[18]

In 1981, the popular black activist Mel King helped organize a grassroots effort, called the Citizens for District Election, which ran a successful referendum campaign mandating a combined district/at-large city council and school committee. Each was given nine district seats and four elected at large. Beginning in 1983, district voting did result in an increase in the number of black elected officials. Despite Reverend Stith's optimism, however, electoral evidence suggests that the addition of at-large seats to a district format restricted the growth of black political power. While the number of black officeholders went up, the increase did not keep pace with demographic changes and has, in fact, maintained a steady proportionality to white seats. Though both are under black leadership, the council went from a black-white ratio of one to nine, to two out of thirteen, and representation on the school committee was diluted, from two out of five, to five out of thirteen. With district/at-large representation, then, blacks went from holding 11 percent to 15 percent of the seats on the council in a city where they are a quarter of the population, and from 40 percent to 38 percent of the school committee in a system where blacks constitute at least 70 percent of the student population.

The fall elections of 1990 dealt another blow to the school committee. As a result of the increasing decline of the system, intensifying racial splits in the administration, and heightened debate about a school "choice" plan, the mayor sponsored an initiative giving his office political control of the membership of the committee. The measure passed, though it was strongly criticized in the black community. Blacks argued that the racial imbalance of the school committee is a likely source of its ineffectiveness; the minority community, its largest constituency, is not fairly represented and, therefore, not adequately defended. Blacks fear that the loss of an elected board leaves them with no formal means of redress or accountability.

Business and "The Partnership"

Next to Reverend Stith's "Campaign for ONE Boston," the most vocal opposition to Mandela came from the black business community itself. The minority community of Boston has had little reason to feel anything but antipathy for "downtown," the local euphemism for big business. Excluded from executive boardrooms and private clubs, blacks and Latinos have come to believe that their interests are of little consequence. Given these feelings, it should not be surprising that when the most exclusive of business groups, the self-appointed 'Vault,' came out against Mandela, many in the black community, including those who opposed the initiative, saw it as an attempt to interfere in an issue internal to the community itself.[19]

The story of business opposition to Mandela is complicated, however, because black business raised money and assumed a major role in the campaign for its defeat. In part their rationale was similar to that of downtown. Minority businesses would not be exempt from the impact of Mandela's development and speculation control laws. More centrally, however, black businessmen and women agreed with the mayor's contention that the health of their enterprises was tied to the economic boom that had swept through the metropolitan area. Particularly for those involved in construction and service provision, there seemed to be no question that their future was inextricably tied to that of downtown and the mayor's set-asides.

To many in black business circles, other important indicators of change in Boston were the initiation of a black seat on the Vault and the success of groups such as "The Partnership." The Vault is an exclusive, self-selecting institution with considerable influence in Boston politics and fiscal planning. The CEOs and corporate presidents that make up its membership have used private and corporate discretionary funds to underwrite large public projects. The expansion of Vault membership beyond the white community is inarguably significant. However, local black leaders have argued that without integration of the management and executive hierarchy of other, major corporations, the position on the Vault is "tokenism." In response to such criticism, the Partnership was created to "strengthen corporate access."[20] Created in 1986, the Partnership described itself as a "multi-racial leadership organization," interested in "intervening quietly but effectively in major issues affecting Boston." One of its objectives was the placement of black professionals in boardrooms and political conference rooms. "Outside critics," the Partnership argued, were important for raising relevant issues and for applying pressure for restructuring the public agenda. It insisted, however, that change would come only through high-level access and the creation of an economic elite. The continued success of the Partnership's ability to influence political appointments and hiring in middle-level management depends upon its ability to both maintain its institutional ties to Boston, and convince business and the mayor of their responsibilities and interests in the minority community.

When the Mandela incorporation movement became a serious effort, the Partnership moved against it. Its position statement was an apt summary of the argument of the black business community as a whole:

> [W]hile no serious person suggests that Boston has solved its racial problems, Boston is making genuine progress and secession is simply not the best way to attack the underlying social and economic problems that remain...Boston is not in so perilous a condition. Much has been done, yet much more needs to be accomplished. The Partnership commends the Mayor's efforts.... Yet we call for Boston's business community to be more forthcoming in investing in the minority community.... This approach we feel will be more productive in the long run in remedying economic imbalance and racial injustice (Minor: 1).

The Partnership charged pro-Mandela forces with the obligation to prove that incorporation "would be economically viable and that political realignment would be beneficial."

Integration and Economic Dependence

The failure of the Mandela referendum has, in many ways, strengthened the belief of many in Boston that blacks are still as committed to integration, and to the same conception of integration, as they were following the successes of the civil rights movement. This is only supposition, however; there was no exit polling or extensive post-election interviewing that could be used as evidence. But explaining Mandela's defeat as a nod to the integrationist impulse is not only too simplistic but quite likely wrong.

Perhaps more than anything, the referendum campaign made clear the difficulties of racial or ethnic nationalist politics—what is coming to be called "identity politics" by some—in a complex urban environment. The city of Mandela, as conceived by its originators, was to be an independent entity, committed to "controlling the land, the buildings [and] the pavements."[21] However, little thought was given to the mechanics of, and constraints on municipal-level policy. For example, the taking of property through eminent domain is an alternative severely limited by Commonwealth of Massachusetts law and the ability to pay a fair price. How would Mandela manage its property rights? How would it provide a lucrative environment for investment, which in most cities requires expensive tax incentives, and also increase the quality of service delivery?

Mandela was not the first proposal of its kind in the 1980s. The leader of GRIP developed the idea from a 1983 *New York Times* article detailing the incorporation of a minority community in northern California. East Palo Alto, a city surrounded by Silicon Valley and its well-to-do suburbs, mirrored the Roxbury-Dorchester area of Boston; both were at least 75 percent minority, lacking in a commercial economic base, and both continued to experience poverty and unemployment while surrounding white residents prospered from the growth of high-tech and service industries. The experience of East Palo Alto, however, should prove that those skeptical of Mandela's viability were correct. East Palo Alto is bankrupt. Its inability to provide services to its citizens forced the surrounding county, with aid from the State of California, to offer short-term contracts for police and emergency crews. More critically, the city continues to be economically isolated from the surrounding area. It has not been able to translate a resolve to defend minority rights into economic development in the absence of an indigenous, independent business base. As conditions have worsened, East Palo Alto has become politically divided.

What are the broader implications of Mandela for both black and urban politics? There are two, perhaps not entirely distinct, issues to be considered, one political, the other economic. The creators of the Mandela referendum began with the basic assumption that the fundamental problem facing Roxbury was its lack of political control over local economic resources. Though this may be true at the margins, it seriously underestimates the complexity of the current political environment of American cities. Urban mayors, once the pinnacle of local power, are now fighting vicious battles with the suburbs. Businesses, educational institutions, and constituents who cannot get what they want from the city are being enticed to move out. Keeping them in the city means allowing them into the administrative coalition. The case of Atlanta is instructive.

In arguing for the Mandela initiative, many of its supporters used Maynard Jackson as an example of what could be achieved with a commitment that focused first and foremost on the interests of the minority community. Clarence Stone's recent study of Atlanta suggests that this reading of the city's politics is not correct.[22] Though development in Atlanta was used to promote opportunities for minority businesses, it had little affect on the poor and was often pursued *despite* opposition from the neighborhoods. Stone argues convincingly that Jackson, like Andrew Young, governs with the advice of a coalition that is "deracialized" and clearly influenced by the business community. Orfield and Ashkinaze, in their 1991 book on the effect of conservative policies on cities, put it this way:

> [L]ocal governments act more as supplicants than as powerful regulators of private business, offering subsidies in efforts to prevent business departures. What city leaders can do to expand black opportunity is significant but limited: provide fair employment and affirmative action within their own staffs, see to it that some minority contractors get included in public contracts, and try to prevent problems such as police brutality.... The institutions and policies that most directly affect the mobility of young blacks are almost all outside the control of city leaders.[23]

The second implication for urban politics that can be gleaned from the Mandela initiative is that the economic structure of cities is also becoming increasingly complex. As the industrial base of the United States continues to adjust to its changed position in the world economy, structural dislocation and changes in federal aid policy increase the burden on already overtaxed state and local budgets. Cities should expect decreasing levels of outside help. Poor neighborhoods like Roxbury will become more dependent on the ability of local politicians to produce alternative sources of revenue and to develop cooperative arrangements for education, police protection, and hospital care with nearby towns and counties for the provision of services. At the same time, as coalitions sustaining local government expand to include private business, they will also move across municipal boundaries.

In comparison with other cities, Boston's black population is remarkably small and, therefore, weak. Though blacks have a natural socioeconomic ally in the poor Irish of Charlestown and "Southie," the busing crisis of the early 1970s stands between the two communities. In all of this, then, Roxbury may be in an unusual situation, but evidence suggests that its circumstances are only more extreme, not atypical. The change in urban politics that has come as a consequence of conservative fiscal and social policy is affecting even those cities, such as Atlanta and Detroit, where blacks are in the majority. Redistribution of wealth and opportunity is not materializing. Local governments have limited resources and little policy discretion. The political power and program initiation that they once wielded has shifted to the state and, in some instances, to private business.

This analysis does not allow much optimism with respect to the situation of Roxbury's black community. Boston and the Commonwealth of Massachusetts are going to be forced, in the coming year, to cut further into the programs that serve the poor. There are some positive suggestions that can be gleaned, however. First, black political activists should shift their focus to the state and toward building state-wide political coalitions. Like Atlanta, the black middle class has left the city for the suburbs. As long as the political battle is waged only in Boston, the influence of the middle class will remain untapped. There are other cities in the state with sizable black communities. Second, blacks must also begin to think about more radical ways of providing decent education and job training. It may be that the current public school system is not salvageable, that the city will have to allow its students to attend classes in the suburbs while it rebuilds from the ground up. This puts the burden on black children, as they are forced to commute when others do not. The alternatives, though, are not much better; reorganizing, hiring and firing teachers and administrators, experimenting with new curricula and requirements may also put two or three graduating classes at risk. Finally, the state must be encouraged to develop programs with private industry that solve location and training problems. For example, businesses located in the suburbs, where entry-level labor is scarce, could be offered help in developing transportation for urban workers in exchange for subsidies on job training.

The problems posed by areas such as Roxbury are of the most difficult to solve. They must be done in such a way so that those already vulnerable are not left more so. "Owning the pavements," as the proponents of Mandela put it, is not sufficient, even in large, prosperous cities. There is no doubt that Boston is still one of the most segregated cities in the country, but in voting against Mandela, the black community made its priorities clear. The difficulties of repairing economic disparities far exceed the power of political good will.

References

Blackwell, James. 1985. "Jobs, Income and Poverty: The Black Share of New Boston." In *The Emerging Black Community of Boston*, ed., Phillip Clay. Boston: Institute for the Study of Black Culture, University of Massachusetts.

Canellos, Peter. 1989. "Court Ruling on Public Housing Puts Suburbs on the Spot." *The Boston Globe*, (28 June).

Clay, Phillip, ed. 1985a. *The Emerging Black Community of Boston*. Boston: Institute for the Study of Black Culture, University of Massachusetts at Boston.

———. 1985b. "Housing, Neighborhoods and Development." In ibid.

Dooley, Raymond. "Proposed Mandela Secession." Unpublished, the City of Boston.

Elliot, Clinton. 1985. "Contractors Hit Secession Strategy." *The Bay State Banner*, (12 December).

Gaston, Maricio and Marie Kennedy. "From Disinvestment to Displacement." Unpublished manuscript, 1985, University of Massachusetts, Boston.

Hinton, Catherine. "The Mandela Referendum of Boston: Integration, Nationalism and the Divided Black Middle Class." Unpublished Senior Honors Thesis, 1989, Harvard-Radcliffe, Cambridge.

Howe, Peter J. 1989. "A Segregated City: The Rhetoric and the Reality of Boston." *The Boston Globe*, (28 June).

Jennings, James. 1985. "Race and Political Change." In *The Emerging Black Community of Boston*, ed., Phillip Clay. Boston: Institute for the Study of Black Culture, University of Massachusetts.

Jones, Andrew and Curtis Davis. 1986. "The Greater Roxbury Incorporation Project: A New Municipality." Unpublished proposal for incorporation.

Kenney, Charles. 1987. "The Aftershock of a Radical Notion." *The Boston Globe Magazine*, (12 April).

Kenney, Charles. "The Politics of Turmoil." *The Boston Globe Magazine*, (19 April).

Jordon, Robert. 1985. "Employment Inequality." *The Boston Globe*, (8 June).

King, Mel. Unpublished memorandum, 27 March 1987.

Lung, Keri. "The Job Linkage Approach to Community Economic Development." Unpublished MCP thesis, 1985, Massachusetts Institute of Technology.

Mollenkopf, John H. 1983. *The Contested City*. Princeton: Princeton University Press.

Minor, Hassan. 1986. "Statement of The Partnership in Opposition to Referendum #9."

The New York Times, (1983). "Incorporation of a Coast Town Divides Community," (17 August).

The New York Times. 1983. "California City Upheld on Vote to Incorporate," (18 September).

Orfield, Gary and Carole Ashkinaze. 1991. *The Closing Door,* Chicago, Ill.: University of Chicago Press.

Perkins, Gregory. "Profile of Roxbury." Unpublished manuscript, 1985, Boston Redevelopment Authority.

Quill, Ed. "Hub Study Puts Mandela in the Red." *The Boston Globe,* (4 October 1986).

Quill, Ed. "Mayor Flynn Sounds Off." *The Boston Globe,* (7 November 1986).

Sege, Irene. 1989. "Study finds Massachusetts Poverty Rate Stalled." *The Boston Globe,* (17 July).

Stith, Charles. 1986. "Vote No: Entire City Making Progress." *The Boston Globe,* (1 November).

Stone, Clarence. 1989. *Regime Politics: Governing Atlanta, 1946-1988.* Lawrence: University Press of Kansas.

Travis, Toni-Michelle C. 1990. "Boston: The Unfinished Agenda." In *Racial Politics in American Cities,* Rufus Browning, Dale Rogers Marshall and David Tabb, eds. New York: Longman Publishers.

Notes

1. John H. Mollenkopf, *The Contested City* (Princeton, N.J.: Princeton University Press, 1983), 142-43.
2. Ibid., 166.
3. Phillip Clay, "Housing, Neighborhoods and Development" in Phillip Clay, ed., *The Emerging Black Community of Boston* (Boston: Institute for the Study of Black Culture, University of Massachusetts, 1985), 201.
4. James Blackwell, "Jobs, Income and Poverty: The Black Share of New Boston" in Phillip Clay, ed., *The Emerging Black Community of Boston,* (Boston: Institute for the Study of Black Culture, University of Massachusetts, 1985) 15-16.
5. Clinton Elliot, "Contractors Hit Secession Strategy," *The Bay State Banner,* (12 December 1985): 1.
6. Blackwell, "Jobs, Income and Poverty," 54.
7. Keri Lung,"The Job Linkage Approach to Community Development." Unpublished Masters thesis in Community Planning. (Massachusetts Institute of Technology, 1985), 28-30. Also see Blackwell, "Jobs, Income and Poverty," 54-56.
8. Gary Orfield and Carole Ashkinaze, *The Closing Door* (Chicago, Ill.: University of Chicago Press, 1991), 54-55.
9. See Robert Jordan, "Employment Inequality," *The Boston Globe* (8 June 1985); Charles Kenney, "The Politics of Turmoil," *The Boston Globe* (19 April 1987); "Special Series on Boston Jobs," *The Boston Globe* (April 1983).
10. Gregory Perkins, "Profile of Roxbury" for the Boston Redevelopment Agency, City of Boston, 1985. Unpublished.
11. Irene Sege, "Study Finds Massachusetts Poverty Rate Stalled," *The Boston Globe* (17 July 1987), 1.
12. Charles Kenney, "The Aftershock of a Radical Notion," *The Boston Globe Magazine,* (12 April 1987): 24-26; Charles Kenney, "The Politics of Turmoil," *The Boston Globe Magazine,* (19 April 1987).
13. Peter J. Howe, "A Segregated City: The Rhetoric and Reality of Boston," *The Boston Globe,* (28 June 1989): 13.
14. Peter Canellos, "Court Ruling on Public Housing Puts Suburbs on the Spot," *The Boston Globe,* (28 June 1989): 1.
15. Maricio Gaston and Marie Kennedy, "From Disinvestment to Displacement." Unpublished manuscript, 1985, 21-22.

16. Phillip Clay, "Housing, Neighborhoods and Development," in Phillip Clay, ed., *The Emerging Black Community*, 189.
17. Many in Boston tell the story of how the opposition tried to defeat O'Bryant by going door to door and plastering car windshields with pictures of him, asking "Do you know who this man is?" The Irish community knew that most people would vote on the basis of ethnic identification. The opposition formed too late, and O'Bryant won the election.
18. James Jennings, "Race and Political Change," in Phillip Clay, ed., *The Emerging Black Community*, 318.
19. Created in 1959 to save Boston from sliding into municipal bankruptcy, the Vault is a self-appointed group of corporate presidents and CEO's that meets on a regular basis to advise the city on fiscal matters. When necessary, the Vault has also used the corporate discretionary and/or personal funds of its members to fund or underwrite community programs and to influence political campaigns. Recently, Ronald Homer, president of the Boston Bank of Commerce, was the first black to be appointed to the Vault.
20. Hassan Minor, "Statement of The Partnership in Opposition to Referendum #9," 1986.
21. Andrew Jones and Curtis Davis, "The Greater Roxbury Incorporation Project: A New Municipality." Unpublished proposal, 1986.
22. Clarence Stone, *Regime Politics: Governing Atlanta, 1946–1988* (Lawrence, Kans.: University Press of Kansas, 1989).
23. Orfield, Gary and Carole Ashkinaze, pp. 24.

Minority Business Enterprise Set-Aside Programs, Disparity Fact-Finding Studies, and Racial Discrimination in State and Local Public Contracting in the Post-Croson Era

Mitchell F. Rice

Louisiana State University

Introduction

Government set-asides, or "sheltered markets" for minority business enterprises (MBEs) are affirmative action programs that provide minority contractors and subcontractors a certain percentage of a governmental jurisdiction's contract dollars. Government set-aside programs were developed under two theoretical assumptions: (1) a redistribution of government's contract dollars to minority-owned firms would provide business these firms could not obtain by themselves, thereby increasing their long-run competitive viability and (2) as subcontractors these firms would develop contacts with larger firms, role models, training, increased business acumen, and greater business potential.[1] The realization of these assumptions would preserve, strengthen, and increase the competitiveness of MBEs to excell in the economic mainstream and participate effectively in both the public and private sectors.[2] The justifications for minority set-asides include: (1) as a way of closing the business "Ownership gap" between minorities and whites; (2) as an economic development tool in the minority community, particularly for creating jobs in high unemployment areas; and (3) as a tool for creating an expanding minority middle class to serve as a role model for minority youth.[3]

Minority Business and Set-Aside Programs: An Overview

Minority businesses are generally small businesses (with less than 100 employees) privately owned and controlled by minority group members.

Minority businesses are clustered in the major urban areas of the country and are primarily engaged in "Selected Services and Retail Trades" (cleaning and janitorial, auto repair, hair care, and etc.).[4] Over the years, minority businesses have found it difficult to raise capital and financing, have limited access to markets, have limited access to credit, have a negative perception from society, and face other problems detrimental to their survival.[5] The U.S. Commission on Minority Business Development, created by the Business Opportunity Act of 1988 (Public Law 100-656), views these problems as critical issues to be dealt with.[6] Historically, because of these issues, minority participation in entrepreneurial activities in the United States has been negligible or nonexistent.[7]

Even though minority-owned businesses appear to prosper, James and Clark have been able to identify three constraints which hinder their development:

> First, most minority-owned businesses are "service performing industries" reliant on consumer expenditures as their market. Second, minority-owned business[es] in general and black businesses in particular are concentrated in economically distressed cities where overall consumer markets are frequently declining. Third, minority-owned business[es are] reliant on minority purchasing power.[8]

Yet, due in part to set-aside programs, minority businesses—particularly black businesses in the construction and business services—have increased dramatically in the U.S. since the early 1980s.[9] According to the most recent data from the U.S. Census Bureau, which has been tracking minority business trends since 1969, there were 424,000 black-owned firms in the United States in 1987 (3 percent of all firms)—an increase of 115,905, or nearly 38 percent from 1982. These firms employed about 220,00 employees (about 5 percent of the minority workforce in 1987) as compared to 121,000 employees in 1982. The number of paid employees in these firms nearly doubled from 38,000 in 1982 to 71,000 in 1987. Black-owned firms generated sales of nearly $20 billion. The average sales and receipts of these firms rose from about $36,600 in 1982 to $46,600 in 1987, a 27 percent increase.[10] Black-owned construction and business services increased by 63.7 percent and 53.3 percent, respectively, from 1982 to 1987.[11]

Furthermore, from an economic perspective, state and local government set-aside programs for minority businesses have led not only to millions of dollars in contracting opportunities, but also to increased minority employment.[12] For example, in Atlanta in 1988, minority businesses received nearly 35 percent of $55 million expended by the city. In Chicago, during the period 1985-1989, minority contractors received more than $307 million from the aviation industry. In 1989 minority firms in Philadelphia received about 15 percent of nearly $62 million in city contracts. Washington, D.C. expended $232 million with minority businesses in 1988.[13] The Metropolitan Washington Airport Authority awarded $60 million (out of a total of $299 million) to minority-owned firms in 1993.[14] In New York state set-aside programs have significantly assisted minority businesses. The Port Authority of New York and New Jersey awarded minority firms $105 million in 1989. The Dormitory Authority of the State of New York provided $62.4 million to minority businesses in 1989.[15] On the employment side, minority firms in Atlanta, as an example, employed some 7,200 individuals. The City of Chicago's set-aside program over the period 1985 through 1988 created an estimated 7,200 to 10,800 new jobs.[16] Thus, for the continuation of state and local governmental jurisdictions, set-aside programs would seem to be critically important to the further development, proliferation, and diversification of minority-owned businesses and to overall minority employment.[17]

Since the Supreme Court's decision in *City of Richmond* v. *J. A. Croson*[18] in early 1989, disparity fact-finding studies have become a focal point in state and local government jurisdictions' MBE set-aside policies. Disparity fact-finding studies, at a cost of some $13 million, have been conducted or are underway in more than sixty jurisdictions around the United States.[19] This chapter discusses the status of MBE set-aside programs after *Croson* and examines the use of disparity fact-finding studies as mechanisms for justifying the adoption or continuation of set-aside programs in state and local governmental jurisdiction. This chapter also provides a discussion of specific analyses that have been major components of disparity fact-finding studies and a summary and discussion of disparity of fact-finding studies conducted in five jurisdictions.

State and Local Set-Aside Programs in the Aftermath of *Croson*

Borchers categorizes public contract preference legislation and resultant legal cases into three classes:[20] (1) Class I cases—purely state and local enhancement, with no federal involvement (the *Croson* case); (2) Class II cases—federal funding contributes to a state or locally administered contract with availability of federal funding depending upon the state/local entity complying with a federal directive to give racial preference (the *Fullilove* case);[21] and (3) Class III cases—the federal government acts directly without using a state/local intermediary (the *Metro Broadcasting* case).[22]

In *Croson*, a majority of the Supreme Court for the first time held that ameliorative race-based preferences developed by state and local governmental entities must meet the "strict scrutiny" standard, as opposed to the "rational relationship" test, in order to withstand challenge under the Equal Protection Clause of the U.S. Constitution. The Court found the City of Richmond's (Virginia) MBE set-aside ordinance to be unconstitutional.[23] In striking down the Richmond ordinance, the Court called into question the constitutionality of hundreds of other similar state/local governmental jurisdictions MBE programs. Nay and Jones speculate that between 564 and 1,394 set-aside programs were affected by the court's decision.[24] In view of the *Croson* decision, seven defects may by identified in state and local jurisdictions MBE programs: inadequate statistics; lack of specific evidence; overly inclusive definition; excessive numerical goal; unlimited duration; failure to try race-neutral remedies; and inadequate waiver procedures.[25]

Opponents in the Set-Aside Battle

The National Associated General Contractors (AGC) of America and state/local chapters have been the primary challengers of set-aside provisions nationwide.[26] The organization has been tracking set-aside policies at the federal, state, and local government levels since the mid-1980s. AGC is a 32,500 member, 8,000 contractor organization. About 95 percent of AGC members are small business.[27] AGC and its minority counterpart organization, the National Association of Minority Contractors (NAMC) are two major opponents in the set-aside issue.[28] AGC views set-asides as "discrimination as a means of correcting perceived discrimination," driving non-MBEs out of business, taking away business, unfair, a monopoly for MBEs and increasing prices.[29] NAMC argues that set-asides are necessary because they "increase productive capacity and competitiveness among contractors. They give a sense of equal opportunity in the marketplace"[30] and "because racial discrimination continues to deprive minority contractors of opportunities open to whites."[31] Other anti-set-aside organizations, such as the Builder's Association of Missouri and the Mechanical Contractors Association of Kansas City, are strongly opposed to the use of a disparity fact-finding study, arguing that:

> We are concerned that the pursuit of such a study and its findings, whatever they may be, will only polarize opinion on special preference programs and possibly lead to costly and unfortunate litigation involving study results and race- and gender-based preferences generally.[32]

Aftermath of Croson

The immediate aftermath of *Croson* led to the judicial dismantling of some set-aside programs in state and local jurisdictions and the voluntary termination/suspension of numerous other programs.[33] About a year and a half after the *Croson* decision, over fifty cases had been filed involving challenges to federal and nonfederal minority set-aside programs and some forty-six jurisdictions had abandoned their programs.[34] Lower court decisions struck down set-aside programs in a number of state and local entities, including the Florida Department of Transportation, state of Michigan, Minnesota Department of Transportation, City of Atlanta, Wisconsin Department of Transportation, City of Philadelphia Public Schools, and Multnomah County, Oregon. Other jurisdictions responded to *Croson* by either changing, suspending, or terminating their programs.

State and local jurisdictions that voluntarily made changes in their set-aside programs to comply with *Croson* include San Francisco; Minneapolis; Phoenix; Denver, State of Oregon, Denver, Colorado; Forth Worth, Texas; the New York/New Jersey Port Authority; and Wilmington, Delaware. Denver, Colorado developed MBE goals on a project-by-project basis. San Francisco changed to a 10 percent bidding preference for MBEs. Minneapolis removed the gender and race qualifications from its set-aside provision to benefit only economically disadvantaged businesses. Phoenix changed its MBE/WBE set-aside to a disadvantaged business enterprise program. Some jurisdictions that suspended/terminated their programs include San Jose, California; State of Colorado; New Castle County, Delaware; Ft. Lauderdale, Florida; South Bend, Indiana; Genesee County, Michigan; Minneapolis, Minnesota; Durham, North Carolina; Guilford County, North Carolina; Lane County, Oregon; and Salem County, Oregon.[35] The State of California enacted a new law in January 1991 that requires minority-owned firms to perform 15 percent of all work carried out under state contract.[36]

As a result of the *Croson* decision and changes in state and local set-aside policies, minority business participation in state and local government contracting declined sharply.[37] The City of Atlanta's minority business participation fell from 37 percent in 1989 to 24 percent by mid-1900.[38] In Richmond, Virginia, minority participation of 32 percent before *Croson* decreased to some 11 percent in 1990. The State of Illinois contracts to minority vendors were off by 50 percent in 1990.[39] In Tampa, Florida, at the end of the first quarter of 1989, total contract awards to black firms dropped by 99 percent; Hispanic firms total contract awards dropped by 50 percent. In Hillsborough County, Florida, a 99 percent decrease in minority contracting opportunities occurred following the judicial termination of the county's set-aside program.[40]

Croson Standards and the Rise of Disparity Fact-Finding Studies

The Croson *Standards*

The *Croson* Court spelled out the criteria for justifying the adoption or continuation of set-aside programs of state and local jurisdictions and, as a result, the decision has greatly affected the evidentiary requirements of enacting or continuing set-aside programs. Under the Court's strict scrutiny approach in *Croson*, a state or municipality burden consists of establishing two important sets of criteria. First, it must demonstrate a compelling state interest by establishing a *prima facie* case of past discrimination and/or discrimination by the local construction industry. In other words, the state or municipality must find that the state or municipality itself discriminated against minority businesses in the past and the effects of past discrimination persist. Second, it must demonstrate that other race-neutral alternatives were carefully considered and the set-aside program adopted was *narrowly* tailored to remedy the effects of past discrimination. While the Court in *Croson* did not define what constitutes adequate consideration of alternatives, it did indicate such alternatives as "simplification of bidding procedures, relaxation of bonding requirements and training and financial aid" assistance to minority/economically disadvantaged businesses.[41] From a theoretical perspective, these nondiscriminatory alternatives would promote economic opportunity for MBEs and maintain equal treatment of nonminorities. In other words, race-neutral alternatives would increase minority participation without stigmatizing MBEs and prevent established minority firms from receiving most contracts. However, Brimmer and Marshall observe that while "race neutral policies are necessary to improve minority business development...they do nothing to see to it that there is a *demand* for the minority businesses' services."[42]

The narrow tailoring race-conscious program requirement must also focus on three other considerations: (1) the flexibility and duration of the program and its waiver provisions; (2) the relationship between the preference and the relevant labor market; and (3) the program's impact upon the rights of third parties.[43] A set-aside program authorized by state/local entities should be limited to only the context and duration absolutely essential to reach the desired end. In other words, a set-aside program should be of limited duration and undergo periodic re-evaluation to assure that it is effectively pursuing a remedial purpose. This review process is critical to the constitutional soundness of the program. A waiver provision to exempt nonminority contractors from set-aside requirements is necessary for particular situations in the event a qualified MBE is unavailable. The narrow tailoring approach also emphasizes that the numerical preference granted MBEs by a set-aside program should not substantially exceed the percentage of MBEs in the relevant industry and that "non-minority businesses should not bear a burden greater than reasonably necessary to effectuate the bona fide remedial purposes of a set-aside program."[44]

The Rise of Disparity Fact-Finding Studies

States, cities, and other governmental bodies have moved to carry out disparity fact-finding studies, sometimes referred to as predicate studies or minority business studies or discrimination studies, for the purpose of providing evidence upon which to base decisions concerning MBE preference programs. These studies attempt to document local past bias against minorities with an attentive focus on economic and business discrimination.[45] According to *Croson*, "where there is a significant disparity between the number of qualified minority contractors willing and able to perform a particular service and the number of such contractors actually engaged by the locality or the locality's prime contractors, an inference of discriminatory exclusion could arise."[46]

Disparity fact-finding studies have been completed or are underway in such jurisdictions as Atlanta; Oakland; New York City; San Antonio; San Francisco; Milwaukee; Hillsborough County, Florida; Tallahassee, Florida; State of Louisiana; State of Louisiana; State of Minnesota; King County, Washington; Maricopa County (Phoenix), Arizona; State of California; Los Angeles; Dade County, Florida; and State of Massachusetts. From a geographic perspective, ten disparity fact-finding studies have been completed or are underway in California (State of California, Contra Costa/Alameda Counties, Hayward, Los Angeles, Oakland, Regional Transit Association of the Bay Area, Sacramento, San Francisco, San Jose, Sacramento Municipal Utility District) and none in Florida (state of Florida/General Services, Dade County, Dade County Public Schools, Hillsborough county, Palm Beach County, Jacksonville, St. Petersburg, Tallahassee and Tampa).[47]

The cost of disparity fact-finding studies has ranged from $60,000 to $791,000. Factors that may influence cost are: the experience of the "consultant expert"; the complexity of the MBE ordinance/legislation; the number, nature, and size of the political entity's population; the size and ethnic diversity of the business community under study; and the nature and scope of the work to be performed.[48] The City of Atlanta paid more than $500,00 for a disparity fact-finding study with noted economists Andrew Brimmer and Ray Marshall. The City of Tampa, Florida authorized up to $175,000 for a study.[49] Several Seattle-Tacoma jurisdictions paid $400,000 to compile a statistical paper trail showing discrimination in the letting of local government construction contracts.[50] The State of Minnesota conducted an in-house fact-finding study that cost approximately $100,00. The Metropolitan Washington Airports Authority, Jacksonville, Florida and New York City have paid to disparity fact-finding study consultants $349,000, $398,000, and $460,000, respectively.[51] A principal reason for the consultant expert is the need for outside expertise to collect and analyze data and perform corresponding economic and statistical analyses.[52] Furthermore, state and local governmental entities would probably prefer to be neutral and unbiased observers in the fact-finding and data collection processes.

Analytical Components of a Disparity Fact-Finding Study

Although the *Croson* court did not clearly articulate what a disparity fact-finding study analysis should consist of, the growing body of disparity fact-finding studies, as well as legal and analytical commentary on the *Croson* case, suggest several specific analysis: contemporary discrimination analysis; utilization analysis; race-neutral alternatives analysis, marketplace discrimination analysis; availability growth analysis by race; and a comparative growth analysis of local MBEs to national MBEs and to local non-MBEs.[53] These analyses must provide proof of direct and deliberate bias and a detailed discussion of "the wealth, health and general opportunities of minorities in a locale." The latter discussions should "analyze both negative and positive implications of such general factors" to minorities' social well-being.[54] The nature and detail analyses of disparity fact-finding studies require the use of legal experts, economists, and statisticians. The justification for set-aside programs is no longer a predominately legal question. Halligan observes that "it now is largely an empirical, quantitative question."[55] These fact-finding studies are available as evidence to the courts and appear to be important factors in the legal shift of recent decisions favoring minority contractors.[56] Table 1 points out the analytical requirements of a disparity fact-finding study. The discussion following examines the procedural approaches and issues involved in several of these components.

Utilization Analysis

A factual predicate is necessary to assure that the public entity has a strong basis in evidence to justify the remedial action. In other words, the factual predicate assures that the preferred class of MBEs in fact has been to subject to racial discrimination and continues to suffer its effects, thereby overriding the consideration of racial-neutral alternatives. This factual evidence should consist of a statistical analysis showing that there is a significant imbalance between the proportion of available minority contractors and subcontractors. This statistical analysis is referred to as a "utilization ration" and employs statistical tests of significance that show whether particular patterns can reasonably be attributed to chance or indicate evidence of discrimination.[57] Simply stated, "the analysis of utilization examines the pattern and level of participation by minority businesses in different contracting opportunities." In question form, the utilization analysis asks what is "the market share that a firm (or group of firms) would have had in the absence of anticompetitive [discrimination] activity?"[58]

Table 1
Analytical Requirements of a Disparity Fact-Finding Study

Historical Discrimination Analysis in Geographic/Jurisdiction Area
A. Descriptive Statistics
Contemporary Discrimination Analysis in Geographic/Jurisdiction Area
A. Descriptive Statistics
B. Anecdotal Evidence
(Interviews/surveys/public hearings with MBE owners, non-MBE owners, trade associations, etc.)
Employment/Income Analysis in Geographic/Jurisdiction Area by Race and Sex
Availability Analysis of MBEs in Market Area
Utilization Analysis of MBEs in government Contracting in Jurisdiction
Market Place Discrimination Analysis in Geographic Analysis in Geographical/Jurisdiction Area
A. Price Discrimination Analysis
B. Bonding Discrimination Analysis
C. Bid Manipulation Analysis
D. Financing Discrimination Analysis
E. Attitudinal Discrimination Analysis
F. Financial Analysis of MBEs and non-MBEs
Population Growth Analysis by Race
Comparative Growth Analysis of Local MBEs to National MBEs and Local Non-MBEs in Business/Trade Industries

Data on utilization of MBEs and non-MBEs are collected from internal records of the pubic bodies under question to provide a standard of comparison. It is important that the analysis go beyond the simple observations that note the small number of minority firms in a geographical area, the statistical disparity between the percentage of prime contracts awarded to minority firms and the percentage of blacks or other minorities in the geographic area, and/or the low minority membership in local/statewide trade associations.[59]

Basing a disparity on population percentage assumes that "minorities will choose a particular trade in lockstep proportion to their representation in the local [or state] population."[60] This is simply balancing and is not a permissible Court goal for race-conscious classification. Evidence of low membership in the relevant trade associations is insufficient by itself to establish discrimination in the relevant industry. Although, if the statistical disparity was great enough, an inference of racial discrimination could be made. Furthermore, Congressional findings of nationwide racial discrimination have lesser probative value at the state/local level.[61] Racial discrimination must be documented with specific local/state instances of individual harm, not generalized notions of group harm. In the words of the Court, "A generalized assertion that there has been past discrimination in an entire industry provides no guidance for a legislative body to determine the precise scope of the injury it seeks to remedy."[62] Stated another way, mere societal discrimination against minorities is not a sufficient predicate for a racial classification because it " is too amorphous and would justify remedies that are ageless in their reach into the past, and timeless in their ability to affect the future."[63]

Availability Analysis

An availability analysis must identify the "shortfall" between the expected number of a state and/or local government minority contractors and the *actual* number. The analysis should also devise a methodology for estimating the number of "deterred" minority businesses.[64] When the shortfall is removed—or when the actual number of minority contractors equals the number of such contractors—one would expect to find absent discrimination, then the set-aside would be removed. The findings from the availability are used to assess the MBE utilization by the public agency to determine whether or not there is a disparity between MBE utilization and the availability of MBEs.

A simple head count as the unit of measurement for availability may not be the most appropriate method of head counting. This method does not consider barriers to entry or expansion of MBE firms in the market area. MBEs and non-MBEs (as a standard of comparison) should be asked "how long they have been in business, what education and experience they have, what their expansion (or construction) trend was, what their single job and annual capacity were,"[65] as well as questions about obstacles to expansion or earlier entry. If the head count to determine availability is utilized, a variety of sources must be consulted including Census data; state and local agencies; federal agencies that do business with minority firms such as USDOT, USDOD, USSBA, and USDOC; U.S. Minority Business Development Agency; national minority business directories; local MBE directories; and state/local chapters of minority trade associations.[66] The objective is to perform a thorough search to identify the availability of MBEs in the market area.[67]

Historical Analysis

Although contemporaneous findings of racial discrimination in the procurement of government contracts cannot be overlooked, and documenting a historical pattern of racial discrimination within a jurisdictions's overall procurement area must be done. Both historical overt barriers (such as discrimination laws) and covert barriers (such as loan and bonding discrimination) should be included. Further, the historical analysis may begin with the earliest verifiable instances of racial discrimination. The gathering of such evidence should consist of confidential interviews/affidavits, factual data and information, and particularized anecdotes of specific instances of discrimination. Evidentiary analysis must also be attentive to the following:

> The existence, nature and operation of an "old-boy network" an how it has or may tend to exclude MBEs from full participation in the marketplace;
>
> the ways in which "business as usual" in current procurement procedures can effectively perpetuate the effects of past and present discrimination;
>
> the need for race-conscious remedies.[68]

Furthermore, anecdotal evidence, interviews, and affidavits must be from reliable and trustworthy sources and should include counter explanation and rebuttals from sources accused of bias. In other words, the gathering of evidence utilizing these approaches must be fair and deliberative. While hearsay may offer a potentially justifying remedy, one-way adversarial untested accusations would simply be biased opinions[69] or "highly conclusory" allegations.[70]

One purpose of demonstrating a historical pattern of racial discrimination is to establish a link between the racial discrimination and "the chilling effect on the formation of minority businesses within the jurisdiction."[71] Another purpose for this kind of evidentiary analysis would be to establish that a state or local government had become a "joint participant" (an active or passive participant) with private industry or other parties in a pattern of racially discriminatory conduct.

Contemporary Analysis

Contemporaneous findings of racial discrimination in procurement should include economic evidence demonstrating statistical disparities in contract awards, capacity utilization for MBEs versus non-MBEs, and the growth rate of MBEs versus non-MBEs. Other sources of inquiry regarding racial discrimination should include: written surveys to MBEs and non-MBEs and extracting data/information from agency/jurisdictions records or accounts payable.[72] Stated more succinctly, statistical data collection should be probative in nature. The purpose of probative statistics is to attempt "to attribute existing business disparities across identifiable groups significantly to their experiences of local discrimination."[73] In other words, "the challenge is to identify and explore whether state and/or local business, legal or other factors either caused or were strongly correlated with any disparity in contracting or other business conditions in the state/local market."[74] Generalized or amorphous findings or wrongdoing by unidentified persons or sectors and generalized findings of societal discrimination are not sufficient to justify a set-aside program. Discriminatory findings must be demonstrably related to the jurisdiction under study and the actions of the jurisdiction must have enlarged or exacerbated the discriminatory impacts against MBEs.[75]

Although absolute national statistics are of lesser value in supporting local MBE programs, certain national data may hold relevance. Cole observes that a discriminatory/contemporary analysis should "compare local business conditions with national conditions and establish the locality's [or state's] relative posture"[76] (if, for example, the locality or state has relatively more minority-owned construction companies and was receiving correspondingly more of the local or state construction business).[77]

Marketplace Discrimination Analysis

Although several sub analyses are required as a part of an overall marketplace discrimination analysis (see table 1), the bonding discrimination sub analysis is of considerable importance. Surety bonds are a form of credit and thus enhance the credit worthiness of contractors, subcontractors, and suppliers.[78] While unavailable bonding in itself is not a racial barrier to business development and growth, a bonding discrimination analysis is necessary to determine if a suretyship is denied on the basis of racial discrimination or simply on the basis of business dynamics (i.e., a newer firm, a small firm, etc.).

Another important sub analysis is an attitudinal discrimination analysis. That is, to what extent white consumers (whether representing government or themselves) dislike purchasing goods or services from minority-owned firms. A finding of attitudinal discrimination may explain why the most abled black individual, unlike the most abled white individual, self selects salaried employment as opposed to self-employment. According to Borjas and Bronars, "The existence of consumer discrimination reduced the gains from self-employment for the most able members of a minority group."[79]

Establishing a Set-Aside Percentage

After specific evidence of discrimination has been established *on the record*, a set-aside program that is adopted must be directly and demonstrably related to that record. According to the Minority Business Enterprise Legal Defense Fund, there are three approaches to devising a set-aside percentage:

> To be on the safe side, the percentage figure for the set-aside should probably be somewhere in between the present percentage of all minority businesses that are capable of doing business with the government, and the *maximum* percentage of the potential business capacity that is currently held by minority firms. This will undoubtedly require the use of an economic expert. Another possibility is to create a sliding scale for the size of the set-aside, gradually increasing the percentage from year-to-year until the maximum is achieved.[80]

In this observation, what is unclear is whether a set-aside percentage figure can be higher than the number of qualified minority firms in the relevant labor market, particularly if it has been established that the number of minority firms would have been higher but for the preclusive practices in contracting trades that created barriers for minorities twenty or thirty years ago.[81] Following the establishment of a set-aside percentage, a set-aside policy should provide for a flexibility in goals and periodic review to ensure that the policy is performing adequately and is still serving its intended purpose. This process should serve to maintain the narrowly tailed focus of the policy.[82]

Another issue that must be addressed in establishing a set-aside percentage is the willingness or unwillingness of businesses—both MBEs and non-MBEs—to participate in public sector contracting. It has been observed that "a disproportionate number of MBEs offer their services to...governments, while many non-MBEs do not."[83] MacManus points out many businesses avoid public sector contracting because such contracting brings slow payment cycles, increased scrutiny, too much paperwork, and decreased profits. Those MBEs that do not participate in government contracting feel that they do not have the ability to compete against larger firms.[84] If these observations are accurate, the question they raise is which MBE firms are to be counted, those seeking business from government and/or prime contractors on government projects or all MBEs, including those not in the government contracting market?

Relevant Market Area

Prior to establishing a set-aside percentage, an important issue that must be resolved is the relevant market that is applicable to MBEs. According to Elzinga and Hogarty, "The delineation of the relevant market has two dimensions: specifying the appropriate product line and delineating the correct geographic market area."[85] Furthermore, "A market encompasses the primary demand and supply forces that determine a product's price and the geographic market area is the are that encompasses these buyers and sellers."[86] In the context of MBEs, a crucial question is, should the MBE set-aside percentage be calculated on the "product market" or the "geographic market"? Product market refers to all businesses that are capable of doing business with government in a specific product area. Geographic market refers to all businesses in a geographic market, regardless of goods and services offered, who are capable of doing business with the public entity. Burman and Coie observe that,

> As long as overall availability and utilization are accurately calculated, it should not be necessary to calculate each narrow market separately. It is often appropriate to look at the "cluster" of goods and services offered to a customer or class of customers, not the individuals items.[87]

Furthermore, because MBEs compete in more than one industry, double counting would most likely occur with the product market approach. moreover, a set-aside percentage with fixed product-by-product or industry-by-industry goals would be expensive and difficult to administer.

The problem with the geographic market approach is defining the geographic boundary. On the one hand, businesses just outside of a defined boundary will often seek some share of their business from surrounding markets. Thus, in the context of MBEs, some firms outside the defined geographic boundary may be able to serve the relevant market, while some inside the relevant market may not be able to serve that market. To determine the geographic market, one strategy is to review the bid/purchasing records of a government for a specified period of time and ascertain the location of some 75 percent of the offerers or sellers.[88]

Summary of Selected Disparity Fact-Finding Studies

Atlanta

The City of Atlanta's disparity fact-finding study consisted of an eight-part 1,100 page report. The study was undertaken at the request of the City of Atlanta, who asked the consultants to conduct "a fact-finding study relating to the review, assessment, and potential reinstitution of the City Minority and Female Business Enterprise Program,"[89] an analysis of discrimination in Atlanta from the Ante-bellum period to the contemporary era. Its overall conclusion was that Atlanta's minority entrepreneurs have a lower success rate in obtaining loans and bonding procuring contracts regardless of their levels of education, training, or business-related experience. The study presented economic data with respect to incomes of blacks and whites and noted that blacks, who are nearly 67 percent of population, received only about 41 percent of the Atlanta's total income. Employing a "Utilization Percentage Ratio," the study found marketplace discrimination in bidding opportunities and bonding, bid manipulation, price discrimination by suppliers, customer/end discrimination, discrimination in financing, and stereotypical attitudes of customers and professional buyers.

The study also found discrimination in several business areas, including construction, real estate, law, architecture, accounting, engineering, commodity sales, security consulting, and energy. To discover anecdotal evidence of discrimination, some 76 interviews were conducted with individuals and firms knowledgeable about business practices in Atlanta (fifty-six were with minority/women-owned businesses). The minority/women-owned business interviews consisted of thirty-six black-owned businesses (including four black females), nine Hispanic-owned businesses (including four females), two Native American-owned businesses (including one Native American female), and one Asian Pacific Islander-owned business. Six of the seventy-six interviews were conducted with past or present public administrators of Atlanta area M/WBE programs.[90]

Milwaukee

The Milwaukee Metropolitan Sewerage District disparity fact-finding study found that prior discrimination in employment and educational opportunities deterred minority businesses from developing necessary, financial, technical, and community support and this discrimination, although not as pervasive, continues in the 1990s. The study observed that "this discrimination has established a hostile environment in which minority individuals and businesses must operate daily," and revealed that many minority businesses had experienced lower ownership rates, limited access to debt and equity financing, significant underrepresentation in the construction industry, lower sales receipts, and lower net worth.[91]

The study conducted interviews with forty-eight minority-owned construction firms in the Milwaukee area, including twenty-eight black-owned construction-related firms. Some 75 percent of black-owned businesses and 32 percent of Hispanic-owned businesses affirmed the existence of racially motivated obstacles within the Milwaukee construction marketplace. Furthermore, a brief historical analysis of racism and discrimination in the Milwaukee area was provided covering education, employment, business with specific attention to minorities, and the construction trades from 1965-1980. Discrimination in the construction trades "were pervasive in reach and substantive in effect and imposed significant constraints on minority training and employment opportunities within the construction trades."[92] The study recommended that the Milwaukee Metropolitan Sewerage District continue its affirmative action efforts and that the evidence of past and current discriminatory activities "provides a proper basis which the District could use to appropriately tailor new race and gender-conscious training, employment and contracting remedies." The study also observed that "race-neutral alternatives have not effectively eliminated discrimination from the Milwaukee marketplace."[93]

Tallahassee

The disparity fact-finding study for the City of Tallahassee used two different relevant time periods, 1973–1983 and 1978–1988, since the city's MBE program had two different starting dates—1983 and fiscal year 1988/89.[94] The initial MBE program included only construction firms. Other firms that could supply goods and services were included in the city's MBE goals in fiscal year 1988/89. Anecdotal data were collected by interviewing more than thirty current and former minority business owners. The interviews focus on the racial environment in Tallahassee and its impact on minority businesses.[95] In the construction area, MBE prime contractors and subcontractors received no city contracts for the years 1973–1975. In 1976 contract awards to minority construction firms did not exceed 1 percent of the city's total contracts. Contract awards to minority construction firms did not exceed 1 percent of the city's total construction contract awards to MBEs with a total of prime and subcontracts awards of about 24 percent.

In the areas of professional services and procurement, MBE contractors in 1988 received their highest contract awards of 10.67 percent and 25.24 percent, respectively. Findings from the availability and utilization analyses led to the observation that "on the whole, MBEs have experienced under-utilization in the expenditures of the City of Tallahassee operating budget."[96] Black firms were underutilized in every year of the period of study except one. The study notes that "black firms have been able to do the work, yet they have not been given ample opportunity to do so" and "the existence of the MBE program has played a significant role in the utilization of MBE firms."[97]

The study recommended that the MBE program be continued with several modifications, including "establishing set-aside percentages and goals based on the availability of MBEs within contracting and procurement categories...reduce the set-aside percentage for women and minorities other than blacks," amend the set-aside regulation "to exclude Alaskan Natives, Aleuts and any other minority groups that do not exist in the service area...establish a mechanism to maintain availability and utilization data which could be analyzed at fixed intervals", and "establish clear program entry and exit criteria and mechanism."[98]

Hillsborough County, Florida

D.J. Miller and Associates' disparity fact-finding study of Hillsborough County, which took six months to complete, revealed that "there is a significant disparity between the development and growth of Black businesses and that of Hispanic and women-owned businesses," and that minority/women business owners' contract and procurement opportunities in Hillsborough County is disproportionate to the minority population percentages.[99] The study provided a trend analysis of growth rates for black, Hispanic, and women-owned businesses in various businesses over a ten-year period, 1972-1982. The analysis showed no growth in the number of black-owned construction firms during this period. Utilizing a minority business "ratio of Black to Hispanic, Black to women and Hispanic to women-owned businesses," the study found that black business formation in the county was "less than 30 percent of that of Hispanics and less than 35 percent of women-owned businesses."[100]

This disparity fact-finding study performed an independent statistical analysis (utilization analysis) of more than 48,000 county expenditures for the ten-year period 1978-1987. The statistical tests at both the 95 and 99 percent levels of confidence showed that while the County purchasing activity with minority/women-owned businesses appeared to be in proportion to their participation numbers, procurement with these firms was not in proportion to overall county minority population.

The availability/capacity of the minority/women business community was determined through survey analysis responses from 276 minority/women-owned firms. Only 60 of the 276 respondents (some 21 percent) had done business with the county (12 blacks, 19 Hispanics, 24 women, 5 other). Less than 41 percent of the respondents had submitted bids to do county work. The black bid rate was the lowest of the three groups, with a rate of 17 percent. Furthermore, of all respondent black business owners had been in business the least number of years and employed the least number of employees per firm. An overwhelming number of respondents (248) indicated that their business could expand if they had more capital. The study concluded that minority businesses "are available for significant participation in the Hillsborough County contract process," and procurement opportunities abound with minority businesses with projected expenditures by Hillsborough County for goods and services of $1.5 billion over the next five years.[101] The study recommends that Hillsborough County continue its set-aside program and that a minority/women "participation goal of 25 percent would not be disproportionate to measures of minority population, or minority business population, or minority business availability, capacity, or a combination thereof."[102]

A Disparity Study Finding of Nondiscrimination

Unlike the disparity fact-finding studies summarized above, the disparity fact-finding study conducted for the State of Louisiana found no evidence of discrimination in the letting and procurement of contracts in the public works arena. The disparity fact-finding study of the State of Louisiana (Louisiana Department of Transportation and Development, LADOTD) was performed by a consortium of university-based investigators and support personnel from Louisiana State University and Southern University.[103] The study has been referred to as the "academic model" type disparity fact-finding study.[104] The study was requested by the Governor's Task Force on Disparity in State Procurement of the State of Louisiana and contracted for by the Division of Minority and Women's Business Enterprise of the State of Louisiana's Department of Economic Development. A principal purpose of the study was "to determine whether discrimination against minorities and women exists in the public works arena and the State of Louisiana procurement system regarding public works."[105] The study defined minority businesses in Louisiana as those owned by blacks, French Acadians, Asians Hispanics, American Indians, and women. In performing a utilization analysis, the study utilized contract award data from LADOTD for the time period 1978–1989 (subcontract awards data) and 1985–1989 awards granted by LADOTD exceeded $1.7 billion.[106] For the period 1973–1,989 LADOTD used 1,632 prime contractors who, in turn, subcontracted with 4,519 subcontractors.

The study also performed historical, survey, employment, and income and population analyses. The historical analysis consisted of twenty-three pages and provided: "[1] brief historical sketches of the original and present conditions of each subgroup of ethnic minorities and women within the state, [2] a brief record of that state highway department, [3] extent of participation, if any, of each subgroup within the highway construction program and [4] summaries and recommendations."[107] The historical analysis uncovered evidence of racial, class, and gender discrimination, especially against blacks and women.[108]

The survey analysis provided data concerning the size and financial strength of the respondent firms, their participation in the pubic works arena, and the ethnicity and genders of the owners. Slightly more than 4,000 surveys (including follow-up surveys) were mailed and only 719 returned surveys were deemed usable—a response rate of 26 percent. The names of the firms that were mailed surveys were obtained from three sources: LADOTD, the *1977 Survey of Minority-Owned Business Enterprises*, and the *Census of Construction Industries for 1967, 1977, 1982*.

According to the survey results, the average white-owned respondent firms had gross receipts in the 1 to 2.5 million-dollar range, while the black-owned firms had gross receipts in the 50,000 to 99,999 dollar range. Fifty percent of the black-owned respondent firms had four employees or less, as compared to only 15.9 percent of the white firms. The survey results also showed that black-owned firms had a success rate of 12.4 percent when bidding for prime contracts and 22.1 percent when bidding for subcontracts over the four-year period from 1985-1989. Seventeen minority-owned firms (6.6 percent) received $36.2 million in prime contract; 257 white-owned firms received $520 million in prime contracts. About 147 minority-owned firms (14.6 percent of all firms receiving subcontracts) received $18.7 million in subcontracts; 858 white-owned firms (85.4 percent of all firms receiving subcontracts) received $52.9 million in subcontracts. For the years 1977-1989, minority-owned firms received no prime contracts the first three years and averaged only three prime contracts per year from 1980–1989. Yet, only four black-owned and seven French Acadian-owned firms receiving major contract awards and twenty-one black-owned, thirteen French Acadian-owned, two Asian-owned, one Hispanic-owned, three American Indian-owned and seventeen women-owned firms receiving subcontract awards responded to the survey.

A statistical analysis of employment in the Louisiana construction industry was performed for the years 1973–1985. According to the study, the coefficients from a linear-probability model did not show widespread employment discrimination during the period. Wage earning differentials between blacks and whites was explained by individual characteristics such as age, sex, occupation, and unionization, not by discrimination.[109] Furthermore, the study pointed out that, as of 1982, there were 1,496 black-owned construction firms in Louisiana (about 6.20 percent of all construction firms in the state), and observed that "based on analysis of census data, there is little or no statistical evidence of discrimination on the basis of race in employment in Louisiana's construction industry."[110]

Interviews were conducted with sixteen firms (five blacks, three hispanics, eight whites). These interviews consisted of three personal interviews and thirteen telephone interviews. An overwhelming majority of white interviewees felt that there was no discrimination in the construction arena of the state procurement system in public works, while some black interviewees pointed out specific instances of discrimination. All of the interviewees thought that race-neutral strategies would help minority-owned firms compete in the public works arena.[111] The overall principal finding of the study was: "there is no statistical evidence of discrimination against minority-owned construction firms in the public works arena in Louisiana."[112]

Weaknesses of Louisiana Disparity Fact-Finding Study

In comparison to the four disparity fact-finding studies reviewed above, the Louisiana Disparity Study appears to have several deficiencies. First, the study interviewed only sixteen construction firms, including only five black firms. Disparity studies of Atlanta and Tallahassee conducted seventy-six (thirty-six blacks) and thirty (minority) interviews, respectively. Of particular note in the Louisiana study is the small number of interviews with black-owned construction firms. While these firms did feel discriminated against, additional interviews with black-owned construction firms would have provided further anecdotal evidence of discrimination. Furthermore, the Louisiana Study included only one interview with a black-owned construction firm that was no longer in business. No interviews were conducted with state officials (past or present) in the Louisiana Department of Transportation or the state office of Minority and Women Owned Business Program or other related state administrators. Perhaps additional interviews would have provided further anecdotal evidence of racial discrimination. Moreover, the Atlanta Study was able to uncover city documents (correspondence) that showed racial discrimination in the awarding of city contracts.

Second, the number of black-owned construction firms that were surveyed, the total number that responded, and the universe that these firms were drawn from is not apparently clear. The response rate does not appear to be representative of black-owned construction firms. Furthermore, the study lacked a thorough availability analysis. It did not utilize a variety of sources in order to identify those minority-owned firms that are available and willing to do business with the state. It appeared to have relied on only three sources to identify minority-owned firms in the State: LADOTD listing, the *1977 Survey of Minority-Owned Business Enterprises*, and the *Census of Construction Industries* (the 1982 issue being the latest year). Survey respondents were asked to indicate their ethnicity. Other, more recent sources, including state and local government certification lists of MBEs and minority trade associations listings and national sources, may have provided more comprehensive listings of black-owned construction firms in Louisiana.

In addition, the census survey data has four important shortcomings: (1) The survey was conducted in 1982, making the data nearly ten years old; (2) The survey does not categorize businesses in a very comprehensive fashion.

(The nine broad categories used by the bureau, which included the construction category, do not indicate the business nature of each firm. In other words, in the construction category, the survey does not report how many firms are paving contractors, etc.); (3) The survey does indicate that it missed some unknown number of firms; and (4) data are published only for local areas with 250 or more minority firms.[113] Furthermore, the firms provided by LADOTD most likely include only LADOTD-certified MBEs, excluding those black firms that have not been certified or have not sought LADOTD contracts.

Third, the study does not adequately address the issues of MBE formation, growth, or capacity. Nor does it address the issue of "deterred" MBEs. What circumstances have prevented the further development of MBEs? Related to these issues is the impact of employment discrimination upon the upward mobility of blacks in the construction industry. The employment analysis did not adequately address and analyze this situation.[114] An important question not answered is, What has been the impact of employment discrimination on the available pool of blacks with adequate backgrounds to establish prime construction firms? The establishment of black prime construction firms would logically develop from blacks who have served as project managers for large white-owned construction firms, a phenomenon that has been quite rare in Louisiana.[115]

Fourth, the time period for the utilization analysis (1985–1989) was at a time when discrimination would least likely occur. The study does not analyze the possible growth of black-owned construction firms as a result of the LADOTD set-aside program. In other words, the study does not track the number of awards and dollar amounts to black-owned firms on an annual basis since the establishment of the LADOTD set-aside program. Nor does the study does mention or analyze the LADOTD set-aside program or affirmative action efforts in the awarding of contracts to black-owned firms. This, of course, would involve a discussion and analysis of two important questions: (1) What are the key features of LADOTD set-aside program? (2) What compliance/enforcement mechanisms are in place and implemented? Moreover, the study did not document any race-neutral strategies/alternatives adopted by LADOTD or their effectiveness in assisting MBEs in obtaining construction contracts.

Fifth, the study compared size and sales of construction firms. However, it did not provide a longitudinal analysis of growth patterns of firms by size, age, or ethnic group. A more comprehensive marketplace discrimination analysis is required that would take into account procurement and contracting patterns in both the public and private sectors. The study did not provide any analysis of MBE utilization in the private sector. The low utilization of MBE construction firms in the private sector may be evidence of marketplace discrimination in the private sector.[116]

Conclusion

The *Croson* decision is a significant development affecting the prospects for minority business development and MBE programs at the state and local levels. The decision subjects state and local jurisdiction, race-conscious, procurement, set-aside programs to a rigorous set of standards. These standards are that set-asides be narrowly tailored, flexible, contain a waiver, be based on local evidence (factual and anecdotal) of discrimination, be logically related to the problem, have a specified time period, and be used after the failure of race-neutral alternatives.

While there is no doubt that these standards will make it more difficult for state and local jurisdictions to employ set-aside programs to remedy the continuing effects of discrimination, disparity fact-finding studies are being utilized to justify the adoption and/or continuation of set-aside programs. A disparity fact-finding study documents specific, local problems of discrimination, provides quantitative estimates of minority under-representation in business activity, and assesses the impact of race-neutral strategies to promote minority business development and utilization.

However, based on the above review of five disparity fact-finding studies, there appears to be several fundamental problems with disparity fact-finding studies relative to discrimination. The first problem has to do with size and experience of minority-owned firms. If state and local governments select firms on the basis of a demonstrated "track record," many minority-owned firms will not be qualified. Furthermore, the size of a firm qualifies it for some jobs but not for others. Thus, firms may have been selected based on what seems to be nondiscriminatory reasons and yet past discrimination may explain why minority-owned firms are smaller and less experienced.

The second problem with disparity fact-finding studies is statistical methodology. Regression analysis is utilized to determine a disparity in the awarding of contracts to majority-owned and minority-owned firms and whether the observed disparity is attributable to racial discrimination after controlling directly for specific variables. According to Lunn and Perry, these control variables, however, would not be able to "reflect the impact of past discrimination on the size and number of minority-owned firms."[117] This is to say that regression analysis cannot explain if more and larger minority-owned firms would be in existence past discrimination. Given these problems, is it correct to assume that a disparity is evidence of past discrimination? Or, would controlling for firm characteristics when assessing the effect of race on contract awards be a more acceptable method for determining discrimination or nondiscrimination? Using the former would most likely require a remedy, while the latter would probably not.[118]

A third problem with disparity fact-finding studies is the difficulty in documenting the chilling effect that discrimination has in deterring minority business entrants. The question here is, Do disparity fact-finding studies attempt to document the numbers of deterred minority businesses? If they do not, the statistical documentation will *understate* the extent and impact of discrimination on minority businesses.

A fourth problem area for disparity fact-finding studies is that they may not sufficiently explain why minority businesses are relatively more common in the service category (both in producer and consumer services) as opposed to the major retail and industry categories. That is, discriminatory barriers are more pronounced in some markets, such as retail and industry, that in other markets. The retail and industry markets are the most competitive, most highly concentrated, and are where market power is the most concentrated.[119]

Finally, disparity fact-finding studies seek to identify "systemic" discrimination rather than "identified" discrimination—that which is perpetuated by specific individuals or sources. While systemic discrimination may justify race conscious programs, it does not necessarily eliminate the perpetuators of discrimination. Identifying sources of discrimination could lead to appropriate sanctions against government agencies and/or administrators, private contractors, and individuals. Nevertheless, a disparity fact-finding study, properly and carefully done, may assist state and local entities in devising MBE set-aside programs that will expand minority access to government contracts.

Notes

1. See Joan G. Haworth, "Minority and Women's Business Set-Asides: An Appropriate Response to Discrimination?—A Partial Response, Poorly Implemented." In U.S. Commission on Civil Rights, *Selected Affirmative Action Topics in Employment and Business Set-Asides*, vol. 1 (Washington, D.C.: U.S. Commission on Civil Rights, 1985): 79–89.
2. See Joseph P. Addabbo, "Statement." In U.S. Commission on Civil Rights, *Selected Affirmative Action Topics in Employment and Business Set-Asides*, vol. 1 (Washington, D.C.: U.S. Commission on Civil Rights, 1985): 72–5.
3. See Timothy Bates, "Minority Business-Asides: Theory and Practice." In U.S. Commission on Civil Rights, *Selected Affirmative Action Topics in Employment and Business Set-Asides*, vol. 1 (Washington, D.C.: U.S. Commission on Civil Rights, 1985): 142–57.
4. See Joyce E. Allen, "The Growth and Diversification of Black Businesses," *Focus* (Joint Center for Political Studies, 18 October 1990 Washington, D.C.): 5–6, 8 and James H. Lowery, "Set-Aside Programs: Viable Vehicles for Change or Threats to the Free Enterprise System?" In U.S. Commission on Civil Rights, *Selected Affirmative Action Topics in Employment and Business Set-Asides*, vol. 1 (Washington, D.C.: U.S. Commission on Civil Rights, 1985): 109–29.
5. See Eugene Carlson, "Black-Owned Firms in the U.S. Are Increasing at Rapid Pace," *Wall Street Journal* (12 September 1990): B10.
6. See "*Richmond v. Croson* Update," *Minority Business Today*, 10 (April 1991):8; U.S. Commission on Minority Business Development, *Interim Report, 1990 Executive Summary*, (Washington, D.C.: U.S. Commission on Minority Business Development, 1990); and Matthew S. Scott, "Will Commission Report on Minority Business Make a Difference?" *Black Enterprise* (June 1991): 102.
7. See Stephen A. Plass, "Judicial Versus Legislative Charting of National Economic Policy: Plotting a Democratic Course for Minority Entrepreneurs," *Loyola of Los Angeles Law Review* 24 (April 1991): 655–89.
8. Franklin J. James and Thomas A. Clark, "Minority Business in Urban Economies," *Urban Studies*, 24 (1987): 497.
9. See Timothy Bates, "Impact of Preferential Procurement Policies on Minority Owned Businesses," *The Review of Black Political Economic* (Summer, 1985): 51–65.
10. U.S. Census Bureau, *Survey of Minority-Owned Business Enterprises* (Washington, D.C.: Government Printing Office, July 1990). However, despite the growth of minority businesses, they still represent only a small percentage of the total of various business and trade sectors. For example, only 7 percent of the 432,000 manufacturing firms in 1987 were minority owned, and 10 percent of retial firms and agricultural services concerns were minority owned. Black-owned businesses represented only 3 percent of all businesses in the U.S. and only 1

percent of the gross receipts. For further discussion of these observations see Jeanne Saddler, "Praise for Health Plan; Review Gap at Minority Firms," *Wall Street Journal* (19 October 1991): B1; and John Grant, "Minority Rules," *Corporate Detroit Magazine* (December 1991): 34–36.

11. U.S. Census Bureau, *Survey of Minority-Owned Business Enterprises*, 1990. Minority-owned firms are heavily concentrated in the tradition fields, that is, the provision of services (barber shops, beauty parlors, shoe shine repair, cleaning and pressing, etc.) and retail trade. These businesses, for the most part, are typically small-scale operations that serve neighborhood markets. These firms are characterized by small size, high failure rates, limited employment potential, low profit margins, and poor growth prospects. The construction business, along with such fields as finance, business services, certain types of manufacturing, and selected professional services, represent several emerging lines of minority business. These firms are large-scale operations in skill-intensive fields. The multiplier effect in the emerging lines of minority business is much greater than in the traditional fields. See Nikolas C. Theodore, "Stimulating Minority Business Development in the Emerging Lines of Minority Enterprise: The Role of Minority Business Set-Aside." Paper presented at the 53rd National Conference of the American Society for Public Administration (Chicago, Ill.: April 1991).

12. For more discussion on this point see Timothy Bates, "Do Black-Owned Businesses Employ Minority Workers?" *Review of Black Political Economy* (Spring 1988): 51–58.

13. These points are discussed by Plass, "Judicial Versus Legislative Charting of National Economic Policy," 658–60 and Michael D. Hinds, "Minority Business Set Back Sharply by Court's Ruling," *New York Times* (23 December 1991): A1.

14. See "In Brief," *Minority Business Entrepreneur* (January/February 1994): 4.

15. See Ylonda Gault, "Set-Aside Ruling Cuts Minority Contracts," *Crain's New York Business* (5 March 1990): 3–4.

16. On these points see Plass, "Judicial Versus Legislative Charting of National Economic Policy," 659–61.

17. The construction industry is the major area of contention in the set-aside issue. The industry is "a mainspring of economic growth and generates significant sales and revenue." In 1991, new construction in the United States was valued at nearly $500 billion, represented by about 6.5 percent of the total business revenues, and amounted to 7.1 percent of the gross national product. For an excellent, concise discussion of these points see Andrew F. Brimmer, "A *Croson* to Bear," *Black Enterprise* (May 1992): 43–44.

18. 109 S. Ct. 706 (1989); 488 U.S. 469 (1989).

19. Minority Business Enterprise Legal Defense and Education Fund, "Factors Affecting the Cost and Performance of MBE Disparity Fact-Finding Studies." (Washington, D.C.: MBELDEF, 1 March 1991) (memorandum).

20. Patrick J. Borchers, "*Croson:* A Look Forward, a Look Back." In American Bar Association, *Minority and Women Business Programs Revisited: Public Contracting in the 1990s* (Dallas, Tex: American Bar Association, 1990): 9.

21. *Fullilove v. Klutsnick*, 448 U.S. 448 (1980).

22. *Metro Broadcasting, Inc. v. Federal Communication Commission*, 11 S. Ct. 2997 (1990).

23. For a discussion of the *Croson* decision see Mitchell F. Rice, "Government Set-Asides, Minority Business Enterprises, and the Supreme Court," *Public Administration Review* 51 (March/April 1991): 114–22; Charles V. Dale, "Minority Business Set-Asides and the Constitution," *Congressional Research Service Review* (September 1989): 6–7; and Bryan B. Chambers, "Looking Back at *City of*

Richmond v. J.A. Croson Co.: Its Effects on State and Local Set-Aside Programs," *Brigham Young University Law Review* (1991): 1633–56.
24. Leslie A. Nay and James E. Jones, Jr., "Equal Employment and Affirmative Actio in Local Governments: A Profile," *Journal of Contemporary Law and Inequality* 8 (1989): 103–47.
25. See National Association of Minority Contractors, *The Impact of the Supreme Court's Decision in the City of Richmond v. J.A. Croson Company on Federal, State, Local Minority Business Utilization Programs* (Washington, D.C.: Government Printing Office, January 1991).
26. See "Opponents Find Common Ground," *Engineering News Record* (June 28, 1990): 11 and Donald P. Merwin, "Behind the Struggle that Divides the Industry," *Highway and Heavy Construction* (February 1990): 20–26.
27. See John W. Sroka, "Minority and Women's Business Set-Asides: An Appropriate Response to Discrimination." In U.S. Commission on Civil Rights, *Selected Affirmative Action Topics in Employment and Business Set-Asides*, vol. 1 (Washington, D.C.: U.S. Commission on Civil Rights, 1985): 90–108.
28. See "AGC Celebrates *Croson*, Promises to Help DBEs," *Engineering News Record* (30 March 1989): 13, 16.
29. See Donald P. Merwin, "How Two Camps Divide Over Programs Fairness," *Highway and Heavy Construction* (March 1990): 36–8, and Donald P. Merwin, "Deep-Seated Differences Keep a Solution at Bay," *Highway and Heavy Construction* (April 1990): 38–41.
30. Cited in Mervin, "Deep Seated Differences Keep a Solution at Bay," 37–38.
31. "Opponents Find Common Ground," 11.
32. Dan Margolies, "Minorities Say MBE Program Failing; Quotas Considered," *Kansas City Business Journal* (14 June 1991): 27–28.
33. See National Urban League, *The State of Black America* (New York: National Urban League, 1990).
34. Margaret C. Simms, "Rebuilding Set-Aside Programs," *Black Enterprise* (September 1990): 33.
35. On these points see Pamela Joshi, "After *Croson*: New Directions for Minority Business Set-Asides," *Focus* (Joint Center for Political Studies, Washington, D.C.), 3–4; "Sinking Fast As Goal Programs Thin," *Engineering News Record* (29 March 1990): 11–2; and Eve Hoberg, "State Suspends Mandate in Minority Hiring Rules," *Rochester Business Journal* (17 September 1990): 4. Most set-aside programs enacted since *Croson* are of three basic types: (1)those targeted at small businesses; (2) those targeted at economically disadvantages businesses; and (3) facially neutral programs with race and gender used as set-aside criteria.
36. Tim Turner, "Contractors Stymied by Law Helping Minority Companies," *The Business Journal* (Sacramento) (27 May 1991): 32, 37.
37. The *Croson* decision generated considerable coverage of set-asides in popular newspapers and magazines. See, for example, Tom Sheerwood, "Memo Questions Legality of D.C. Minority Pacts; Proposed Law Changes Infuriated Barry," *Washington Post* (21 July 1989): C1; Carolyn Wake, "Level the Playing Field for All Competitors," *USA Today* (15 March 1989): 8A; Bruce Fein, "The Court is Right to Stop Pampering Minorities," *Newsday* (3 July 1989): 41; Robert Pear, "Courts are Undoing Efforts to Aid Minority Contractors," *New York Times* (16 July 1990); A1; Dawn Garcia, "Ruling May Undercut Some Programs," *San Francisco Chronicle* (6 February 1990): A7.
38. See Q. Sabir, "Affirmative Action Watch," *Black Enterprise* (October 1990): 24.
39. See Paul Reidinger, "Life after *Croson*," *ABA Journal* (October 1990): 3.
40. Plass, "Judicial Versus Legislative Charting of National Economic Policy," 657–59.

41. See 109 S. Ct. 729. An interesting question that can be raised concerning race-neutral alternatives is, How extensive should be the use of race-neutral alternatives before moving to a race or gender based alternative? In *Coral Construction v. King County*, the district court states that "*Croson* does not compel the county consider every imaginable race-neutral alternative, nor try alternatives that would be plainly ineffective." See 719 F. Supp. 734, W. D. Washington, at 737, note 6 (1989).
42. Andrew F. Brimmer and Ray Marshall, *Public Policy and Promotion of Minority Economic Development: City of Atlanta and Fulton County, Georgia* (Parts I–VII) (Atlanta, Ga.: 29 June 1990): part I: 11.
43. On these points see Ronald L. Taylor, "The Equal Protection Dilemma of Voluntary State and Local Set-Aside Programs for Minorities and Women," *Houston Law Review* 27 (1990): 45–78.
44. Ibid., 65–66.
45. See Jason Upright, "Study Confirms Florida's Need for Preference Program," *Orlando Business Journal* (7 December 1990): 13, and "New York Mayor Plans to Increase Contracts Given to Minorities," *Wall Street Journal* (12 February 1992): C11. More specifically, disparity fact-finding studies seek to provide careful, deliberative documentation to the following questions: (1) Is there substantive evidence of historical and contemporary discrimination against persons in the class of individuals to be assisted by a set-aside program? (2) Is there substantial evidence of government participation in the discrimination, or passive discrimination in the otherwise established discrimination? (3) Have non-race neutral alternatives been ineffective and have the reasons for their ineffectiveness been explained? and (4) Is there substantial evidence of discrimination and to minimize adverse impact on those affected by the set-aside program remedy?
46. 109 S. Ct. 728.
47. MBELDEF, "Factors Affecting the Cost Performance of MBE Disparity Fact-Finding Studies," (1991 memorandum).
48. Ibid.
49. MBELDEF, "Factors Affecting the Cost Performance of MBE Disparity Fact-Finding Studies," (1991); and "AGC Celebrates *Croson*, Promises to Help DBEs," 13, 16.
50. "Set-Aside Programs Are Getting New Life," *Wall Street Journal* (16 January 1990): B1.
51. See Ken Nickolai, "Implementing *Croson*: Applying Illogic to the Elusive and Concluding the Obvious," *William Mitchell Law Review* 17 (1991): 497–537 and MBELDEF, "Factors Affecting the Cost Performance of MBE Disparity Fact-Finding Studies," (1991 memorandum).
52. John M. Gruenstein, "Documenting Discrimination with a Statistical Disparity Model: The City of San Francisco. In American Bar Association *Minority and Women Business Programs Revisited: Public Contracting in the 1990s* (Dallas, Tex.: American Bar Association, 1990): sect. G.
53. See Dave Miller and Midge Sweet, "Eye of the Beholder," *Minority Business Entrepreneur* (January/February 1994): 24–32.
54. Patrick Halligan, "Minority Business Enterprises and Ad Hoc Hypotheses: Guidelines for Studies by Local Governments," *The Urban Lawyer* 23 (2) (Spring 1991): 249–79.
55. Ibid., 262.
56. "*Richmond* v. *Croson* Update," *Minority Business Today* 10 (Spring 1991): 8. There have been at least thirty federal court decisions interpreting the *Croson* rulings with more than half upholding minority business set-aside provisions.

57. Gruenstein, "Documenting Discrimination with a Statistical Disparity Model," sect. G: 3–6.
58. David J. Burman and Perkins Coie, "Predicate Studies: The Seattle Model." In American Bar Association, *Minority and Women Business Programs Revisited: Public Contracting in the 1990s* (Dallas, Tex.: American Bar Association), sect. E.
59. See 109 S. Ct. 725–7.
60. 109 S. Ct. 728.
61. Edward D. Rogers, "When Logic and Reality Collide: The Supreme Court and Minority Business Set-asides," *Columbia Journal of Law and Social Problems* 24 (1990): 117–68.
62. 109 S. Ct. 724.
63. 109 S. Ct. 723.
64. Barry Goldstein, "Set-Asides After City of Richmond v. *Croson*." In Committee on the Judiciary, House of Representatives, *Minority Business Set-Asides* (101st Congress, 1st Session, Government Printing Office, January, 1990): 35–42.
65. Burman and Coie, "Predicate Studies," sect. E: 14.
66. Anthony W. Robinson, "Satisfying the *Croson* Standard." In Committee on the Judiciary, House of Representatives, *Minority Business Set-Asides* (101st Congress, 1st Session, Government Printing Office, 1990): 56–64.
67. Ibid., 59–62. Some interesting questions that must be raised at this point are: What if *no* minority firms are identified in the availability analysis? Does this mean there is no disparity and, hence, no evidence of past discrimination? Or, what if one or two minority firms received unusually large contracts that could in effect eliminate the disparity in the market based on contract awards? See Nickolai, "Implementing *Croson*," (1991): 502–13.
68. Ibid., 60–61. A "good old boy network" may be described as an informal network in which contracts go to friends, fellow club, union, and association members, business associates, and others. It is difficult to prove that this network is a source of discrimination because the members of the network protect themselves very well. See Lillian Ejebe, "Set-Aside Programs in Minnesota: The Effects of City of Richmond v. J.A. Croson Co." *Mitchell Law Review* 17 (1991): 467–95. According to Andrew Brimmer, in the construction industry, "The old boy network [is] composed entirely of white males." See Brimmer, "A Croson to Bear," 14.
69. Halligan, "Minority Business Enterprises and Ad Hoc Hypotheses," 260–62.
70. See National Association of Minority Contractors, *The Impact of the Supreme Court's Decision in the City of Richmond v. J.A. Croson Company on Federal, state, Local Minority Business Enterprise Utilization Programs*, 6–7.
71. Robinson, "Satisfying the *Croson* Standard," 56.
72. Ibid., 57–58.
73. John A. Cole, "Analysis in Support of MBE Programs." In committee on the Judiciary, House of Representatives, *Minority Business Set-Aside Programs*, 101st Congress, 1st Session (Government Printing Office, January 1990): 111.
74. Ibid., 111.
75. Halligan, "Minority Business Enterprises and Ad Hoc Hypotheses," 258–65.
76. Cole, "Analysis in Support of MBE Programs," 112.
77. Ibid., 112.
78. Halligan, "Minority Business Enterprises and Ad Hoc Hypotheses," 262–7.
79. George J. Borjas and Stephen G. Bronars, "Consumer Discrimination and Self-Employment," *Journal of Political Economy* 97 (3) (1989): 581–605.
80. Robinson, "Satisfying the Croson Standard," 57.
81. John Payton, "The Meaning and Significance of the Croson Case." In Committee on the Judiciary, House of Representatives, *Minority Business Set-Aside*

Programs, 101st Congress, 1st Session (Government Printing Office, January 1990): 13–34.
82. Robinson, "Satisfying the *Croson* Standard," 56–58.
83. Burman and Coie, "Predicate Studies," 9.
84. Susan S. MacManus, "Why Businesses Are Reluctant to Sell to Governments," *Public Administration Review* 51 (July/August 1991): 328–43.
85. Kenneth G. Elzinga and Thomas F. Hogarty, "The Problem of Geographic Market Delineation in Antimerger Suites," *The Antitrust Bulletin* (1978): 45–81.
86. Ibid., 47.
87. Burman and Coie, "Predicate Studies," 9.
88. Ibid., 14.
89. Brimmer and Marshall, *Pubic Policy and Promotion of Minority Economic Development*, Part I, 69.
90. Ibid., Part II.
91. Conta and Associates, *A Study to Identify Discriminatory Practices in the Milwaukee Construction Marketplace* (Milwaukee, Wis.: Conta and Associates, February 1990), ii.
92. Ibid., ii.
93. Ibid., i, iii.
94. MGT of American, *Final Report: City of Tallahassee MBE Fact-Finding Disparity Study* (Tallahassee, Fla.: MGT of America, Inc., 1990).
95. Ibid., 27.
96. Ibid., 128. A debate exists over which is a better measure of success in government contracts going to minority firms; the number of contracts secured or the total dollar volume of business to minority firms. MacManus observes that "the argument for regarding the number of contracts as the better measure of success is based on the relatively small size of most minority firms and the perception that MBE program participants are relatively new businesses. The major argument for treating the total dollar volume of contracts received is the multiplier effect—the notion that larger contracts actually benefit a greater number of minorities because they tend to go to larger firms that hire more minority employees." See MacManus, "Minority Business Contracting with Local Government," 458.
97. MGT of America, *Final Report*, 136: iii.
98. Ibid., v–vi.
99. D. J. Miller and Associates, *Hillsborough County Disparity Study* (Atlanta, Ga.: D. J. Miller and Associates, 1990): 10.
100. Ibid., 57, 10.
101. Ibid., 11.
102. Ibid., 13.
103. John Lunn and Huey Perry, *An analysis of Disparity and Possible Discrimination in the Louisiana Construction Industry and State Procurement System and Its Impact of Minority and Women-Owned Firms Relative to the Public Works Arena* (Baton Rouge, La.: April, 1990).
104. John Lunn and Huey Perry, "Academic Model Louisiana." In American Bar Association *Minority and Women Business Programs Revisited: Public Contracting in the Late 1990s* (Dallas, Tex.: American Bar Association, 1990), sect. F.
105. Lunn and Perry, *An Analysis of Disparity*, ix.
106. Ibid., 15.
107. Ibid., Appendix C, 231–54.
108. Ibid., 253.
109. Ibid., xii.
110. Ibid.

111. Ibid., 139.
112. Ibid., 145. According to Nickolai, "A statistical disparity may *not* be found for two reasons: (1) if the firms are being used roughly in proportion to their availability; or (2) there are no significant number of firms available with owners having specified race or gender characteristics." See Nickolai, "Implementing *Croson*," 527.
113. Marc Bendick, Jr., "The Croson Decision Mandates That Set-Aside Programs Be Tools of Business Development." In Committee on the Judiciary, House of Representatives, *Minority Business Set-Asides*, 101st Congress, 1st Session (Washington, D.C.: Government Printing Office, January 1990): 93–105.
114. Minority Business Enterprise Legal Defense and Education Fund, *Deficiencies in Louisiana Fact-Finding Study* (Washington, D.C.: MBELDEF, 1990) (Memorandum).
115. Ibid.
116. Ibid.
117. John Lunn and Huey Perry, "The Impact of the *Croson* Decision on Affirmative Action Programs." Unpublished Manuscript, 1991.
118. Ibid.
119. See J. Heywood, "Market Structure and the Pattern of Black-Owned Firms," *Review of Black Political Economy* 16 (Spring 1988): 65–72.

Racial Formation in Zimbabwe

Vernon D. Johnson

Western Washington University

In the postwar era a voluminous literature has grown up around the issue of race in international relations (Segal, 1967; Franklin, 1968; Shepherd, 1970; Kuper, 1975; Lauren, 1988). Michael Omi and Howard Winant have made a significant contribution to our understanding of racial conflict in *Racial Formation in the United States* (1986). Although their theory pertains to only one country, it may have broader application. The United States was born from European settler colonialism during the seventeenth century. Frederickson (1981) has shown that white settler colonial development in the United States and South Africa have many commonalties. The thrust of this paper is to extend the comparative analysis of racial formation under white settler colonialism to include a case like Zimbabwe, which is even more divergent from the United States.

Omi and Winant define "racial formation" as "the process by which social, economic and political forces determine the content and importance of racial categories, and by which they are in turn shaped by racial meanings" (61). The ideology of white supremacy determines the meaning of race under settler colonialism. But in the post-war era white supremacy is eventually challenged by racial ideologies among the subordinated and race relations become politically contested. In applying racial formation theory to Zimbabwe several questions will be addressed: (1) How were European* racial ideology and meanings transferred to colonial Southern Rhodesia? (2) How did the political economy of settler colonialism induce the formation of racial consciousness and identity among Africans in Southern Rhodesia? (3) What role did racial consciousness play in the development of nationalism among Africans? (4) How did racial and ethnic identity interact and compete for the allegiance of African guerrilla movements during the war for independence? (5) To what extent are the politics of post-colonial Zimbabwe racially contested?

The Concept of Race in Social Science

Omi and Winant criticize three major paradigms of race relations—ethnicity, class, and nationalism—in American social science over the last half century.

The ethnicity paradigm was the first to view race as socially, rather than biologically, determined. It saw races as types of ethnic groups, and held that, at least in America, minority races would eventually assimilate to the mainstream of society (Park, 1950; Myrdal, 1962), or, at any rate, that plural cultures might remain intact, but increasingly take part in pluralist competition with other interest groups (Kallen, 1924; Glazer and Moynihan, 1970).

The racial conflicts of the 1960s popularized two other paradigms: those of class and nationalism. Class theories—whether neo-classical, (Friedmann, 1962; Williams 1982) reformist (Wilson, 1981), or Marxist (Boggs, 1970)—interpreted racial conflict as a type of class conflict for a liberal position. Nationalists' theories saw racism as a product of colonial subjugation of various peoples at the hands of white Europeans (Carmichael and Hamilton, 1967; Acuna, 1981).

Omi and Winant (1986: 52 and 53) argue that each of the three paradigms is deficient, because they view race as a product of something else (class exploitation or colonial domination), or as a subset of some larger phenomenon (ethnicity). Consequently, theories deriving from each paradigm argue or imply that racism can be eradicated in the same way as, or along with, that broader phenomenon.

Omi and Winant maintain, as do others (Gossett, 1965; Burkey, 1978), that race is *socially constructed* out of the initial contacts between Europeans and people of color during the period of mercantilism beginning in the fifteenth century. They end by telling us "that United States racial dynamics are the subject of permanent political contestation" (1986: 143). Thus, for Omi and Winant, race is an independent phenomenon whose dynamics must be addressed in and of itself. But they caution us against panaceas that could one day harmonize race relations or completely assimilate races. For them "race will always be at the center of the American experience" (1986: 6). The thrust of this chapter is to extend the comparative analysis of racial formation under settler colonialism to include a case like Zimbabwe, which is even more divergent from the United States. The question for this study is whether or not race continues to be central to the experience of a very different kind of post-white settler colonial social formation such as Zimbabwe.

Racial Ideology as a Global Phenomenon

In colonial Rhodesia, settlers brought with them ideas about race that had been crystallizing for generations within European civilization. The normal ethnocentric instincts all cultures exhibit toward outsiders became more pronounced as European powers expanded their reach globally, and as the axis of power in Europe shifted to the north. The expansion of empire into the Americas brought a series of rationalizations of the system of slavery that crystallized it as an institution to be supplied only from black Africa. This was largely a pragmatic matter owing to the locus of slave-based sugar production shifting from the Mediterranean to the Atlantic islands off the coast of Africa (Drake, 1990: 232–34).

Positive images of black people abounded in Mediterranean Europe across the medieval period. The eclipse of the Iberian states as sea powers by Great Britain meant the control over the slave trade by a nation with virtually no first-hand experience with Africans. The British image of blackness had always been loaded with negative passion (Drake: 273). Therefore, when they inherited a system of black slavery, it allowed those passions to emerge full-blown. Although Europe had had many experiences with Africa and had produced a variety of images both positive and negative of black people over the centuries, it is ironic that "before the end of the seventeenth century, Britain had become the primary source of information and speculation about the assumed proclivities and capabilities of Africans" (Drake: 269).

With science and the Industrial Revolution, European power to control the other peoples they encountered grew. European desire to understand humanity as they were coming to know the natural world in general increased apace. Scientific categorization led to scientific racism and the consolidation of an ever-hardening racial ideology by the mid-nineteenth century. With racial ideology came a narrative concerning the meaning of racial categories. These racial meanings had to do with the social stereotypes surrounding racial categories. To be white anywhere in the world meant being civilized, intelligent, hardworking and (relatively) morally upright, while blackness imparted primitiveness, stupidity, bestiality, indolence, and moral turpitude (Lauren, chap. 1).

This chapter is particularly concerned with the manner in which racial ideology and meanings were manifested in state policy in Zimbabwe during the colonial and early post-colonial period. The state is the social institution that exerts control through law and force over certain peoples and territory (Skocpol, 1979: 22). States everywhere are concerned with economic affairs. A strong and productive economy is an important factor in generating political order and stability. The colonial state is intimately involved in the economy, because state policy is the vehicle through which the foreigners can mobilize the indigenous population to produce to meet the needs of the metropole. This analysis will observe the manner in which colonial state policy acted to institutionalize in Zimbabwe racial ideology and meanings already established globally.

Race and the Colonial Situation

Modern colonialism is a product of the geopolitical competition among the great capitalist powers in the era since 1492. The colonial social formation features a capitalist economy, a repressive state, and a plural society. Naked strategic considerations involving competing calculations about military security were, undeniably, a stimulus to colonization. But once a piece of ground was held, its economic exploitation was imperative, lest it become a drain on the metropolitan treasury. A repressive state machinery designed to discipline the local population to work and otherwise function in the interest of metropolitan capital was also necessitated.

The colonial situation is said to produce a plural society, which includes discrete cultural groups with divergent aspirations for themselves (E.A. Walcker in Balandier, 1970: 33). Plural communities converge in the colonial setting "where economic forces are exempt from control by social will" (Furnivall, 1956). In plural societies "there is no common social will," the only common standard is profit, and "the only common deity is Mammon" (1956: 306–08).

Ethnic and linguistic groups are, in Furnivall's terms, clearly communities within colonial social formations. Furnivall (1956: 307) argues that races are not communities, but aggregates of individuals. Europeans work and live there, but they establish few lasting ties. They seldom have families with them. "The club and not the home is the centre of social life." For natives, he finds "their horizon is contracted to their lives as cultivators and their social life is less comprehensive than before." Traditional village socioeconomic life is eroded under the pressure of market relations induced from the outside, so that each *race* is "a crowd and not a community" (Furnivall: 307).

The colonial economy is geared for metropolitan profit and creates a plural society, and the colonial state exists to enforce the economic will of the metropole. However, Furnivall's hypothesis about racial groups would not seem to hold in a *settler colonial situation*. One indicator of the deeper level of oppression in settler colonialism lies squarely in the fact that Europeans develop what they hope will be lasting communities. Entire families move into the colony, land is made available to them by dispossessing the natives, and a full community life takes shape. A settler social will is evident from the very beginning, and it can come into conflict with the strict economic calculations at the metropole. We shall see how settler interest came into conflict with those of the British South Africa Company in Southern Rhodesia.

The situation of Africans is very different. Various ethnic groups retain their distinctness, though ethnic identities do undergo changes in response to colonization (Vail, 1989). However, the fundamental logic of their cultural life is undermined by their loss of political, and consequently, economic autonomy. Their predicament is further complicated by the fundamentally racial logic of colonialism that disparate African ethnic groups are all viewed as natives. The European design is one of domination over people considered to be backward; and in most of Africa that goal was realized.

With the establishment of European control native communities are all seen as factors to be exploited in the economic development of the colony. Native workers from all over the colony are recruited for work, to do different work than Europeans, and always subordinant to Europeans. The races are also residentially segregated. Yet, natives tend to retain their cultural identities. The fact of discrimination and subordination against them by race does not immediately manufacture a racial affinity among them. Natives then, are a "crowd" in the way Furnivall argues. They are brought together to work by day and they return to their culture by night. The similarity in their situation does not make them the same people.

A global white racial consciousness existed and informed settler treatment of natives the world over. In cases of white settlement a settler social will certainly emerged; but no black consciousness existed at the time of colonization. So no collective will projecting the way of life and aspirations of black people under the evolving colonial system was possible. Colonialism introduced Africans to the global political economy as subordinant actors based upon their physical appearance. In order to eradicate that subordination Africans would have to accept their admission to the system on racial terms, acquire racial consciousness, and begin to exert their own social will upon the colonial order.

The Early Colonial Period and the Politics of Ethnicity (1890–1923)

The original settlers in Southern Rhodesia came primarily from South Africa and had been part of the evolving white supremacist project there. Southern Rhodesia was formed as part of the "Scramble for Africa" after the Berlin Conference of 1884–1885. Cecil Rhodes, the South African gold and diamond magnate, started the British South Africa Company (BSAC) in 1889 and received a royal charter to explore the Zimbabwean plateau (Fredrickson: 178–79). Through state policies of political disenfranchisement and economic subjugation, they impelled disparate African ethnic groups to formulate racial consciousness and racial ideology. Two broad linguistic groups of Africans inhabited the plateau: the Ndebele and the Shona. The Ndebele were related to the Zulu of South Africa, who had been in present day Zimbabwe since the late 1830s. The Ndebele, under their king, Lobengula, were a powerful, warlike people who controlled the southwest portion of the plateau bordering South Africa. The Shona speakers had occupied the plateau for nearly a millennium (Beach, 1980: 16–17).

The BSAC charter was based upon an earlier concession, the Rudd Concession, under which the king permitted mineral exploitation in his dominions in return for weapons, a steamboat, and money. The concessionaire also verbally agreed to abide by Ndebele law, stay away from towns and settlements, and bring no more than ten white men into the country. The charter, on the other hand, gave the company comprehensive powers for the governance and economic development of the territory (Blake, 1978: 47–54).

The BSAC commanded the settler state and the colonial economy. As such, it was the bearer of racial ideology and meanings in that part of Africa. The preamble of the charter nicely incorporates the totality of the company's mission empowering it for "promoting trade, commerce, 'civilization' and good government" (Blake: 53) The charter called for the protection of European and African interests in Rhodesia; but in any conflict between the two, the combination of British strategic interests in the region, the company's interest in returning a profit, and the fact that being African meant being uncivilized, predisposed that African interests would not be seriously entertained by the colonial state. (Mutambirwa, 1980: 213).

In 1896, first the Ndebele and then the Shona rose up against the settlers. The Ndebele sued for peace after two months of fighting, but the Shona fought on until they were crushed in 1897. After the settler victory in "the risings," the foundations for the colonial system were secured. Legally the Ndebele and Shona had theoretical access to the British government in London, but Africans had no rights in areas coveted by Europeans. For their part the settlers sought representation in the colony's executive council to gain a direct voice in administration. In 1898, Britain handed down the Southern Rhodesian Order in Council, which gave the company and settlers the ability to set up a legislative council. The company appointed five members and the settlers elected four. The franchise was based upon ownership of a certain value of property and literacy qualifications. Since African cultures in Zimbabwe were non-literate and held different conceptions of property than Europeans, few Africans were able to qualify to vote at that early date in colonial history. Only fifty-one Africans voted in the first election (Blake: 150). The

British Colonial Office, through a Resident Commissioner, reserved the right to block legislation prejudiced against Africans; but over time the interests of settlers, the Crown, and the company overshadowed those of Africans. The settlers desired a permanent white enclave in Central Africa. Britain sought eventual union of Rhodesia to South Africa, and the company simply wished to return profits to its investors. The issue of the African franchise was not so salient in 1898. Both the Ndebele and Shona were preoccupied with sustaining their own social institutions, not participating in colonial ones. A black racial consciousness had yet to form that perceived itself to have been treated unjustly by being denied the vote.

When it became apparent that Rhodesia was not the new "El Dorado," farming came to be viewed as the key to the colony's future, with greater attention given to land tenure. As a consequence, the racial nature of the economy was revealed. As the BSAC awarded or sold land to settlers, reserves were established for the Ndebele as early as 1895, and after 1898 for the Shona. In 1902, about 21 percent of the country's territory was set aside for reserves. Until 1898, all land in the country was theoretically available to Africans and Europeans who possessed the "capital and techniques" to develop it.

Whites, however, feared direct economic competition with Africans, and there were reports of Africans being denied the ability to buy land (Wills, 1973: 41). Still, settlers had to rationalize their undertakings. Racial meanings and ideology that had been evolving internationally served them well. The Anglican Diocese of Mashonaland reported in 1902 that

> the Christian faith...recognizes inequalities existing individuals and races arising from the fact that neither individuals nor races are born with equal facilities or opportunities...and the only way to fit the natives of Africa to fill the place intended for them in the Commonwealth is by the disciplinary influence of the Gospel. This Gospel involves the training of the native in a sense of responsibility to himself, to his neighbor and to the state. (Mutambirwa: 77–78)

The colonial press joined the chorus. The *Bulawayo Chronicle* put forward the view that Africans "are barbarians...[that] must be treated by the government as...a people still in its childhood," while the *Bulawayo Express* exclaimed "the whites will not reckon the blacks as equals, and if they did it would simply mean the degeneration of the whites" (Mutambirwa: 78–80). To be African meant being irresponsible, barbaric, childlike, and degenerate.

In such an ideological setting any rationalization of land policy could only be at the expense of African interests. As more whites arrived seeking to become farmers, the Legislative Council was pressured to roll back the size of the reserves. Following the report of the Southern African Native Reserves Commission in 1914, Britain approved a one million acre reduction in reserve lands, and more than that was actually taken. A.J. Wills (1973: 199) nicely sums up the way racial ideology informed deliberations of the colonial government toward agricultural competition between Africans and Europeans:

> In allocating land between native reserves and areas available for European occupation, two sets of values were applied. For Europeans it was essential to provide the maximum opportunity, which was the life spirit of the enterprise. Towards the African people the Land Commission was moved by the wish to

protect...Manifestly, the African could not compete in capital or techniques. The purpose of demarcating reserves, therefore, was to ensure that Africans would not be "bought out," but would be always sure of land.

The Commission went on to say that "the natives have, of course, no united policy and are, as a people, almost inarticulate" (1973: 200).

The need to protect Africans then, was said to arise from their lack of unity and inability to speak for themselves. The Land Commission, however, did interview several chiefs and headmen. They expressed almost universal dissatisfaction with the amount and quality of land available on the reserves (Mutambirwa: 144). So Africans were able to articulate their concerns, but no attention was paid to them.

The response of both the Ndebele and Shona to the first generation of colonial rule was, for the most part, cultural and ethnic rather than broadly racial. (See Ranger, 1968a; 1968b; 1970.) Lobengula's policies had been geared toward maintaining, and indeed extending, Ndebele political and cultural suzerainty over the plateau, and Ndebeles certainly saw themselves as distinct from, and superior to, the Shona.

The Shona had their internal rivalries, but they spoke mutually intelligible dialects; and those of them who remained outside direct Ndebele rule retained their cultural identity. The sense of indignation that caused the Ndebele to fight in 1893 was an expression of Ndebele ethnic nationalism against the intruders. Although there apparently was some contact between Ndebele and Shona spirit mediums during the 1896 risings, each group rallied essentially to protect its own way of life.

In the period between 1898 and World War I, the attention of the Ndebele focused around the issues of restoring their monarchy and access to land. The earliest petitions were heard on the issue of the monarchy. Two of the late King Lobengula's sons, Njube and Nguboyena, became involved in a series of schemes to resurrect the monarchy. Petitions were made to the Chief Native Commissioner and eventually the High Commissioner. None of these thrusts were taken seriously by the colonial government.

As the kingship issue waned in importance after 1909, land pressures increased. Ndebele became squatters in their own country as whites bought or were allotted land. They were subjected to rents, grazing and dipping fees and "thousands were evicted" by the early part of this century. (Ranger, 1968b: 219) Their grievances were heard by the government at periodic *indabas* (councils of chiefs), but nothing was done to alleviate the situation.

In 1919, the British Privy Council determined that the Crown, not the British South Africa Company, owned the land of Southern Rhodesia. Because the settlers were pressing for self-government at that time, there was an opening for an "African voice" to be heard (Ranger, 1970). Nyamanda, the eldest son of Lobengula, mobilized traditionalist and educated Ndebele and African migrants from South Africa around "the restoration of the Ndebele kingship and of the Ndebele homeland" (Ranger, 1968b: 220). He also developed strong ties to the South African Native National Congress, which had experience in petitioning white authorities. The Congress chaplain Henry Reed Ngcayiya agreed to carry Ndebele grievances to London. Reverend Ngcayiya eventually gained an interview with a Colonial Office official. Still, the petition was denied. Even when the Ndebele developed modern interest group techniques, they still failed to gain redress for their grievances. The Shona responded to their defeat of 1897 in three ways, each of which demonstrated that they had yet to acquire a racial consciousness.

Some Shona continued the warrior tradition, which had kept the Zimbabwean plateau free from Portuguese control since the sixteenth century. The paramount chief Mapondera had taken his people to Mozambique in 1894 to participate in the risings of the Barwe Shona against the Portuguese. Thus, Mapondera was not around to experience the defeat of 1897. Between 1900 and 1904 Mapondera mounted a campaign to regain Shona independence in north-central Mashonaland. Mapondera was defeated and imprisoned in 1904. Nonetheless, the Shona in Mozambican border areas were not pacified until 1917. Rumors of renewed risings circulated in Mashonaland throughout this period.

The majority of the Shona focused on local communal pursuits, particularly on the agrarian economy. Far fewer Shona than Ndebele worked in the European wage laboring economy before World War I. Shona peasants produced food for mine workers and the growing towns, and many prospered. Only on the eve of the war did European agriculture become competitive with that of the Shona. Terrence Ranger (1970: 15) observes that:

> [T]he economic opportunity did enable the Shona to turn inward to their own local situation. Shona "traditional" life and ways were at least an economic success in this period even if there had been a collapse of military institutions and a serious erosion of the political.

Shona ethnic politics retained its vitality. Competition over "chiefships... positions of influence as headmen or councillors...all of this continued to absorb a great deal of Shona political energy" (1970: 3) Chiefs and headmen continued to control the allocation of land in the reserves, and local office holders served to represent the interests of their people vis-à-vis the colonial authorities.

Shona also adopted the Christian religion in the hopes of turning its power to their advantage. By the period of World War I, Matthew Zwimba had formed the White Bird Mission, which blended Christianity and traditional Shona spirituality. Zwimba's work, unique at the time, was a forerunner of religious nationalist movements that would worry colonial authorities into the 1920s and 1930s.

The foundations of a political economy based upon racial domination were in place as the 1920s began. But African politics remained essentially ethnic, looking backward toward cultural traditions as a way of sustaining beleaguered peoples.

Emergent Racial Consciousness (1923–1939)

The growth of colony-wide racial consciousness among Africans was accelerated by the establishment of responsible settler government that consolidated racial, political, and economic institutions. After a 1922 constitutional referendum, the settlers achieved "responsible government" and Company rule came to an end. "Responsible government" was a thirty-five-member legislative assembly and a six-member cabinet under a Premier (later known as a Prime Minister). Policymakers in Britain and white settlers in Southern Rhodesia were of the same mind as to the separation between the races—the convention that Great Britain would not interfere in the colony's domestic affairs, though it held the legal power to do so. Britain could veto any legislation "that discriminate(d) against Africans (except in respect to arms and liquor)" (Blake: 187–92). The High Commissioner (British Ambassador) for South Africa retained control over native land purchasing rights, reserves, and representative councils. The franchise was restricted to persons twenty-one years old and greater, earning 100 pounds per year, or possessing property valued at 150 pounds (Blake: 192). These restrictions assured that at the electoral level Africans interests would not be recognized. Of the nearly 15,000 votes cast in the referendum, only sixty were by Africans (Mutambirwa: 197). Simultaneously, at the lobbying level, African political organizations were simply too weak to gain serious attention.

Modern interest groups expressing an inchoate black nationalism did, however, begin to appear around the time that responsible government was established. All three of these early nationalist organizations were dominated by Africans from neighboring colonies (either South Africans, Northern Rhodesians, or Malawians). Each organization directed its lobbies toward the legislative assembly rather than London, and their aspirations were increasingly colony-wide. However, for each the organizational reality was regional. The Rhodesian Bantu Voters' Association (RBVA) was centered in Matabeleland. Its leadership was dominated by black South Africans who had migrated north, and almost all of the rest of its membership was Ndebele. The founder, Abraham Twala, was himself a Zulu from South Africa, and he considered the Shona to be unready for modern politics (Ranger, 1970: 90–93). The program of the RBVA initially revolved around efforts to obtain the franchise for more Africans and find liberal white candidates to represent African interests in the legislative assembly. But under the leadership of Martha Ngano, the Bulawayo chapter of the RBVA adopted a more grassroots approach, focusing on issues pertinent to the common people, such as "destocking and dipping and land shortage" (Ranger, 1968b: 224).

In Mashonaland modern politics was initiated by the Rhodesian Native Association (RNA) under the leadership of Eli P. Nare. The RNA represented the "progressive Shona farmers." Its program was more accommodationist than that of the RBVA, seeking to work in cooperation with the Native Department rather than posing demands to it. The RNA was interested in increasing African educational opportunities, making more private lands available for African purchase, expanding the African franchise, and having direct access to government official. Despite its territory-wide aspirations, the RNA showed its limitations by using anti-Ndebele rhetoric in its pronouncements.

In the central areas of the country, the Gwelo Native Welfare Association (GNWA) was established in 1924. It was a social welfare association. The GNWA was established around Gwelo, but it had both Shona and Ndebele membership and its influence spread quickly into Matabeleland. Over time it also acquired national aspirations and its name changed to the Southern Rhodesian Native Welfare Association, and finally to the African Welfare Association (Ranger, 1970: 108). Although the RBVA and the GNWA, in particular, had made considerable impact among the peasantry, their roots were not very deep and the government still did not take them seriously.

A trade union movement also emerged in the late 1920s. The South African-based Industrial and Commercial Workers Union (ICU) sent Robert Sambo up to Southern Rhodesia to organize in 1927. The ICU represented the first expression of working-class consciousness. It was also the first organization to seriously attack tribalism and actively promote a national identity. An example of the typical rhetoric propagated at ICU meetings is instructive, "You cannot conquer the white man because they are united. If you fight one white man the whole group will come upon you. Do not say 'I am a Blantyrer or a Sindebele.' Then we shall obtain our country" (Ranger, 1968b: 229). In practice the ICU sent a Shona, Masoja Ndlovu, to organize in Bulawayo, and a Ndebele, Charles Mzingeli, to head up its efforts in Salisbury.

Despite its progressive style of organizing, the ICU ran into a number of difficulties. It organized in the towns in a migratory economy. The people it sought to organize retained deeper roots in rural areas. In fact, many of them were from other colonies in southern Africa. Issues of family and land tenure acted to strengthen, and even reformulate, ethnic ties and counter any concrete movement around racial identity. Yet, the ICU extended the discourse on black nationalism to workers residing throughout Southern Africa. In doing so, it planted seeds that the post-war generation would bring to full flower.

The impetus for greater black racial identification came as a response to white strides to impose their social will in public policy. A number of restrictive laws were passed that would distinguish Southern Rhodesia from colonial development in the rest of British Africa. "The Vagrant's Act was directed against Africans without jobs or land to return. The African Registration and Identification Act required Africans to carry passes. The African Affairs Act was a general act to control Africans" (Kapungu, 1974: 30).

Most importantly, the land issue had to be settled once and for all. The Morris Carter Commission was established in 1925 to survey African and European opinion on the disposition of the 76 million acres of land remaining outside the Native Reserves (including land already occupied by whites). Hundreds of Africans of every political persuasion were heard by the Commission. Many opinions were expressed, but generally it was clear that Africans wanted access to more land (Ranger, 1970: 174–83).

By 1925 Europeans privately owned 31 million acres of land in both urban and rural areas. Africans held 20.5 million acres, all but 47,000 of which were on the reserves. The Carter Commission recommended that 17 million additional acres be allocated to Europeans and 6.8 more acres be designated for "native purchase." Europeans were to receive the more arable lands in areas closer to paved highways and railroads, while Africans were to be relegated, generally, to more marginal areas. In a country with one million Africans and 50,000 Europeans such an allocation, if adopted, would place serious constraints upon African agriculture. Many whites at the time viewed the Commission's report as benevolent toward Africans who lacked the capital and know-how to compete successfully with European commercial farmers. It would assure that Africans would retain some land as progressive settlers streamed into the country. Yet Europeans resented "African farmers...competing at cut prices with access to markets which Europeans regarded as their own" (Blake: 201). Such pronouncements by Europeans covered their fear of competition from African peasants producing at less overhead.

In the aftermath of the Carter Commission visit, black nationalist aspirations toward territory-wide organization grew. In 1926, the RNA asked the government to allow it to organize in the reserves nationally, and form a Native Advisory Council. The Southern Rhodesian Native Welfare Association also sought to recruit among all Africans. The Land Apportionment Bill was based upon the recommendations of the Carter Commission. As it was before the legislative assembly in 1929, African interest groups met jointly to discuss it under the sponsorship of the RBVA. They universally rejected the bill. During the debate the language of European-African racial conflict could be heard (Ranger, 1968b: 229). But territory-wide organization around the precepts of black nationalism was yet to be realized. The government understood this, and never seriously considered African objections. The Land Apportionment Act became law in 1931.

As Europeans sought to perfect their control over African labor, the Industrial Conciliation Act that "restricted Africans from qualifying for apprenticeships or skilled work, and from joining trade unions" was also passed in 1934 (Kapungu: 29). As the racial political economy crystallized during the 1930s, the Southern Rhodesian African National Congress emerged to make another thrust at territory-wide organizing. It too had limited success, but it did survive into the 1950s, linking the elements of early nationalism to the more mature, post-war mass nationalist movements (Ranger, 1968b: 230–31).

It must also be noted that, for the most part, the Ndebele and Shona masses remained at the level of ethnic nationalism as World War II approached. The Matabele Home Society dominated Ndebele politics after 1929, focusing on the old issues of land and the restoration of the monarchy. An additional concern for them now was the condition of the Ndebele in urban areas. Independent churches, led mostly by migrants from Nyasaland, were formed and became prominent among the Shona, melding black nationalism with Christianity.

The beginnings of an African racial consciousness were apparent. Some Africans had begun to think racially, and they had appropriated modern interest group techniques, but they had yet to mobilize the peasant masses for racial politics. On the eve of World War II, African nationalism did not pose a threat to European nationalism in Southern Rhodesia. Because of this telling political weakness, Africans continued to be ignored by colonial authorities.

World War II, Greater Participation in the Global System, and a Mature Racial Consciousness (1939–1963)

What Southern Rhodesian Africans were unable to achieve by their own devices during the interwar years was made more possible by the global forces unleashed during the Second World War. These forces were both ideological and material in nature. At the ideological level the war extended the developing discourse on human rights to actors from every corner of the colonized world. Foremost among human rights issues at that time was self-determination of peoples. With the inception of the League of Nations following World War I, self-determination of peoples was made an international issue. Although the rhetoric of self-determination was focused on the European world, it was utilized to justify nationalist movements, particularly in Asia, in the interwar period. Self-determination was given further force after World War II, because the two post-war superpowers, the United States and the Soviet Union, were both anticolonial. The two great colonial powers, France and Great Britain, were militarily and ideologically spent after the war, and thus, in no position to oppose the inclusion of the principles of self-determination into the United Nations charter (Hargreaves, 1988: 56–59).

The issue of race was also politicized on a global scale by the war. The dynamics set in motion by the war acted to sharpen Africans' racial consciousness at the material level of human activity, and at the ideological level, as well. At the material level, the war had the effect of undermining the colonial order. The war required the total effort of the belligerents, including the full mobilization of the colonies. African soldiers fought in metropolitan armies, learned to operate modern military technology, and travelled overseas. Africans were participating in the modern world. The combat itself had a telling effect. Fighting alongside white soldiers, killing the white enemy, watching the defeat of white countries at the hands of the Japanese in the Pacific—all of these experiences helped to demystify the power of white people in the eyes of the colonized (Sithole, 1968: 49–53).

Upon returning home, African veterans found the usual racial discrimination of colonialism. In Southern Rhodesia black veterans received less-attractive benefit packages than their white counterparts. As time passed they had the added insult of seeing the former enemies, Italians and Germans, immigrate into the colony and advance rapidly as white settlers. Additionally, black peasants and workers experienced harsher state policies during the war. The Land Apportionment Act was made more restrictive, and the Industrial Conciliation Act was enforced more tightly. These policies, visited equally upon Shona and Ndebele, made "them conscious of common disabilities that transcended tribal ties" (Mtshali, 1967: 86). The basis of a movement for self-determination based on race was laid.

It was in this racial consciousness among Africans the trade union movement took hold after the war, "In 1945 J.Z. Savanhu, a leader of the African Workers' Trade Union, declared: 'The old African of tribalism and selfishness has died away. Africans realize as never before that united they stand and divided they fall.'" (Utete, 1979: 43). Later that year, African workers successfully struck against the Rhodesian Railways, winning "higher wages, improved working conditions, and the recognition of their union" (Utete: 87–88).

However, railway workers were only one special interest. The late 1940s saw the emergence of a multiplicity of black organizations, each with its own rather narrow constituency. A key figure in melding these diverse elements into a broader movement was Benjamin Burombo. He was the founder of the British African Voice Association (BAVA) in Bulawayo in 1947. BAVA sought to press for the redress of the grievances of all Africans. In 1948 a general strike broke out among African workers across the country. The generally horrid pay, conditions of work, and residence for Africans fueled the walkout. Burombo and BAVA were involved, at least in encouraging the strike, and perhaps instigated it. The strike was crushed by the police and army after ten days, but a commission was established to determine the causes of the strike and make recommendations. The commission called for the creation of Native Labor Boards to represent the grievances of African workers (Shamuyarira, 1965: 36–37).

Burombo and BAVA were also active in rural areas, especially in opposition to the Land Husbandry Act of 1951. The act was meant to privatize land tenure and lower the number of cattle in the native reserves as ways of decreasing soil erosion and increasing productivity. Of course Africans had no say in its passage or implementation. By the 1950s this was unacceptable (Utete: 45): "[T]he rural areas became centres of struggle against the regime(with)...mass refusals to apply for land permits; destruction of government property such as cattle dipping tanks; [and] violence against all rural agents of the settler regime." These tactics did not cause the regime to falter. BAVA was banned in 1952, but a colony-wide, race-based nationalism was germinating.

The proposed amalgamation of Northern and Southern Rhodesia and Nyasaland into federation would be the issue that would allow African nationalism to mature. The Central African Federation was born in 1953. The preponderant interests in this new formation were domestic agricultural and manufacturing capital in Southern Rhodesia and British investment capital. State priorities under federation included economic development and "racial partnership." Economic development was to be based upon the industrial infrastructure of Southern Rhodesia, the revenues generated from Northern Rhodesian copper mines, the vast reservoirs of cheap African labor available in each territory, and British and domestic capital.

The notion of "racial partnership" was particularly troublesome at that time in history. It was a concession to the changes in global ideology resulting from World War II and the formation of the United Nations. Global racial ideology had changed drastically since the war. Africans had become equals to Europeans in their humanity. Europeans and their institutions were everywhere under scrutiny for the possibility that they were racist. As the federation was being established, the racial regime of colonialism was already being dismantled in Asia and the winds of decolonization were blowing in Africa.

It was in this context that white settlers in Central Africa connived to establish an independent state based upon a racial partnership that was only a smoke screen for continued racial domination. It was to be the ideological answer to rising African nationalism to the north and rigid apartheid to the south. Southern Rhodesian Prime Minister Godfrey Huggins called it a partnership between "a horse and rider" in which African beasts of burden would be ridden toward economic development and prosperity by Europeans (Kapungu: 38).

Until federation, Southern Rhodesian constitutions had been implicitly racial by using literacy, income, and property stipulations to limit African voting. The federal constitution now explicitly provided for African representation. Seven of the thirty-five seats in the legislature were reserved for members elected to represent African interests, and two more were appointed for the same reason (Palley, 1966). The African petty bourgeoisie, because of its representation and ability to vote, was seen as a buffer against the continuing growth of African nationalism. But during the years of federation, a succession of organizations carried the banner of an increasingly aggressive nationalism.

The City Youth League (CYL), formed in 1955, was the first black organization to oppose the federation. It continued the confrontational politics of BAVA, daring to identify government administrators with responsibility for native affairs as "racialists." Much to the chagrin of the government, it also further cemented the coalition between an African middle-class leadership and African workers by leading a boycott against the Harare bus system.

In 1957 the CYL merged with a rejuvenated ANC of Bulawayo to form a new territory-wide ANC. The new organization coalesced Shona and Ndebele in an unprecedented mass movement. Its program called for "national unity...in true partnership, regardless of race, colour or creed...(and) is equally opposed to tribalism" (Shamuyarira: 46). In 1959 the ANC took up the struggle against the Land Husbandry Act, bringing suit against the government in a number of cases. Some estimates put its membership at 250,000. It was banned that same year. But the ANC had made its contribution to the movement by bringing Shona and Ndebele together and articulating a consciousness of race, as well as a vision for a nonracial and nontribal society.

In 1960 the nationalist movement regathered itself as the National Democratic Party (NDP). Its manifesto called for universal adult suffrage and black majority rule. This was an advance upon the ANC policy of a mere increase in African voting. The Central African Federation disintegrated in the early 1960s, as black rule in Northern Rhodesia and Nyasaland became a foregone conclusion. In the south, where white power was greater, the black nationalist NDP boycotted the referendum over yet another white supremacist constitution in 1961. White voters ratified the constitution by a two-to-one margin. The NDP was banned following widespread violence in African areas later that year (Blake: 333–40).

The political center was vacated in 1962 as Europeans and Africans coalesced around mutually antagonistic, racially based programs. Europeans formed the Rhodesian Front Party (RF), which opposed forced racial integration and majority rule. Africans regrouped under the Zimbabwe African Peoples' Union (ZAPU), which supported majority rule. In the ensuing elections, which ZAPU boycotted, the RF won a majority and the polarization of races was complete. ZAPU began to send youths abroad for guerrilla training in 1962 and terrorist attacks on whites areas began. Those actions, however, were intended to pressure the settler regime into changing its policies, not to overthrow it (Hudson, 1981: 43–48).

By 1963 Zimbabwean Africans had developed a racial consciousness for the political purposes of national liberation. They had come to understand and accept the importance of race as an organizing principle of the colonial order. They realized that a transethnic and racial political movement would advance the cause of decolonization. But as of 1963, they were faced with an intransigent and well-armed settler regime. As Zimbabwean Africans groped for a successful strategy for decolonization, ethnic cleavages would appear in the liberation movement.

Racial and Ethnic Consciousness in the Late Colonial Period (1963–1979)

Joshua Nkomo was the President of ZAPU. He toured abroad in 1961 and 1962, rallying international support for majority rule, but he had no program to counter the emergence of the RF. Criticism of Nkomo's leadership eventuated in a split in the nationalist forces. Nkomo had favored establishing a government in exile, while other leaders wished to build a stronger base inside the country. In August 1963, Reverend Ndabaningi Sithole, Robert Mugabe, and others formed the Zimbabwe African National Union (ZANU). Sithole and Mugabe were Shona and ZANU would be socially rooted in the Shona people. ZAPU, like its predecessors, was bi-ethnic, and would remain so until the 1970s. So ethnic cleavage, per se, did not cause the split. Many key Shona politicians stayed with ZAPU, including party chairman James Chikerema and guerrilla leader Rex Nhongo.

The RF government under Ian Smith made its Unilateral Declaration of Independence (UDI) in 1965. In 1966 ZAPU and ZANU attempted ineffectual guerrilla insurgencies. Ethnic conflicts affected each party's ability to pursue armed struggle. ZAPU's cohesion began to unravel after Nkomo went to jail in 1964. In his absence James Chikerema, a Shona, was acting president. By 1970 Chikerema was being accused of running the party on the basis of tribalism and nepotism. Eventually, Chikerema and other leading Shonas were forced out of ZAPU and it became a predominantly Ndebele party. Chikerema's faction formed the Front for the Liberation of Zimbabwe (FROLIZI) in 1971. The new party was composed primarily from the Zezuru tribe of the Shona ethnic group.*

At the same point ZANU became a party mostly composed members of the Karanga and Manyika tribes of the Shona. After Karanga-Manyika competition led to the deaths of "over 250 ZANU cadres," including party chairman Herbert Chitepo, ZANU split into Karanga and Manyika factions in 1975. These cleavages occurred while Reverend Sithole and Robert Mugabe were in prison. Upon his release that year, Sithole, himself a member of the small Ndau group of Shona, linked up with the Karanga faction. Meanwhile, Mugabe, a Zezuru, joined the guerrillas fighting from Mozambique and garnered mostly Zezuru, Karanga and Manyika backing (Sithole, 1980: 26–30).

Despite its internal problems, ZANU had decided to step up its guerrilla operations as early as 1969. The party requested permission from the ruling party of Mozambique, FRELIMO, to operate from Tete province along the northeastern border of Zimbabwe. FRELIMO resisted for three years hoping that ZAPU, like itself a Soviet client, would undertake guerrilla operations instead. Finally, in 1972 ZAPU admitted it had no influence in the Shona regions of northeast Zimbabwe. At that point FRELIMO gave ZANU the green light to operate from Mozambique (Martin and Johnson, 1981: 16–19). It was this political-military strategy in which broad Shona ethnicity was crucial that propelled ZANU to electoral victory in 1980. Although it was primarily a Manyika and Zezuru party until 1975, by the time of the Lancaster House talks in 1979 it was operating in nearly all Shona-speaking areas of the country. ZANU's resolution in waging the war and its ability to mobilize

---

* "Ethnic group" will be used here to denote the larger cultural grouping composed of any number of communities speaking mutually intelligible dialects and interacting for economic and other cultural purposes. "Tribe" refers to these smaller communities. Sithole [1980] identifies six distinct Shona and two Ndebele tribes.

voters across Shona ethnic groups outflanked the machinations of all other parties as the transition to majority rule took place.

Although ethnicity played a crucial role in the internal politics of the Zimbabwean revolution, all nationalist parties, revolutionary and accomodationist, projected themselves as anti-racist to global society. The "Salisbury Declaration," prepared jointly by all of the nationalist parties in 1974 (Nyangoni and Nyandoro, 1979: 296), proclaimed:

> We assume that on this demand for independence there is no difference among Rhodesians of all races. But there has until now been a difference on the kind of independence which Zimbabwe must have. The Rhodesian Front has, in the past, sought independence on the basis of minority rule. We reject that. The independence we still seek, is independence on the basis of majority rule.

Institutionalized racial discrimination was receiving increasing attention as a human rights problem in the post-war era. United Nations-sponsored trade sanctions against apartheid South Africa had been in place since 1963. The United Nations Charter had proscribed racial discrimination and in 1965 the General Assembly passed the International Convention on the Elimination of All Forms of Racial Discrimination (Hannum, 1992: 64). That same year the UN initiated voluntary economic sanctions against Rhodesia for its refusal to accept black majority rule. By 1968 the sanctions were universal and mandatory for UN members (Strack, 1978: 16–22).

As the Lancaster House Conference to settle the Rhodesian conflict unfolded in 1979, all the African parties sought a constitutional order that would provide for black majority rule. Racial equality was a human right in the post-war global setting, and black Zimbabweans had developed a racial consciousness and built a movement in response to the indignities of white settler colonialism. Yet, as we have seen, the nationalist movement became fractured along ethnic lines, and ethnic consciousness played a crucial role in ZANU's victory. It was not just the fact of Shona ethnicity, but the use of the Shona warrior tradition and religion as tools of mobilization that propelled ZANU to ascendancy (Lan, 1985). ZANU's guerrilla organization, The Zimbabwe African National Liberation Army (ZANLA) operated in some Ndebele areas of the country during the war, but they failed to broaden their strategy to incorporate Ndebele culture into their conception of nationalism. Consequently, Ndebele seeking independence supported ZANLA during the war, but voted for ZAPU candidates in the 1980 elections (Ranger, 1985: 216). This ethnic cleavage would continue to plague Zimbabwe after independence.

Race and the Post-Colonial Political Economy

As a result of the Lancaster House Agreement, black Zimbabweans attained full citizenship of their country, but issues of race would still plague the country. Of the 100 seats in the House of Assembly, twenty were reserved for whites, though they were far less than 5 percent of the population. A few thousand white farmers still controlled most of the really good farm land in the country. According to the constitution, the representative system could not change until 1987, and land reform could not occur until 1990. Thus, after nearly a decade of guerrilla war, Zimbabwe still had a racial constitution.

In what came as a surprise to many observers, Robert Mugabe and ZANU-PF won a clear majority of fifty-seven seats in the House of Assembly in the 1980 elections. (PF is the acronym for the Patriotic Front, the diplomatic alliance formed between ZAPU AND ZANU in 1976. In preparation for the 1980 elections ZAPU changed its name to PF-ZAPU, and ZANU became ZANU-PF.) The Mugabe government embarked upon a policy of "national reconciliation." In Mugabe's own words (Novicki, 1982: 5):

> There has been the political thrust to try and unite Zimbabweans in spirit, one might say, and make them accept one another. Whatever we did by way of integrating the army also had to be done among the people, integrating them in spirit and getting them to accept that they are now one society, whatever political affiliations they owe, whatever ethnic groups they belong to, whatever religion they believe in.... So we have been preaching from the mountain a sermon on national reconciliation...we went about it by establishing a government of national unity, by inviting ZAPU to join the government and also appointing two or so whites in government so as to make the population see that we were no longer living in the past. We no longer were at war with each other.

Within the overall framework of national reconciliation there has been political contestation, and some of it has been over matters of race. Much of the social discrimination against blacks was actually dismantled under the government of Bishop Muzorewa. The notorious Land Tenure Act had been amended in 1977 to end racial allotment of agricultural land (Tartter, 1981: 201–02). Many other racial issues could be dealt with summarily by ZANU-PF, because it controlled the Parliament. The biggest issues facing the Mugabe government were the implementation of an equitable minimum wage for Africans and the movement of significant numbers of Africans into the middle and upper levels of the civil service. The minimum wages for farm, domestic, and industrial workers were raised. The percentage of Africans in the civil service went from 40 percent in 1980 to 60 percent in 1982, with Africans holding roughly half of the senior positions (Curtin, 1983: 107; *Africa News*, 1982: 4–5).

Another major racial issue in newly independent Zimbabwe was land reform. If meaningful land redistribution could not be achieved, the years of bloodshed would become dubious for many Africans; but sweeping land reform was precluded until 1990 by the constitution. African agriculture had been confined to tribal trust lands since the 1930s, and most of those areas were grossly overpopulated by people and cattle by 1980. The Mugabe government has been trying to purchase land on a willing seller-willing buyer basis. It had planned to resettle 162,000 families on such a basis, but by 1989, only about 50,000 families had been resettled. Even someone as highly placed as Senior Minister Joshua Nkomo was not above discussing land reform in racial terms. Talking to a group of white commercial farmers in Bulawayo, Nkomo described landless black peasants as "squatters in their own country." He continued, declaring (*Sunday Mail*, 1989): "Only 4,400 white commercial farmers own the best land in the country, but what of the ten million blacks in the communal areas and other displaced people? Can we say then that we are free if we don't have land which we fought to get?"

However, as the debate unfolded, it became clear that the government had no intention of expropriating land on a wholesale basis. There is so much unused and underused land in commercial farming areas that the government seems to be leaning toward acquiring only those kinds of land, while leaving white farmers who have continuously occupied and worked their land alone.

In addition, the government is giving more attention to the redevelopment of communal lands. Under white settler governments it was enough to simply crowd Africans onto these lands without assistance. The Mugabe government is recognizing that the productivity of communal lands might be increased with more ease than commercial lands can be converted to peasant-style production. As issues of the sheer government capacity to administer land reform have surfaced, technocrats wishing to avoid policies that could hamper Zimbabwe's success in agriculture have dominated decision making. In the process there has been a tendency to deracialize land reform politics (Herbst, 1990: 52–62). Nevertheless, the present pattern of land ownership in Zimbabwe is racial in its origins. Everyone is well aware of that, and the government's ability to maintain a technocratic approach to the issue depends upon population growth and continuing pressures on communal lands, the related issue of unemployment and underemployment in the agrarian and urban sectors, and the way prominent politicians might choose to manipulate racial rhetoric at some future date.

The issue of black advancement in the private sector is even more explicitly racial. It is actually the same issue as affirmative action in the United States. In 1989, the Confederation of Zimbabwe Industries reported that blacks occupied 78 percent of the positions in junior management, 64.5 percent in mid-management, and 37.5 percent in senior management (*Financial Gazette*, 18 August 1989). These figures represent impressive gains from the pre-independence period, when virtually no blacks were employed in private sector management. Nonetheless, charges of racism in hiring and promotion policies can frequently be heard. On 3 December 1988, a columnist for the *Herald* reported that many blacks in the private sector felt as if they were "window dressing" with no real authority in their companies (Ngwenya, 1988). The *Sunday Mail* (26 February 1989) discovered that the Harare Sheraton Hotel was allegedly paying white managers more than blacks at the same positions. After President Mugabe called attention to the continuing need for black advancement in his Independence Day speech in April 1989, black businessmen began lobbying him to take action on the problem (*Herald*, 12 August 1989). At a conference on black advancement, Dr. Brigid Strachan made the following observation (Zenenga, 1990):

> Looking more generally at black managerial advancement, the response of industry since 1980 has been to sweep the issue under the carpet as long as possible. There has always been a reluctance to speak honestly and openly. The only conclusion one can draw from this is that there is still a significant amount of racial prejudice.

The prejudice to which Dr. Strachan refers is politicized when public institutions are asked to take stands and make policy. Even though whites remain such a small percentage of the population in Zimbabwe, their continuing influence over the economy is likely to be a bone of contention for some time to come.

Jeffrey Herbst has argued that in another generation or so race will cease to be an issue in Zimbabwean politics. He says that there is an agreement "which is never discussed but is generally understood," that the present generation of white industrial and agrarian entrepreneurs and managers can stay, but their children should be encouraged to make their lives outside of Zimbabwe. Foreign-based firms wishing to dispose of their operations in Zimbabwe "can have their funds remitted only if the purchasers are Black Zimbabweans, Black Zimbabwean co-operatives, or the government." Herbst concludes that "Zimbabwe, therefore, will become like Kenya or Zambia," another country where settler colonialism failed, most whites left, and the politics of race becomes irrelevant (222–24).

If Herbst is right, the thesis of Omi and Winant regarding the relatively permanent political contestation of race in the United States cannot hold for Zimbabwe. From the evidence provided here, it is apparent that however short-lived racial political contestation will be in Zimbabwe, it certainly continues to preoccupy the country today, more than a decade after independence. Whites who control the industry and most of the best farm land in Zimbabwe are in many ways locked into the economy. If they sell their land to the government they get paid in Zimbabwe dollars. The children of white Zimbabwean capitalists may be discouraged from staying in the country, but they may still hold the title to property and enterprises from outside. Absentee landlordism is already a problem in agriculture. When the absentee landlords also happen to be white, and the growing numbers of land hungry peasants are black, race is inextricably linked to the policy debate.

The passage of the 1992 Land Acquisition Act has reinvigorated racial political contestation. The law permits the government to purchase land at a price it sets, rather than the market value. It represents a renewed effort by the government to resettle African peasants according to the mandate of the revolution. White farmers and the international donor community are understandably nervous, but Mugabe is facing elections in 1995 and needs to shore up his rural base (Meldrum, 1993). Under this scenario, racial contestation over agricultural land could continue for quite some time.

Ethnic conflict also plagued the Mugabe government. In the course of the integration of the two guerilla armies into one, violence erupted in 1981. Before the fighting ended, 300 men were killed, another 6,500 were disarmed, and three battalions were liquidated. In 1982 large caches of arms were found in ZAPU's possession. Over 4,000 Ndebele troops deserted the armed forces, and by the summer antigovernment guerrillas were active in Matabeleland. Mugabe sent the elite and all-Shona Fifth Brigade into Matabeleland to quell the insurgency. It accomplished its ends brutally, as 2,000 people were reportedly killed (Scarritt, 1990: 261). After much jockeying back and forth, ZANU-PF and PF-ZAPU signed a unity agreement in 1987 and merged into one party. Since that time ethnicity has become less important as a formal cleavage in national politics.

In the 1990s Zimbabwe is still a plural society. Africans retain their ethnic differences and distinct communal ways of life. Though it has not been observed in this article, white Zimbabweans also have developed their own ethnicity based upon a common way of living. Both black and white also possess a racial identity that determined the life chances of their forefathers. Racial identity continues to be a factor in determining their socioeconomic position today, and their opportunities for the future. Although black Zimbabweans now have a social will related to ending racially based injustices, they also have a cross-cutting social will connected to their ethnicity. The black race still resembles Furnivall's "crowd." It is ethnically divided and the potential for ethnic conflict to become repoliticized is always alive. But at another level, black Zimbabweans are also now a political community with recognized common interests in relationship to the whites remaining in the country. As long as whites retain the socioeconomic advantages created by settler colonialism, racial political contestation will continue to haunt the country.

References

Acuna, Rodolfo. 1981. *Occupied America: A History of Chicanos,* 2nd ed. New York: Harper and Row.
Adamson, Walter L. 1980. *Hegemony and Revolution: A Study of Antonio Gramsci's Political and Cultural Theory.* Berkeley: University of California Press.
Africa News. 1982. Zimbabwe: "Economic Planners Face Dilemmas," April 5, 1982, 5-6.
Arrighi, Giovanni. 1970. "Labour Supplies in Historical Perspective: A Study of the Proletarianization of the African Peasantry in Rhodesia," *Journal of Development Studies,* 6: 3, 197-236.
Balandier, Georges. 1970. *The Sociology of Black Africa.* New York: Praeger Publishers.
Beach, D. N. 1980. *The Shona and Zimbabwe: 900–1850.* Gweru, Zimbabwe: Mambo Press.
Blake, Robert. 1978. *A History of Rhodesia.* New York: Alfred A. Knopf Publishers.
Boggs, James. 1970. *Racism and Class Struggle.* New York: Monthly Review Press.
Burkey, Richard M. 1978. *Ethnic and Racial Groups: The Dynamics of Dominance.* Menlo Park, Calif.: Cummings Publishing Company.
Carmichael, Stokely and Charles V. Hamilton. 1967. *Black Power: The Politics of Liberation in America.* New York: Vintage Books.
Chengeta, J. Zvogbo. 1980. "Rhodesia's Internal Settlement (1977-1979): A Record." *Journal of Southern African Studies,* (January).
Curtin, Virginia Knight. 1983. "The Social and Economic Transformation of Zimbabwe." *Current History,* (March): 106-9, 129-130.
Drake, St. Clair. 1990. *Black Folk Here and There: An Essay in History and Anthropology,* vol. 2. Los Angeles: Center for Afro-American Studies, UCLA.
Financial Gazette. 1989. "Advancement is Significant, but Momentum Must be Maintained." August, 18.
Franklin, John Hope, ed. 1968. *Color and Race.* Boston, Mass.: Houghton Miflin Company.
Frederickson, George M. 1981. *White Supremacy: A Comparative Study in American and South African History.* New York: Oxford University Press.
Friedman, Milton. 1962. *Capitalism and Freedom.* Chicago, Ill.: University of Chicago Press.
Furnivall, J. S. 1956. *Colonial Policy and Practice: A Comparative Study Burma and the Netherlands India.* New York: New York University Press.
Glazer, Nathan and Daniel P. Moynihan. 1970. *Beyond the Melting Pot.* Cambridge, Mass.: M.I.T. Press.
Gossett, Thomas F. 1965. *Race: The History of an Idea.* New York: Schocken Books.
Gramsci, Antonio. 1971. In *Selections from the Prison Notebooks of Antonio Gramsci,* ed., Hoare, Quintin and Smith, Geoffrey Nowell. London: Lawrence and Wishart.

Hannum, Hurst. 1992. *Autonomy, Sovereignty and Self-Determination: the Accomodation of Conflicting Rights.* Second printing. Philadelphia: University of Pennsylvania Press.
Hargreaves, J. D. 1988. *Decolonization in Africa.* New York: Longman, Inc.
Herbst, Jeffrey. 1990. *State Politics in Zimbabwe.* Harare, Zimbabwe: University of Zimbabwe Publications.
Hudson, Miles. 1981. *Triumph or Trajedy? Rhodesia to Zimbabwe.* London: Hamish Hamilton.
Kallen, Horace. 1924. *Culture and Democracy in America.* New York: Boni and Liveright.
Kapungu, Leonard T. 1974. *Rhodesia: The Struggle for Freedom.* Maryknoll, N.Y.: Orbis Books.
Kuper, Leo. 1975. *Race, Class and Power: Ideology and Revolutionary Change in Plural Societies.* Chicago, Ill.: Aldine Publishing Company.
Lan, David. 1985. *Guns and Rain: Guerrillas and Spirit Mediums in Zimbabwe.* Berkeley: University of California Press.
Lauren, Paul Gordon. 1988. *Power and Prejudice: The Politics and Diplomacy of Racial Discrimination.* Boulder, Colo.: Westview Press.
Leys, Colin. 1959. *European Politics in Southern Rhodesia.* London: Oxford University Press.
Mandanza, Ibbo, ed. 1987. *Zimbabwe: The Political Economy of the Transition, 1980-1986.* Harare, Zimbabwe: Jongwe Press.
Martin, David, and Phyllis Johnson. 1981. *The Struggle for Zimbabwe: The Chimurenga War.* New York: Monthly Review.
Maxey, Kees. 1975. *The Fight for Zimbabwe: Armed Conflict in Southern Rhodesia Since UDI.* London: Rex Collings.
Meldrum, Andrew. 1993. "The Poor Pay the Price." *Africa Report,* (July-August): 63–67.
Meredith, Martin. 1979. *The Past is Another Country: Rhodesia, 1890-1979.* Andre Deutsch.
Mtshali, B. Vulindlela. 1967. *Rhodesia: Background to Conflict.* New York: Hawthorne Books, Inc.
Mutambirwa, James A. C. 1980. *The Rise of Settler Power in Southern Rhodesia (Zimbabwe), 1898-1923.* Teaneck, N.J.: Farleigh Dickinson University Press.
Myrdal, Gunnar. 1962. *An American Dilemma: The Negro Problem and Modern Democracy.* Twentieth Anniversary Edition. New York: Harper and Row.
Ngwenya, Ron. 1988. "Window Dressing in Private Sector's Corridors of Power." *Herald (Zimbabwe),* (3 December 1988).
Novicki, Margaret A. 1982. "Robert Mugabe, Prime Minister of Zimbabwe." *Africa Report,* (September-October): 4-9.
Nyangoni, Christopher, and George Nyandoro. 1979. *Zimbabwe Independence Movements: Selected Documents.* New York: Barnes and Noble.
O'Meara, Patrick. 1975. *Rhodesia: Racial Conflict or Coexistence?* Ithaca, N.Y.: Cornell University Press.
Omi, Michael and Howard Winant. 1986. *Racial Formation in the United States: From the 1960s to the 1980s.* London: Routledge and Kegan Paul.
Palley, Claire. 1966. *The Constitutional History and Law of Southern Rhodesia, 1888–1965.* Oxford, England: Clarendon Press, 1966.
Palmer, Robin. 1977. *Land and Racial Domination in Rhodesia.* London: Oxford University Press.
Park, Robert E. 1950. *The Collected Papers of Robert E. Park.* Everett Hughes ed. Glencoe: The Free Press.
_____. 1985. *Peasant Consciousness and Guerrilla War in Zimbabwe.* Harare, Zimbabwe: Zimbabwe Publishing House.

_____. 1970. *The African Voice in Southern Rhodesia: 1898-1930.* Evanston, Ill.: Northwestern University Press.
Ranger, Terrance O. 1968a. "The Nineteenth Century in Southern Rhodesia." In *Aspects of Central African History*, ed., Terrance O. Ranger. Evanston, Ill.: Northwestern University Press.
_____. 1968b. "African Politics in Twentieth-Century Southern Rhodesia." In *Aspects of Central African History*, ed., Terrence O. Ranger. Evanston, Ill.: Northwestern University Press.
Roosevelt, Franklin D. 1960. "President Roosevelt Reports on the Atlantic Charter." In *The Shaping of American Diplomacy, ed.,* William A. Williams. Chicago, Ill.: Rand McNally and Company.
Samkange, Stanlake. 1969. *Origins of Rhodesia.* New York: Praeger Publishers.
Scarritt, James R. 1991. "Zimbabwe: Revolutionary Violence Resulting in Reform." In *Revolutions of the Late Twentieth Century*, ed., Jack Goldstone, et. al. Boulder, Colo.: Westview Press: 235–71.
Segal, Ronald. 1967. *The Race War.* New York: Bantam Books.
Shamuyarira, Nathan M. 1965. *Crisis in Rhodesia.* London: Andre Deutsch, Ltd.
Shepherd, George, Jr. 1970. *Racial Influences on American Foreign Policy.* New York: Basic Books.
Sithole, Masipula. 1980. "Ethnicity and Factionalism in Zimbabwe Nationalist Politics." *Ethnic and Racial Studies,* (January): 17–39.
Sithole, Ndabaningi. 1968. *African Nationalism,* 2nd ed. London: Oxford University Press.
Skocpol, Theda. 1979. *States and Social Revolutions.* Cambridge: Cambridge University Press.
Smith, Donald. 1969. *Rhodesia: The Problem.* London: Robert Maxwell.
Stoneman, Colin. 1981. "Agriculture." In *Zimbabwe's Inheritance, ed.,* Colin Stoneman. New York: St. Martin's Press: 127–49.
Strack, Harry R. 1978. *Sanctions: The Case of Rhodesia.* Syracuse, N.Y.: Syracuse University Press.
Sunday Mail (Harade). 1989. "Land Imbalance Problem Still Haunts the Nation."
Tartter, Jean R. 1981. "Government and Politics." In *Zimbabwe: A Country Study,* ed., Harold D. Nelson. Washington, D.C.: American University Foreign Areas Studies Series: 185–234.
Utete, C. Munhamu Botsio. 1979. *The Road to Zimbabwe: The Political Economy of Settler Colonialism, National Liberation and Foreign Intervention.* Washington, D.C.: University Press of America.
Vail, Leroy, ed. 1989. *The Creation of Tribalism in Southern Africa.* Berkeley: University of California Press.
Williams, Walter E. 1982. *The State Against Blacks.* New York: McGraw-Hill.
Willis, A. J. 1973. *An Introduction to the History of Southern Africa,* 3rd ed. New York: Oxford University Press.
Wilson, William J. 1981. *The Declining Significance of Race,* 2nd ed. Chicago: University Press.
Wiseman, Henry and Alastair Taylor. 1981. *From Rhodesia to Zimbabwe: The Politics of Transition.* New York: Pergamon Press.
Zenenga, Hatred. 1990. "Still Too Much Prejudice." *Herald (Zimbabwe),* (1 February).

Affirmative Action: The Quality of the Debate

Sue Davis

University of Delaware

Stephen L. Carter, 1991; *Reflections of an Affirmative Action Baby* (New York: Basic Books) xii + 275 pp. ISBN 0-465-06871-5 (cloth).

Frederick R. Lynch, 1991; *Invisible Victims: White Males and the Crisis of Affirmative Action* (Westport, Conn.: Praeger) xvi + 237 pp. ISBN 0-275-94102-7 (paper).

Bron Raymond Taylor, 1991; *Affirmative Action at Work: Law, Politics, and Ethics* (Pittsburgh, Pa.: University of Pittsburgh Press) xvii + 251 pp. ISBN 0-8229-5454-2 (paper).

Ronald J. Fiscus, 1992; *The Constitutional Logic of Affirmative Action* (Durham, N.C.: Duke University Press) xviii + 150 pp. ISBN 0-8223-1206-9 (cloth).

The controversy generated by affirmative action programs during the last almost thirty years seems to be endless. The debate, which continues unabated as we approach the end of the twentieth century, is often acrimonious, at least in part because the stakes seem quite high—access to elite colleges and professional schools and lucrative careers. The absolute certainty with which each side holds its position and the vast distance between them may have much to do with the harsh terms in which the debate is so frequently conducted. All of this is clearly reflected in the four books reviewed in the present essay. Anyone who reads these books will be moved to ask what the current debate is likely to contribute to our understanding of the issues surrounding affirmative action. Is the debate advancing a more thorough understanding of those issues in a way that might help to provide the basis for their eventual resolution? Or, is it merely rehashing the old arguments?

All four authors consider questions that are at the center of the debate. Do preferential policies reinforce racist stereotypes by promoting the view that people of color are unable to compete with white males? Does affirmative action harm innocent white males by excluding them from jobs and promotions for which they are qualified and that they, therefore, deserve? Do race-conscious hiring policies result in the placement of unqualified individuals? Does the presence of those individuals then threaten the efficiency of our institutions? Or, is it possible that affirmative action, insofar as it promotes genuine diversity, will have a transformative, enriching effect, and will help to create institutions that will serve all of the people? Does affirmative action enjoy popular support? Or, do preferential treatment policies elicit widespread opposition? It is noteworthy that the very formulation of some of the questions is likely to promote discord rather than harmony. Such issues aside, however, it seems most useful to examine the four books in the context of the way each author approaches and proceeds to answer the major questions.

In *The Constitutional Logic of Affirmative Action*, Ronald J. Fiscus provides a tightly argued, persuasive philosophical-legal defense of proportional quotas. At the core of his argument is a rejection of the assertion that affirmative action harms innocent white males. Beginning with the premise of inherent racial equality at birth, he easily deduces that all racial disparities can be attributed to racism. Without racism, he reasons, members of different racial groups would be found in different occupations in proportion to their percentage in the general population.

Proceeding from the principle of inherent equality to address the "innocent persons" argument, Fiscus reasons that proportional quotas are not unfair to white males—they do not take away anything to which any individual had a right or a claim. For example, if whites and blacks constituted 80 percent and 20 percent of the population respectively, a proportional quota would guarantee to whites 80 percent of the positions and 20 percent would be guaranteed to blacks. For whites to obtain more than their 80 percent would be for them to benefit from racial discrimination. Fiscus's defense of affirmative action is based on the principle of distributive justice; he rejects the idea that racial preferences may be justified on the grounds of compensatory justice. Thus, in his view affirmative action should be justified on the basis of the claim an individual or group has to the positions, advantages, or benefits they would have been awarded under fair conditions, not on the idea of providing a way of compensating those who have been harmed by discrimination.

Fiscus examines the Supreme Court's decisions regarding affirmative action to demonstrate that the justices (as of 1989) accepted the argument that affirmative action programs punish the innocent. Accordingly the Court has held that particular programs violate the Equal Protection Clause of the Constitution or a provision of the federal law. Fiscus's approach would provide a stronger constitutional basis for affirmative action by shifting the focus from questions of guilt or innocence to questions of right—not "Who is to blame for racism, but What would the group members have naturally attained?...[and] what they [white people] would be entitled to in a nonracist society" (p. 45).

Fiscus would apply the principle of proportionality to undergraduate and graduate admissions, blue collar as well as professional hiring and promotions, and layoffs. While he concedes that his apparently simple principle would be complex in its application, he maintains that any problems in calculating and implementing proportional quotas would be manageable and the solutions would be based on constitutional standards.

The problem with the argument becomes readily apparent when one considers the gaps between political theory and the reality of American politics, and between constitutional theory and judicial decision making. The Supreme Court would not look favorably upon the type of legal-constitutional argument that Fiscus advances; likewise, public opinion would condemn the replacement of a system perceived to be based on equal opportunity with one of proportional quotas. Indeed, his argument would most likely be labelled radical, extreme, divisive, perhaps even racist by those with more traditional views (remember Lani Guinier?).

Fiscus' "exercise in logic" (p. 37) constitutes a valuable contribution to an understanding of the issues surrounding affirmative action insofar as it demonstrates how education, jobs, and other valuable resources would be distributed in a nonracist society. White males who are convinced that they are the innocent victims of "reverse discrimination" are highly unlikely, however, to be moved by Fiscus' defense of proportional quotas. Frederick R. Lynch's *Invisible Victims: White Males and the Crisis of Affirmative Action* attests to the resentment and hostility with which affirmative action policies are received by some white men.

While Fiscus explains that proportional quotas do not harm white males, Lynch insists that affirmative action policies do indeed harm innocent white men by excluding them from the jobs for which they are clearly more qualified than members of the favored groups. Moreover, he asserts, it is difficult to discuss the issue because of the force of the taboos suppressing the discussion of racial problems and policies. This "New McCarthyism," according to Lynch, has stifled discussion of affirmative action by its victims as well as by social scientists, journalists, policy makers, and corporate and government elites. As a result, confusion about affirmative action abounds. He alleges that the victims themselves are often not even aware of the extent of their victimization; they are reluctant to complain, and they have no recourse to justice.

To support his assertions, Lynch presents the results of interviews with 34 subjects who believed that they had either lost a job or a promotion because of affirmative action. As he explains, he obtained his subjects by "networking," seeking people who were "reasonably sure" that they were victims of "reverse discrimination." It hardly seems necessary to discuss in any depth the methodological problems that Lynch's study contains. He does not seem to be as interested in examining attitudes about affirmative action as he is in demonstrating that it is unfair to white males—a task he makes easy by limiting his study to the attitudes of a self-identified group of individuals who perceive themselves to be the victims of such policies.

Moreover, it is impossible to determine from Lynch's study whether his subjects actually were harmed by affirmative action. Each subject told the interviewer that he had not received a job or a promotion because of a policy of preferential treatment and that he was passed over in favor of someone less qualified. For example, one of Lynch's subjects, Ed Coles (not his real name), was not hired for a tenure track position at the university where he had filled a position for one semester. Instead the department chose a black candidate with a doctorate from a much less prestigious institution than the one where Coles obtained his. Additionally, Lynch reports, the chair of the department was a radical feminist much concerned about the plight of South Africa. Apparently, that information was sufficient to convince the author that Ed Coles was an innocent victim harmed unfairly by a racial preference. The reader, however, should not be so easily convinced. What precisely were the qualities that the department was seeking in a new faculty member? What were Coles's qualifications? How did he perform in the temporary position? What was the nature of his interaction with the faculty? Lynch never explores such issues. Even if he had provided more information about the circumstances of his interviewees' disappointing experiences, Lynch's results would warrant extreme caution. Given the fact that the subjects were self-identified victims of racial preferences, would they be likely to admit to marginal employment record, or to appearing late, even unprepared, for an interview?

Lynch's methodology is so seriously flawed that it leaves the reader unconvinced of anything except the author's agenda. Indeed, *Invisible Victims* is little more than a polemic thinly veiled as social science. As such, it does little to contribute to the quality of the debate over affirmative action. In fact, several of Lynch's contentions will only serve to heighten the acrimony. He chooses to emphasize but not to support or even examine, for example, the assumption that qualified white males are often passed over in favor of less-than-qualified females and nonwhites.

Still, from a purely impressionistic standpoint, many white males seems to feel that they are at a disadvantage in their professional lives as a result of affirmative action. Resentment on the part of white males is an issue that needs to be examined. Is it as prevalent as Lynch would have us believe? If so, perhaps the resentment is a result of lack of information or misunderstanding about affirmative action policies, distortions or insensitivity by administering personnel, possibly even unfair administration of preferential treatment programs. In that case, there are a number of steps employers might take. Educational programs to explain and justify hiring and promotion policies and sensitivity training would be helpful, for example. If managers stopped making such comments as, "I would love to give you a job but the federal government says I have to hire a black," and "She only got the job because she is a woman," resentment might just begin to decrease.

While Lynch's study fails to shed any light on such issues, Bron Raymond Taylor's far more thoughtful and methodologically sound, *Affirmative Action at Work: Law, Politics, and Ethics* explores ways in which employers might convince individuals who perceive themselves to be unfairly disadvantaged by racial preferences that such policies are justified and that they are fair. Taylor explores attitudes toward the idea, practice, and rationales of affirmative action through interviews, surveys, and participant observation at the California State Department of Parks and Recreation. Unlike Lynch, who focuses entirely on the perceptions of white males, Taylor examines responses of white women, nonwhite men, and nonwhite women as well as white men.

Taylor designed his study to address a complex series of questions that surround the debate over affirmative action. His interest is primarily in discovering links between attitudes about affirmative action and moral reasoning and values. Thus, Taylor manages to move far beyond a simple analysis of employees' attitudes by locating those attitudes in the framework of a variety of moral/ethical/political theories that concern such broad themes as individualism-communitarianism, equal opportunity, and distributive justice. He then utilizes his analysis to suggest which type of arguments in favor of affirmative action might be particularly effective. Finally, he provides some practical advise for organizations with affirmative action programs.

Although it is not surprising, it is significant that Taylor finds a relationship between individualism and opposition to affirmative action. The more individualistic one's outlook, he holds, the more likely one is to oppose affirmative action. Conversely, the more concern one expresses for the group or the social whole, the more likely one is to approve of affirmative action. Further, non-whites and white women are much more likely than white men to express group-focused ideals and concerns and to support affirmative action. The most important variable associated with attitudes about affirmative action is membership in an ethnic or gender group—another important, but not surprising, finding.

More surprising is Taylor's discovery that there is a higher level of support for affirmative action among white males than impressionistic accounts have led us to believe. He classifies 45 percent of the white men he surveyed as consistent supporters of affirmative action, and another 17 percent as a swing group (supported affirmative action in general but rejected most preferential affirmative action practices). Moreover, many of the white men who expressed support for the principle of equal opportunity, a belief that individual initiative is the key to success, and agreed that affirmative action violates the rights of white men, nevertheless supported preferential treatment programs. The author surmises that since a substantial proportion of respondents supported affirmative action even though they perceived it to be in conflict with equal opportunity, it is useful to turn to consequentialist arguments—it benefits either society or women and non-whites—to explain their support. Still, Taylor concludes, because individualism is so dominant in American culture, the arguments for affirmative action that will be most successful will be based on liberal principles, such as enhancing equality of opportunity rather than modifying it. Taylor's interpretation of the attitudes about affirmative action goes a long way to explain why arguments like Fiscus', as scrupulously reasoned and logical as they are, so often elicit negative responses: they are too inconsistent with American liberal values.

Does affirmative action stigmatize its beneficiaries? Taylor avers that it does not. He found that when employees discover new opportunities for advancement that were previously denied to them, their self-esteem increased. Moreover, he discovered that the exposure of white men to members of other racial groups resulted in a decline in a belief in the inferiority of people of color.

In contrast, the assertion that racial preferences perpetuate racist stereotypes is central to Stephen L. Carter's *Reflections of an Affirmative Action Baby*. Carter, a professor at Yale Law School, does not use questionnaires or interviews to analyze affirmative action. Instead, he relies primarily on his own experience and keen insights. The result is a highly readable, frequently personal narrative that provides a valuable addition to the debate on affirmative action. Indeed, Carter's discussion is strongest where Fiscus' is most lacking: *Reflections of an Affirmative Action Baby* emphasizes the need to explore the issues surrounding affirmative within the context of a racially conscious society. Given that context, affirmative action programs promote the idea that people of color are unable to compete with whites for scholarships, for college, graduate, and professional school admissions, for jobs, and for promotions. Since racial preferences are based on the proposition that the achievements of their beneficiaries would be fewer if the preferences did not exist, all arguments for affirmative action, Carter emphasizes, entail the assumption that people of color cannot compete on the same playing field with people who are white. Carter vehemently rejects that assumption.

He alleges that affirmative action programs have come to focus increasingly on the value of diversity. He finds the notion that more African American students should be admitted to professional schools because they will bring a different perspective to the educational process and, in time, to their chosen profession, particularly dangerous. It encourages the "best black" syndrome, according to which people of color are judged by a separate standard from whites and it is assumed that the "best black" candidate will never be as good as the best candidate. Certain forms of affirmative action, including setting aside test scores, hiring from separate lists, set-aside programs, and commitments to hire a pre-set number of minorities, are especially effective in promoting the "best black" syndrome. It is important to note, as Carter does, that preferential treatment programs did not create the syndrome but that they do nothing to refute, and indeed, they reinforce it. Additionally, the emphasis on the value of diversity assumes that all African Americans share a distinct outlook and set of values. Thus, ironically, "diversity" provides a mold into which many individuals do not fit.

Carter acknowledges that he is likely to be labelled a "black conservative" as a result of his *Reflections*. In fact, when Derrick Bell recently observed that black people gain enhanced standing when they "tell white people what they want to hear about blacks," he referred to the enormous attention Carter's book has received. Many will disagree with Carter's objections to affirmative action, but even a cursory reading of *Reflections of an Affirmative Action Baby* makes it clear that his position defies any label. Carter distinguishes his views from those of black neoconservatives like Thomas Sowell by explicitly rejecting the proposition that an unfettered market will remove the barriers to racial equality without the assistance of government programs. Affirmative action, quips Carter, is "Racial Justice on the Cheap" (the title of chap. 4, pp. 71-95), an inexpensive way to create an appearance of social change. But it is not a solution to the increasing income inequality among African Americans and, indeed, it does nothing for those most in need as the benefits fall to those least in need of them. Programs directed at improving education, particularly for young children, in order to prepare them to compete later for admission to college, would be far more effective than affirmative action but they would also be more expensive.

Although he opposes affirmative action in what he sees as its present form, Carter seems to approve of some race-conscious selection programs. He emphasizes that affirmative action should be a program to help a critical mass of African Americans gain the necessary training to meet the standards of their chosen fields. An "opportunity-based" affirmative action program would use a degree of racial consciousness in college and professional school admissions, and possibly in financial aid decisions. Such programs would provide highly motivated people of color who have shown the greatest potential a chance at advanced training that they might not otherwise have. Carter envisions an affirmative action pyramid in which the role of preference would narrow as one moves upward. A slight preference is justified in college admissions as a matter of giving lots of people from different backgrounds the chance to obtain an education at an elite college or university. But he claims that when one's training is finished, the case for preference evaporates.

Still, Carter maintains, even the minimal preferences of the pyramid will perpetuate the perception that excellent blacks are only the best blacks rather than simply the best. What is the solution then? Excellence that will refute all racist stereotypes. Carter calls for a commitment to "battle for excellence, to show ourselves able to meet any standard, to pass any test that looms before us, in short, to form ourselves into a vanguard of black professionals who are simply too good to ignore" (p. 60).

Of the four books discussed here Carter's is the most accessible and seems to offer the most thoughtful analysis of actual effects of affirmative action upon its beneficiaries. Still, the reader cannot help but wonder about Carter's basically simple solution: hard work and excellence. Black leaders have offered such advice before: Frederick Douglass, Booker T. Washington, and W.E.B. DuBois, plus a wide variety of others. But has not American history demonstrated that hard work and even incontrovertible evidence of excellence can easily be disregarded?

To what extent do the authors whose work is discussed here contribute to the debate by improving our understanding of the issues surrounding affirmative action? Do the ways in which they answer the questions posed at the outset of this essay suggest that there is any common ground on which the opposing sides of the debate might meet? While Taylor finds no evidence that affirmative action stigmatizes its beneficiaries, Carter's conviction that it does is central to his opposition to racial preferences. Lynch maintains that preferential treatment programs do not help minorities but do a great deal of harm to white males. Fiscus argues that affirmative action in the form of proportional quotas is the only way to distribute resources in a just society. How do the authors stand on the question of whether affirmative action is a useful tool in the quest for racial justice? Carter and Lynch argue that it is not. But their apparent agreement on the level of a simple yes or no masks their fundamentally different conceptions of racial justice. For Taylor and Fiscus, affirmative action can serve as a means to achieve racial justice. Yet they differ on the basic issue of what an affirmative action plan should be. The four books discussed here reflect the absence of agreement—indeed, the polarity of positions on fundamentally important issues.

Nevertheless, three of the authors (Lynch is the exception) have undertaken a thoughtful and badly needed search for some sort of middle ground between the contending sides in the debate on affirmative action. Each in his own way has tried to move the debate forward, to improve its quality, and to transcend the old acrimony. It remains for readers to assess the extent to which they have been successful.

References

Bell, Derrick. *Faces at the Bottom of the Well: The Permanence of Racism*, (New York: Basic Books, 1992), 124, 116.

Mozambique's Descent into Hell

Robert Fatton, Jr.

University of Virginia

William Finnegan, 1992; *A Complicated War: The Harrowing of Mozambique.* (Berkeley: University of California Press) xiv + 325 pp. ISBN 0-520-07804-7 (cloth).

This intelligent, lively, and informative book is a remarkable journalistic account of Mozambique's tragic political and economic disintegration since gaining independence from Portugal in 1975. Finnegan offers a superb analysis of the domestic and international forces that have precipitated and exacerbated the savage war waged by the Resistencia Nacional Mocambicana (RENAMO) against the once-Marxist government of the Frente de Libertacao de Mocambique (FRELIMO).

Finnegan traces the development of RENAMO from its early roots in the white Rhodesian and South African security apparatus to its rather autonomous life as a quasiterrorist guerilla movement benefitting from the serious failures of FRELIMO. RENAMO was created in 1976 by the Rhodesian military-intelligence services from a "gang of former Portuguese soldiers and secret police, FRELIMO deserters, and escaped prisoners who had fled Mozambique" (p. 31). RENAMO's original purpose was to undercut FRELIMO's aid to the Zimbabwe African National Union (ZANU), which was struggling against Rhodesia's white rulers. With the coming to power of ZANU and Zimbabwean independence in 1980, RENAMO looked like a "spent force," but it was taken over and reinvigorated by the South African military. With South African help, RENAMO escalated its largely indiscriminate violence against people, clinics, rural health posts, and schools. In 1988, the U.S. State Department estimated that 100,00 civilians had been murdered by RENAMO in what it described as "one of the most brutal holocausts against ordinary human beings since World War Two." Finnegan reports also that, at the end of the 1980s, RENAMO had forced the closure of 46 percent of Mozambique's health-care network and destroyed or incapacitated 3,000 schools. Teachers and health workers became prime targets of RENAMO's carnage; hundred of them were either killed, kidnapped, or mutilated. RENAMO caused not only massive human suffering, it also contributed to the collapse of an already weak and underdeveloped economy.

Mozambique's fragile infrastructure was left largely in ruin by RENAMO's destructive military power. With an agricultural sector ravaged by war, the country's foreign exchange was depleted because peasants ceased producing export crops and reverted, wherever possible, to subsistence production. By 1987, money had lost its value as consumer goods were virtually nonexistent and as food shortages became a daily reality. In an economy plagued by the necessities of warfare and where neither import nor export was possible, conditions of acute and all-encompassing scarcity became the cruel norm. Mozambique's vast peasant majority had barely the means to clothe and feed itself as Finnegan's depressing depiction of naked and malnourished rural folks attests. To these injuries of war must be added the devastation of natural disasters. In the early 1980s a vicious cycle of floods, cyclones, and drought led to the destruction and the starvation of 100,00 Mozambicans. By the 1980s it was nevertheless painfully clear that it was the war that was mainly responsible for the misery of Mozambique's 16,300,000 people: it killed an estimated 900,000, created more than 3,000,000 refugees, and caused more than 8,000,000 to face starvation or severe food shortages (pp. 4–5). Not surprisingly, Finnegan discovered that Mozambicans were haunted by what they called "calamidades."

These huge "*calamidades,*" however, were not pre-ordained. In fact, the fundamental question is why FRELIMO's huge popularity, which derived from a protracted struggle of liberation, failed to sustain the promises of independence? Why, in short, did Mozambique descend into hell? Finnegan convincingly shows that the causes of the country's collapse are multifold.

In the first place, there is the thoroughly deficient legacy of Portuguese colonialism, which left Mozambique with inadequate and undeveloped administrative, financial, educational, and health systems. Colonialism had failed to impart to Mozambicans the sense of belonging to a coherent modern nation-state. In fact, when FRELIMO assumed power in 1975, the very notion of Mozambican nationhood had yet to be firmly established. The sense of nationhood remained weak in spite of the long war of liberation and the coming of independence. As Finnegan reports, after more than ten years of FRELIMO power, many peasants could not name their President, Joaquim Alberto Chissano (p. 18). The mechanisms of political participation and administrative regulation were weak and contributed to Mozambique's acute economic and social crisis. Natural disasters, as we have seen, exacerbated the situation. However, external military and economic forces lying outside of the control of FRELIMO, domestic policies enacted by FRELIMO itself, and the burden of Mozambique's own social history were the three single most important causes of the descent into hell.

The rise of RENAMO and the devastation it wrought would have been impossible without the strong military support of South Africa. In the late 1970s and early 1980s the apartheid regime determined that it faced a "total onslaught" from communist forces, and that it would consequently launch it own "total strategy" to preserve white minority rule (pp. 237–39). This strategy called for the militarization of South African society and the destabilization of the frontline states of Southern Africa, particularly Mozambique and Angola. Using RENAMO as a surrogate, South Africa waged an effective "low-intensity conflict" against FRELIMO and Mozambique's first President, Samora Machel. The goal was not the total annihilation of FRELIMO, but rather to "put Machel on his knees" (p. 79). Machel, who died in October 1986 in a plane crash, had attempted to set Mozambique on a socialist course and had given military and diplomatic support to South Africa's leading liberation movement, the African National Congress (ANC). Ruthlessly opposed to FRELIMO'S socialist experiment and determined to undermine the ANC, the apartheid regime waged a relentless campaign of destabilization against Mozambique.

The campaign succeeded. Incapable of resisting, let alone challenging, South Africa's vastly superior military and economic power, FRELIMO eventually capitulated and signed the Nkomati accord in 1984. The accord was Mozambique's acknowledgement that it could no longer withstand South Africa's military offensive or economic strangulation. Nkomati symbolized the extinguishing of Mozambique's radical socialist aspirations and the victory of South Africa's hegemony. Destabilization had worked. As Finnegan points out, "From Pretoria's standpoint, [it] was a huge success. The ANC was ousted. The Frelimo government was crippled. The economy was destroyed. The specter of a thriving black socialist state on its borders had been exorcised. The dreaded Soviets were no longer even in the picture" (p. 239). In exchange for signing Nkomati, FRELIMO obtained South Africa's promise to cease assisting RENAMO. That promise, however, was persistently broken, even if South Africa scaled down its military support for the terrorist organization. Only with the ascendancy of President F.W. de Klerk's reformist policies in 1990 did South Africa truly begin to respect the Nkomati agreement.

By that time, however, RENAMO had acquired an autonomy of its own; with or without South African support it continued to wage the war. Mozambique's agony was no longer, if it ever was, a simple military problem stemming from South Africa's external aggression; it was also a testament to FRELIMO's own inadequacies. By the end of the 1980s, "the evidence," as Finnegan reports, "was everywhere that RENAMO and the anarchy in Mozambique had long since become a fundamentally political problem—a painful reflection, that is, of profound internal conflicts" (p. 253).

However brutal and repressive its tactics may have been, RENAMO had nevertheless acquired a social base in Mozambican society. RENAMO's strategy of mass terror and maximum destruction confirmed Finnegan's assumption that the movement had "come from Hell," (p. 25) but it was a strategy that had "discernible motives" (p. 58) RENAMO'S *bandidos* were bent on wiping out any symbol of FRELIMO's success and "finishing off the people of Samora Machel" (p. 88). Terror became the principal means to that end. Violence, however, was not the only tactic used by RENAMO in its effort to isolate FRELIMO and gain support. Wherever it could, RENAMO effectively bolstered traditional political authorities, customs, and religious beliefs, all of which had been emasculated by FRELIMO's Marxist drive to modernity. RENAMO was thus reviving and enlisting the alienated forces of "tradition" to wage war against FRELIMO (pp. 61–66). In the areas under its control, RENAMO reinstalled the traditional authorities whom FRELIMO had deposed. The petty chiefs, called *régulos* or *muenes*, who had worked for the Portuguese as tax collectors, and the village elders or *mambos*, were all rehabilitated by RENAMO.

In addition, RENAMO fully exploited the pervasive popular attachment to indigenous religion that FRELIMO had attempted to sever. The prestige and legitimacy of traditional religious leaders such as the *curandeiros* (healers), or *feiticeiros* (witch doctors), or *profetas* (prophets), or *espiritistas* (spirit mediums) were effectively manipulated by RENAMO's rebels, the *matsangas*, to enlist rural support and build an aura of invincibility. As Finnegan points out:

> RENAMO used *curandeiros* both to gain the respect of peasants and to give its fighters courage. I heard stories of RENAMO being led into battle by a *curandeiro* waving a goat's tail and of rites meant to make warriors invisible to their enemies.... And RENAMO's alliance with the supernatural also seemed to be accepted at face value by many ordinary Mozambicans. In every part of the country I visited, I heard people say that the *matsangas* were "bulletproof," that they were "immortal." (p. 64)

RENAMO, in spite of any clear ideological vision, was thus rooting its struggle in the revival of what FRELIMO condemned as "obscurantist traditions." The enduring power of these traditions, as Finnegan astutely explains, greatly contributed to the widespread appeal of "social banditry" as a form of violent resistance against the infringements of a distant and often exploitative coercive central authority (p. 252–55). The *matsangas* understood that peasant mind set well and tapped into this reservoir of rural resentment to undermine FRELIMO's centralizing pretensions. In fact, Finnegan concludes that, given Mozambique's historical realities, FRELIMO's Socialist Project was an impossibility. As he put it: "FRELIMO's leadership—modern men all—undoubtedly found it hard to accept that a successful secular state was an impossibility at Mozambique's state of development.... This was, nonetheless, the conclusion that the country's deterioration increasingly suggested. The pieces were too small, the structures of power too dense and personal, the people too soaked in the sacred" (p. 243).

Finnegan's words, however, smack too much of a pessimistic determinism. While it is true that Mozambique's descent into hell has been precipitous, it might well have been averted were it not for South Africa's campaign of destabilization. Once that campaign was underway, it unleashed a series of chain reactions that undermined and ultimately destroyed FRELIMO's socialist project. The vision of an egalitarian, industrializing, yet austere society was not utopian. During the war of liberation, Mozambicans had actually begun to create, as Finnegan himself shows, a better world, and they hoped that it would flourish and come to maturity with independence. It was South Africa's military and economic strangulation of Mozambique that caused the vision to turn into a nightmare. There was nothing inherent in FRELIMO's governance that had to lead to the current disaster.

This is not to deny that many of the policies enacted by FRELIMO were ill-planned, poorly pursued, and absurdly grandiose. Moreover, FRELIMO lacked the trained personnel to run the excessively centralized economy that it wished to create. It used authoritarian methods to launch an unpopular program of agricultural collectivization. The party alienated traditional authorities unnecessarily instead of seeking to gradually win them over to new structures of popular government. In its zeal to impose an urban-oriented and urban-dominated socialist project, FRELIMO lost its rural base and had little power to stop the brutal ascendancy of RENAMO. Such failures were in and of themselves neither inevitable nor irreversible.

The war, however, exacerbated FRELIMO's weaknesses, enhanced its authoritarian tendencies, and overwhelmed its limited resources. The conflict destroyed whatever opportunity FRELIMO may have had to reassess its socialist project; it foreclosed any imaginative popular process of democratization, and it facilitated the emergence of right-wing forces within FRELIMO itself.

The devastation brought about RENAMO and South Africa, coupled with the collapse of the Eastern bloc as a source of foreign assistance, forced FRELIMO to engage in a series of compromises that ultimately transformed it from a revolutionary socialist movement into a conservative government beholden to international capital. As its options became increasingly limited, Mozambique turned to the World Bank and the International Monetary Fund for help. In fact, its growing right-wing enthusiasm went so far that FRELIMO declared its support for Ronald Reagan's re-election (p. 181).

With the acceptance of a structural adjustment program sponsored by the IMF in 1987, the detour to the right set in motion by the Nkomati Agreement had become the final journey. While the program generated an appearance of urban renewal, it failed to improve the miserable lot of most Mozambicans. As Finnegan reports, the harsh devaluation of the metical backed by the IMF meant that "so few Mozambicans could afford to buy anything that, for the ordinary workers, money still meant far less than access to a vegetable plot did. Meanwhile, in rural areas...there was less to buy than ever" (p. 40).

The IMF program also generated a process of increased social stratification and dependence on foreign assistance. Mozambique was becoming a haven for the aid industry, or what Graham Hancock has called the "Lords of Poverty."[1] In fact, for many Mozambicans, the immense power that international organization exercised over their own affairs, and the presence of hundreds of foreign experts living in privilege amidst mass poverty, meant the arrival of a new colonialism. This new colonialism contributed to the resurrection of old depravities; prostitution at the service of foreign customers, colonial-style compounds for the white "lords of poverty," and a small "comprador" class of Mozambicans dependent on the financial largesse of alien institutions. Not surprisingly, Mozambican "clerks, drivers, translators, liaisons, and trainees who worked for the foreigners and were paid partly in hard currency—thus escaping much of the privation that afflicted their compatriots—[were dubbed] 'the new *assimilados*'" (p. 101).

Under Portuguese colonialism, the *assimilados* were those Africans who, having adopted the Portuguese way of life and obtained a certain level of education, achieved a status that differentiated them from the rest of the population. Like their forerunners, the new *assimilados*, thanks to their connections to foreign institutions and experts, represented an embryonic ruling class. They were the privileged few who managed to acquire some wealth with which to escape the poverty of most Mozambicans. The emergence of this new class indicated that the earlier commitment to equity and self-reliance was increasingly a thing of the past. Mozambique was fast resembling the typical African state: a dependent economy at the service of an urban privileged elite who had made its peace with international capital.

A new colonialism was indeed in the making; FRELIMO's socialist project was no longer. In 1989, FRELIMO officially buried its original agenda when it dropped all reference to Marxism-Leninism and class struggle from its party platform. A new liberal constitution adopted in 1990 legalized a multiparty political system, promised future free elections, and celebrated the virtues of the market economy. In the process, FRELIMO started negotiating with RENAMO, thus abandoning its longstanding policy of refusing to talk to "bandits." Ending the war had become the single most vital issue confronting FRELIMO. The vision of a prosperous, socialist commonwealth had completely vanished, summarily displaced by the mere hope of halting the descent into hell. In the meantime, as Finnegan's sad last words indicate, people continue to sob over the tragedy of a generation lost in the killing fields of Mozambique.

Notes

1. Graham Hancock, *Lords of Poverty*, (New York: The Atlantic Monthly Press, 1989).

Democracy in America and the Representation of African Americans

Robert C. Smith

San Francisco State University

Carol M. Swain, 1993; *Black Faces, Black Interests: The Representation of African Americans in Congress* (Cambridge, Mass.: Harvard University Press) xi = 275 pp. ISBN 0-674-077615-x (cloth).

In democratic societies, legislation and representation are inextricably linked, such that a defining property of a legislative institution is the extent to which it fully or equitably represents the people that constitute the polity. Indeed, in its narrowest modern usage the term legislation itself may be understood as a general rule of broad application enacted by a broadly representative body. In the American context it is precisely because of their lack of representativeness that it is thought improper or illegitimate for executive and judicial institutions to legislate. The President and the Supreme Court of course do from time to time legislate through executive orders and judicial decrees, however, it is considered constitutionally inappropriate. John Stuart Mill stated the case for the necessary relationship between legislation, representation, and democracy in his 1869 treatise *Considerations on Representative Government*:

> In a really equal democracy, every or any section would be represented, not disproportionately, but proportionately. A majority of electors would always have a majority of the representatives but a minority of electors would always have a minority of the representatives, man for man, they would be as fully represented as the majority; unless they are, there is not equal government, but government of inequality and privilege: One part of the people rule over the rest: there is a part whose fair and equal share of influence in representation is withheld from them contrary to the principle of democracy, which professes equality as its very root and foundation. (Mill 1869, 1958: 146)

It is these principles of legislative legitimacy and equality in representation that Carol Swain challenges in her book on the representation of African American interests in Congress.

Swain advances two interrelated arguments in *Black Faces, Black Interests*. First, that blacks as a minority do not require representation in the Congress "man for man" because whites can represent the interests of blacks as well as and, in some cases, perhaps better than blacks. Second, given that whites can represent blacks as well as blacks themselves, Swain challenges the post-civil-rights-era strategy of the Justice Department, the courts, and the civil rights lobby of drawing legislative district lines so as to enhance the opportunities to elect black representatives.

Swain seeks to sustain these arguments on the basis of case studies of nine black and four white members of Congress. The black representatives are placed in four categories based on the racial and ethnic composition of their districts. The first category is what she calls "Historically Black," districts with large black populations that have elected blacks for ten years or more. These include former Congressman George Crockett of Detroit and former Congressman William Gray of Philadelphia. The second is "newly black," districts with smaller black populations usually drawn pursuant to court order. These include former Congressman Mike Epsy's Mississippi delta district and John Lewis' Atlanta district. The third category she labels as "heterogeneous," districts that include blacks, whites, and Latinos with no group having a majority. Here she includes the Los Angeles district of Mervyn Dymally and the Queens district of Floyd Flake. The final category of black representatives include three members who represent districts with a white majority, Berkeley's Ronald Dellums, Gary's Katie Hall, and Kansas City's Alan Wheat. The white representative studied included two from districts with black majorities (former representatives Peter Rodino of Newark and Lindy Boggs of New Orleans) and two from districts with high but less-than-majority black populations (Congressmen Tim Valentine of North Carolina and Robin Tallon of South Carolina). Swain's purposes in selecting this diverse category of cases is to show first that the racial composition of a district has no relationship to the member's representation of black interests; second, that whites can effectively represent the interest of blacks; and third that blacks can represent the interests of whites without sacrificing black interests.

At the outset Swain defines and operationalizes interest and representation. She employs Hanna Pitkin's (1972) familiar typology of representation in terms of "descriptive," the statistical or demographic correspondence of representatives with their constituents and "substantive" representation in terms of the correspondence between the representatives' goals and those of their constituents. She writes that the "objective interests" of blacks is to end the wide disparity in social and economic well-being between the races and that blacks believe, correctly or not, that an activist federal government that pursues redistributive programs and increased social welfare expenditures is the best way to reach this goal. This concept of the interests of blacks is used to determine the substantive dimension of representation. This is done by calculating the scores of members of Congress on a series of scales that purport to measure support on roll-call votes for civil rights and redistributive policies.

In addition to roll-call analysis, Swain used several other methods in her research, including interviews with members of Congress (including fourteen present or former members not included in her thirteen case studies) and their staffs and field observations with eleven of the members in their districts. (She reports that both Congressmen Crockett and Gray from the two historically black districts refused her requests to accompany them on their district visits.) The results of her inquiry may be simply stated: on roll-call votes on issues relevant to black interests, in the ethnic and racial composition of their staffs, in service to constituents in the districts and in overall style of representation, white representatives in her sample represented black interests as well as (in a couple cases she judges better) did the blacks.

What is to be made of Swain's arguments? First, there are methodological problems, some acknowledged, that make it difficult to accept the validity and reliability of the empirical findings. Second, even if one accepts as valid the conclusion that whites can represent the interests of blacks as effectively as blacks, the normative implication that she draws about the strategy of legislative districting does not follow. That is, one could very easily accept the proposition that some whites in Congress, no matter the racial composition of their districts, represent the interests of blacks but nevertheless support strategies to maximize the election of blacks, given their disproportionate underrepresentation in the House (at the time of her study, prior to the 1990 redistricting, blacks constituted 6% of the House compared to their 12% of the population).

Turning first to the methodological problems, Swain herself notes (p. 230) that "it is not certain whether these findings can be generalized," pointing to the absence of Republicans in her sample and the possibility that the time span for the data collection may have distorted member activity given the impact of Jesse Jackson's 1988 presidential campaign. These are limitations for sure but they strike me as rather minor given other problems in the design and execution of the research.

First, while the number of cases in her sample is adequate given the size of the various universes, it is not clear how the cases were selected, specifically if they were drawn randomly. This is particularly a problem with the two high black population districts, the most problematic of her cases both empirically and normatively. The criteria for high black population (35–39 percent) seems arbitrary, narrowly tailored to fit the two Congressmen selected. Swain offers no explanation or rationale for this figure. It seems to me a more appropriate figure would have been 25–49 percent. This figure represents a large number of people (more than 120,000) and a significant voting bloc, twice the size for example of the national black electorate. Using this figure, at the time of Swain's study there were thirty-three high black population districts, which yields a larger universe from which to draw the sample and may have resulted in different conclusions about the extent to which white southern Democrats represent black interests as effectively as blacks. But even Tallon and Valentine may not be said to represent black interests as effectively as blacks since on both the civil rights and social welfare rating scales their scores are 20–25% below the average for the Congressional Black Caucus (CBC) and the typical white northern urban Democrat. Thus, by even this admittedly crude measure blacks would have enhanced the representation of their interests by replacing these white representatives with blacks.

The use of rating scores on roll-call votes is a crude indicator of black interests for two reasons. First, frequently by the time an issue reaches the floor for a final role-call vote it has usually been so substantially modified, often watered down, in the party caucus and authorizing and rules committees that it bears little resemblance to what black interests might require. It is probable that if Swain had examined the work of her sample in the Democratic caucus and in the committee process that a more substantial difference in the representation of black interests by black and white representatives might have been observed.

Roll-call analysis is also a crude indicator of the representation of black interests because the range of issues that come to the House for floor votes are so narrow, so constricted, in terms of dealing with the realities of the black condition that they do not constitute good measures of support for black interests as understood by blacks in Congress or the black mass public. That is, it is unlikely you would find substantial support (even among northern urban Democrats) for a ghetto Marshall plan or a meaningful full employment program, standard items on the post-civil-rights-era black agenda. For example, since 1981 the CBC had proposed a series of alternative budgets that reflected its understanding of the nation's priorities and its view of a minimal program to deal with the problems of black and poor people. Described by the *Washington Post* as the only truly liberal budgets during the Reagan era of the several Caucus budgets that came to vote in the 1980s, none received more than sixty-one white votes (Smith, 1992: 115).

Reflecting on the failure of his Democratic colleagues to support the Caucus budgets, Congressman John Conyers said during the 1982 floor debate, "And it is about time we get a little bit of respect or criticism for the nature of our work product. We bring you millions of Democratic votes to the Halls of Congress and the national ticket, more than anybody else, excluding nobody. And they are watching you. And I want to say time is running out. You are not going to explain in a long hot summer why 70 people out of a majority of Democratic body could not do anything but give us a nodding tip of the hat" (Congressional Recrod, 1982: 111524). Similarly reflecting on the lack of support from southern Democrats Congressman Major Owens said "It should be noted that there are more than 50 white members of the Congress who represent a substantial black population.... If the congressmen in this House would begin to truly represent their constituency there would be enough votes to pass the CBC budget" (Congressional Record, 1984: 2379).

Interestingly in terms of white support for black interests in the Congress, in general there is no relationship between support for the CBC budgets and the percentage of blacks in a congressman's constituency. For example, the most enthusiastic supporters for the budgets during the floor debates were Congresswoman Rose Mary Oakar of Ohio and Congressman David Bonior of Michigan, each representing districts with black populations of about 1 percent. During the 1984 debate Congressman Bonior remarked, "I think if you were to present to the people of this country the numbers that have been laid out here in terms of the deficit, in terms of tax-equity, in terms of domestic programs and in terms of needs to cut defense, and took away all the labels conservative caucus, Black Caucus or freeze, and had them pick, I think you would be very surprised at the numbers of people in this country that would identify themselves with this particular program.... I have maybe 1-1/2 percent black population but I think this resolution fits very closely the needs of the people I represent" (Congressional Record, 1984: 2377).

The CBC budgets are a better indicator of what blacks in Congress consider black interests than the typical roll-call vote on civil rights and social welfare expenditures. Support for them shows, as Swain argues, that some whites in Congress can represent the interests of blacks and that blacks in Congress can develop programs and policies that represent the interests not just of blacks but of all Americans. But in a sense this finding—whether based on the routine roll-call votes examined by Swain or on support for the Caucus budgets—is simply documentation of the obvious. Clearly, *some* whites in Congress *sometimes* represent *some* of the interests of blacks. Otherwise, no legislation *for* the interests of blacks would be enacted since in the last hundred years there has usually been no black representation in the Senate. The problem is not, as Swain contends, that some black politicians argue "that only blacks can represent black interests" (p. 276). Rather, the argument is first that relatively few whites in Congress are prepared to support the kind of legislation (the Caucus budget, for example) that offer a realistic chance of bridging the gap in social and economic well-being between the races. Second, given the historic racial cleavage in American society and the disproportionate representation of whites in Congress, blacks who argue for increased representation of their own do so not because they believe that only blacks can represent blacks, but rather, because they believe that as a minority they, like the majority, deserve equality in representation. This was the consistent argument of black challengers to white incumbents (such as Lindy Boggs and Peter Rodino) who represented districts with black majorities during the 1980s (Smith, 1986: 189–316).

It is this historic racial cleavage, coupled with inequality in representation, that has lead blacks in the post-civil-rights era to pursue strategies that would enhance their opportunities to elect blacks to Congress and other offices. As Pitkin (1972: 213) writes, "[D]eep cleavages in a society [on the basis of ethnicity or class] are likely to give rise to descriptive representation as a means to substantive representation." In other words, to the extent that a discrete group of citizens have or perceive themselves to have problems or interests that set them apart from their fellow citizens, they will seek representation by "one of their own" as one means to advance their interests in the political process.

To challenge, or, as she puts it, "question this strategy," is in the final analysis the real, underlying purpose of Swain's book, believing as she does that "[r]ace relations suffer when electoral remedies favor one racial group over another or in environments where candidates can engage in racially polarizing tactics without fear of defeat" (p. 203). Creating districts to facilitate the election of blacks, she argues, encourages racial polarization and inhibits the development of "broad coalition building across racial groups" (p. 203). The questioning of this strategy is not new with Swain. On the contrary, conservative scholars and jurists have advanced this argument for more than two decades, most notably in Abigail Thernstrom's *Whose Votes Count? Affirma-*

tive Action and Minority Voting Rights, and in the writings of Michael Barone in *The Almanac of American Politics,* and elsewhere. Most recently it was stated by Justice O'Connor in *Shaw v. Reno* (1993), a decision questioning the constitutional validity of 1992 redistricting strategies that resulted in the election of twelve new black members of the House. In her opinion for the Court's five-person majority in *Shaw,* Justice O'Connor wrote that drawing district lines on a racial basis "reinforces racial stereotypes and threatens to undermine our system of representative government by signaling to elected officials that they represent a particular racial group rather than their constituency as a whole" (p. 18). What is new about Swain's work is that she attempts to support what are largely philosophical and ideological arguments with empirical research; empirical research that is of questionable validity and generalizability.

Philosophical and ideological questions aside, it is not likely that the interest of blacks in a serious, well-crafted, well-funded, long-term program to deal with the problems of the so-called "black underclass" will find majority support in Congress, probably because there is no majority support in the country. This is the inference to be drawn from the watered-down Humphrey-Hawkins Act passed in 1978 and the response of the Democratic majority in the House to the Caucus alternative budgets. That is, even if blacks achieve proportionate representation in both the House and Senate, it would not likely result in congressional responsiveness to black interests in terms commensurate with the needs of the black community. This is why Lani Guinier (1991) proposed the radical idea—and in the context of contemporary American politics it is indeed radical—of "proportionate interest" representation which would guarantee to a "disadvantaged and stigmatized minority group" not just fair representation in terms of numbers but also a fair chance of having its policy preferences satisfied. The fate of her nomination to head the Justice Department's Civil Rights Division as well as the Court's decision in the *Shaw* case suggests that blacks are not likely—unless there are radical changes in American politics—to find equitable representation descriptively or substantively. Thus, Guinier is also correct in her critique of post-civil-rights-era black political strategy when she suggests that blacks need to look beyond the routines of redistricting and elections toward development of new theories of community-based mobilization and organization and political parties organized around a specific set of demands or interests, what she calls a "political program."

References

Congressional Record-House, May 24, 1982; April 5, 1984.
Guinier, Lani. 1991. "The Triumph of Tokenism: The Voting Rights Act and the Theory of Black Electoral Success." *Michigan Law Review,* 89.
Mill, J. S. 1869. 1958. *Consideration on Representative Government.* Indianapolis, Ind.: Bobbs-Merrill.
Pitkin, H. 1972. *The Concept of Representation.* Berkeley: University of California Press.
Shaw et al. v. Reno, Attorney General et al., 92 U.S. 357 (1993) (slip opinion).
Smith, Robert C. 1992. "Politics is Not Enough: On the Institutionalization of the African American Freedom Movement." In *From Exclusion to Inclusion: The Long*

Struggle for African American Political Power, R. Gomes and L. Williams. New York: Greenwood Press.

———. 1986. *When Majority Black Districts Elect White Representatives: Case Studies in Race and Representation.* Unpublished monograph prepared for the Joint Center for Political and Economic Studies, Washington.

Book Reviews

Mario Antonio Rivera, *Decision and Structure: U.S. Refugee Policy in the Mariel Crisis* (Lanham: University Press of America, 1991) ISBN 0-8191-8389-x (cloth);
and
Michael Fix, ed., *The Paper Curtain: Employer Sanctions' Implementation, Impact, and Reform* (Santa Monica: Rand Corporation, 1991) ISBN 0-87766-550-8 (paper).

A national debate on immigration has been escalating over the past two years. Perhaps this is to be expected inasmuch as such debate seems to ebb and flow with boom and bust cycles of the economy. However, as economic conditions in the country have worsened in the current period, legitimate debate on policies and issues related to immigration have often become intertwined with xenophobic reactions of citizens and organized anti-immigrant groups, particularly in states considered to be major points of entry. As a result, harsh and restrictive "anti-immigrant" bills have flooded state legislatures. In this dilemma of rising debates and reactions, the two works to be reviewed in these pages are especially significant.

Marco Antonio Rivera's *Decision and Structure: U.S. Refugee Policy in the Mariel Crisis*, is a well-written and well-documented case study of the Mariel boat lift and refugee crisis of 1980 and the disjointed performance by the United States government during that crisis. During the Mariel episode of U.S. immigration history, 125,000 Cubans were boat lifted from Mariel, Cuba to Key West, Florida. This massive migration, different in racial and class composition from previous professional, skilled, and largely white Cuban migration, eventually involved an enormous investment of resources by the United States. However, the author persuasively argues that this investment came without commensurate human and policy accomplishments on the part of the United States government. Particularly impressive was the author's well-explored attention to and documentation of structural difficulties, bureaucratic mistakes, and presidential missteps that occurred during the crisis. Rivera makes a forceful case for his conclusion that an organizational and diplomatic policy failure resulted.

Professor Rivera speaks with considerable authority on the interworkings of the Carter administration on immigrant and refugee affairs, inasmuch as he worked during and immediately after the Mariel episode as a research analyst with the Cuban-Haitian Task Force and, later, in the Office of Refugee Settlement.

He was, therefore, in a privileged observer role, which provided him with access to memos, correspondence, edicts, and conversations concerning the Cuban boat lift and its resulting repercussion on U.S. immigration and refugee policy. Within this context, Professor Rivera offers a careful and detailed analysis of federal multigovernmental involvement that ultimately led to policy failure. Evidence of the involvement of over twenty-five U.S. government agencies and private-voluntary agencies in some aspect of this crisis is offered as testimony to what the author characterizes as a lack of purpose and guidance from the White House.

Rivera carefully documents and analyzes federal interdepartmental rivalry, meddling, and poor communication in the first two chapters. However, as compelling as these chapters were, I found the sections in the third and fourth chapters dealing with federal executive and legislative branch interactions in the framework of intergovernmental relations even more compelling.

Rivera's attention to the urban impact of refugee settlements and costs is also important, although somewhat abbreviated and limited by the extent to which the urban literature was not consulted. This may be seen as a significant omission given the (1) strength of past and especially current state and local actions seeking to "recoup" costs from the federal government associated with immigrant settlement and servicing in host state; (2) increasingly harsh tone of the debate between states and localities on immigration servicing and funding; and (3) escalating debate among counties and municipalities concerning proper local jurisdictions for immigration affairs.

As important as this work is in exploring intragovernmental as well as intergovernmental relations during a "crisis situation," Rivera's work contains a number of significant problems. First, although he refers to his book as an historical case study, it truly is not very historical at all. This is an important point inasmuch as the author intended this work to be, in his own words, "a historical summary of the Mariel crisis and its antecedents" and a "critical policy analysis based on this history" (p. 1). However, if the historical context is overly abbreviated and therefore flimsy, does it follow that the analysis will be based on soft, if not equally flimsy, ground?

On this point, in the historical backdrop of the Mariel episode, the author covers a period from 1849 to 1980 in three pages contained entirely in the Introduction—hardly paying sufficient attention, much less detail, to this history of immigration, related public policy, and governmental relations between Cuba and the United States. While minimal attention is devoted to policy relations between the two countries on immigration issues, the devastating economic blockade enforced against the small island nation by the United States from 1960 to the present is scarcely mentioned. In the same vein, while he briefly acknowledges a dependency theory on U.S. and Cuban relations in the modern era, the author does not make any substantial connections between historical relations of domination by one country over an entire hemisphere with current policy relations and governmental (including paramilitary) practices. Nor does he address the consequences of actions and practices of such domination, including perhaps the Mariel chapter of U.S.-Latin American immigration and refugee history.

The work would also have been stronger had it made reference to other groups which are, aside from Cubans in the context of the Mariel refugees, struggling for the status of political refugees (Salvadorans, Guatemalans, and Haitians). Although the author frequently refers to Haitian undocumented immigration, the reader gets the impression they are forced on him by Carter administration and Congressional categorical lumping of Cubans and Haitians in the early 1980s.

Finally, Professor Rivera often uses terms that are not substantiated, but which undoubtedly give strong clues to this own ideological preferences in his coverage and analysis of Cuban-U.S. relations in this "crisis." For instance, on page 171 he states that the Mariel boat lift exemplified an "assault on American sovereignty by the Cuban Government," and he dismisses strong anti-immigrant nativist histories by simplistically claiming that a "generous outlook on immigration is part of American culture" (p. 184). On this point, he also claims that the Carter administration's mishandling of the crisis was in large part responsible for "fanning a xenophobic reaction to Cuban immigration" (Introduction). In fact, xenophobic reactions to immigrants have long been a part of the American experience. A more extensive exploration, and balanced reading, of the history of immigration and of relations between the United States and Cuba would have improved this already significant work immensely.

Recent hearings held by the Judiciary Committee of the House of Representatives on the impact of employer sanctions in controlling immigration flows reflect the cornerstone importance these sanctions were given in the Immigration Reform and Control Act of 1986 (IRCA). However, far from having a clear impact on immigration control, the debate on sanctions continues to escalate as much of the discussion over illegal immigration continues to center on efforts to stem the flow across the border, particularly from Mexico. Significant portions of the current debate on immigration range from a recent call by the Orange County Grand Jury (in Southern California) for the federal government to declare a three-year moratorium on immigration and efforts to create a national identification card system to beefing up border protection and patrols and toughening up employer sanctions.

In *The Paper Curtain: Employer Sanctions' Implementation, Impact, and Reform,* editor Michael Fix offers us a significant collection of important Reform and Control Act (IRCA) in three cub forms: Implementing Employer Sanctions, Employer Compliance with IRCA Paperwork Requirements, and Reform Options. These subtopics become the three essential parts of the book.

There are four primary conclusions reached by the authors. First, the number of undocumented workers coming across the Mexican border has increased since 1990, four years after the passage of IRCA. Second, agricultural jobs in particular continue to be a "magnet" for immigration workers. Third, the introduction of employer sanctions as part of IRCA appears to have increased the incidence of national origin and citizenship discrimination. Fourth, despite the problems with the employer sanctions program, it should be retained as an integral part of immigration control and reform. These last two conclusions are most interesting and, apparently, somewhat contradictory. Inasmuch as employer sanctions represent the keystone to the 1986 IRCA, the findings, reported in the General Accounting Study (GAO) in 1990, that a link existed between employer sanctions and "widespread discrimination" against "foreign appearing" job applicants, has forced a fierce debate about their demise from IRCA. The GAO report gave cause to making the issue of employer sanctions as much "an immigrations matter as a civil rights question" (p. 1). Thus, a central question raised throughout this work is, Are the costs of sanctions proving to be worth the price given IRCA's apparent role in increasing discrimination, on the one hand, while diminishing the impact of undocumented immigration flows, on the other?

Always controversial, the employer sanctions provisions of IRCA prohibit three types of activity on the part of employers: (1) the knowing hiring of unauthorized (undocumented) workers; (2) continued employment of known unauthorized (undocumented) workers; and (3) hiring of any individual without verifying the identity and authorization of the worker to work (p. 11).

Although the employment sanctions of IRCA are the focus of all chapters, other immigration control programs and activities are also discussed. Of particular interest were those authors (such as Rolph and Robyn and Zimmerman) who provided a context to discuss the considerable intergovernmental tension unleashed by IRCA.

The authors, primarily mainstream social scientists, are experts on immigration policy and evaluative outcomes representing the Rand Corporation and the Urban Institute collaborating under a Ford Foundation grant. However, in representing almost exclusively mainstream currents, little attention was paid to some of the more progressive works and authors. This was an oversight.

While the manuscripts are well written, analytic, and important to the ongoing debate cresting in recent House hearings, the overall work was limited in that not a single Latino author or scholar was included among the seventeen authors credited with the twelve manuscripts. Estaben Flores of the University of Colorado, Gilbert Cardenas of the University of Texas at Austin, Rodolfo de la Garza of the University of Texas at Austin, F. Chris Garcia of the University of New Mexico, Harry Pachon of the Claremont Graduate School, Marta Lopez-Garcia of California State University at Los Angeles, Jorge Bustamante of the Colegio de Mexico, Raul Fernandez of the University of California at Irvine, Leo Estrada of UCLA, and Gloria Romero of California State University at Los Angeles, among others, have all published significant works and studies on Latino immigration and current immigration laws. All should have been strongly considered as part of this study/scholarly pool on this project. That lack of Latino scholarly participation and insight is a significant oversight.

James A. Regalado
Director and Associate Professor
Edmund G. "Pat" Brown Institute
of Public Affairs
California State University,
Los Angeles

John Rawls, *Political Liberalism* (New York: Columbia University Press, 1993) xxxiv + 401 pp.; ISBN 0-231-05248-0 (cloth).

Since the publication of *A Theory of Justice* (Cambridge, Mass.: Harvard University Press) in 1971, John Rawls has been the most prominent moral and political philosopher in the English-speaking world. *Theory of Justice* makes major substantive and methodological contributions. Rawls argues for his now-famous principles of justice—the first establishing equal liberties, and the second, the "difference principle," holding that inequalities must benefit the "least-advantaged" members of society—through a form of social contract theory, familiar from works by Hobbes, Locke, Rousseau, and Kant. "Justice as fairness," as Rawls calls his view, is established by showing that inhabitants of a hypothetical "original position," behind a "veil of ignorance," which eliminates knowledge of their particular characteristics and situation, would choose the two principles of justice over possible alternatives. Rawls appears to make great claims for his principles, which are said to hold "sub specie aeternitatis" (*Theory*, p. 587).

In responding to criticisms of *Theory of Justice*, Rawls has appeared to shift his ground. In a series of articles in the late 1970s and 1980s, which have themselves attracted enormous attention, Rawls develops a sociological defense of justice as fairness, as the view of justice best suited to contemporary liberal societies. *Political Liberalism* is a fully worked account of Rawls's new position. It is comprised mainly of revised versions of seven of his previous publications. Only two of these, "The Basic Structure as Subject" (1978) and "The Basic Liberties and Their Priority" (1982), are presented virtually unchanged.

The starting point of Rawls's new position is the diversity of contemporary liberal societies. Political liberalism's task is to find principles of justice that people with strongly different moral, religious, political, and philosophical views can accept in spite of their differences. Rawls attempts to develop what he calls a "political conception of justice," which can provide a basis for agreement among different groups, and so contribute to stable democratic societies.

In contrast to other moral doctrines, a political conception of justice is neither "general in scope" nor "comprehensive." By the former, Rawls means that a "political" view does not address a wide range of questions, but focuses mainly on central political and social institutions. In contrast to a comprehensive doctrine, which "covers all values and virtues within one rather precisely articulated system" (p. 13), a political view attempts to stay on the philosophical surface, not being dependent on controversial philosophical views. Rawls's aim is to create an "overlapping consensus." Different groups in society will be able to accept a set of principles to adjudicate important political issues, though they disagree about wider philosophical questions, and accept these principles for different reasons. In a diverse society, general agreement on comprehensive views could be achieved only through the oppressive use of state power. In addition, it is essential that the use of coercion, which characterizes the political domain, be justifiable to all members of society. An overlapping consensus enables each individual to accept the principles in question from his own point of view. Rawls emphasizes political philosophy's practical aim, "The aim of justice as fairness, then, is practical: it presents itself as a conception of justice that may be shared by citizens as a basis of reasoned, informed, and willing political agreement. It expresses their shared and public political reason" (p. 9).

In order to accomplish its practical task, a view of justice must be rooted in ideas that are "implicit in the public political culture of a democratic society" (p. 13). Presumably, in spite of their other differences, people subscribe to at least some common political ideas. Rawls focuses on the idea of society "as a fair system of cooperation" between people, and a view of people as possessing certain "moral powers," which they should be concerned to develop. Properly fleshed out, these fundamental ideas give rise to his distinctive principles of justice.

Though it departs significantly from *Theory of Justice* in various ways, *Political Liberalism* defends similar principles of justice. In addition, despite Rawls's concern with the political culture of liberal societies, he also retains a semblance of the original position. Rawls argues that his political conception of justice should be developed in two stages. In the first, representative individuals behind the veil of ignorance develop the best possible principles of justice for liberal society. These are applied to society in the second stage, in which the aim is to construct an appropriate overlapping consensus. Rawls argues that the task of "political constructivism" accomplished in the first stage should be independent of the particular features of liberal societies, including the views of diverse groups. Its content "is not affected in any way by the particular comprehensive doctrines that may exist in society" (p. 141). To proceed otherwise would be "political in the wrong way" (p. 142). He is deeply concerned with showing that the desired overlapping consensus is more than a mere "modus vivendi," in essence a truce between different groups, entered into out of self-interest and adhered to only out of weakness (Lecture IV). Briefly, an overlapping consensus goes beyond a *modus vivendi*, in that its principles are accepted in their own right, as ends in themselves. Rawls appeals to basic facts of moral psychology, that as people engage in cooperative activity with others over a long period of time, cooperation will eventually come to be viewed as good in itself. Thus, an overlapping consensus should not be threatened by a change in the balance of contending groups, which could upset a *modus vivendi*.

As one would expect, *Political Liberalism* is a rich work, which I cannot discuss adequately in this brief space. Among the many striking features of the book I have not mentioned is Rawls's attempt to work out a conception of public reason. Recognizing the distance between comprehensive views, he argues that effective principles of justice must be accompanied by general agreement on criteria through which arguments should be assessed, and in regard to such important liberal virtues as civility, intellectual tolerance, and fairmindedness (esp. Lecture VI). However, it is also clear that, as was the case with *Theory of Justice*, there is much with which to disagree. I will briefly suggest one possible line of criticism here.

Rawls's two-stage procedure can be questioned. Though this particular process appears to be necessary to defend the two principles of justice and to justify retention of the original position from which they are derived, one must wonder about the separation between the stages. The development of an overlapping consensus would fulfill Rawls's hope for genuine political agreement, which he believes "would complete and extend" the development of liberal thought over the last three centuries (p. 154). But in the meantime, political philosophy must provide a remedy for breakdowns in a society's shared political understandings (pp. 44-46). It is not clear how differences between groups can be dealt with if their actual views must be set aside. Rawls concedes that particular principles of justice fail if they cannot gain the requisite social support (pp. 65–66), and accordingly, that parties in the original position are "to select (if possible) principles that may be stable, given the fact of reasonable pluralism" (p. 78). This last quotation suggests that the two stages are not as separate as Rawls otherwise asserts.

Rawls perhaps fears that negotiating from the actual views of contending groups will yield political principles that are not sufficiently liberal. But if the two-stage model is cast aside, it is not clear why his principles of justice would be chosen over other doctrines as the basis for an overlapping consensus. Rawls gives little indication of how political conflicts can be reconciled through mutual appeal to principles other than those to which contending parties actually adhere.

In spite of these and other reservations, *Political Liberalism* is a philosophical event. It is a work that everyone interested in political philosophy must read and ponder. Like *Theory of Justice*, it is likely to dominate discussion throughout the field for some time to come.

George Klosko
University of Virginia

Paul C. Light, *Monitoring Government: Inspectors General and the Search for Accountability.* (Washington, D.C., The Brookings Institution) viii + 274 pp.; ISBN 0-8157-5256-3 (cloth).

The search for governmental accountability has been illusive, somewhat like the search for the Loch Ness Monster or Big Foot. Many claim to have seen them, but no one has yet produced them. The same thing is the case with governmental accountability. Paul Light, professor of public affairs at the University of Minnesota concludes that accountability still has not been achieved, although that was the hope of those who created the office of Inspectors General (IGs).

The Inspector General Act of 1978 created Inspector's General in each of the major federal departments. They were charged with the responsibility of conducting audits and investigations; reviewing existing and proposed legislation and regulations for possible impacts on economy and efficiency; and coordinating relationships among governmental agencies to promote economy, efficiency, and effectiveness. This isn't something that excites the imagination, but Light does a fine hob of breathing life into the question and, in the process, showing us why bureaucracies are bureaucratic. The Act was a part of the reforms that began in the late 1960s and 1970s, all of which were aimed at curtailing that independence of bureaucracy. But, unfortunately, the IGs used compliance during the 1980s, which is a top-down method of command and control that envisions a highly bureaucratic system in which, Light notes, "workers have no role in accountability except to do exactly what they are told, with supervisors always watching." This, of course, is a recipe for stifling initiative (which may be what the Reagan administration wanted anyway).

Instead, the Inspectors General could have used performance (i.e., specifying performance outcomes and using positive incentives), or capacity-based methods (i.e., recruiting good people and providing adequate resources). But throughout the 1980s they did not do this because these methods are more expensive, take longer to implement, and are not as rewarding politically.

Better yet, says Light, they should use a post-bureaucratic model in which the government is customer driver and service oriented, but he doubts that Congress or the President are ready to embrace this approach. Light also suggests strengthening the evaluation capacity of agencies. This would indeed help, especially if the emphasis is on process rather than outcome evaluation because the former is directed at discovering which implementation factors lead to more successful outcomes. This can help agencies improve what they are doing, especially if a stakeholder approach is used. In such an approach, the perspectives of all stakeholders in a program—the clients, targets, or victims, as well agency groups—are included. Outcome evaluation, on the other hand, looks only at the extent to which goals have been achieved and, as was discovered in the 1970s by evaluators, the results are seldom, if ever, used by agencies. Consequently, evaluation by itself will not ensure accountability, but it can help improve the performance of agencies. This is already being done to a certain extent by the Program Evaluation and Methodology Division of the General Accounting office, but I doubt that evaluation will *ever* be the major factor in determining what governmental agencies do or don't do.

In the eleven chapters of the book, Light takes us through a discussion of the three methods of accountability, a short history of the concept the internal working of IGs, and an evaluation of their effectiveness. Chapter 1 focuses on the three types of accountability; chapter 2 is a brief history of the IG concept; chapter 3 describes why Congress wanted IGs; chapter 4 discusses the difficulties they faced as they tried to get established; chapters 6 and 7 tell us the way the Reagan and Bush administrations used the IGs (Bush had much less interest in fraud busting so IGs were relegated to a back seat); chapters 8 and 9 describe how IGs work; chapter 10 evaluates their effectiveness; and chapter 11 considers a broader role for the IGs.

How effective have the IGs been? Light tells us that they have been effective from an organizational perspective because they have become more independent and have increased their staff. They also have accumulated huge savings and ferreted out wrongdoing. But the amount of waste that Reagan claimed existed in government was grossly exaggerated says Light, and more importantly, effectiveness means more that just getting your agency to grow and save money. A broader definition includes questions of how professional are the offices, how deep is the coverage, how great are the savings, how good are the cases, and how visible are the results.

Using these measures, Light concludes that IGs are not very effective. Not many agencies pay attention to IGs findings (IGs have no enforcement powers); the public hasn't become more trusting of government during the time IGs have existed (actually they have become much less trustful); the government is a little less vulnerable to waste, fraud, and abuse, but we don't really know how much less; and while the government is producing some outcomes of greater public value as the result of IGs, unless the capacity of government is increased, all we may get from the IGs is more bureaucratic inertia. Light concludes (p. 224) that, "After all the statistical accomplishments are totaled and all the staff and budget increases reviewed, government appears no more accountable today that before the IG Act."

So the search for accountability goes on. Perhaps the problem is that we are looking for the wrong thing; perhaps there is no such thing as accountability, just as there is no Big Foot or Loch Ness Monster, although it is titillating to think there is.If accountability means having administrative agencies do exactly what Congress intends and no more, then it is not achievable for three reasons: (1) the intentions of Congress are seldom, if ever, clear; (2) it is impossible to completely eliminate the discretion of street-level workers, and; (3) as Michael Lipsky has noted, they engage in policymaking when they interpret and apply rules and regulations.

If, on the other hand, accountability means getting administrators to do the best job they can while implementing the often vague and sometimes poorly designed legislation, and they do this because they are dedicated professionals rather than because their supervisors are watching, then accountability is achievable. But this doesn't mean they will do what the statute intends, for they will continue to adapt and change programs to fit local needs. Moreover, this is a long-run strategy as Light says, and it is not likely that Congress or the President will buy into it because it is more fun and politically advantageous to bash those "government bureaucrats." Moreover, in our system of checks and balances and separation of powers, the executive will make policy when it implements statutes and these policies will not be the same as those of Congress, especially when the Congress is controlled by the opposite political party, as the Reagan and Bush administrations demonstrated.

In any event, Light's excellent book is well worth reading and using in college political science and public administration classes because it tells us a lot about the inner workings of the agencies that are supposed to govern us.

Dennis J. Palumbo
Regents Professor of Justice Studies
Arizona State University

George C. Edwards III, John H. Kessel, and Bert Rockman, eds., *Researching the Presidency: Vital Questions, New Approaches* (Pittsburgh: University of Pittsburgh Press, 1993) x + 496 pp.; ISBN 0-8229-2727-9 (cloth); 0-8229-5494-x (paper).

The field of presidential studies has fought long and hard for recognition from the other domains of political science. While political scientists have been writing about the chief executive at least since the days of E.S. Corwin, research on the presidency has been castigated as bad history or little more than biography. Some friendly observers in other subfields have gone so far as to argue that the whole enterprise of a political science approach to the presidency is doomed by the fact that it explores a phenomenon in which $n = 1$, thus making irrelevant many of the techniques of contemporary social sciences.

Because of these criticisms, scholars of the American presidency have been especially self-conscious about conceptual and methodological questions. In the 1970s, Hugh Heclo surveyed the available literature on the presidency and concluded that it suffered from a surfeit of "didactic" tomes that were of little real value. He called for more and better empirical studies. Since then, presidential scholars have regularly reflected on the scope and methods of their subfield, in the process winning status as an organized section of the American Political Science Association and producing not only interesting scholarship but a considerable body of work on the enterprise of presidential studies itself.

One of the leaders in this undertaking has been George Edwards, who was the co-editor of a 1983 volume on *Studying the Presidency*, (University of Tennessee Press). He and a number of others in the field have devoted much of their careers to increasing the rigor of research on the nation's highest office. *Researching the Presidency* is but the latest product of that effort, the fruit of a 1990 conference in Pittsburgh sponsored by the National Science Foundation. Its focus is identified in its subtitle, *Vital Questions, New Approaches*.

Parts I and III survey the scope of presidential studies. Rather, they sketch some of the domain of the field. Chapters on presidential selection, personality evaluation, and sources of power present a rough outline of the major issues explored in contemporary research, although constitutional and legal issues are largely ignored. As is generally the case in survey volumes of this sort, the chief value of individual chapters is their synthetic quality: they provide a good introduction, summary, and sophisticated assessment of the literature on a particular issue. The best "scope" chapters are those by Erwin Hargrove and Karen Hult. Hargrove provides an instructive discussion of presidential personality and leadership style that puts such classic works as Lasswell's analysis of political man, the Georges's study of Woodrow Wilson, and Barber's typology in context with Greenstein and Burke's analysis of Vietnam decisionmaking. Hult examines research on presidential advisory decisions, drawing together such works as Allison's conceptual models of foreign policy advice, public management literature, and Wyszomirski's studies of domestic decision structures. Her bibliography is especially helpful to those taking a first look at this area.

Part II focuses more on the methods of presidential research, with an emphasis on theoretical approaches to studying the chief executive. Whereas Edward and Wayne's *Studying the Presidency* spent considerable space on sources of information, the contributors to this volume are more concerned with overarching schemes for examining the subject: organization theory, leadership theory, formal theory, rational choice modeling, and how to bring more rigor to qualitative as well as quantitative research. The book's emphasis on "New Approaches" is as advertised: the aim of the contributors is to explore the "cutting edge" of presidential research. But the "cutting edge" represented here is that of a dagger rather than a sword: narrow. The chapters in this section are useful and interesting, but generally dominated by approaches drawn from economics or econophilic social science.

What the book lacks is a good analysis of approaches to the study of the presidency drawn from normative theory, law, and political history. Works such as those in Cronin's *Inventing the American Presidency* (University Press of Kansas, 1989), Bessette and Tulis's *The Presidency in the Constitutional Order* (Louisiana State University Press, 1981), Hargrove and Nelson's *Presidents, Politics, and Policy* (Knopf, 1984), Spitzer's *President and Congress,* (McGraw-Hill, 1992) or Koh's *The National Security Constitution* (Yale University Press, 1990) have no real place here. It is unfortunate that this is so, but to some extent it is inevitable.

It is too bad that the book does not make room for such works, because this literature have tremendously enriched our understanding of the presidency and its place in the American political system. In the wake of Vietnam, Watergate, and the Iran-Contra affairs, scholars have found normative and constitutional questions to be some of the most important and challenging ones they can address. Research in these areas has also been useful to the nation. But it is somewhat predictable that they would not find a place in this volume, because the orientation of the book is clear: it tends to place the scientific over the political in its approach to political science. Works that use alternative approaches and methodologies—even ones that are intellectually sophisticated and new to the average social scientist—are not even in the ball park of a book such as this one.

In the end, *Researching the Presidency* makes a valuable contribution to the growing literature on presidential studies. But it is an incomplete contribution, because of what it excludes. Those who want a good overview of this field and its literature would do well to read this book in conjunction with others, most notably the earlier volume on *Studying the Presidency* and some of the works mentioned above. That survey of the literature offers a more comprehensive view of what is going on in presidency research than the admirable but flawed volume under review.

Ryan J. Barilleaux
Miami University (Ohio)

Patricia W. Ingraham and David H. Rosenbloom, eds., *The Promise and Paradox of Civil Service Reform* (Pittsburgh: University of Pittsburgh Press, 1992) x + 329 pp.; ISBN 0-8229-3716-6 (paper).

The Civil Service Reform Act of 1978 (CSRA) was a landmark in legislative success for the administration of President Jimmy Carter. The promise of the legislation was improved management of the federal bureaucracy and increased responsiveness of the public service to the public through the president. The paradox of the reform effort lies in what has resulted from the legislation and what contributed to those results. Ingraham and Rosenbloom have pulled together a collection of essays that analyze the policymaking process leading to CSRA and evaluate the successes and failures of the policy as it has been implemented.

The major intent of this collection of essays is to examine the collective impact of each of the major components of the CSRA. The authors represent leading experts in the field of public personnel management. Many of the contributions came from a symposium on Ten Years of Civil Service Reform held at the Maxwell School of Citizenship and Public Affairs at Syracuse University.

In an introductory essay, Patricia Ingraham provides the framework for the analysis with perceptive insight into the reform effort and the processes by which it occurred. She also outlines the promise of reform that serves as the base for evaluation of CSRA for the other authors. Ingraham notes that the fundamental problem of contemporary public administration is finding a replacement for the politics/administration dichotomy and suggests that it also is the leading concern of proponents of civil service reform. Additionally, the roles of the three branches of government under the U.S. constitutional system emerge as concerns in the reform decisions.

The unprecedented comprehensiveness of the reform proposals of the Carter administration added to the complexity of the decision-making process and the difficulty in achieving the results expected of it. In a second essay, Ingraham goes on to explain that to understand the design and outcomes of CSRA, it is necessary to recognize that (1) only the fringes of the system were addressed; (2) widely accepted but untested assumptions about professional management and political control were built into the legislation; and (3) assumptions that private sector practices could be transferred effectively to the public sector were incorporated into critical elements of the reform.

The overall assessment of the authors included in this volume is that CSRA failed in achieving its promises. Each of the essays addresses a specific element organized around four themes: (1) designing change; (2) institutions of reform; (3) civil service process and procedure; and (4) the lessons of reforms.

In designing change, the reform effort promised improved management and increased responsiveness of the system while protecting against political abuses. As suggested by several of the authors, improved management did not result, partly because of structural difficulties and conflicts among competing government agencies. These themes appear throughout the volume. Instead of improving management, political responsiveness became an overriding concern of the Reagan administration with Dan Devine as Director of the Office of Personnel Management. The highly partisan activity of Devine led to decreased morale in the public service and a sense of alienation from the system. At the same time, the constant bureaucrat bashing and the many ethical scandals of the Reagan administration brought the image of the public service to new lows. While the Bush administration reversed some of the these trends, the promise of the CSRA got lost in the implementation of its various provisions. Some of the problems also were attributed to the fact that the act was so broad that it encompassed conflicting values and expectations to gain political support.

The structure of reform also has its impact. Reorganization is a very difficult, time-consuming process. Larry Lane suggests that in the process of reorganizing, policymaking, and program development, the federal personnel community was left out (pp. 107–111). The results are predictable: lack of enthusiasm for the changes and essentially placing the public service on the fringes of government activity.

Examination of the institutions of the public service, Office of Personnel Management (OPM), Senior Executive Service (SES), Merit Systems Protection Board (MSPB), Office of Special Counsel, and Federal Labor Relations Authority (FLRA), also suggests lack of success of the reforms. While authors find some successes in the Merit Systems Protection Board and Federal Labor Relations authority, even they are tempered by haunting problems in timeliness, judicial review of their actions, and perceptions of lack of fairness.

Reforms always are limited by the expectations various participants have for their outcomes. The political process that leads to policy enactment requires compromise and often, acceptance of conflicting values. Whether the outcomes reflect success depends upon the perspective of the evaluator. The authors in this volume, for the most part, represent public administration experts who have a strong desire to see the personnel management system operate in a rational manner to improve public service management and service to the polity. They had high hopes that the civil service system, which was the result of many years of incremental policy, would be thoroughly reformed to achieve the lofty objectives espoused by the president. It is very likely that many of those who bought into the reform did so because they had other expectations. As Chester Newland, Larry Lane, and Paul Light point out, many elements of the proposals finally settled upon by the President represented compromises with influential interest groups. Similarly, the process through congress further reflected lobbying by affected interests. The result was a reform falling short of the original promise. Implementation with changing administrations led to new twists in the meaning of the CSRA.

For policymakers, the CSRA represents an almost unique effort. Rarely does one see such a comprehensive approach to policymaking. While some of the authors acknowledge the comprehensiveness of the effort (especially Ingraham), most tend to focus on the specific elements and do not celebrate the fact that CSRA made public personnel management a major focus of public attention for many years. Although the negative image of the public service was used to gain acceptance for reform, the fact that attention was paid to improving the system placed personnel management at the center of public management discussion. Clearly, the effort fell short of the expectations generated for it. If the Carter administration had been re-elected, it is possible that the reforms would have been sustained and institutionalized in a fashion that would have met many of the expectations.

It is difficult to assess the entire effect of CSRA. This volume goes further than any effort at evaluation. It is insightful in documenting what led to the passage of CSRA and how it fared in implementation. The reader is left with the sense that the major problem in realizing the promises of the reform is based on the fact that there really is little consensus on the fundamental questions it attempted to address. As Paul Light suggests, there are three important questions: (1) How many political appointees is too many?; (2) What are the baselines against which to measure reform?; and (3) Just how important is pay, anyway? Because there is not agreement even on these basic questions, the reforms are unlikely to meet expectations.

This book should be of great interest to scholars of public personnel management as well as public policy analysis. It provides insightful analysis of personnel issues from the perspective of effective government and it analyses the policymaking and implementation processes in detailed fashion. One essay, "The Senior Executive Service in Australia," seems out of place as it is the only one with a comparative bent. Although CSRA is mentioned in the essay, it is not the focal point of analysis of the Australian case.

N. Joseph Cayer
Arizona State University

Harold E. Cheatham and James B. Stewart, eds., *Black Families: Interdisciplinary Perspectives* (New Brunswick, N.J.: Transactions, 1990) vii–xv + 403 pp.; ISBN 0-88738-812-4 (paper).

This collection of articles is the product of a 1985 conference at Pennsylvania State University entitled: "The Black Family: Contemporary Issues and Concerns." The resultant volume is a very useful scholarly endeavor that utilizes various disciplinary studies to increase knowledge about black families and to examine similarities and differences among black families, taking into account ecological and class factors. Also, in a culturally pluralist context, it examines social issues and cultural adaptations relevant to black family life in St. Vincent, West Indies, Nigeria, and West Indian immigrants in the United States.

The strength of this volume is mostly at the micro level of testing factors affecting the functioning of the family and at the mezzo level of historically and culturally examining such institutions as the black church and black hospitals. While asserting that social-ecological issues are effected by political economy decisions, the volume does not engage the social politics and budgetary politics of the Reagan-Bush era and its impacts on the black family and the black community. In this regard it seems to avoid political engagement to enhance its particular sociological perspective. There are perhaps some gains but also some losses in this approach.

The eighteen articles in this collection all make some contribution to understanding different aspects of the functioning of the black family. In this brief review, it is not possible to give all of them the attention they might deserve, so I will only try to highlight some main trends and emphases.

The Stewart article, "Back to Basics: The Significance of DuBois's and Frazier's Contributions for Contemporary Research on Black Families," demonstrates how these classical works provide the foundation blocks for more contemporary studies about the black family. The contemporary split in the black community between a stable, albeit often threatened, middle class and a black poor community encompassing a sometimes violent and socially disorganized very poor segment can be traced back to analyses by DuBois and Frazier on the impact of slavery on black Americans. Stewart recalls DuBois's observation that while slavery involved oppression and forced human degradation, it also involved a forced assimilation which affected the development of the black leadership class—later referred to as the "Talented Tenth."

DuBois observed that:

> while to some extent European family morals were taught the small select body of house servants and artisans, both by precept and example, the great body of field hands were raped of their own sex customs and provided with no binding new ones. Slavery gave the monogamic family ideal to slaves, but it compelled and desired only the most imperfect practice of its most ordinary mortals. (p. 12)

Frazier noted the disruption of the slave economy on the family life of slaves while emphasizing the importance of the slave mother as a bearer of intergenerational stability. He had observed that in the slavery period:

> [o]nly the bond between the mother and her children continually resisted the disruptive effect of economic interests that were often inimical to family life among slaves.... [U]nder all conditions of slavery, the Negro mother remained the most dependable and important figure in the family. (p. 12)

While late in his career Frazier moves closer to an ethnic conscious notion of black development in American society, for much of his career Frazier developed a sociological interest in "objectifying" the problems of black families and the notion that the development of an urban black proletariat would enhance the black family's stability and its eventual assimilation into American society. On the other hand, DuBois was more concerned with examining how black institutions such as the black church would improve the status of black Americans and subsequently enhance integrationist goals.

Nonetheless, both DuBois and Frazier were concerned with the impact of migration, unstable industrialization trends, and urbanization which was contributing to a developing pattern of unwed motherhood among poor black families in America. Stewart notes that their research was a precursor of contemporary insights as to how "the process of de-industrialization...is currently disproportionately affecting African-Americans and the lives of black families" (p. 24).

Some of the articles dealing with specific institutions are noteworthy. Thomas Poole's article on the black church points out how such churches served as the focal points for economic cooperation and education as well as a place to develop community leadership and political skills. While the black church served as a community development resource, it tended not to make a significant contribution to the political agenda of the black community. With some exceptions such as T. Wyatt Walker and Martin Luther King, Jr., and today perhaps Jesse Jackson, it has tended to be accommodationist and subject to what Edward Wilmont Blyden termed "bourgeoisification." Nevertheless, by seeking to sustain the health of African-American families under contemporary ecological stresses, black churches, such as the African Methodist Episcopal Zion Church and the Progressive National Baptist Church, continue to play a significant role in the survivalist strategies of the black community. What they seem to do best is to conduct "their ministry" to the family.

Mitchell Rice provides an excellent review of the courageous role of black hospitals in providing care to the black community, in spite of significant deficiencies in resources, from the 1850s to the 1960s, and their demise in the wake of the combination of the Civil Rights Act of 1964, the implementation of the (Hill-Burton) Hospital Construction Act, and the subsequent implementation of Medicare and Medicaid. The Barbee Myers article on hypertension is also a health-related study that indicates that adiposity and weight are significant predictors of hypertension as is examination of a parent's medical history. These findings are combined with a literature review which notes that life and security-threatening events—low income and lack of education, particularly in an urban environment—are also important precursors of hypertension within the black population. In order to understand the prevalence of this condition in the black community, she suggests combining a psychosocial and a biological risk factor approach.

A number of the articles deal with male/female relations. Noel Cazenave and Rita Smith are concerned that a number of their respondents viewed black male/female relationships negatively. They suggest that one way of improving such relationships is to develop mutual support around the interests of children. Michael Williams rejects polygamy as a strategy for dealing with the declining male to female ratio in the black community. His argument that economically successful black women should "marry down" probably asks too much of successful black women. His suggestion that they marry Caribbean or African men could highlight problems of cultural difference, especially when such men operate within authoritarian, patriarchal, male-dominated systems.

A number of the articles raise issues of concern with respect to the development of social policy. Wilhelmine Leigh's article on federal housing policies demonstrates that despite the 1948 *Shelley* v. *Kramer* case, in which the Supreme Court held that courts could not enforce restrictive covenants, and the 1968 Fair Housing Act and other state fair housing acts, blacks lack equal access to suitable housing in safe and nonsegregated areas and are also often denied access to market information. Moreover, even the utilization of federal programs such as Section 235 mortgage insurance and Section 8 rental subsidies indicates problems in securing black families equal opportunities to develop ownership or rentership in safe and nonsegregated areas.

Lois Benjamin and James Stewart's article on welfare dependency point out that "feel good" programs improving one's sense of self-efficacy are insufficient to reduce welfare dependency and that what is more central are "coordinated labor market, housing, educational, and child care policies" (p. 258). The need for multitiered interventions with black youth to deal with problems of education, mental health, and violence in poor areas is noted by Jewel Taylor Gibbs. Robert Hill's article provides a thoughtful analysis of federal programs that have helped enhance status rights and economic rights of African-Americans as well as addressed the remnants of institutional discrimination such as redlining and discriminatory zoning in education. He speaks highly of the Earned Income Tax Credit, which removed 4 million working poor families from the tax roles, 25 percent of whom were black. Hills criticizes William Julius Wilson's analysis of the social problems of the black ghetto poor and Wilson's perhaps overly optimistic portrayal of the dramatic rise of the black middle class since the Civil Rights Act of 1964—a criticism sociologists Andrew Billingsly and Bart Landry also have made. In defense of Wilson, one may note that his "hidden agenda" offers effective programs and a reasonable strategy for meeting the needs of poor black families. Hill's article really does not do so. Also, even those who criticize Wilson as not pointing out the economic and social vulnerability of the black middle class do not question the significant movement of middle-class black Americans into economic areas from which they previously had been formally and informally barred.

This is a very useful and probing multifaceted volume on the black family. It is problem focused on a number of levels. Its analysis and prescriptions are most sharply focused on the micro and mezzo levels. Its discussion of political-economic interventions clearly identifies current problems, but does not grapple sufficiently with the need to point out the political interventions needed. This monumental task could perhaps be the subject for another conference. (In the wake of the Bush-Reagan social policies of the 1980–1992 period, we may all underestimate the extent to which policies of social reconstruction and reclamation are needed.)

Howard A. Palley
University of Maryland at Baltimore

David W. Rohde, *Parties and Leaders in the Postreform House* (Chicago: University of Chicago Press, 1991) xii + 232 pp.; ISBN 0-226-72407-7 (paper).

David Rohde has written a most important book about the changing nature of political parties in the House of Representatives. What Rohde describes and analyzes is the growing strength of political parties at the governing level in American politics. His concerns are with the causes and consequences of this impressive, and largely unanticipated, change. In the course of his examination Rohde successfully undercuts the conventional wisdom that political parties in Congress are not very important in understanding institutional decisionmaking. Rohde demonstrates that unlike party in the electorate, which has remained weak for over two decades, party in government in the United States Congress is stronger than at any point since the early years of the New Deal. True, American congressional parties are not as strong as in some parliamentary systems. But given the context of the American political system, political parties in Congress have reached an unusual level of importance, especially in the House of Representatives.

The book is nicely organized in a manner that first informs the reader of the body of literature on the decline of parties in Congress and then allows Rohde to present his evidence on party resurgence. Thus, instead of serving as a critique of the existing literature, Rohde's writing credits the comprehensive body of literature on which he is able to build. Although at times he correctly notes some of the shortcomings of earlier research, Rohde's goal is not one of refutation. Instead, his research should be seen as a significant substantive extension. But Rohde's extension is also an important departure from that literature. This is clear from the data he presents at the end of chapter one that documents, through the use of party unity scores, the growth in party votes and party unity scores in the House since the early 1980s. It then is the task in the remaining chapters to address significant questions about this resurgence of party: What role did congressional reforms play in the strengthening of party? How much of the change was influenced by alterations in membership composition? How has the majority party leadership contributed to the advancement of party? What has been the reaction of House Republicans to a more unified Democratic party and a more effectively equipped majority party leadership? What effect have the Reagan and Bush presidencies had on the level of partisanship? Why has partisanship in the Senate grown less rapidly than in the House? In each instance Rohde confronts the question at hand like a puzzle to be unraveled and then proceeds, often in an original manner, to lead the reader to a solution.

After a careful discussion of the literature on parties in the House and the decline of party, Rohde presents a thorough examination of congressional reforms of the 1960s and 1970s and their consequences for political parties and leaders in the House. In this section Rohde performs several important services for the reader. First, he presents the different tracks of the reform movement: removing power from committee chairs, increasing the power of the Democratic party and its leadership, and the development of what Rohde labels "collective control of power." Second, he examines and explains why strong leadership and increased party unity were not immediately forthcoming once reforms were in place. In this regard Rohde's discussion of the constituency base of Democratic House members is particularly crucial. The growing homogeneity of Democratic members was a necessary, but not sufficient, factor in the resurgence of party. Rohde's analysis of the changing party support levels of southern Democrats from the 1950s through the 1980s provides empirical support for those who argue that the impact of the Voting Rights Act was lagged. He supplements these findings with data on the decline in membership in the Conservative Democratic Forum.

Among the most attractive features of Rohde's analysis is the way in which he goes beyond the use of collective measures of party unity to demonstrate the change in Democratic party cohesion over time. To ensure that his finding about increased Democratic cohesion is not a function of a changing issue mix, he develops cohesion scores for five different substantive areas over seventeen Congresses. Similarly, he examines cohesion levels on different types of votes (final passage, suspensions, amendments, and procedural). This is the only way to make meaningful comparisons on party voting across time because electronic voting (which started in 1973) changed the mix of roll-call votes. Prior to that time, roll calls were largely limited to final passage votes and rarely taken on amendments. Rohde is to be applauded for taking this step. It is a major corrective for an obvious flaw in previous work that has compared levels of party voting over time. The richness of Rohde's work is evident in his examination of the role of party on key issues. He is able to demonstrate the disappearance of sectional conflicts in the Democratic party on race, budget, and defense issues. In addition, by using the voting record of Jamie Whitten, Rohde makes a strong case for the importance of caucus elections of committee chairs and the support of senior members for party positions.

Much of Rohde's work focuses on the Democratic party in the House and its leaders. In fact, Rohde finds that is where the biggest change occurs. However, he does not neglect the Republicans. His study of their responses to a stronger majority party in strategy and tactics and in internal party contests is well documented. Most valuable is his analysis of the impact of presidencies on partisanship in the House. His division of presidential position roll-call votes into those on which the president favored passage and those on which the president opposed passage offers a new perspective on the effect of divided party government.

My enthusiasm for this book is only tempered by a couple of relatively minor reservations. The first of these is substantive. Rohde nicely demonstrates the impact of a range of conditions on the growth of partisanship. Many of these conditions are not sufficient but are necessary ones. Yet Rohde never clearly establishes the size of the contribution that each makes. Is increased party homogeneity more important than the increase in leadership powers or the presidential influences? About as strong a conclusion as Rohde is willing to offer comes on page 174, where he argues: "The reforms...were not a substitute for shared policy preferences among Democrats. They could not create consensus where none existed." The ability to give some weight to these different factors is particularly important in attempting to estimate the likelihood that House Democrats will retain a high level of cohesion with a Democratic presidency.

Second, I am surprised by the amount of copyediting oversights in a book prepared by the University of Chicago Press. For example, in several instances the Reagan budget initiatives are dated as being in 1987 not 1981. In another case the data in a table and the interpretation of it in the text are inconsistent. (I believe the data in the table should be reversed.) Perhaps as a former journal co-editor, I am more sensitive than others to editing matters. But a book of this substantive quality should not have such blemishes.

In sum, *Parties and Leaders in the Postreform House* should be on the required reading list not just for congressional specialists, but for serious students and scholars of American politics. It not only informs the reader of significant changes that have occurred in American politics since the 1950s, but it establishes more refined ways of examining the changing strength of parties in legislative institutions. David Rohde has established a new bench mark for the study of political parties in Congress.

Bruce Oppenheimer
Vanderbilt University

H. Mark Roelofs, *The Poverty of American Politics: A Theoretical Interpretation* (Philadelphia: Temple University Press) xvi + 276 pp.; ISBN 0-87722-877-9 (paper); ISBN 0-87722-878-7

The principal theme of this essay is stated by the author in this way,

"As we have pushed forward with our analysis of the American political system, the argument has been studded with analytical assertions one by one, for example: that the system is essentially schizophrenic between its religious and secular impulses, that the founding fathers were intellectually and theoretically confused, that the presidency is simultaneously too strong and too weak, that the Congress is a legislative body only in myth, that bureaucracy does not 'belong' in America, and many more" (pp.181). This summary captures the somewhat acerbic and quixotic quality of this work, but this tone does not adequately convey its underlying seriousness.

Having been subjected to a great many celebrations of the American Constitution and the institutions and political dynamics that have developed under its aegis, this gentle blasphemy is refreshing. Having been equally subjected to a wide variety of critical writing that is often thought-provoking, if bombastic, and rarely instructive, Roelofs's book is mildly shocking and more than a little engaging.

Turning to the genesis of the trouble with American politics, the confusion of the founding fathers is portrayed as rooted in their unsuccessful efforts to adopt "community-loving social democracy seeking broad goals of social justice, and, at the same time, a freedom-loving, privatistic, interest-seeking liberal democracy with powerfully sustained elitist tendencies" (p. 1). This, he says (pp. 2-5), has led to five central additional paradoxes:

- The United States is and is not a judaic-Christian nation.
- It is and is not a democracy.
- The principal powers of government are both separated and overlapping.
- The U.S. presidency is both too strong and too weak.
- Parties are both essential to political function in the U.S. polity and non-existent.

Formidable myth and ideology are required to render this sensible. Myth "is the total process by which Americans traditionally legitimize themselves and the power constructs they erect over themselves." The U.S. myth is then comprised of two components: identification of the U.S. people as a "people in history," and the direct legitimization of governments and their operative powers (p. 18). The United States is "the total process by which Americans traditionally have come to govern themselves in actual daily practice" (p. 18). These two concepts generate the U.S. images of itself "in practical, operative ideology, a liberal democracy, and, in aspiring myth, a social democracy" (p. 56). The one primal note of resonance between these two is the "moral autonomy of the individual." However, this is buried under the rubble created by the explosive encounter of these concepts. "The social democratic vision summons the individual to obey God.... Meanwhile, the liberal democratic vision summons the same individual to a life of self-aggrandizement" (p. 56).

We have, then, a beginning functional way of beginning to explain some of the cross-cutting currents in American political history, especially in the past generation or so. Goldwater, the self-proclaimed libertarian, nonetheless became the hero of some of the most authoritarian political tendencies. Johnson at once passed the Civil Rights Act and the

Voting Rights Act, even as he was building up the forces of violence in Southeast Asia to enforce democracy in that foreign land. George Bush at once claimed his Christian heritage and at the same time mounted a plainly racist campaign to become president. No doubt such contradictions could be found in the statements and practices of most major U.S. politicians.

This is a very interesting book, and we should all read it. But, as is the case with most interesting books, it can be challenged on a number of grounds. First, what Roelofs describes as paradoxical in U.S. political thought and action may be common in politics in most modern industrial states. Consider the French and Italian political economies, characterized by multiplicities of political parties, each of which often seems to speak with a forked tongue. Even in Britain there is a stark contrast between the mythic and ideological notions of democracy and what is actually practiced, at least as regards people of color, to say nothing of the Irish question.

Second, looking at two of the principal nominal founts of wisdom in the industrial West, Freud revealed the flawed nature of the concept of rationality in understanding human behavior, and Marx, if nothing else, identified the omnipresence of conflict and contradiction in human societies. Again, the most elemental perspective of Roelofs resonates with earlier work.

Third, in a postscript, Roelofs ponders the endurance of the U.S. system, furrowed as it is with paradox and perplexity. In a concluding comment, he says this: "So, the system endures. But is mere endurance a value to be admired without qualifications? Is stability in a sore place a good? The quality of what endures is also to be questioned. Is a perpetually self-impoverishing politics going to be efficient enough, good enough, and competent enough to see the nation into the next century?" In itself, this is not a very novel question, as we address ourselves to the apparent sea change of the transition from Reagan/Bush/Quayle to Clinton/Gore. What makes it interesting is that it is at the end of a very interesting and engaging essay which seeks to dissect and analyze some of the basic organs of American political thinking using some new and interesting slices.

The detailed specification of the tensions and paradoxes in U.S. political thought is very helpful, and it is to be hoped that the more lofty thinkers in the Clinton/Gore administration will read *The Poverty of American Politics*, and find that it enhances their understanding and enriches their formulation of new myths, ideologies, and above all, actions to successfully address the crisis that now confronts us.

William W. Ellis
Library of Congress

Gregory R. Weiher, *The Fragmental Metropolis: Political Fragmentation and Metropolitan Segregation* (Albany: State University of New York Press, 1991) xi + 225 pp.; ISBN 0-7914-0564-8 (paper).

In recent years, the burgeoning scholarship on the subject of urban political change and development is indicating that this subfield of political science is regaining a place of prominence, which it lost after the turbulent era of the 1960s and early 1970s. Older and newer themes and issues are converging in a discourse that is both intellectually stimulating and socially pragmatic. Such inner-city policy problems as poverty and unemployment, educational underdevelopment and family instability, racism and urban renewal, and political powerlessness and alienation are receiving new attention as urban scholars analyze the changing character of today's urban scene: de-industrialization and the rise of the postindustrial city, international economic restructuring and the emergence of the global city, the micropolitics of schooling and the managerial crisis in education, public-private partnerships and the dynamics of regime politics, the urban dispossessed and a rising cynicism, the increasing racial/ethnic diversity of cities and growing racial/ethnic antagonism, biracial coalitions and the politics of deracialization, and the process of gentrification and racial/class residential segregation. Clearly, scholarly attention to this new urban reality is central to contemporary political and socioeconomic research.

Residential segregation continues to infect the social body of urban America. The exclusion of African Americans from many all-white neighborhoods is widespread. Chicago, Cleveland, Detroit, Milwaukee, and Newark generally are considered the most racially segregated localities. The level of residential segregation exceeds 80 percent in cities such as Atlanta, Baltimore, 2Birmingham, Boston, Dallas, Fort Lauderdale, Houston, Indianapolis, Jacksonville, Los Angeles, Memphis, Philadelphia, Pittsburgh, and St. Louis. Truly integrated communities are still exceedingly rare.

The book reviewed here makes an important contribution to the study of urban politics by explaining residential segregation as a dimension of urban political and social fragmentation. Although much of the research that deals with urban behavior has examined urban political behavior, decisionmaking, and policy problems by concentrating on largely informal arrangements and dynamics, the book under review signals a return of attention to formal structures in order to arrive at a better explanation of urban social and political dynamics.

In *The Fractured Metropolis*, Gregory R. Weiher argues that the urban political boundary system in the United States provided a concrete focal point for the types of information people use to decide where they want to live. This bounding of political space permits an interaction of geography, demography, and human cognition that tends to result in residential segregation or fragmentation by race and class. It is Weiher's view that division or fragmentation is fundamental to American society and culture; for historical reasons, this phenomenon has become deeply embedded in all aspect of America's social, political, and economic life. This is the context in which Weiher presents a theory of urban governmental or jurisdictional fragmentation and ultimately an argument about the character of contemporary residential segregation based on racial and socioeconomic categories. Definite historical borders serve to demarcate the residential space wherein people with notable characteristics initially come to build their homes. Although many urban analysts employ the term "homogeneity" in reference to this residential dynamic, Weiher considers this concept misleading and speaks rather of jurisdictional "eccentricity" because population compositions rarely are totally uniform. Assuming reasonable degrees of residential mobility, the interrelationship between jurisdictional boundaries and individual and household preferences—concerns about family, security, and lifestyle—operates as a dynamic mechanism that influences succeeding household seekers in their decision to select or to avoid particular residential spaces on the basis of their relative homogeneity with respect to the racial and socioeconomic characteristics of their populations.

Additionally, Weiher contends that the dynamic and complex interaction between municipal or political boundaries and jurisdictional "eccentricity" structures urban and suburban ecological setting by sorting desirable and undesirable residents. Especially in suburban areas, relatively homogenous white communities use political boundaries as a means to attract more privileged white individuals and families and as a strategy to exclude and redirect low-income and non-white invaders. Although Weiher examines this metropolitan compartmentalization with respect to race, education, and occupation, it is the matter of race—and particularly practices that whites employ to exclude African Americans—that captures his greatest attention. He remarks that overt mechanisms of racial segregation employed prior to the eruption of civil rights policies have been replaced by new covert strategies that are changing the patterns of residential discrimination beyond compartmentalization by race. In the emerging transition from intrajurisdictional sorting strategies to interjurisdictional ones, Weiher observes, the more encompassing category of socioeconomic class (one that includes, but is not limited to, race) is utilized. Under these circumstances, jurisdictional boundaries simplify and structure information about what it will be like to live in a given community. That is, repeated white exclusionary activities against African Americans create the impression that a community is closed to them. The impression that such activity is likely to continue constitutes the information on which African American household seekers base their locational decision. Weiher suggests that formal jurisdictions transmit such information more powerfully than do the less formal neighborhood designations and concepts because they represent the convergence of political, economic, and social characteristics of a place with firm geographical referents. Thus, political boundaries are ways of organizing metropolitan space.

The strength of this book is its provision of an interesting and original interpretation of urban political fragmentation. It gives the reader considerable insight into the dynamics of contemporary residential segregation and the complementary strategies of exclusion and recruitment employed by relatively homogenous jurisdictions. It also has some weaknesses. This is most apparent in the book's empirical content. In chapter 4, he tests the hypothesis that, increasingly, racial and socioeconomic segregation varies more at the level of municipal boundaries (interjurisdictional) than at the level of neighborhood boundaries within municipalities (intrajurisdictional) by using census-tract data taken from Cook County, Illinois, and Los Angeles County, California. However, defending this strategy on statistical reasoning, Weiher eliminates the main cities (Chicago and Los Angeles), as well as municipalities under 10,000 from the analysis. As such, Weiher's strategy basically excludes the areas in which local neighborhoods might be thought of as the more important focal points for racial and socioeconomic sorting, not to mention the huge segments of the population and the locus of the natural area and social area analysis literature. We are scarcely surprised that Weiher's data support his hypotheses.

In chapter 5, Weiher hypothesizes that municipalities whose boundaries coincide with those of functional jurisdictions are more homogenous than those municipalities whose boundaries cross functional jurisdictions, which are viewed in terms of the information dynamic as ambiguous for future residents rather than serving as the basis for polarized local communities within the municipality. Utilizing data from suburban St. Louis County, Missouri (again he excludes the city), with school districts as the functional jurisdiction, Weiher confirms his main hypothesis but shows some variation regarding the dynamic. Unified municipal and functional jurisdiction boundaries structure and transmit clearer informational cues than boundaries that cross. Additionally, the data suggest that split municipalities tend to be less eccentric than unified municipalities. In view of these results, it is not altogether understandable why chapter 6, reports on a case study of Richmond Heights, an empirical example of an extreme form of crisscrossing political boundaries; for this dynamic is what Weiher's investigation had shown as the less typical, not hypothesized contradiction between population groups.

As an introduction to each of these three empirical chapters, Weiher details at length the text's theoretical argument; this seems redundant. Moreover, he inserts a model that is purely formal and not directly pertinent to the analysis that follows. In the final chapter, Weiher defends the view that the outcomes emerging from his analysis of metropolitan ecological fragmentation are not reducible to economic market mechanisms; rather, he argues for the primacy of political dynamics in the context of America's pluralist governmental tradition.

Notwithstanding these criticisms, *The Fractured Metropolis* presents a thoughtful discussion about the significance of urban political boundaries and information transmission and their influence on residential selection and patterning. Residential segregation on the basis of race and class continues to deform metropolitan America's political culture and human ecology. Weiher explains why.

Floyd W. Hayes, III
Purdue University

Sean M. Lynn-Jones and Steven Miller, eds., *America's Strategy in a Changing World* (Cambridge: The MIT Press, 1992) XVII + 398 pp.; ISBN 0-262-62085-5 (paper)

During the Cold War, the United States had a clear vision of and purpose in the international system. Foreign policy problems were simply defined and solutions were implemented with relative ease because both were determined by the Cold War imperative; the containment of Soviet ideological, economic, and military influence. The Cold War afforded the U.S. many opportunities to expand its global presence and pursue its ideological and material interests. Today visions of the global order are not so lucid; problems are not easily discerned and foreign policy choices have become difficult. Ironically, the "new post-Cold War" era has increased the range of foreign policy choices available to the U.S. In the timely volume, *America's Strategy in a Changing World*, edited by Sean M. Lynn-Jones and Steven Miller, a group of foreign policy and international relations specialists examine the multiple dilemmas, challenges, and policy options that the U.S. faces in the new global order. The volume is divided into two parts. The preface chapter, authored by Miller and Lynn-Jones, provides an excellent introduction to the post-Cold War foreign policy debate. The volume was put together to serve as a complement to an earlier publication from the MIT Press entitled, *The Cold War and After: Prospects for Peace*.

Part I of the volume includes three essays that examine the nature of the post-Cold War international system and the probable impact that it will have upon long-standing strategic doctrine. The essays provide an overview of the foreign policy options available to the U.S. While each author highlights very different options, all seem to agree that the U.S. should continue to promote its values in the international system—the spread of democracy and an open international economy.

Robert Jervis's article, "The Future of World Politics: Will it Resemble the Past," sets the tone for the articles that follow. He offers a cautionary proviso for those attempting to use the past to predict the future, particularly in a rapidly changing world in which many of the agreed upon generalizations and laws about international relations may not remain valid. He states: "If our laws are not timeless—if history resembles an arrow—some of what we have learned will not help us understand the future" (p. 9). He concludes that the post-Cold War foreign policy debate will be one that addresses questions about the extent of future U.S. global involvement, its policy goals, values, and trade-offs in the new international order.

Terry Diebel points out in his article, "Strategies Before Containment: Patterns of the Future," that American national security goals—physical security, value projection, and economic prosperity—have not changed. Therefore, the traditional approaches to security—balance of power strategy, collective security, hemispheric defense, and isolationism—need not be abandoned in the future. He advocates the formation of trading blocs or protectionism as of means of assuring U.S. economic prosperity. The U.S. should concentrate on the development and maintenance of a successful and prosperous domestic economy. A successful U.S. economy could become an example to the rest of the world, therefore enabling the U.S. to globalize and project its values in the post-Cold War international system.

In "A Defensible Defense: America's Grand Strategy After the Cold War," Robert Art advocates the continuation of an internationalist posture by the U.S., even though it is secure in the wake of the Soviet collapse because of its nuclear weapons and relative geographic isolation. He believes that a radical retrenchment of U.S. global military forces in the 1990s could destabilize the international system. He argues that in spite of the changed global environment, a reduced but continued military presence in Europe, East Asia, and the Persian Gulf will assure a level of international stability.

International stability will be conducive to U.S. interests, values, and prosperity.

Part II of the volume is entitled, "Dimensions of U.S. Strategy After the Cold War." This section is a collection of essays that examine specific challenges to the U.S. security policy in the post-Cold War era. The topics range from Soviet and Eastern European disintegration and reconstruction, the Middle East, War, Peace, Arms Control, to the future of the Third World.

Ted Hopf's essay entitled, "Managing Soviet Disintegration: A Demand for Behavioral Regimes," looks at some of the problems created by Soviet disintegration. Hopf argues that while the Soviet collapse ended the Cold War, Western security is still threatened by the number of nuclear arms controlled by Moscow, the proliferation of weapons of mass destruction in the new non-Russian republics, and the hostility and conflict that could emerge among the new republics in post-Soviet Eastern Europe. Hopf argues that the U.S. has a stake in the evolution of a "peaceful and democratic order" in the region, and the security of the Russian republic. This outcome can be facilitated by the creation and enforcement of a policy framework that links policies towards the new Eastern European and former Soviet Republics to behavioral standards for their armed forces, security policy, foreign conduct, and domestic affairs. He believes that a system of inducements and penalties would encourage Eastern European nations to adhere to those standards. The "carrot and stick" behavioral regime would promote pacific relations among the nations in the region and avert behavior that would destabilize the new international order.

In another essay that addresses the problems created by the emergence of a post-communist order in Eastern Europe, F. Stephen Larrabee looks at the demographic phenomena of East to West migration stimulated by the end of the Cold War. He argues that while nationalist and economic tensions are predictable sources of hostility and conflict in Europe, the relaxation and/or elimination of East to West travel restrictions has led to a new and often ignored source of conflict in Europe. The new levels of East to West migration have already caused substantial domestic and social problems in Germany, for example. It is grappling with the domestic problems of social violence, economic pressures, and social tensions associated with the new refugee crisis.

Three selections in Part II of the volume examine the issues of collective security, peace, war, and arms control. Charles and Clifford Kupchan's essay, "Concerts, Collective Security, and the Future of Europe," advocates the development of a more cooperative security framework in Europe. They suggest that an arrangement built on existing regional institutions like the Conference on Security and Cooperation in Europe (CSCE) would be feasible. The CSCE, for example, could serve as the foundation for Europe's new security system. The Kupchans suggest that the institutionalization of cooperative behavior among Europe's major powers is one of the best ways to oppose aggressors and create stability in an increasingly anarchic post-Cold War international system.

Richard Betts, on the other hand, argues that the collective security systems idea is an old one, but one that should not come of age, because it may create a more dangerous post-Cold War international environment. In the article, "Systems for Peace or Causes of War? Collective Security, Arms Control, and the New Europe," Betts contends that collective security systems are unreliable guarantors of security because they do not effectively build in an "automatic element" that commits member states to engage in war. He also argues that the implementation of a collective security system risks turning minor disputes into major wars among states, because states are committed to war regardless of their individual interests and preferences. Finally, such arrangements undermine more effective individual national security preparations.

With the end of the Cold War, the U.S. is no longer able to justify actions in the world that often contradicted its basic ideological values of political freedom and human rights, especially in the Third World. Richard Herrmann's article, "The Middle East and the New World Order; Rethinking U.S. Strategy After the Gulf War," explores the events leading to the war. He concludes that U.S. policy in the region must emphasize democratization and multilateralism in order to prevent the continued reliance upon military force and support of repressive regimes in the region. He concludes that during the Cold War, the U.S. failed to understand the dynamics of change in the Arab world, which created the Gulf crisis.

For Steven David, the Third World is and will continue to be of importance to global stability after the Cold War. He observes in the article, "Why the Third World Still Matters," that the end of the Cold War will not lead to the resolution of conflict in Africa, Latin America, and Asia. Also, the spread of weapons technologies and the continued U.S. dependency upon imported oil make it necessary for it to retain interventionist capabilities in the Third World. Steven Fetter's essay, "Ballistic Missiles and Weapons of Mass Destruction: What is the Threat? What Should be Done?" argues that global security threats posed by the spread of ballistic missiles and weapons of mass destruction in the Third World can only be thwarted by a combination of security guarantees, multilateral arms control, and export controls backed up by sanctions.

Relations between the U.S. and Japan will be of particular importance in the future. In the article, "Beyond Mutual Recrimination: Building a Solid U.S.-Japan Relationship in the 1990s," I. M. Destler and Michael Nacht examine the increased tensions between the U.S. and Japan. The collapse of the Soviet Union, the decline in U.S. economic security, and the rise of Japanese economic influence in the global system are identified as the underlying causes of U.S.-Japanese tensions. The authors argue that the U.S. and Japan should strengthen their bond of interdependence in order to maintain healthy relations. The bond should be one that is conducive to economic competition and friendship. A competitive economic alliance is preferable to economic warfare.

The collection of essays in this volume are thought provoking, well written, and of value to readers concerned about the evolution of U.S. policy in the complex post-Cold War international system. The authors provide a wide range of opinions and analyses. One major criticism of the volume, however, is that the authors almost consistently deal with issues and strategies that already exist. The authors seem to make the assumption that despite the end of the Cold War, continuity will remain in U.S. foreign policy goals and values. The tone of the volume seems to be that of "plus c'est change; plus c'est la meme chose." In other words, the external context in which the U.S. must pursue and preserve its goals and values has changed, but its goals and values have and will not change. Therefore, the task ahead is to develop a post-Cold War foreign policy from existing policy options, not the recreation of U.S. foreign policy or the international system.

Clearly, the volume is not an attempt to develop new and innovative ideas, or even to forecast the emergence of new U.S. foreign policy dilemmas. Although the specific choices and problems that the U.S. will face in the future cannot be fully anticipated, some attempt could have been made to explore new and innovative alternatives, given that the U.S. is in the position to significantly shape the post-Cold War order. Notwithstanding these observations, the essays are a competent and useful beginning in the post-Cold War debate that is guaranteed to continue during the next few years.

Walton L. Brown
Central Connecticut State University

Scot Mainwaring, Guillermo O'Donnell, and J. Samuel Valenzuela, eds., *Issues in Democratic Consolidation: The New South American Democracies in Comparative Perspective* (Notre Dame, Ind.: University of Notre Dame Press, 1992) vii + 357 pp., ISBN 0-268-01210-5

The time has probably arrived for observers to write of a new dynamic in Latin American politics. With the democratic transitions of the 1980s virtually complete, scholars are beginning to discuss the particular set of problems related to the consolidation of the democracies established at the end of the arduous transitions from authoritarian rule. As hard won as the creation of democratic regimes was to achieve, harder still is the challenge of keeping the fragile democracies of Latin America alive.

The editors of this volume have assembled a number of essays which attempt to map out the new terrain of democratic consolidation. Their major concern is to alert their readers of the remaining obstacles in achieving full and lasting democratic politics in the region. They also offer strategies that might be used in overcoming these obstacles.

On the whole the essays make two essential points. One is that the patterns of politics that emerged during the transition from authoritarian rule determine the long-run outcomes of consolidation; and the second is that the prospects for successful consolidation should be measured with a yardstick of caution. In fact, each of the authors in this volume goes to some lengths to outline the many obstacles that might stall successful democratic consolidation.

The authors of these essays identify several political patterns which they believe represent real impediments to democratic consolidation. Some focus on the persistence of authoritarian elites in the ruling coalitions of the new democracies (O'Donnell, Hagopian); others cite the daunting and chilling presence of the military in post-authoritarian democratic politics (Valenzuela, Aguero). Still others point to the weakness in democratic beliefs and institutions within civil society itself (Conaghan).

The authors arrive at their conclusions using a variety of methodologies. In some instances arguments are buttressed by detailed case studies. In others a logical scheme is judged more effective in laying out an argument. Adam Przerowski, for example, relies innovatively on the game theory to flesh out the logic that connects transition with consolidation politics. Guillermo O'Donnell and J. Samuel Valenzuela also are consciously schematic in their discussions.

In any event all of the authors offer intriguing insights. O'Donnell makes several provocative observations. He notes, for example, the possibility that consolidation may proceed toward unsuccessful outcomes. O'Donnell distinguishes these outcomes as "sudden" and "slow death." By making this distinction, O'Donnell aims to warn that a consolidation can be derailed as much through a quick and unexpected turn of events as through a gradual and corrosive diminishing of confidence in democratic politics.

J. Samuel Valenzuela also makes a strong contribution. Basing his discussion on the Chilean experience Valenzuela observes that a formal restoration of democratic institutions and procedures may in fact camouflage the enormous constraints placed on civilian leaders in important policy areas. The extraordinary prerogatives enjoyed by the Chilean armed forces over both military and economic policy tellingly illustrate the extent to which civilian authority remains beholden to authoritarian elites.

The essays assembled here suggest the direction that the study of Latin American politics is presently taking. One genuine departure made by the authors is their placing explicit emphasis on political variables as the center of discussion. Where other older and more widely debated theories of Latin American politics, such as dependency theory, are couched heavily in political economy, these discussions of democratization more self-consciously define the starting point of their analysis in such factors as representative institutions, elections and parties, and elites' fashioning of the procedures for contesting and transferring power. Recognizing such a perspective makes it easy to see how and why Robert Dahl's classic *Polyarchy* casts a large shadow over the authors.

This shift in focus is, in fact, a welcome counterweight to what perhaps has been an overemphasis on political economy in the literature. However, this shift also carries with it several shortcomings. For example, as consolidation process evolves further in Latin America questions about the very nature of democracy will have to be aired. This is reflected in the fact that Latin American political actors express fundamental disagreements over the meaning of the concept. The concept of democracy is somewhat elastic. Its meaning for individuals can vary depending on such factors as socioeconomic status, political experience, or ideological disposition. Certainly workers and dissident intellectuals share notions of democracy that differ substantially from those of established elites. Brazilian intellectuals such as Francisco Weffort and Marilena Chaui, both of whom closely identify with Brazilian workers' movement, offer a somewhat broader definition of democracy in their writing than one limited to elections, parties, and the other institutional aspects of democratic politics.

The role of social movements in the consolidation process also requires more attention than provided in this volume. Such movements as the Christian base communities, feminism, the Greens, and the protests of racial minorities have contributed in significant ways to the consolidation process. They have created the kind of space within civil society for citizens to question in improprieties of authoritarian rule and to fashion the vehicles through which citizens attempt to make democratic values pervasive norms in every day life. These movements suggest that the consolidation process involves more than changes in institutions, procedures, or elite conduct. Their emergence indicates the profound changes taking place in the political culture of Latin America. Dealing analytically with these changes will require revising the minimalist definitions of democracy on which current discussions of consolidation are based.

In any event this volume promises to remain one of the seminal guides for research on democratic politics in Latin America. The intriguing insights and the significance of the questions posed should concern both students of Latin American politics and those who wise up to track the evolution of democratic politics into the next century.

Michael Mitchell
Arizona State University

Editor's Postscript:
Regime Issues and a Study Agenda

Within the terms of this volume, there are regime issues the study of which would add clarity in a science of politics. This has particular relevance to those African American political scientists who join in any of the criticisms of the discipline itself already mentioned. But it cannot be limited to those colleagues alone. As Robert Brisbane once observed, "We don't own this field" (Brisbane, 1970).

1. *There is a need for serious re-evaluation of the predicates of the racial regime.* Cedric Robinson's article should encourage the question of what are the intellectual underpinnings of the racial regime, and what are the terms in which they are challengeable. The present and the perceptible future both are sanctified by an image of what the past has approved. The terms of political debate are governed, in part, by people's images of what they themselves are. Americans' ability to take constructive action is undermined when they believe that there is nothing important to correct. That ability is undermined when they believe that the bad situation is something that no sensible person wishes, or has ever wished, to correct. The seriousness of the matter is enhanced by the growth of doctrines of "original intent."

Scholars, African Americans among them, know the proposition that stratification could, or should, be grounded on the claim of Africans' biogenetic inferiority to Europeans. (This was asserted by many, including the great Thomas Jefferson, in 1782, six years after the Declaration of Independence. [Jefferson, in Koch & Peden, 1944: 255–62.]) The legitimate desire to recognize the historic power of racism, however, gives sanction to the belief that no significant white person has ever disputed with other persons the proposition that Africans are inferior beings. *The available evidence should convince us that this is sufficiently incomplete as to be wrong.* American elite opinion divided on this issue in the eighteenth century. John Jay expressly declared the hope that the American polity ultimately would be open to all, without regard to "color" (Morris, 1969). Hamilton stated unsentimentally the belief that the "faculties" of the Africans were probably not very different from their own (Hamilton, 1960: 414). Such divisions in white elite opinion have ebbed and flowed throughout the past two centuries. Moreover, the divisions on race have not been consistently in keeping with the alignments variously designated as as "conservative," "radical," "progressive," "liberal," or otherwise.

The issues raised in Robinson's paper, and in Henry's, remain in the polity and in political science in contemporary forms. One of the questions that persists is how to estimate, and to explain, the severity and the consequence of white hostility toward persons of African descent. This is present in new literature such as the recent books of Sniderman and Piazza (1993) and of Feagin and Sikes (1994), who bring nearly opposite views to the same question. In broad terms, the differences between Sniderman and Piazza, on one hand, and Feagin and Sikes, on the other, are differences about what to believe about white opinion in this decade.

Sniderman and Piazza recognize that race is a continuing issue in politics and policy, but assemble data that they interpret to mean that "[r]acism is not built-in to the American ethos" (Sniderman & Piazza, 1993: 175). Feagin and Sikes, proceeding from less systematic, but more intensively human, data reach the opposite conclusion.

2. *There is need for follow-up analysis of the extent of change that has already taken place at the level of processes and institutions.* But the evaluation of change is complex, and is one to which different scholars, and others, attach very different weights. Social fences used to constrain African Americans to designated portions of the economy and polity in an extreme degree. Against that baseline of almost total exclusion, change is unquestionable. Eddie Williams and Milton Morris thus say, "The political arena, once virtually closed to most blacks, is now wide open" (Williams & Morris, 1993: 418). The fact of being visible as an African American no longer, *in and of itself,* constitutes a total bar to a person. Williams and Morris illustrate their point, referring to Supreme Court appointments (Marshall and Thomas), the roles of General Colin Powell, described as "almost matter-of-factly ... appointed chairman of the Joint Chiefs of Staff," Representative William Gray's time as Majority Whip, the third-ranking leadership position in the House of Representatives, and Ronald Brown's chairmanship of the Democratic National Committee.

Since Williams and Morris wrote their essay, General Colin Powell has become the subject of intense speculation as a possible presidential candidate; Ronald Brown has, with three other African Americans, entered the President's Cabinet; and former Congressman Gray has achieved very high responsibility and visibility as the President's special advisor on Haiti.

Social scientists and journalists note the hundreds of African American mayors. Political scientists can, however, go into such matters more deeply.

(a) The number of mayors is large, considering a baseline close to zero prior to 1967, the year Richard Hatcher was elected in Gary, Indiana and Carl Stokes in Cleveland, Ohio. However, it is only a token of what constitutes an increase in power. It is a small proportion of mayors. On the other hand, the severity of racial division in the urban electorate (Kleppner, 1994; Banks, [forthcoming]; Grimshaw [forthcoming]; and, Wright [forthcoming]) means that many of these mayors exist in highly tenuous circumstances. In addition, the decisional scope of most of the African American mayors is rather narrow. They hold the honorific title, often by virtue of being presiding officer of the city council in city-manager governments. In most of those cases, the administrative authority of the city—with discretion over information, money, and coercive force—is in the hands of the manager. Twenty-six of the mayors are in cities with populations over 50,000 persons, and some of these also are city-manager governments. What is equally noteworthy is that each of the prime cities that have been over one million in population for most or all of this century has had an African-American mayor once so far, but in no city except Detroit has an African-American mayor been succeeded directly by an African-American mayor. Finally, even when the mayors are chief executives, the capacity for action, beyond the important, but necessarily restricted, function of managing current city details, means that most pledges of social policy change lie beyond their capacity to redeem. For example, some of the sources of discretion available to mayors in the past, and even to the first wave of African-American mayors, are removed by the powerful weapon of judicial decision at the highest level. Peter K. Eisinger thus wrote:

> [B]lack professionals in Norfolk grew to nearly perfect proportionality from a baseline of next to nothing. Black workers achieved a nearly perfect fair-share in New Orleans, increasing their numbers by two-thirds. In Little Rock, there was a dramatic gain in the number of black administrators, and there was a similar gain in Oakland. But nothing equals the change that occurred in Oklahoma City, where the black administrator fair-share score went from a mere 2 in 1973 to 129 in 1980. (Eisenger, 1983: 48)

This form of power in the ability to hire and fire public employees, more or less at will, is now being limited by the Supreme Court. As the Court has decided that the municipal work force has First Amendment protection against political firing, it may well have incidentally deprived African-American mayors of one of the historic means of exercising urban power, namely the patronage. The Court, similarly, by its limitation of the right of municipal governments to adopt "set-aside" policies, has similarly restricted one of the historic instruments of urban governance. For these and other reasons, the African-American mayors are, to some degree, coming to the control of offices, but not equally to the accession to power.

(b) The problem of evaluation includes still other inquiry into the structure of power. In American local government, there is a honeycomb of offices. At the level of the 3,000 counties, more or less, there are sheriffs, assessors, chancery clerks, county clerks, auditors, treasurers, prosecuting attorneys, and so on. Each of these offices contains some duties and some powers that are part of the structure of power. In the past, these offices were controlled chiefly by political groups that were not favorable to the civil-rights movement, and the residues of such control are to be found in most local governments today. In some modest degree (but only in modest degree), African-American participation has had an effect. (For instance, Richard M. Daley and Carol Moseley-Braun were both chosen for the Cook County, Illinois, ticket by a political agreement between Mayor Harold Washington and one of the more adaptable leaders of the Irish Democratic faction. [Kleppner, 1994])

To illustrate the point that the structure of power at the local government level is still largely what it was before, we might note the important office of prosecuting attorney, called by various other names in various jurisdictions. They place the crucial role, generally beyond even judicial review, not only in *criminal* prosecution, but the "term is also used respecting civil litigation, and includes every step in action, from its commencement to its final determination" (*Black's Law Dictionary*, 1991: 849). These law officers also play an important role by advice, advocacy, and interpretation what other public officials do in a broad range of public policy actions.

In the slightly more than 3,000 counties, there are about 2,300 "chief prosecutors," meaning the people who head the offices, generally by popular election. It is doubtful if there are as many as ten African Americans in such offices in the entire country, and it is doubtful if any were elected prior to the middle of the 1980s. We note this in such detail here only to reiterate the simple point: the structure of power (even if defined as local officeholding) is a dense structure, we have said "honeycomb," and African Americans have at that level penetrated only marginally into the honeycomb.

Presence in Congress is also noteworthy. Congress was the institution where, at least during the first part of this century, the old racial regime had its strongest hold. That has changed, at least since the 1960s. The duration of the change has yet to be estimated. In the 1992 election, some thirty eight African Americans were elected to the United States House of Representatives. One version of the problem is acutely defined by the question of who, or what, "represents" African Americans in the Congressional process, or what the weight and leverage of African American members of Congress may be in the overall system. These members, the one Republican exception apart, play a significant role in the Democratic caucus and, through that means as well as others, play a significant role in the House itself. But a large share of these members were elected under district plans sanctioned by courts, under the terms of the Voting Rights Act. The fact that the very interpretation of the Act itself is open to severe challenge means that the political security, and thus growth in influence, of such members is somewhat less than it would otherwise be. (This is touched upon in the public controversy about the nomination and views of Professor Lani Guinier and the academic controversy about the research and views of Professor Carol Swain. [See Smith, 1994]) If white legislators were to represent African-American constituents, in policy as well as in "casework," about as well as they represented white constituents, then presumably there would be less importance attached to the election of African-American legislators. By the same measure, if white voters were as likely to vote for African-American candidates as for white candidates, there would be less importance attached to geographical units designed to maximize the likelihood of African Americans' winning. These hypotheticals, however, are sufficiently far from current reality that few observers take them seriously.

3. *There is, from the viewpoint of overcoming rigidity, a need for a closer look at the institutions of the society, and what predictions one should draw from one's knowledge of them.*

(a) We may take it for granted that the interest group is a crucial American institution. If the interest group is so taken as fundamental, there is a notable obscurity about the interests and representation of African Americans. There may even be some question about how a group so large as the African American population can, as a group, be represented. The argument can be made that one of the sources of rigidity is the incapacity of a potential claimant to press its claim with force. This assumes that the source of the incapacity is not the strength of the opposition, but the weakness or lack of skill of the group making the claim. It can be argued that experience shows African-American to be generally too cautious. That type of explanation is implicit in many of the views put forth, within the African-American population, and it fits themes seeking deliverance and wishing for defiance that are found in African-American culture. (Holden, 1973) No political scientist that I know has, however, actually examined the options in a sustained manner.

For example, what explains the desire and the ability of some presumptive leadership claimant to continue the process of defining the very name by which the group will be known? Why are people who profess to assert leadership ashamed or reluctant to assert the needs of the emergent middle class or of the serious element whom one has called Working Class Respectables (Holden, 1973)—the two elements of the population crucial to the civil-rights movement of the 1950s and early 1960s?

If rigidity within a fluid system is a significant question, then some political scientists might inquire more deeply into what is involved in social reconstruction. There can be no harder intellectual and practical problem. It is probable that any adjustment between any group A and group B depends, among other things, on the ability of the leadership of each group to constrain the more rebellious members who threaten the other group. Yet the current public focus on social disarray, exaggerated perhaps by television, is related to the troubles of young men who project themselves upon the rest of the world, and the predictable response of the rest of the world to respond chiefly by making the coercive institutions (police, corrections, etc.) the primary social custodians. It is very doubtful that such moral authority can be achieved in any population in the near term, if it is absent. The question is whether it can be achieved at all.

This is a fundamental problem for any group, and any kind of group. The scholarship in contemporary political science does not yet adequately discuss the problem, no matter what the social origins of the scholars. There is, in the same way, a need to know how capital is aggregated and turned into socially useful results. We need to think more about the capability of so large a group as the African-American population to alter matters that are unfavorable. There are also external influences that should be considered. Some questions are more remote, but very important. Students of African-American politics have not yet considered the impact on interest-group politics of an instantaneous communication technology. It may well be that lobbyists make deals, or assist in complex negotiations, as they have done at least since the eighteenth century. CNN may well have the function chiefly of disrupting negotiations. Does the emergence of the instantaneous, worldwide, communication system enhance opportunities or diminish them? How does group A (e.g. African-American) make a deal with some group B, if the deal *is* psychologically surprising or logically incongruous, when every aspect of the deal now becomes susceptible to global politics-as-theater. How is this likely to affect the seriousness, and the effectiveness, of African-American leaders who, in recent years, have often had difficulty establishing a psychological link with a broader audience? .

(b) In light of the presumptive importance of the Presidency, how might colleagues studying the Presidency (as cited in Barilleaux, 1994) forecast the further development of policies relating to the relationship between citizens in different racial groups? (Holden, 1993). In the representative process embodied in the Congress, how, at the end of one century and the beginning of another, should we conceive the leadership process and its relations to the presumptive interests of racial minorities? (Smith, 1994.)

(c) If, for example, parties are more important at the governing level (Oppenheimer, 1994), what is to be said of the prospect for more effective representation that ultimately might diminish the racial quality of the American regime? If "party sorting" is occurring, shall we anticipate that partisan politics will become more racialized, on the expectation that African Americans will be grouped into one party, or shall be we believe that they will be redistributed into whatever parties exist?

The same kind of inquiry is raised by issues of civil service, bureaucracy, and the administrative process. Since the African-American population, and possibly other nonwhite minorities, lives with a notable subjectness to administrative discretion, may we assume that the Inspector General process (Palumbo, 1994) is simply "color blind" or that reform of the process by which career administrators are recruited, installed, and displaced is itself neutral (Cayer, 1994).

(d) Above all, if policy is taken as the product of politics, and racial difference is significant in politics, then the consequence will be seen in policy benefits and burdens. Despite the great concern with "race," the oncoming generation of scholars—African American and otherwise—has yet to establish an effective coverage of the range of public policies that relate to the subordination or equalization of the white and African population streams. It is, for example, common observation that the employment prospects of African Americans diminish because employment itself is more threatened in the contemporary economy than it used to be.) It is even more common to observe that the African-American population, *en bloc*, has a less-than-desirable level of schooling.

It should also be noted that, at no point since the Employment Act of 1946, has national policy seriously contemplated, as a practical, political, and economic proposition, to bring African-American rates of employment up to the white rates of employment. Even with a recent increase in political science literature about race, policy, and political economy, one is aware of little discussion about how to forecast the political consequences of a market economy characterized by severe racial inelasticities. Even less so does one note signs of thinking about the consequences for the American polity—including the possibilities for further reducing racial disparity—of the middle-term consequences of corporate downsizing on a world scale.

4. *Finally, the question of the role of African Americans in relation to others brings us to the ever-recurrent fundamental of politics: an accurately predictive theory of political integration and its converse, disintegration.* The question of how, how far, and at what rate the American racial regime is changing brings us back to that subject. In the 1950s and 1960s, Karl W. Deutsch and various associates dedicated a great deal of energy to studying the problems of political integration, chiefly among nation-states. The problem of sociopolitical integration at the nation-state level is at least as crucial, and recent experience in several countries reminds us of the continuing potentiality of disintegration.

At one level, it is manifest in the reality that the American urban setting is now multiethnic, including multiracial (as it was in the long-ago past sometimes biracial), and multinationality. No one could, as a practical matter, ignore the simultaneous coexistence and hostility of African Americans and Koreans in some cities, even though we should know enough to believe that the public press reports these relationships with more drama than detailed accuracy. Nor could anyone, as a practical matter, ignore or fail to notice the complex relationships of African Americans and American Jews (Washington, 1984; and, Holden [forthcoming].) If the public press could be treated as reliable, then we would rely on a newspaper account of guard-prisoner troubles in the prison at Rikers Island in New York City. The allegation is that the African-American guards abused and denounced Hispanic prisoners, in more or less the same way that white guards have been known to abuse African-American prisoners (*New York Times*, 9 May 1994). In this particular case, this is racism, and not mere racial stratification. Some analysis of these multiple minority situations is starting (Jackson & Preston as cited in Stewart, 1994, 341–44; Jennings, 1993), though such literature is very new.

The Zimbabwean case points to the same theoretical issue in the form of a problem about the magnitude and duration of conflict between groups called "races." It is apparent that there is nothing "primordial" about the social identities of groups that are linked by some putative ancestral identity. Nonetheless, such groups can persist for very long times, and can re-emerge as carriers of conflict when the conflicts were thought to have died. What seems imperative is a deeper understanding, from present facts, of what levels and forms of conflict are to be forecast, over what periods of time, and by what means they may be resolved.

Summary

In review of the regime concept and its relationship to race in American politics, we suggest some possibilities where new lines of work would be helpful. We do not suggest, or believe, that political scientists will make decisions about power. But in the critical questions of race and power, the areas of action may be constrained by better knowledge. The possibilities of change in the racial regime, we thus say, relate to five issues: (1.) a better understanding, from a new study, of the predicates of the racial regime; (2.) evaluation of the extent and form of change in the structure of power, with its dense honeycomb of offices; (3.) a new assessment of the key processes institutions (especially interest group, Presidency, legislature, and parties); (4.) policy and the associated burdens and benefits and their distribution; and (5.) *an accurately predictive theory of political integration and its converse, disintegration.*

References

Banks, Manley Elliott. Forthcoming. "Political Support Attitudes Toward an African American Regime" *National Political Science Review,* vol. 6. New Brunswick, N.J.: Transaction Publishers.

Black's Law Dictionary, Abridged Sixth Edition. 1991. St. Paul: West Publishing Company.

Brisbane, Robert. Comment to Matthew Holden, Jr., at Morehouse College, 1970.

Cayer, N. Joseph F. 1994. Review of *The Promise and Paradox of Civil Service Reform*, ed; Patricia W. Ingraham and David H. Rosenbloom. In *The Racial Regime: Rigidity within Fluidity*, ed., Matthew Holden, Jr., New Brunswick, N.J.: Transaction Publishers.

Eisinger, Peter K. 1983. *Black Employment in City Government, 1973–1980*. Washington, D.C.: Joint Center for Political Studies.

Feagin, Joe R. and Melvin P. Sikes, 1994 *Living With Racism: The Black Middle-Class Experience*. Boston: Beacon Press.

Grimshaw, William J. Forthcoming. "Race and Reform: Minority Empowerment and the White Liberal Question" *National Political Science Review*, Vol. 6. New Brunswick, N.J.: Transaction Publishers.

Hamilton, Alexander. 1960. "A Proposal to Arm and Then Free the Negroes." In *The Negro in American History. III. Slaves and Masters 1567–1854*. With an Introduction by Charles H. Wesley. Encyclopedia Brittanica Educational Corporation.

Holden, Matthew, Jr. Forthcoming. "What Black and Jewish Leaders Should Know and Do." In volume forthcoming, ed., Samuel DuBois, Cook. New Orleans: Dillard University.

———. *The Divisible Republic*. (New York, Abelard-Schuman, 1973.)

Jay, John. *The Federalist*. With an introduction by Edward Mead Earle, no. 2. New York: Modern Library, 9.

Jennings, James, ed. 1993. "A Special Issue on the Political and Social Relations Between Communities of Color." *Trotter Review*, 7:2 (Fall), entire issue.

Kleppner, Paul. 1994. "Mayoral Politics Chicago Style: The Rise and Fall of a Multi-Ethnic Coalition, 1983–1989." In The Racial Regime: Regidity within Fluidity, ed., Matthew Holden, Jr. New Brunswick, N.J.: Transaction Publishers.

Koch, Adrienne, and Peden, William, eds. 1944. *The Life and Selected Writings of Thomas Jefferson*. Edited and with an Introduction by Adrienne Koch & William Peden. New York: The Modern Library.

Oppenheimer, Bruce. 1994. Review of David W. Rohde, *Parties and Leaders in the Postreform House*, see Kleppner.

Palumbo, Dennis. 1994. Review of Paul C. Light, *Monitoring Government: Inspectors General and the Search for Accountability*, see Kleppner.

New York Times, Monday, 9 May 1994.

Smith, Robert C. 1994. "Democracy in America and the Representation of African Americans." Review of Carol M. Swain, *Black Faces, Black Interests: The Representation of African Americans in Congress*," see Kleppner.

Sniderman, Paul M. and Thomas Piazza. 1993. *The Scar of Race*. Cambridge: Belknap Press of Harvard University Press.

Stewart, Joseph. 1994. Review of Byron Jackson and Michael Preston, *Racial and Ethnic Politics in California*. In (*National Political Science Review*, vol. 4.New Brunswick, N.J.: Transaction Publishers.

Washington, Joseph R., Jr., ed. 1984. *Jews in Black Perspectives: A Dialogue*. Rutherford, N.J.: Fairleigh Dickinson Press.

Williams, Eddie and Milton Morris. 1993. "Racism and Our Future." In *Race in America: The Struggle for Equality*, ed., Herbert Hill and James E. Jones, Jr. Madison: University of Wisconsin Press.

Wright, Sharon. Forthcoming. "Political Organization or Machine?: The Power of Ford Endorsements in Memphis Mayoral Elections." *National Political Science Review*, vol. 6. New Brunswick, N.J.: Transaction Publishers.

Invitation to the Scholarly Community

The *National Political Science Review (NPSR)*, a refereed publication of the National Conference of Black Political Scientists, is seeking to expand its contributor and subscriber base.

The *NPSR* was conceived with emphasis particularly on theoretical/empirical research on politics and policies that advantage or disadvantage groups by reason of race, ethnicity, or gender, or other such factors. However, as a journal designed to serve a primary audience of political scientists, the *NPSR* welcomes contributions on any important problem or subject in the discipline of political science.

The *NPSR* also seeks to embrace the socio-political dimensions of all disciplines within the social sciences, broadly defined. Generally, the *NPSR* seeks to incorporate analysis of the full range of human activities which undergird and impinge upon political life. Thus in addition to contributions from political scientists, the *NPSR* seeks relevant contributions from historians, sociologists, anthropologists, theologians, economists, ethicists, and others. The *NPSR* strives to be at the forefront of lively scholarly discourse on domestic and global political life particularly as disadvantaged groups are affected. While not meant to be exhaustive, the listing below is illustrative of the different areas of scholarship which the *NPSR* wishes to draw upon.

Public policy (general)	Political development
Health policy	Economics
Social policy (general)	Law and legal studies
Educational policy	Criminology/criminal justice
Environmental policy	Race and ethnicity
Science and technology policy	Women/gender politics and policy
Policy history	Anthropology
Communications and media	City planning
History	Public administration
Sociology	Language and communication
Philosophy	Ethics
African studies	Religion and theology

The *NPSR* welcomes conventional manuscripts as well as research notes on important issues. The *NPSR* is particularly interested in contributions which set forth research agendas in critical scholarly areas within the context of past scholarship and ongoing contemporary developments. In this regard, the Editor encourages collaborative efforts by two or more contributors which may encompass one or more manuscripts.

The *NPSR* is seeking individuals to serve as reviewers of manuscripts in a wide range of areas. Individuals wishing to serve as reviewers should submit a resume and a cover letter stating the particular areas of specialization in which they wish to review. Correspondence should be sent to the Editor at the address provided below.

Manuscripts submitted for publication should not exceed thirty typewritten pages double-spaced, inclusive of notes and must be prepared according to guidelines of the *Chicago Manual of Style*. Three hard copies (with the author's name on one copy only) must be provided along with one computer diskette (3.5") in WordPerfect for Macintosh. An abstract of no more than 150 words should appear below the title and before the beginning of the text. Tables, figures, and graphs must be submitted in camera-ready form upon acceptance for publication. For tables, use a uniform typeface (preferably Times Roman). Use three rules: one under the table head; one under the columnheads; and one under the table body but above any notes. Column heads are 9/11 Bold, caps and lower case; body is 9/11 upper and lower case, column centered; notes are 8/10 upper and lower case, flush left. "Note" or "Source" is italic followed by a colon.

Correspondence and manuscripts should be sent to: Georgia A. Persons, Editor, *National Political Science Review*, School of Public Policy, Georgia Institute of Technology, Atlanta, GA 30332. Phone: (404) 894-3196. Fax (404-853-0535. Matters regarding reviews of books should be sent to Paula D. McClain, Book Review Editor, *National Political Science Review*, Department of Government and Foreign Affairs, 232 Cabell Hall, University of Virginia, Charlottesville, VA 22901.